Using Windows 8

Using Windows 8

Jane Holcombe
Charles Holcombe

McGraw Hill
Connect Learn Succeed™

The McGraw-Hill Companies

USING WINDOWS 8

Published by McGraw-Hill, a business unit of The McGraw-Hill Companies, Inc., 1221 Avenue of the Americas, New York, NY, 10020.

This book is printed on acid-free paper.

1 2 3 4 5 6 7 8 9 0 QDB/QDB 1 0 9 8 7 6 5 4 3

ISBN 978-0-07-759176-2
MHID 0-07-759176-3

Senior Vice President, Products & Markets: *Kurt L. Strand*
Vice President, General Manager, Products & Markets: *Brent Gordon*
Vice President, Content Production & Technology Services: *Kimberly Meriwether David*
Director: *Scott Davidson*
Senior Brand Manager: *Wyatt Morris*
Executive Director of Development: *Ann Torbert*
Development Editor: *Alan Palmer*
Digital Development Editor: *Kevin White*
Marketing Manager: *Tiffany Russell*
Project Manager: *Kathryn D. Wright*
Senior Buyer: *Carol A. Bielski*
Designer/Cover Designer: *Jana Singer*
Interior Designer: *Laurie Entringer*
Cover Image: © *Dave Cutler Studio, LLC*
Content Licensing Specialist: *Joanne Mennemeier*
Media Project Manager: *Cathy L. Tepper*
Typeface: *10/12 Palatino*
Compositor: *Aptara®, Inc.*
Printer: *Quad/Graphics*

Library of Congress Cataloging-in-Publication Data

Holcombe, Jane.
Using Windows 8 / Jane Holcombe, Charles Holcombe.
pages cm
Includes index.
ISBN 978-0-07-759176-2 (alk. paper) -- ISBN 0-07-759176-3 (alk. paper)
1. Microsoft Windows (Computer file) 2. Operating systems (Computers) I. Holcombe, Charles. II. Title.
QA76.774.M434H65 2014
005.4'46–dc23

2012039896

www.mhhe.com

dedication

We dedicate this book to our friend Jeanne Stevens, whose exceptional salsa enriched our lives, and who willingly took care of our dogs while we worked to meet deadlines.

About the Authors

JANE HOLCOMBE (A+, Network+, MCSE, CTT+, and former MCT) was a pioneer in the field of PC support training. In 1983, while working for a financial planning company, she moved the accounting and client-management operations to IBM PCs. This required the use of three different operating systems to run the selected software and installation of a local area network for sharing the accounting system and client files. The project revealed the potential of networked PCs in business, and Jane found appropriate training for herself and the staff. Between 1984 and the mid-1990s she was an independent trainer, consultant, and course content author, creating and presenting courses on PC operating systems, and through the late 1980s and early 1990s she taught these courses nationwide. She also coauthored a set of networking courses for the consulting staff of a large network vendor. In the early 1990s, after working with both Novell and Microsoft server operating systems, Jane focused on Microsoft operating systems. She achieved her Microsoft Certified Training (MCT) and Microsoft Certified Systems Engineer (MCSE) certifications in 1996 and later updated the MCSE twice for new versions of Windows. Since 2000, she has worked primarily as a technical writer and technical editor.

CHUCK HOLCOMBE has a high-tech computer background in the nuclear and aerospace fields. In his 15 years at Control Data Corporation he was successively a programmer, technical sales analyst, salesman, and sales manager in the field marketing force. He ran the Executive Seminar program, was Control Data's liaison to the worldwide university community, and was a market development manager for Plato, Control Data's computer-based education system. For the past 30 years he has been an independent trainer and consultant. He has authored and delivered many sales and negotiation training courses and is a skilled writer and editor. For a while he claimed he was semiretired, but helping to write books like this one and editing for *The eLearning Guild* for the past several years is far too much work for him to be able to say that anymore.

Together the Holcombes have authored 10 books, including the *MCSE Guide to Designing a Microsoft Windows 2000 Network Infrastructure* (Course Technology), both the *A+ Certification Press Lab Manual*, and the *MCSE Certification Press Windows 2000 Professional Lab Manual* (McGraw-Hill/Osborne). They have authored three editions of *Survey of Operating Systems*, contributed chapters to *Mike Meyers' Guide to Managing and Troubleshooting PCs*, *Michael Meyers' All-in-One A+ Certification Exam Guide, 5th Edition*, and *Windows 2000 Administration* (McGraw-Hill/Osborne). They wrote several chapters for the *Peter Norton Introduction to Operating Systems, 6th Edition* (McGraw-Hill), three editions of the *CompTIA A+ Certification Study Guide*, and most recently, this book, *Using Windows 8* (McGraw-Hill).

About the Contributors

This book was greatly influenced by the comments, suggestions, and feedback from the following group of dedicated instructors. To them we give our heartfelt thanks.

Technical Editors

Gerlinde Brady	*Cabrillo College*
Brenda Neilsen	*Mesa Community College*
Mike Peterson	*Central Oregon Community College*
Kevin Lee	*Guilford Technical Community College*

Reviewers

Frank Abnet	*Baker College of Owosso*
Wilma Andrews	*Virginia Commonwealth University*
Ralph De Arazoza	*Miami Dade College*
Ralph Argiento	*Guilford Technical Community College*
Patricia Avent	*Tennessee Technology Center at Covington*

David Barnes	*Penn State, Altoona*
Robert M. Benavides	*Collin College*
Gina Bowers-Miller	*Harrisburg Area Community College*
Gerlinde Brady	*Cabrillo College*
Taha Ben Brahim	*Auburn University*
Peggy Burrus	*Red Rocks Community College*
Lee Cottrell	*Bradford Pittsburgh*
Gary DeMarco	*Empire College*
Charles DeSassure	*Tarrant County College-SE Campus*
Ryan Donham	*Empire College*
Jean Finley	*Asheville-Buncombe Technical Community College*
Lynnette Garetz	*Heald College*
Terri Helfand	*Chaffey College*
Barbara Jauken	*Southeast Community College*
Annette Kerwin	*College of DuPage*
Diane Kosharek	*Madison Area Technical College*
Charles Lake	*Faulkner State Community College*
Marjean Lake	*LDS Business College*
Rich Lanigan	*Centura College*
Christine Lazaro	*Gateway Technical College*
Kevin Lee	*Guilford Technical Community College*
Yin Lemley	*Pensacola State College*
Julie Lewis	*Baker College*
HuiLiang Low	*Joliet Junior College*
Al Mangini	*Tri-State Business Institute*
Amelia Maretka	*Wharton County Junior College*
Santiago Martinez	*FastTrain College*
Roberta Marvel	*Casper College, Casper*
Martha S. McCreery	*Rend Lake College*
Sue A McCrory	*Missouri State University*
Peter Meggison	*Massasoit Community College*
Shayan Mirabi	*American Intercontinental University*
Mike Morris	*Southeastern Oklahoma State University*
Tamar Mosley	*Meridian Community College*
Eddie Nestingen	*Globe University*
Brenda Nickel	*Moraine Park Technical College*
Brenda Nielsen	*Mesa Community College*
Patricia Partyka	*Schoolcraft College*
Banks Peacock	*Wayne Community College*
Mike Peterson	*Central Oregon Community College*
Ram Raghuraman	*Joliet Junior College*
Terry Rigsby	*Hill College*
Antoon W. Rufi	*ECPI University*
Theresa M. Savarese	*San Diego City College*
Steve Schwarz	*Raritan Valley Community College*
Bonnie Smith	*Fresno City College*
Nathan K Stout	*University of Oklahoma*
Kasia Taylor	*Anne Arundel Community College*
Mike J. Tetreault	*McHenry County College*
Paul Weaver	*Bossier Parish Community College*
Marcia Welch	*Highline Community College*
Charles R. Whealton	*Delaware Technical & Community College*
Diana Wolfe	*Oklahoma State University-OKC*
Nancy Woodard	*Moraine Valley Community College*
Mary Ann Zlotow	*College of DuPage*
Matthew D. Zullo	*Wake Technical Community College*

Acknowledgments

It was with mixed emotions that we listened to sponsoring editor Paul Altier and development editor Alan Palmer speak about a need for a Windows 8 textbook because, at the time, Windows 8 was still very far on the horizon. We began by writing a proposed outline that they sent to instructors at dozens of schools. From the feedback we received we finalized the outline and began researching and writing as soon as the Developers' Preview of Windows 8 became available. When the Consumer Preview was released we researched and rewrote. Of course, this was followed by the Release Preview and the Release to Manufacturing. Shampoo, rinse, repeat. With each iteration the outline and content changed; writing a textbook for a brand-new version of Windows is indeed challenging.

Our goal is not to provide an encyclopedic "all you need to know" book of Windows 8, but to get you started, and to introduce you to some of the differences between this version of Windows and any version you've used in the past. We also wanted to show you practical ways to work, how to make Windows secure, and how to have a little fun along the way.

It takes a village to write even a modest book like this, beginning with knowledgeable technical editors and peer reviewers who scrutinized each chapter and gave us invaluable feedback on the relevancy and accuracy of the content. We can't imagine writing a book like this without their guidance.

We thank every member of the talented team of people at McGraw-Hill who ensured the book's integrity. They include Wyatt Morris, Alan Palmer, Kathryn Wright, Jana Singer, and Joanne Mennemeier. We particularly want to thank Alan for his unstinting support, unwavering positive attitude, and professionalism.

We are thrilled with the fresh, creative design for this edition, and we greatly appreciate the expertise of Kathryn Wright, Jana Singer, and the production group. They all worked hard to make the book look wonderful. Creating and laying out the many elements of this complex book design was a huge task, and they handled it with aplomb.

We truly appreciate all who worked hard to make this book what it is.

Thank you!

About This Book

Important Technology Skills

Windows 8 is a dynamic operating system (OS) that offers a wide variety of applications and capabilities, from virtualization to managing mobile apps. To become proficient in any OS, however, you need certain basic computer skills.

This book will help you build a foundation for success by introducing you to fundamental information about the operating system itself, a needed basis for working with computers at any level.

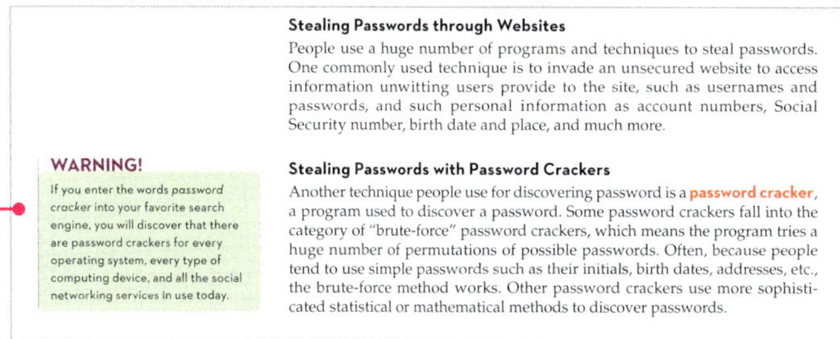

Stealing Passwords through Websites

People use a huge number of programs and techniques to steal passwords. One commonly used technique is to invade an unsecured website to access information unwitting users provide to the site, such as usernames and passwords, and such personal information as account numbers, Social Security number, birth date and place, and much more.

WARNING!

If you enter the words *password cracker* into your favorite search engine, you will discover that there are password crackers for every operating system, every type of computing device, and all the social networking services in use today.

Stealing Passwords with Password Crackers

Another technique people use for discovering password is a **password cracker**, a program used to discover a password. Some password crackers fall into the category of "brute-force" password crackers, which means the program tries a huge number of permutations of possible passwords. Often, because people tend to use simple passwords such as their initials, birth dates, addresses, etc., the brute-force method works. Other password crackers use more sophisticated statistical or mathematical methods to discover passwords.

Warnings create a roadmap for success.

Create a Password Reset Disk

Windows allows the currently logged-on user to create a **Password Reset Disk** to use in case of a forgotten password. This is very important to have, because if you forget your password, and an administrator resets the password using User Accounts or Local Users and Groups, when you log on using the new password you will lose access to some items. These include files that you encrypted when logged on with the forgotten password. When you reset a password with a Password Reset Disk, you can log on using the new password and still have access to previously encrypted files.

You have this advantage only if you think to create a Password Reset Disk before you forget the password! If you need to create a Password Reset Disk for a computer on a network (domain), search the help system for Password Reset Disk and follow the instructions for a computer on a domain.

The Password Reset Disk is both a convenience and a threat. You have to create the password reset disk only once, regardless of how many times you may later change the password. It is a convenience in that you make it one

Encryption is a very advanced feature that you should use only after studying it carefully. It would take more than a chapter just to talk about encryption in depth!

Notes create a roadmap for success.

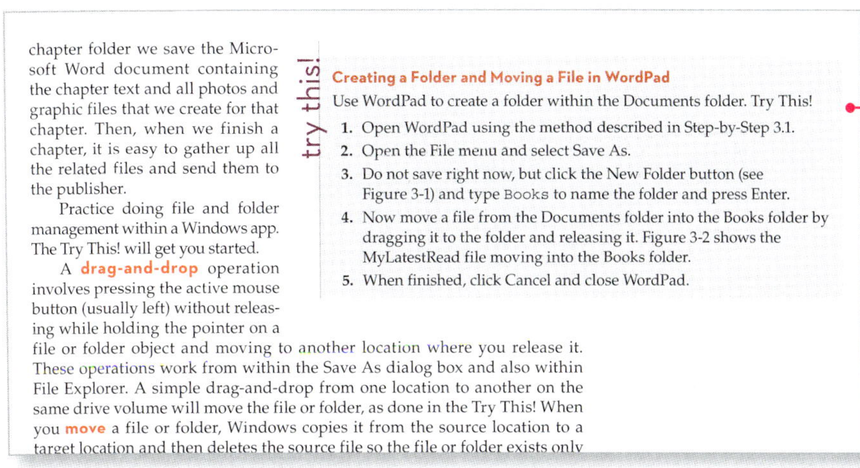

chapter folder we save the Microsoft Word document containing the chapter text and all photos and graphic files that we create for that chapter. Then, when we finish a chapter, it is easy to gather up all the related files and send them to the publisher.

Practice doing file and folder management within a Windows app. The Try This! will get you started.

A **drag-and-drop** operation involves pressing the active mouse button (usually left) without releasing while holding the pointer on a file or folder object and moving to another location where you release it. These operations work from within the Save As dialog box and also within File Explorer. A simple drag-and-drop from one location to another on the same drive volume will move the file or folder, as done in the Try This! When you **move** a file or folder, Windows copies it from the source location to a target location and then deletes the source file so the file or folder exists only

try this!

Creating a Folder and Moving a File in WordPad

Use WordPad to create a folder within the Documents folder. Try This!

1. Open WordPad using the method described in Step-by-Step 3.1.
2. Open the File menu and select Save As.
3. Do not save right now, but click the New Folder button (see Figure 3-1) and type `Books` to name the folder and press Enter.
4. Now move a file from the Documents folder into the Books folder by dragging it to the folder and releasing it. Figure 3-2 shows the MyLatestRead file moving into the Books folder.
5. When finished, click Cancel and close WordPad.

Try This! exercises to reinforce the concepts.

Effective Learning Tools

The design of this colorful, pedagogically rich book will make learning easy and enjoyable and help you develop the skills and critical thinking abilities that will enable you to adapt and troubleshoot problems. Jane and Chuck Holcombe's proven ability to explain concepts in a clear, direct, even humorous way makes this book interesting, motivational, and fun.

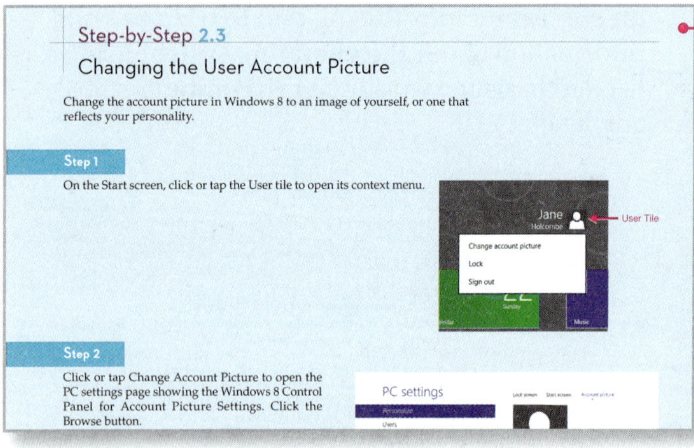

Step-by-Step exercises put concepts into practice.

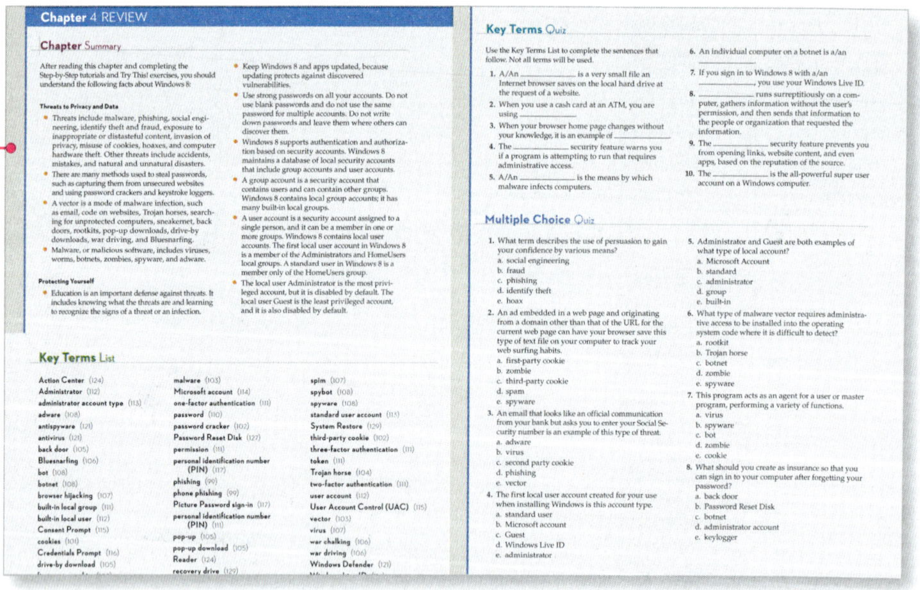

Chapter Review sections provide summaries, key terms lists, and a variety of questions and projects for students.

Each chapter includes:

- **Learning Objectives** that set measurable goals for chapter-by-chapter progress
- **Four-Color Illustrations** that give you a clear picture of the technologies
- **Step-by-Step Tutorials** that teach you to perform essential tasks and procedures hands-on
- **Try This!** Sidebars that encourage you to practice and apply the concepts in real-world settings
- **Notes** and **Warnings** that guide you through difficult areas
- **Chapter Summaries** and **Key Terms Lists** that provide you with an easy way to review important concepts and vocabulary
- **Challenging End-of-Chapter Tests** that include vocabulary-building quizzes, multiple-choice questions, essay questions, and on-the-job lab projects.

Contents

Introduction

What Will You Learn?

Are you ready for a new experience? Windows 8 comes with a brand new GUI and the ability to work on a wide range of computers from desktops to tablets. As such, it works with the conventional mouse and keyboard on a PC or laptop, but it is also optimized to work with the latest touch screens on new tablet computers. This book leads you through your first encounter with Windows 8 and shows you how to perform daily tasks, as well as implement security, share files and printers on a network, and work with your music, video, and photo collections.

- **Chapter 1,** "Windows 8 Overview," begins by defining operating systems in general, why we need them, and what they do for us. Then it introduces you to Windows 8 and its features. Finally, you'll learn how to start up and log in to Windows 8.
- **Chapter 2,** "Navigating and Customizing the Windows 8 GUI," will guide you through the new Windows 8 GUI and the slightly modified Windows 8 Desktop. Then you will learn how to customize Windows 8 to make it work for you, beginning with Ease of Access settings, disabling a Lock Screen, locating tools for customization, changing the User Account picture, making changes to the backgrounds on both the Start Screen and the Desktop, and modifying power options.
- **Chapter 3,** "Windows 8 File Management and Printing," begins with basic file management facts and tasks with hands-on Step-by-Step Exercises on file management from within a Windows app as well as from File Explorer. Then, you will go beyond the basics and learn how to manage Windows 8 Libraries, use the Windows 8 Search functions, and tasks involving removable storage media. Learn how to back up and restore files and how to install local and network printers in Windows 8.
- **Chapter 4,** "Windows 8 Security," details the potential threats to privacy and data and then describes how you can protect yourself through education and good security practices. If your best efforts do not protect you, then follow the instructions at the end of this chapter on how to recover from damage to the operating system and your data.
- **Chapter 5,** "Using Windows 8 on a Network," details how to share files and printers in Windows 8 using a HomeGroup among computers with Windows 8 or Windows Vista. Then it describes how you can share files and printers with older versions of Windows via Public Folders. Learn how to use the Internet Explorer 10 Web browser in both the Windows 8 GUI as well as the Desktop GUI, and how to configure Internet Explorer 10 security features. Also learn how to send and receive email in Windows 8 using its Mail app.
- **Chapter 6,** "Music, Video, and Pictures in Windows 8," first surveys digital media basics and then presents several options for managing and playing media in Windows 8, beginning with an overview of Windows Media Center, a full-featured program that must be added to Windows 8 at a price. Then it moves to those apps bundled with Windows 8 that provide most, if not all, of the tools you need for your media collections including the Music, Video, and Photos apps.

How Will You Learn?

We don't want to give you an encyclopedia of information because it can feel like you're standing in front of an information fire hose, and we've been there ourselves many times in the past decades. Rather, keeping in mind that "less is more," we present just the key points about Windows 8 and guide you in your own exploration of the specifics of this new and very different version. One book simply can't give you everything you need to know about using Windows 8; rather, we hope to get you started in exploring the new experiences in Windows 8, whether on a desktop PC, laptop, or tablet. And Windows 8 on these platforms will look and feel much like the Windows 8 Phone. You can apply the skills you learn working with the Windows 8 GUI to using a Windows 8 Phone device.

Each chapter uses many techniques to help you learn. We start by listing learning objectives, followed by a lucid explanation of each topic supported with real-world experience and a liberal use of graphics and tables. To give you hands-on experience, each chapter contains detailed Step-by-Step tutorials and short Try This! exercises to reinforce the concepts. To build vocabulary to help you "talk the talk," each chapter contains computer term definitions, highlighted in a Key Terms list.

We've also included Tips, which provide handy pieces of knowledge to use with your desktop OS. Warnings will help you prevent mishaps.

You can measure what you've learned with end-of-chapter Key Term, Multiple-choice, and Essay quizzes. In addition, Lab Projects challenge you to independently complete tasks related to what you've just learned.

Let's Get Down to Work

Okay, enough of this introductory stuff. This is the last time in this book that you'll see so many words without illustrations. From now on, it's downright exciting. Learn a lot and *have fun*!

Supplements

For teachers using this book in the classroom, a powerful collection of teaching tools is available online at www.mhhe.com/holcombew8 including:

- An Instructor's Manual that maps to the organization of the textbook and provides additional instructor tips and activities to use with the book.
- A test bank for each chapter, available online in either Word or EZ Test format.
- Engaging PowerPoint slides on the lecture topics, including key points and all figures and illustrations from the chapters.

chapter 1

Windows 8 Overview

"They must often change, who would be constant in happiness and wisdom."

—Confucius

Learning Outcomes

In this chapter, you will learn how to:

- LO **1.1** Describe why you need computer operating systems and how operating system functions help you.
- LO **1.2** List important features of Windows 8, select an appropriate Windows 8 Edition for a computing device, and provide the names for the two architectures that Windows 8 supports.
- LO **1.3** Start up and log in/sign in to Windows 8.
- LO **1.4** Log off/sign off Windows 8 and power off a computer.

Over the decades from World War II to the dawn of the twenty-first century, computers evolved from enormous and very expensive single-purpose tools owned by government agencies or other large organizations to devices owned and used by ordinary people. Similarly, the form and substance of operating systems—the software that controls computers—has changed. Whereas someone using an early single-purpose computer had no concept of an operating system, today's user is aware of both the operating system and the many applications running on that computer. Users experience an operating system through a colorful graphical user interface (GUI) with a variety of graphical screen objects they can manipulate to perform a broad spectrum of tasks. Moreover, users have a selection of operating systems to choose from—limited, in part, by the choice of computing device.

A desktop computer is a computer designed to spend its useful life in one place—normally a desktop—in contrast to a laptop, which is portable and designed to spend its useful life in multiple locations—in contrast to a touch-enabled tablet PC, which has a touch screen as both its main output and input device. Tablets are also called slates, but in this book we will use the term *tablet* for all such devices. Then there are smartphones—those feature-rich handheld devices that are both cell phones and computing devices. Each of these categories can be further divided into various configurations, some of which blur the lines between the categories, but these are the main categories discussed in this book. In spite of the ever-increasing sales of tablets, we believe that PCs are not about to disappear from the desktop, nor do we believe that laptops will go away too soon. Therefore, we designed this book to teach you how to use Windows 8 on a laptop/desktop, while paying attention to how you will use Windows 8 in the future on tablets.

This book explores the Windows 8 operating system. We begin in this chapter with an overview of operating systems and an introduction to basic tasks for successfully starting up and shutting down or signing off from Windows 8. The real introduction to the new Windows 8 user interface begins in Chapter 2, where you will learn more about navigating the Windows 8 GUI and customizing the Start screen. In the following chapters, you will learn how to work with the Windows 8 file and printing systems, secure your Windows 8 computer, use Windows 8 on networks, and have fun with the digital media features of Windows 8.

LO 1.1 | What Is an Operating System and Why Do You Need One?

An **operating system (OS)** is a group of programs bundled together as a single product. Its purpose is to manage system resources and give a user control of a computer and all its components and peripherals. A variety of other software products, called applications (or "apps"), interacts with an OS to make a computer a useful tool for users. An **application** or **app** is software created for performing a set of tasks, such as word processing, using a spreadsheet, database management, creating a presentation, graphics editing, creating videos and music, and much more. Popular applications include business productivity tools bundled together in suites, such as Microsoft Office or Open Office.

In 1949, *Popular Mechanics* published the following prediction: "Computers in the future may have only 1,000 vacuum tubes and perhaps only weigh $1^1/_2$ tons." They had no idea how inventions such as the transistor and the integrated circuit would lead to smaller computer circuitry. Over the years, computers not only became physically smaller, but they also became vastly more powerful than their predecessors. And vastly cheaper!

Operating systems, as separate entities, did not exist in the early years of computing. Changes in the capabilities of computers, as well as in how we use them, led to the need for operating systems. The most important change was from single-purpose computers to multipurpose computers.

Single-Purpose Computers without Separate Operating Systems

Early computers, such as those used during World War II and for the next few decades, were mainly single-purpose computers. They were single purpose in the sense that a computer would simply sit idle until a user loaded a program and data into it. The program would then solve a single problem, and, when finished, the computer would again sit idle waiting for the next program to be loaded.

Today, a **single-purpose computer** permanently contains the program code for only a single set of tasks, as well as the code to control the computer itself. Today's single-purpose computers are not the PCs and laptops we use. Rather, they are most often hidden. In fact, your car may have dozens of single-purpose computers, each of which is a single chip with all the hardware and software required to perform a certain function. This tiny computing

FIGURE 1-1 A recent example of a PC

device is a **microcontroller**, embedded in many products you use every day, such as appliances, toys, consumer electronics, and tools.

Multipurpose Computers with Operating Systems

In the decades immediately following World War II, dedicating a single computer to an individual was a notion that seemed far-fetched. Beginning in the mid-1970s, as certain technological advances made it possible, we saw the emergence of such groundbreaking computers as the Apple I and Commodore PET, mostly among hobbyists. The Apple II, introduced in 1977, was the first consumer-grade computer at an affordable price, and soon programmers wrote useful apps for it, such as VisiCalc, the first spreadsheet app for personal computers.

IBM's introduction of the IBM PC in 1981 seemed to legitimize the idea of **personal computers (PCs)** for use in business and government. Today's desktop (see Figure 1-1) and portable computers are greatly improved, much faster, smaller, and better versions of those of the 1980s.

Desktop, laptop, and touch-enabled tablet computers, as well as smartphones, are multipurpose computers. A **multipurpose computer** has the potential to perform a variety of functions, depending on the application software installed. The typical computing device contains many application programs. Although you cannot add much in the way of hardware to a tablet PC or smartphone, today thousands of applications are available for these handheld computers.

For a multipurpose computer to be successful, it needs to be highly configurable, meaning that you can add the application software and the hardware peripherals to the computer to make it the tool you need. To create reports, you need word-processing software, such as Microsoft Word. To print the reports, you need a printer. If you edit photographs, you would install photo-editing software, such as Adobe Photoshop, and if it were in your budget, you might install a pen tablet to use in place of a mouse for photo editing.

Functions of Operating Systems

Multipurpose computers that you can configure from a huge selection of hardware and software require sophisticated operating systems capable of managing all types of components, interacting with application software, taking input from users, and sending output to devices. In computer parlance, the term **input** refers to moving any type of data into the computer (such as typing on a keyboard or clicking a mouse). **Output** refers to any data that comes from the computer (such as anything on the monitor, printouts, or sound). Together they are called **input/output (I/O)**. All of this requires that an OS perform a large number of functions, and we can break these functions into several broad categories: the user interface, device management, job management, task management, memory management, file management, and security. These functions fit together like a puzzle to form an operating system (see Figure 1-2).

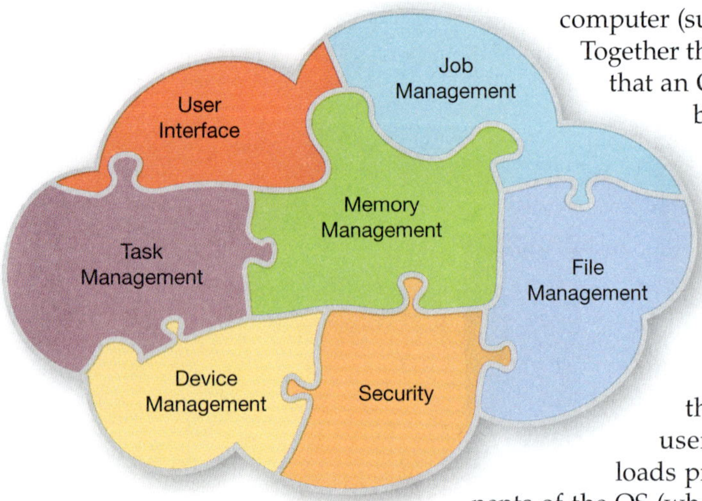

FIGURE 1–2 The functions of an OS fit together like a puzzle.

User Interface

The **user interface** is the hardware and software that allow the user to communicate with the OS. The user interface includes the command processor that loads programs into memory, as well as the visual components of the OS (what you see when you look at the display). On a computer running DOS or Linux without a graphical shell, this visual component consists of a character-based command line that provides only sparse amounts of information. This is the **command-line interface (CLI)**. Figure 1-3 shows the classic **DOS prompt** CLI of Microsoft MS-DOS: white characters against a black screen, with a blinking object that resembles a character-width underline. This is the **cursor**, and it marks the point at which characters you type will appear on the command line. The command prompt passively waits for you to type a command at the keyboard. Only a limited set of characters can appear on the screen, each in its own little equal-sized grid of space.

To become proficient at working in a CLI, you must memorize the exact commands and their modifiers and subcommands and enter them without typos. For instance, "dir" is a command for some CLI operating systems and the Command Prompt in Windows that lists all the files in the current location. On the other hand, a **graphical user interface (GUI)** uses both textual and graphic elements, taking advantage of a computer's graphics capabilities to make it easier to use. This is because the user manipulates graphical elements to perform tasks such as system and file management and running applications. For

FIGURE 1–3 The DOS prompt

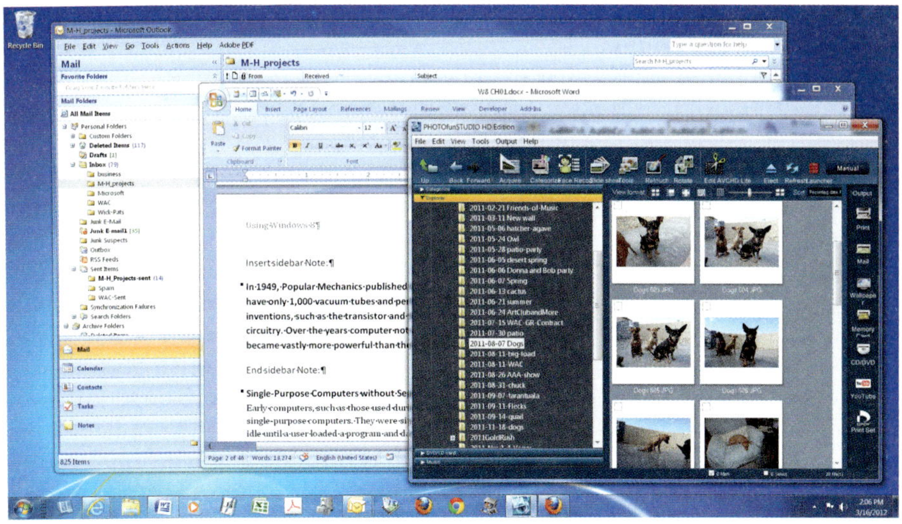

FIGURE 1-4 The Windows 7 GUI

instance, Microsoft Windows provides an information-rich GUI, fully integrated into the OS. Through this GUI, you communicate with the OS and the computer. The GUI offers menus and graphical objects that you select when you want to perform a task list starting a program or opening a word processor file or spreadsheet. Figure 1-4 shows the Windows 7 GUI, and Figure 1-5 shows the Windows 8 Metro GUI. We'll introduce Windows 8 in this chapter and further explore the two Windows 8 GUIs (that's right, plural) in Chapter 2.

Although you do not have to memorize many commands, working within a GUI does require learning the meaning of the various graphical pieces that make up the GUI and how to navigate among these pieces to find your programs and data. In addition, you must learn how to make a program become active (load into memory) so that you can get your work or play done.

An important and common graphical element in many GUIs is the **window**. This object, from which Microsoft Windows gets its name, has a clearly defined boundary, much like a window on a building. Like a physical window, the GUI window object gives us a view into something. In a GUI, each app can open one or more Windows containing the data you create and modify with that app. For instance, when working in a word processor, the contents of the file you are creating or editing are contained in a window.

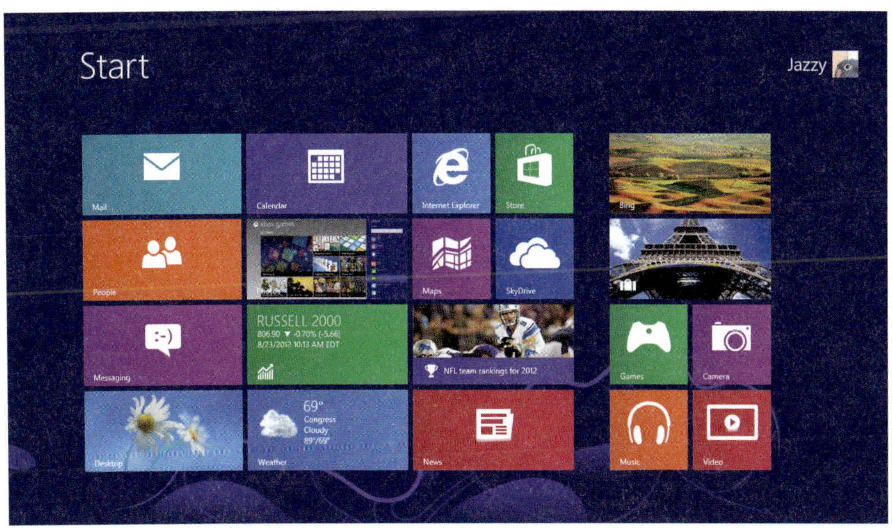

FIGURE 1-5 The Windows 8 Metro GUI

The distinction between move and copy will be defined in Chapter 3, as well as techniques for choosing copy or delete.

GUI windows contain many buttons and menus for the variety of tasks you can do in each application.

In a GUI OS, such as Windows, a graphical **pointer** replaces the cursor, and you can move it around by moving a pointing device—usually a mouse, trackball, or touchpad (on a laptop). The pointer can have a variety of shapes, and it allows you to select or manipulate objects in the GUI, replacing the arcane commands entered in a CLI. For example, to delete an item, you use your mouse to drag and drop it into the Recycle Bin, a GUI object that accepts files and folders and deletes them (learn more about how the Windows Recycle Bin works in Chapter 3). **Dragging** is the action of pointing to an object and holding down the left mouse button while moving the mouse until the object is at the destination you select. Then, when you release the mouse button, you have either moved the object or copied it to the new location, depending on the option you selected. On a touch screen, you can achieve the same results by touching an onscreen object and moving your finger to the destination. By contrast, in a CLI, you type a command such as "delete report.txt."

When working on a touch-screen device, such as a tablet, you manipulate objects by touching them onscreen and using a variety of gestures.

Device Management

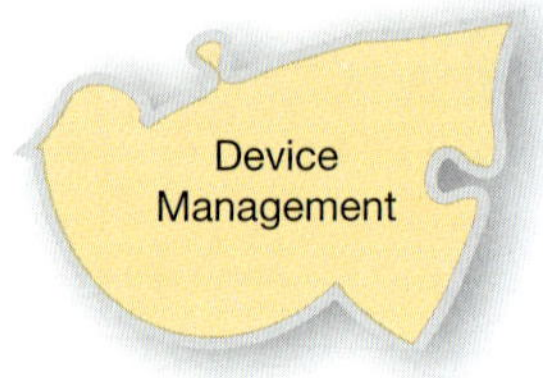

The **device management** function provides control over each hardware device by using special software called **device drivers** that install in the operating system. Manufacturers create device drivers that are unique to the device and to a specific OS. For instance, a printer will come with drivers for several OSs. There will be one for each supported version of Windows, and one for each version of the Mac OS. Most common printer device drivers support these two families of OSs, and many of them also come with drivers for Linux. The device driver contains the commands the device (or rather, its BIOS) understands and uses these commands to control it in response to requests from the OS. You need a component-specific device driver for each unique hardware component with which the OS interacts.

Job Management

The **job management** function controls the order and time in which programs run. Two examples of OS components that perform this function are a scheduling program that schedules other programs or batch files to run on a certain day and time, and a print program that manages and prioritizes multiple print jobs.

Task Management

The **task management** function exists in multitasking OSs, such as Windows, Linux, and Mac OS X. **Multitasking** means that a computer is simultaneously running two or more programs (tasks).

Task management controls the **focus**, the program that has the user's attention at any given moment, which is the top window or the application that is running full screen. It allows the user to switch between tasks by giving the focus to the application the user brings to the foreground. In Windows, this is the current open window—the window that is on top of other windows on the screen and that receives input from the keyboard when the user types.

In reality, a computer cannot simultaneously run more tasks than the number of CPUs that exist within the computer. A **central processing unit (CPU)**, also called a processor, is an integrated circuit (chip) that performs the calculations, or processing, for a computer. Until several years ago, most desktop and laptop computers had only a single CPU, but an OS, such as Windows, could switch between tasks so fast that it seemed to be executing a number of tasks or processes at the same time. A **process** is, essentially, a program running in memory; you can see the list of active processes running in Windows 8 in Task Manager, as shown in Figure 1-6. The Windows OS consists of many processes, as do each of the running applications.

Today, a typical CPU is actually multiple CPUs (or cores) in one package called a multicore CPU. Such a CPU can do true multitasking, simultaneously running a separate process on each core. Still, in Windows 8, many running processes are not associated with a window or other GUI element, so that, even with a multicore CPU, the number of simultaneous tasks running in memory at one time far exceeds the number of CPUs. Therefore, the OS continues to switch between running tasks so rapidly that it seems like true multitasking.

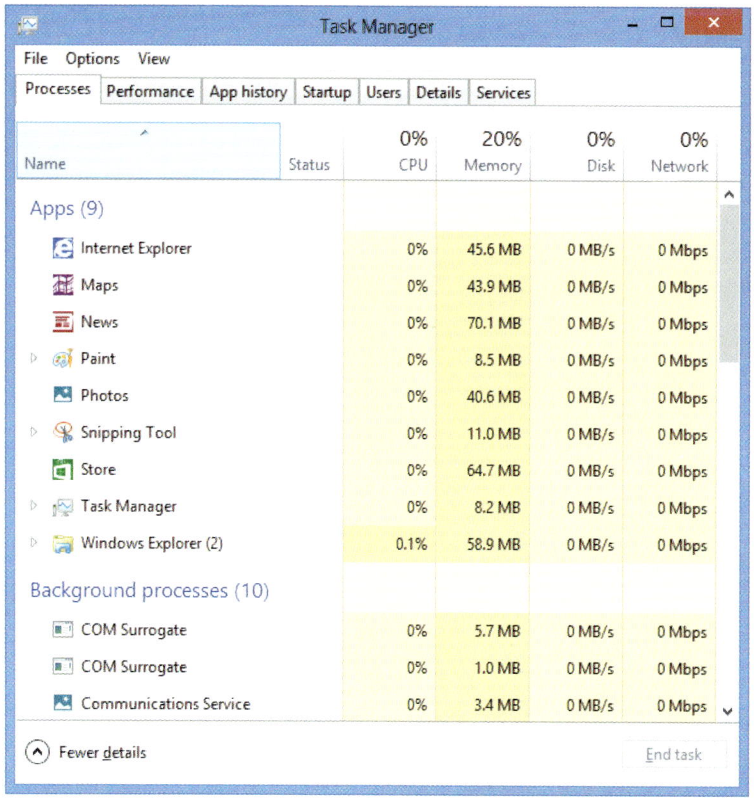

FIGURE 1-6 Active processes displayed in Windows 8 Task Manager

Memory Management

Memory is composed of the physical chips that store programs and data. There are two basic types: read-only memory (ROM) and random access memory (RAM). ROM chips store programs that hold their contents when a computer's power is off, and RAM is a computer's temporary working space that holds program code and data only when the computer is powered up. RAM chips lose their contents when the power is off.

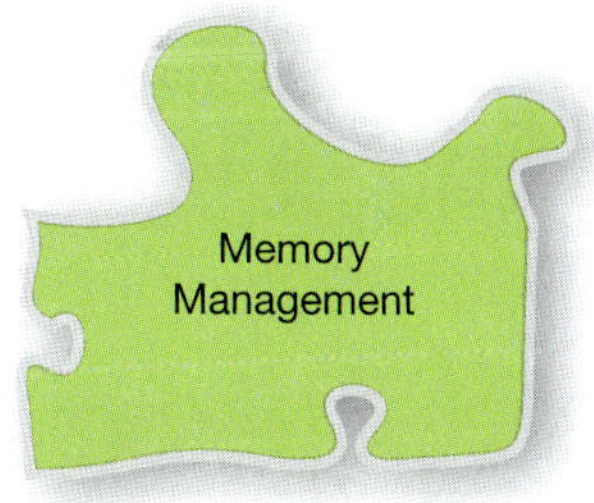

There's Memory and Then There's Mass Storage When you purchase a computer, one of the most important features to consider is the amount of RAM installed in the computer. The more memory it has, the better, although we'll look at some limits later when we talk about 32-bit and 64-bit computers and OSs. Today's typical consumer-grade computer may have 4 to 12 gigabytes (GB) of system memory. The **memory management** OS function manages the placement of programs and data in memory, keeping track of their locations to make optimal use of it.

> When we talk about an active program, we often say that the program is running in memory.

You might hear someone say, "I saved my document to memory." Saving a file copies it from memory to a more permanent storage device, such as a hard drive or flash drive, which is a **solid-state drive (SSD)**. A hard drive is a mechanical device containing metallic platters that spin while arms holding read/write heads float over the surface, storing and retrieving files. Although today's hard drives are far faster than earlier drives, they are still much slower than SSDs, which have no moving parts and consist of nonvolatile integrated circuits. Nonvolatile means that the contents of the memory do not go away when the computer power is off. The down side of SSDs is they are much more expensive per gigabyte than hard disk drives.

Neither a hard drive nor an SSD is main system memory, but is instead a "drive" that you see in Windows with a letter label, such as C or D. Mass storage is persistent, meaning that when you turn off the power to your computer, the saved data remains intact. However, the system memory that your OS and applications use while the computer has power to it is volatile, and the contents disappear when the computer power is off.

Sometimes Memory Is Virtual There is one exception to the distinction between mass storage and system memory: **virtual memory**. In today's OSs, memory management includes the use of virtual memory via a memory management component, the **virtual memory manager (VMM)**. The VMM uses a portion of a hard drive or an SSD as main system memory, allowing Windows to store more code and data in memory than the physical system memory can hold. The virtual memory manager moves code and data, as necessary, to a portion of the drive the OS previously defined as virtual memory.

Without virtual memory, you would be made aware of running out of system memory for your apps and data because the OS would warn you that you were running out of memory and require you to shut down one or more programs before attempting to load another one. With virtual memory, the VMM constantly makes decisions about what code and data to move to virtual memory (also called the swap file) so that you have room to open new programs. The program you are currently using is said to be in the foreground, whereas the inactive, but open, programs are said to be in background—whether they are in system memory or in virtual memory. As you switch between programs, the VMM must quickly reload into system memory what it needs from virtual memory.

File Management

File management, also referred to as data management, is an OS function that allows the OS to read, write, and modify data while managing the storage of the data.

File Systems Each OS supports at least one **file system**, the logical structure used on a storage device to store files, as well as the code within an OS that allows it to store and manage files on a storage device. A logical structure is a way of using software to create a sort of bookkeeping method on a hard disk. Examples of file systems are FAT and NTFS. The FAT file system was first widely used by the DOS operating system of the 1980s, and it is named for one of its logical structures, the file allocation table (FAT). NTFS is a more advanced file system used in Microsoft Windows on large storage devices, such as hard drives, for more than 15 years. NTFS is now the default Windows file system.

When an OS uses a file-system initializing technique called **formatting**, it writes the logical structure of a file system to a storage device, thus mapping the logical organization of the file system to physical locations on a hard disk, SSD drive, or optical disc storage device.

The logical structure of a file system stores metadata—data about the stored files, such as the file size, name, and location—on the storage media. Normally, a single storage device will have only a single file system, residing in a single area defined as a **partition**, but most OSs permit a storage device to have more than one partition. One partition may be an entire physical drive volume or just a portion of a drive, and it is assigned some identifier. In Windows this is a drive letter followed by a colon, such as C:. We often call this a **logical drive**.

Files, Folders, and Directories The logical structure of a file system organizes data into entities called **files** that are saved to storage devices. A file may hold a single document or an entire book, a single database record or an entire database, graphical images, video, and much more. File management also allows users to organize their files, using other special files that act as containers. Each of these special files, called a **folder** or a **directory**, can contain files as well as other folders (or directories). These two words are interchangeable; the term *directory* came into use with early non-GUI operating systems, and the term *folder* came into use after the folder analogy first appeared in GUI OSs, along with an icon representing a paper folder. Figure 1-7 shows a Windows 8 File Explorer window with yellow folder icons to the left of folder names.

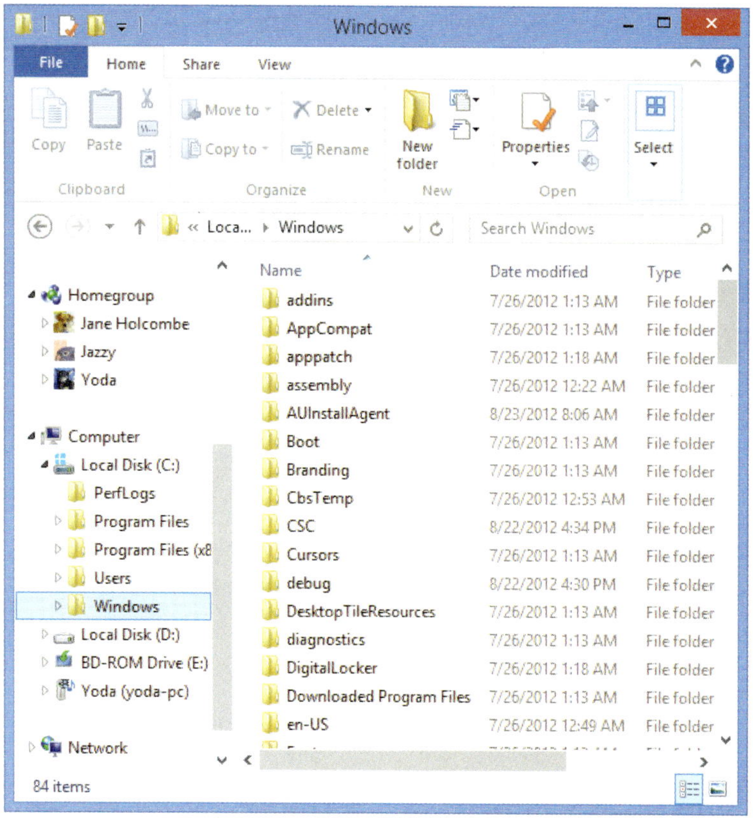

FIGURE 1-7 Windows 8 folders

Security

The **security** function of an OS may restrict what someone can do on a computer and it can include many features, including one that provides password-protected authentication of the user before allowing access to the local computer. For example, Rachel is the accounting clerk in a small company. She has confidential information on her computer, and she doesn't want just anyone to be able to walk up to her computer and access the information stored there. Rachel can set up her computer so that anyone getting into it must log on with a username and password from a user account. A user account is nothing more than a name and an associated password stored inside the PC or on a network **server**, a computer that provides one or more services to other computers on a network. A computer that connects to servers and benefits from the services is a **client** or **workstation**. A desktop OS, such as Windows 8, includes software to allow the computer to be a client to certain types of servers when connected to a network; therefore, Windows 8 is also called a Windows client.

Security is a large topic—one that would take many books and weeks of your time to master, but it is dangerous to use a computer of any type today without understanding common security threats and the steps you can take to protect your computer and yourself from those threats. Therefore, Chapter 4 is devoted to computer security basics.

LO 1.2 | Introducing Windows 8

Overall, Microsoft's Windows 8 has many improvements over previous versions, and some surprising new features. If you dig deep enough you will find hundreds of changes in Windows 8, but many are of interest only to developers writing Windows 8 applications. For our purposes we will briefly highlight a short list of improved or new features.

Windows 8 New or Improved Features—The Short List

Following is a short list of the new or improved features in Windows 8 that we believe are significant to most users.

Windows 8 Is Faster and Smaller

Windows 8 startups are lightning fast. Need we say more? On the newest, even moderately priced, desktop PCs, if you count the seconds while Windows starts up, you won't get to "five." Windows 8 uses less memory than Windows 7 does, which was itself more memory efficient than previous versions.

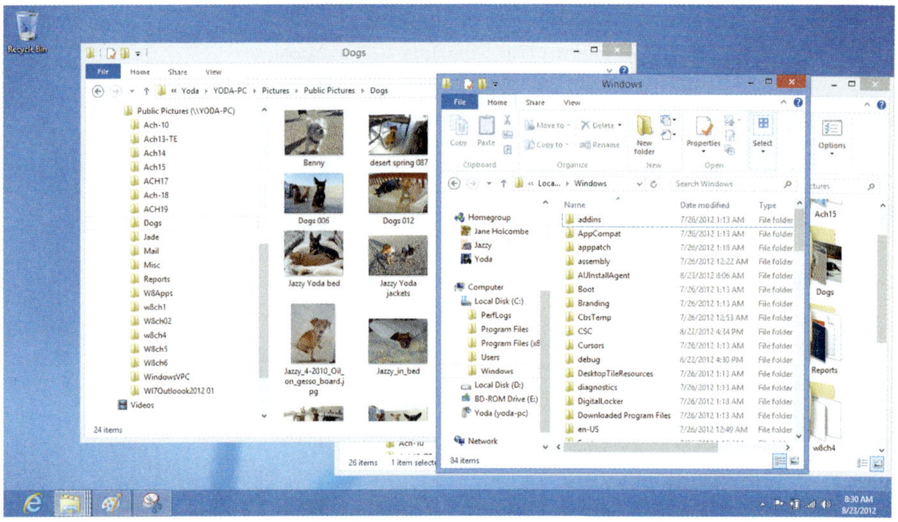

FIGURE 1-8 The Windows Desktop

Windows 8 Has Two GUIs

Windows 8 has two GUIs: Metro and the traditional Windows Desktop. We will explore these two GUIs in Chapter 2, but until then, here is a brief overview of Metro and Desktop features.

The Metro GUI Windows 8 **Metro** is an updated version of the Metro GUI found on Microsoft Windows Phone 7.5. Metro is anchored by the Start screen (as shown earlier in Figure 1-5), with its lack of 3D effects and simple rectangular tiles. All Metro apps are written specifically for the new Metro interface and operate in full-screen mode without frames (windows).

Updated Windows Desktop Windows 8 has a second user interface: a traditional Windows desktop based on **Windows Explorer**, the program that provides the classic Windows Explorer Desktop, shown in Figure 1-8. This GUI lets you run old-style Windows apps and access many Windows components that have come over into Windows 8 dressed in their old clothes. Microsoft refers to this interface in Windows 8 as the **Desktop**.

The apps that ran well under Windows 7 will do so in the Desktop in Windows 8. The traditional Windows Explorer Desktop is slightly updated, but the Start button (also called the Start Orb) and the Start menu, as we knew it in previous versions of Windows, is gone. Also, each Windows Explorer (now called File Explorer) window now has a Ribbon replacing the old-style menu bar, and file copying anywhere within Windows 8 is faster and easier, as you will learn in Chapter 3.

Spell Check for All Metro Applications

Metro applications are designed especially for Windows 8 Metro, and one of the great features of these apps is how they work together. For example, universal spell check across all Metro apps is part of that feature. Even the onscreen touch keyboard uses spell check.

Enhancements to the Desktop on Multiple Displays

Our favorite desktop improvements are in the way Windows 8 works with multiple displays. For instance, when you extend the Desktop to both displays (rather than duplicating it on each) the taskbar extends to all displays. Although it is nice to have the extended taskbar, we like being able to display the Metro Start screen on one display and the Windows 8 Desktop on the other.

Metro Apps Are Always On and Always Connected

This feature keeps your Metro apps up-to-date even when Windows is in standby, meaning that your Metro apps for email, VoIP, instant messages, and streaming content will continue to work in the background, as long as your computer is on the Internet.

Improved Task Manager

Windows Task Manager (shown earlier in Figure 1-6) is the go-to applet for seeing what is running on your computer and for stopping problem applications. In Windows 8 it is both more powerful and easier to use, with many functions, such as the ability to disable one or more startup applications and restart Windows Explorer if you have a problem with the Desktop. Task Manager now has the processes organized into categories with a descriptive name so that you know the app or service to which the process belongs.

Client Hyper-V Now Part of Windows 8

Okay, this gets a bit techie, but this is a great feature for people who want to create programs for Windows or test a new operating system without dedicating an entire computer to it. In fact, that's how we first experienced Windows 8 while preparing to write this book—we installed special software, called a **hypervisor** on a Windows 7 computer, and used it to create a **virtual machine**, a software simulation of a computer. We then installed Windows 8 into that virtual machine so that we could run Windows 8 within a window on our Windows 7 computer, grab screenshots, and write about it—all on the same physical computer. We also installed it directly on another computer for further testing and to see how it performed outside the constraints of a virtual machine. When Windows 8 is installed directly on a computer (not within a virtual machine), you can create virtual machines in Windows 8, using its built-in, advanced hypervisor, **Hyper-V**.

Windows 8 Versions and Editions

A **version** is a major release of the Windows operating system, with major changes to the core components of the operating system, as well as a distinctive and unifying look to the GUI. That makes Windows 8 itself a discrete version, as was Windows XP, Windows Vista, and Windows 7. An **edition** is a separate Windows product with features aimed at a certain type of user. Many editions can exist for a traditional version, such as Windows 7 or Windows 8.

Windows 8 for Different Architectures

Windows 8 now supports different computer architecture. A **computer architecture** is the basic design of a computer, describing the data pathways and the methods the computer's CPU uses to access other components within the computer. At the heart of a computer's architecture is the CPU itself and the chipset. The chipset consists of one to four chips that provide the pathways to all the components in a computer. The two major computer architectures supported by Windows 8 are the Windows/Intel (Wintel) architecture and the ARM architecture by ARM Holdings, Inc.

Windows 8 Support for Wintel Derived from "Windows" and "Intel," the **Windows/Intel (Wintel) architecture** is the Windows-compatible architecture found on most desktop and laptop computers. The leading manufacturers of CPUs

A computer architecture is also called a **platform**.

and chipsets for this architecture are Intel and AMD, but the architecture originated with Intel. AMD is a major competitor and supplier. This architecture is also referred to as the **x86/x64 architecture** because of the 32-bit (x86) and 64-bit (x64) implementations. In this book we use "Wintel" to refer to both the 32-bit and 64-bit architectures unless we make a statement that is true only of the one or the other. Versions before Windows 8—created for PCs, laptops, and tablets—supported only the Wintel architecture.

Many of us were hoping that Microsoft would bring out a version of Windows with just a few editions, rather than the many editions per version that they have brought out since Windows XP. Happily, they have announced only two retail editions and the nonretail Enterprise edition for Wintel systems, and we describe them next.

Windows 8 The Windows 8 edition is the standard Wintel edition targeting consumer PCs, laptops, and tablets with all the basics of Windows 8. You can directly upgrade to this edition from Windows 7 Starter, Home Basic, and Home Premium editions. Here is a feature list of this edition:

- Directly upgradable only from Windows 7 Starter, Windows 7 Home Basic, and Windows 7 Home Premium editions.
- Remote Desktop client allows Windows 8 to connect to Remote Desktop host computer over a network.

Windows 8 Pro The Windows Pro edition is for the user who needs better security through BitLocker and BitLocker To Go, Encrypting File System, Group Policy, and Remote Desktop (host). You can upgrade to this edition from Windows 7 Professional and Ultimate editions. The following are the major features that separate this edition. Some of these are reason enough to select this edition over the standard Windows 8 edition.

- All the features of the Windows 8 edition.
- Upgradable from Windows 7 Professional or Ultimate editions
- If your school or employer has a Microsoft Active Directory Domain, the Domain join feature allows you to log in.
- If your school or employer has a Microsoft Active Directory Domain, Windows 8 Pro can participate in Group Policy, the Domain's policies-based management system.
- Remote Desktop host allows a Windows 8 Pro computer to host incoming Remote Desktop sessions so that you can access your computer over a network when you are away from it.
- It has the full disk-encryption features of BitLocker and BitLocker To Go.
- Encrypting Files System (EFS) lets you encrypt individual folders (and content) and drives, rather than the full-disk encryption of Bit Locker and BitLocker To Go.
- Client Hyper-V allows you to run Windows clients in a virtual machine on the local computer.
- The Boot from VHD feature lets you boot your computer from a virtual hard disk (VHD) in Hyper-V. A **virtual hard disk (VHD)** is a file containing whatever can exist on a physical hard disk, including an installation of an operating system. So, when you choose to boot from a VHD, the VHD is searched for the startup files of an OS.
- You can purchase Windows Media Center for your Windows 8 Pro computer. It is not available for Windows 8 or Windows 8 RT editions.

TABLE 1-1 Windows 8 32-bit or 64-bit Memory Minimums and Limits on Wintel Systems

	32-bit Windows 8	64-bit Windows 8
Minimum Required Memory	1 GB	2 GB
Maximum RAM Memory	4 GB	192 GB

Windows 8 Enterprise This edition is for the corporate environment and includes exclusive features for the corporate environment. It is not available at retail, but through volume-licensing arrangements between Microsoft and large organizations with hundreds or thousands of computers.

32-bit and 64-bit Distributions The Wintel editions come in both 32-bit and 64-bit distributions (usually packaged together). All things being equal, a 64-bit OS will be faster than its 32-bit counterpart. However, another important difference is in the address space that can be accessed by the OS and the software it supports. The address space includes addresses that the CPU can access. These addresses point to locations in system memory installed on the main circuit board (the motherboard) and the RAM and ROM for various peripherals installed in your computer. Table 1-1 shows the minimum and maximum amount of addressable memory for each 32-bit or 64-bit Windows 8 version. Notice that 64-bit Windows 8 uses a maximum of 192 gigabytes of RAM, while the 32-bit version uses a maximum of 4 gigabytes.

You can run 32-bit Windows on a 64-bit Wintel computer, but you cannot run 64-bit Windows on a 32-bit Wintel computer.

Windows 8 Support for the ARM Architecture Windows 8 also supports the **ARM architecture** built around the ARM CPUs created by ARM Holdings, Inc., of Cambridge, England (www.arm.com), for use in smartphones and tablets. Manufacturers of smartphones and tablet computers require extremely small CPUs and other circuitry. The CPU manufacturer ARM created the powerful, ultra-small CPUs that are popular in mobile devices, and Windows 8 supports ARM-based chips from NVIDIA and Texas Instruments. We call the ARM CPU and supporting circuitry the ARM architecture. Further, the traditional ARM architecture is 32-bit, but a 64-bit version of this architecture is on the horizon, so you will eventually see a distinction made between 32-bit ARM and 64-bit ARM—but not just yet.

Windows 8 RT Windows RT is the Windows 8 edition for the ARM architecture, although in the technical press (and in Microsoft's technical blogs) it is also called Windows 8 on ARM (WOA). This edition is not sold at retail as a separate product, but comes preinstalled on new ARM-based PCs and devices. Because this is the first version of Windows to have an ARM edition, you cannot upgrade to this edition. You must buy a computer or device with it already installed.

- It includes device encryption, a feature similar to BitLocker and BitLocker To Go.
- It comes with Metro-style Office 15 apps (Word, Excel, PowerPoint, and One Note 15).

However, there is a trade-off for supporting such dissimilar architectures: Windows RT edition has only one user interface: Metro, and does not support applications written for previous versions of Windows. It requires newer programs written especially for the Windows 8 Metro interface on mobile devices using the ARM architecture. It does not have the Storage Spaces technology, and Microsoft does not include Windows Media Player for this edition.

Support for Computers with Traditional ROM BIOS as Well as UEFI-compliant Computers

A computer chipset is made up of nonvolatile chips (that won't erase when power is removed) containing program code. A generic term for this hardware-software combination is **firmware**. Arguably, the best known firmware in the chipset is the system **ROM BIOS (read-only memory basic input/output system)**. System ROM BIOS (most often simply called "BIOS") contains the program code (the basic input/output system) that informs the processor of the devices present and how to communicate with them. Additionally, most components and peripherals have their own BIOS with program code for operating that component. The device driver for a component is an extension of that component's BIOS.

Although Microsoft continues to support the standard BIOS found in PCs extending back more than 30 years, Windows 8 also supports systems that comply with a new specification, the **Unified Extensible Firmware Interface (UEFI)**, which goes beyond the decades-old limits of the traditional PC BIOS to enable the OS to interact more closely with modern computing hardware. UEFI-compliant chipsets may still have the traditional BIOS, or they may have only a UEFI-compliant BIOS replacement. We expect UEFI to eventually replace the old PC BIOS.

LO 1.3 | Starting Up and Logging In to Windows 8

Here is an overview of what to expect when you turn on your computer and log in/sign in to Windows 8.

Starting Fresh in Windows 8

The first time you start up a new Windows 8 computer—or when you install Windows 8—you select personal preferences for your computer, such as the language you use, and time and currency formats. When you install it yourself from a retail edition of Windows 8, you will also need to provide a product key for activation. This is not necessary when you buy a new device with Windows 8 preinstalled. This product key is a long series of numerals and letters that comes with your purchase, either on the packaging if you purchase it on disc or with the download if you purchase it online.

During **activation**, your installation of Windows communicates with Microsoft to verify that you are using a valid (not pirated) distribution of Windows, but it does not send personal information to Microsoft. Validation is mandatory to use Windows 8. You can skip it temporarily if your computer has no connection to the Internet when you install Windows 8, but it will remind you, and if you have not validated within 30 days, Windows will fail to start.

Do not confuse activation with **registration**, which is not mandatory, but totally voluntary. Windows 8 may prompt you to register a new computer with Windows 8 installed or when you install it yourself. Registration does gather the personal information you provide, and Microsoft uses it to send you information and offers. We have always been grateful that Microsoft separates these two and does not require that you provide personal information in order to use their products. We have used software from other sources that did require registration (at least an e-mail address) along with validation.

FIGURE 1-9 The Windows 8 Lock screen. Use the arrow keys or, on a touch screen, the swipe action to move to the Login screen.

Starting Up Your Computer

When you turn on your computer, the OS starts up. We call this initial waking up of an OS a **bootup**, a term derived from the expression "lifting yourself by your own bootstraps" or "booting up." Most of today's OSs are quite complex, consisting of hundreds of software components and settings, and every time such an OS starts up, it pulls together these components and applies settings to rebuild itself in memory. Its main component, the **kernel**, remains in memory while the computer is running, managing low-level (close-to-the-hardware) OS tasks.

Windows 8 bootup works well with a touch-first device, as well as with those depending on the more conventional keyboard and mouse input devices. Moreover, with each version of Windows, Microsoft has worked to shorten the time between turning on the power switch and logging in, and in Windows 8 this time is negligible on most systems. Figure 1-9 shows the Lock screen that displays in Windows 8 when it first starts up, when you lock your computer (see page 18), and whenever a lack of activity triggers your system's screen saver.

The Windows 8 Lock screen is a great feature on a touch-screen computer or device, protecting you from running a program by accidentally touching the screen. However, on a desktop or laptop without a touch screen, opening the Lock screen is an unnecessary step, so in Chapter 2 we show you how to disable the Lock screen.

Windows 8 Login/Sign In

The security function in Windows 8 protects your computer from unauthorized access. It achieves this through several methods that we will look at more closely in Chapter 4. For now, let's examine the first line of defense: the **mandatory login**. This is based on a security accounts database containing user accounts. Each account contains, at minimum, a user name and password. It may be a local account within the computer; it may reside on a network server; or it may be your Web-based Microsoft Account. For our purposes, we will begin with a local account.

The login process provides authentication and authorization. **Authentication** is the validation of a user account through credentials, such as a username and password, confirming *who you are*. Authentication occurs before the Windows security components give you access to a computer or network.

Authorization determines *what you can do*: usually through permissions to a resource. During login, the first resource you are authorized to access is the computer itself. Further access to files and other resources will require authorization that is usually done without your knowledge, using your login credentials—unless you attempt to do something you are not authorized to do.

With a mouse, click and drag from the bottom of the screen up; with the keyboard, use one of the arrow keys; or use a swiping motion on a touch screen to close the Lock screen and open the Login screen. The Login screen contains a **User tile,** a square tile containing an image that you can alter to represent yourself. The User tile has a user name next to it as well as a box for entering a password. Depending on the configuration of Windows 8 on your computer, you may or may not need to provide credentials before accessing the Windows 8 GUI. This may seem to contradict the "mandatory login" feature of Windows, and we will explain more about this later in Chapter 2 when we discuss automatic login.

If you need to log in, follow the instructions on your screen. The most common login requires a user name and password, but Windows 8 supports other methods, which we look at in Chapter 2.

When you are logged in, whenever you attempt to access a resource, such as a file, folder, program, or printer, the security system will continue to check your authorization to take the action you attempt, such as reading, modifying, deleting, or printing.

Step-by-Step 1.1

Starting Up and Logging In to Windows 8

Let's walk through starting up and logging in to your Windows 8 computer. In this step-by-step exercise, you will need the following:

- A computer with Windows 8 installed
- Any credentials required to log in, such as username and password

Step 1

Turn on your computer.

Step 2

When the Lock screen appears, use the method appropriate for your computer to slide it off and reveal the Login screen. To reveal the Login screen on a touch screen, swipe from one of the edges toward the middle with a finger. On a computer with a mouse, drag from the bottom edge toward the middle of the screen, or press one of the arrow keys on the keyboard.

Step 3

When the Login/Sign in screen appears, enter or select your username and type in your password. To submit the password, perform one of these actions: on a keyboard press the Enter key; use a mouse to click the arrow; or on a touch screen, tap the arrow.

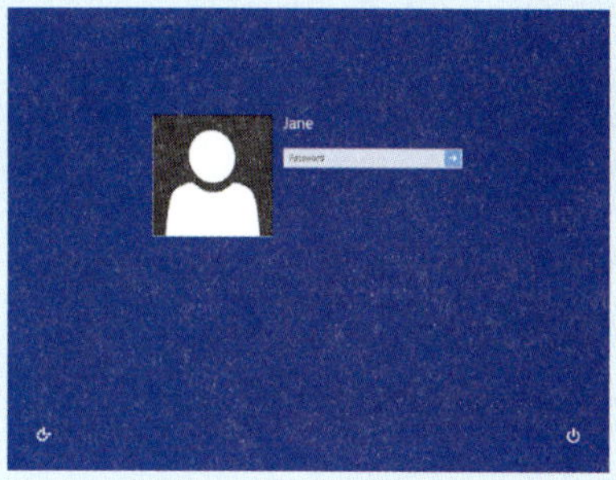

Step 4

The Start screen will display, with a small version of the User tile in the upper right. You are ready to work in the Windows 8 user interface.

LO 1.4 | Logging Off and Shutting Down Windows 8

Logging off and shutting down are two separate operations, although shutting down does include logging off. There are alternatives to fully shutting down Windows 8, such as Sleep and Hibernate. You also can choose to Restart Windows 8. Let's look at all these options and how you select them.

try this!

Sign Out from the Start Screen

Sign out from the Windows 8 Start screen. Try This!

1. From the Start screen, tap or click the User tile.
2. From the User tile context menu, tap or click Sign Out.
3. Sign in again.

Logging Off/Signing Out

If you walk away from your computer while logged in, anyone who happens upon the unattended computer can access all your programs and data. In an attempt to avoid anyone having access to your computer and data, Windows 8 automatically locks the screen after a predetermined interval of inactivity. When it does this, it logs you out and the Lock screen displays, but your desktop and open apps are maintained. When you return, you will need to provide your credentials at the Login screen to get back to your desktop and resume your work.

However, if you rely on the automatic lockout, you still leave your computer vulnerable for a while, and this may not be acceptable if you keep sensitive information on your computer or if you are logged on to a network where your account gives you access to such information. To secure your computer, get into the habit of taking some action before leaving your computer unattended. One action is to log off, which we will look at first, but other options exist, as you will see next. Microsoft now calls this action signing out, and the choice you see on your screen is **Sign Out**. No matter what you call it, you are no longer logged in/signed in, and access is now denied to anyone who cannot provide the correct login/signin.

FIGURE 1-10 Click or tap the username or User tile to display its context menu.

You don't need to keep that boring User tile that comes with Windows 8. Notice the Change Account Picture option in Figure 1-10. You can add any picture you want. Learn how to do this in Chapter 2.

Signing Out from the Start Screen

From the Start screen, tap or click the User tile in the upper-right corner. A context menu appears with options, as shown in Figure 1-10. If you click or tap **Lock**, your open apps will be suspended, but not closed, and the Lock screen will display. If you select Sign Out, your programs will close and you will log off. In both cases, the Lock screen will immediately appear, but the computer will remain on.

Signing Out, Shutting Down, and Restarting from the Windows Explorer Desktop

If you are in the Desktop, as shown earlier in Figure 1-10, you can press the Windows key to open the Start screen, and use the method described above to sign out. Optionally, you can stay in the Windows Explorer Desktop and use the Alt+F4 key combination, which will close the current open window. Repeat until all windows are closed and the Shut Down Windows dialog box appears, as shown in Figure 1-11. Use the up or down arrow key to

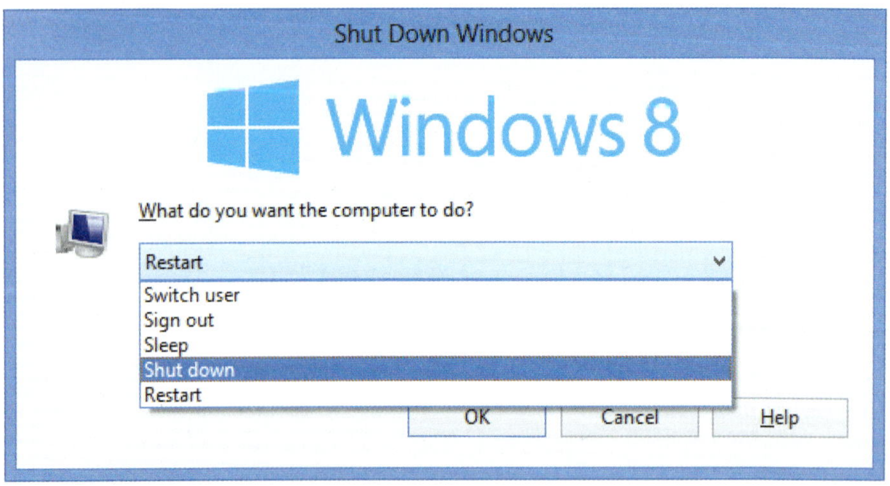

FIGURE 1-11 Use the up or down arrow keys to move through the choices in the open Shut Down Windows dialog box.

move through the choices, select Sign Out, and press Enter. Now you are logged off. Learn why and when you would use Switch User in Chapter 5, and learn more about the Shut Down and Restart options next.

When they first encounter Windows 8, veteran Windows users ask, "Where in Windows 8 can I select Shut Down or Restart?" If you are in the Windows Explorer Desktop, open the Shut Down Windows dialog box, as described previously, and select **Shut Down** or **Restart**.

try this!

Restart from the Shut Down Windows Dialog

After working in the Windows Explorer desktop, you can opt to use the Shut Down Windows dialog box to restart or shut down Windows 8. Try This!

1. From the Start screen, click or tap the Desktop tile.
2. Now press Alt+F4 to open the Shut Down Windows dialog.
3. Click the down arrow to see all the choices, as shown in Figure 1-11, and select Restart.
4. Click OK to restart your computer. After it restarts, log in again.

Shut Down and Restart from the Start Screen

The Windows Shut Down dialog is really part of the past, but you can use a newer method to shut down or restart Windows 8 from either the Start screen or the Desktop. With your mouse or finger, swipe into the right corner, pause until the ghosted image of the Charms bar displays, and then move up to open the Charms bar as shown in Figure 1-12. Then tap Settings. This brings up the vertical **Settings bar** on the right side of the screen, as shown in Figure 1-13. On a keyboard, the faster way to the Settings bar, skipping the Charms bar, is the Windows key+I shortcut. At the Settings

try this!

Restart the computer from the Power Button

This method is available from both the Windows Explorer Desktop, the Start screen, or any app. Try This!

1. From anywhere in Windows 8, either go right to the Power button with Windows key+I or use the mouse or gestures to swipe from the bottom right up until the Settings bar displays, and then tap or click the Power button.
2. In the Power button's menu, select Restart.
3. After Windows 8 restarts, log back in.

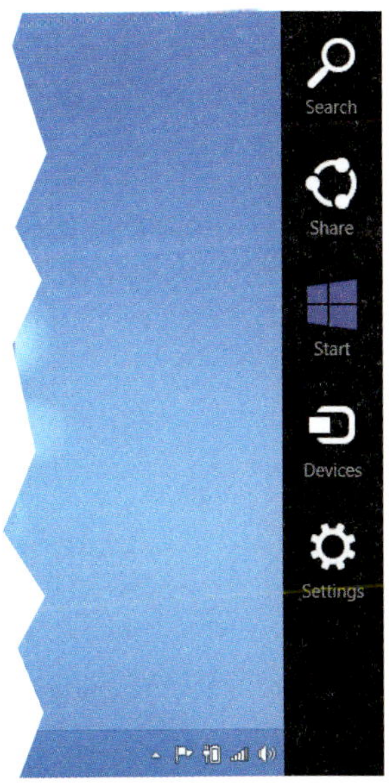

FIGURE 1-12 The Charms bar displays on the right side of the screen.

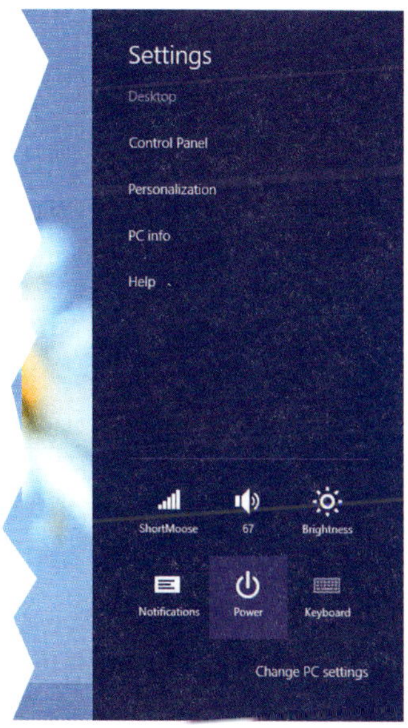

FIGURE 1-13 The Settings bar on the right side of the screen contains the Power button.

The Settings bar is contextual, meaning that it will have different options, depending on the context. For instance, if you are at the Start screen when you call up the Settings bar, the title at the top will read "Start," as shown in Figure 1-13. But if you bring up the Settings bar from an application, it displays the name of the application at the top, and the links immediately below the title will be appropriate for that application. If you open the Settings bar while at the Windows Explorer Desktop, the title will be "Desktop."

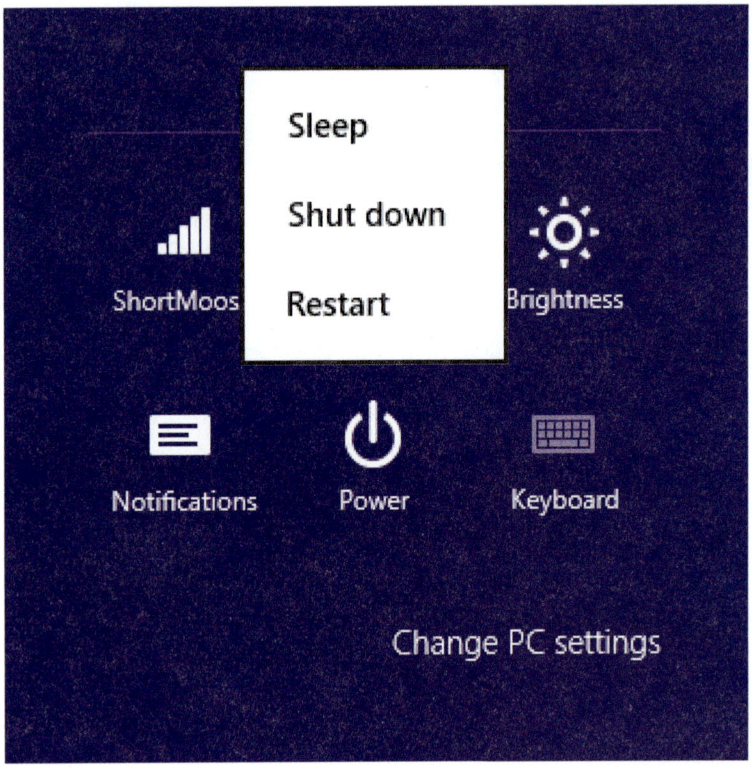

FIGURE 1-14 Click the Power button to access the options for Shut Down and Restart.

bar, locate the Power button in that bar and tap or click it to display the Power menu shown in Figure 1-14.

When you select Shut Down, Windows 8 closes all your open apps, logs your account off, and turns off your computer. Select Restart when you want Windows 8 to close your open apps, sign out of your account, remove Windows from memory, and restart your operating system. This is called a reboot.

What Happens During Windows 8 Shut Down?

When you shut down your Windows 8 computer, Windows uses a form of hibernation—not the entire saving-all-your-programs-and-data hibernation in previous versions of Windows—but a hibernation of the Windows OS kernel, as it appears in memory at the moment you shut down. This is saved to disk. One of the reasons Windows 8 startup is so fast is that it simply brings the Windows kernel out of hibernation, fully configured and ready to run. This startup using the hibernated OS is called **Hybrid Boot**. This partial hibernation shut down, and the related Hybrid Boot process, are enabled by default.

> Regardless of how you select Shut Down or Restart, if you have data files open, Windows will prompt you to save files—one prompt per open data file. Pay attention, and choose to save your files. Better yet, before you choose Shut Down or Restart you should save each open file.

> Depending on how Windows 8 is configured, you may see another Power option: Hibernate. We define Sleep and Hibernate briefly here, so that you can understand what happens if you make these choices. In Chapter 2 you will learn how to add or remove them from the Power menu and the Windows Shut Down dialog box.

> Hibernate may not be a good choice on a computer using SSD storage, because these devices can be written to only a limited number of times in the same location. This is not usually a problem with normal usage, but the hibernation file adds additional usage. Some experts question the wisdom of using Hibernate, because it may shorten the life of an SSD device. This may explain why it is optional in Windows.

Sleep Versus Hibernate Power Options

Sleep

If you select **Sleep**, the computer stays on, in a very low-power mode; applications stay open, but the screen turns off. Wake up your computer (resume) by clicking, tapping, or pressing keys, and the Lock screen displays. Move to the Log In screen, enter your password, and you will be back to your Start screen and able to return to all your open apps, just the way you left them. When is this an appropriate choice? One scenario is on a laptop, tablet PC, or smartphone when you are working with open apps but have been briefly interrupted—say to board a plane or bus. Select Sleep mode. Then, when you're settled in your seat, resume, and you can get right back to work. Do not use this for a lengthy period because when the battery runs out of power, Sleep mode ends. Microsoft has some safeguards built in, but we have never been comfortable using Sleep for an extended time period. We tend to never use this mode on our desktop PCs, but some people like using it.

Hibernate

When you select **Hibernate**, Windows saves to disk what is essentially an image of the contents of RAM, including the OS, your running apps, and all the data you are working on. This is all saved in a file named hiberfil.sys. Then it shuts down your computer. When you turn on the computer, Windows comes out of hibernation mode, an action called **Resume**. During Resume, the image on disk is quickly loaded into memory, and all your apps are open with all your open files. In Windows 8, Hibernate is not available as an option from the Power button in Settings until you enable Hibernate through Power Options, as shown in Step-by-Step 2.4 in Chapter 2.

Chapter 1 REVIEW

Chapter Summary

After reading this chapter and completing the Step-by-Step tutorial and Try This! exercises, you should understand the following facts about operating systems in general and Windows 8 specifically:

What Is an Operating System and Why Do You Need One?

- An operating system (OS) is software that allows the user to interact with the computer hardware without having to know the details of how to do it.
- An application is a program that performs sets of tasks that make a computer a useful tool.
- Early computers were huge single-purpose machines with operating system functions built in.
- Today's smartphones, as well as desktop, laptop, and tablet computers, are multipurpose computers that typically contain many applications.
- The functions of an OS fall into several broad categories: user interface, job management, task management, memory management, file management, device management, and security.

Introducing Windows 8

- Windows 8 has many new or improved features that make it faster and leaner.
- Windows 8 has a new GUI called Metro in which apps written especially for Windows 8 and Metro run. Windows 8 also supports a more traditional Windows Explorer-based desktop in which older Windows apps run.
- Windows 8 supports two major hardware architectures: the x86/x64 Wintel architecture, common on desktop and laptops, and the ARM architecture designed for mobile devices.
- Windows 8 for ARM will not run older Windows programs; it will run only programs specifically written for Windows 8 for ARM in the Metro GUI. Windows 8 for Wintel will run both traditional Windows applications and applications written for the Metro interface on Windows 8 for Wintel computers.
- Windows 8 comes in editions; some are available at retail, some only as preinstalled on computers, and some through a special licensing arrangements offered to large organizations.

Starting Up and Logging In to Windows 8

- You select your personal preferences for your computer when you first start up a new computer with Windows 8 preinstalled or during an installation of Windows 8.
- Retail versions of Windows 8 require a product key for activation, which ensures that the distribution of Windows 8 is legitimate. Activation for retail editions of Windows is mandatory, and such an installation of Windows 8 will fail to run if not activated with a valid key within 30 days of installation.
- You may be prompted to register Windows 8, but this is entirely optional and requires that you provide personal information, such as a name and e-mail address.
- When you start up a Windows 8 computer, it displays the Lock screen. Use an arrow key or a swiping gesture on a touchpad to close the Lock screen and open the Log In screen.
- Logging in serves to authenticate who you are, and authorizes you to access the computer. Further access to files and other resources requires authorization that is usually done without your knowledge, unless you attempt to do something you are not authorized to do.

Logging Off and Shutting Down Windows 8

- Logging off closes your open apps and logs your account off Windows 8, displaying the Lock screen. Windows 8 now uses the term **Sign Out** in place of Log Out.
- Shut Down closes all your open applications and powers off your computer. Shut Down also does a partial hibernation, saving an image of the OS kernel from memory to disk so that each startup does not have to involve loading and configuring the kernel to run on your computer. The kernel is loaded from disk, fully configured.
- Restart shuts down both Windows and your computer and restarts it again.
- Sleep saves all your running apps, and you can resume your work immediately.
- When you hibernate Windows 8, it saves to disk an image of the contents of RAM, including the OS, your running apps, and all the data you are working on. This is in contrast to the partial hibernation (only including the kernel) that Windows 8 does every time you shut down.

Key Terms List

activation (14)
app (2)
application (2)
ARM architecture (13)
authentication (15)
authorization (15)
bootup (15)
central processing unit (CPU) (6)
client (9)
command-line interface (CLI) (3)
computer architecture (11)
cursor (4)
Desktop (10)
device driver (6)
device management (6)
directory (8)
DOS prompt (3)
dragging (6)
edition (11)
file management (8)
file system (8)
files (8)
firmware (14)
focus (6)
folder (8)
formatting (8)
graphical user interface (GUI) (4)
Hibernate (20)
Hybrid Boot (20)
Hyper-V (11)
hypervisor (11)
input (3)
input/output (I/O) (3)
job management (6)
kernel (15)
lock (18)
logical drive (8)
mandatory login (15)
memory (7)
memory management (7)
Metro (10)
microcontroller (3)
multipurpose computer (3)
multitasking (6)
operating system (OS) (2)
output (3)
partition (8)
personal computer (PC) (3)
platform (12)
pointer (6)
process (7)
registration (14)
Restart (19)
Resume (20)
ROM BIOS (read only memory basic input output system) (14)
security (9)
server (9)
Settings bar (19)
Shut Down (19)
single-purpose computer (2)
Sign In (18)
Sign Out (18)
sleep (20)
solid-state drive (SSD) (7)
task management (6)
Unified Extensible Firmware Interface (UEFI) (14)
user interface (3)
User tile (16)
version (11)
virtual hard disk (VHD) (12)
virtual machine (11)
virtual memory (8)
virtual memory manager (VMM) (8)
window (5)
Windows Explorer (10)
Windows/Intel (Wintel) architecture (11)
workstation (9)
x86/x64 architecture (12)

Key Terms Quiz

Use the Key Terms List to complete the sentences that follow. Not all terms will be used.

1. A/an _____________ takes care of the interaction between a program and a computer's hardware, freeing application programmers from the task of including such functions in their programs.
2. The _____________ is the main component of an OS that always remains in memory while the computer is running, managing low-level OS tasks.
3. If you save confidential data on your local hard drive, you should be using an operating system that includes a/an _____________ function, which protects local files and folders from unauthorized access.
4. An operating system that uses _____________ will allow you to simultaneously run more programs than the physical system memory of the computer will hold.
5. When you run several applications at once and switch between them, you are experiencing the _____________ feature of an operating system.
6. Interaction with a computer involving getting data and commands into it and results out of it is called _____________.
7. In the Windows GUI, a _____________ is an object that represents a container for files and other objects like itself.
8. Software that allows the operating system to control a hardware component is a/an _____________.
9. A/an _____________ is a computer that provides services to other computers on a network.
10. Metro is the name for a Windows 8 _____________.

Multiple-Choice Quiz

1. Which of the following is an example of a Windows file system?
   a. NTFS
   b. ROM BIOS
   c. folder
   d. directory
   e. partition
2. After reading this chapter, which of the following do you believe accurately describes the overall trend in computing during the past 60-plus years?
   a. Toward physically larger, more powerful computers
   b. Toward physically larger, less powerful computers
   c. Toward physically smaller, less powerful computers
   d. Toward physically smaller, more powerful computers
   e. Toward physically smaller, single-use computers
3. In addition to the PC computer architecture based on the Intel and AMD CPUs, Windows 8 also supports a CPU developed for smartphones and tablet. Which of the following refers to that CPU?
   a. x86
   b. ARM
   c. x64
   d. Wintel
   e. Metro
4. When Windows 8 first starts up, which screen displays?
   a. Task Manager
   b. Hyper-V screen
   c. Start screen
   d. Login screen
   e. Lock screen
5. When you buy a printer or other peripheral, what type of software comes with it that you need to install to allow the OS to control the printer?
   a. Task Manager
   b. application
   c. device driver
   d. Metro app
   e. job management
6. Which of the following actions is mandatory before you can access Windows 8?
   a. Backing up all data
   b. Connecting to the Internet
   c. Logging on with credentials
   d. Double-clicking the Start button
   e. Rebooting
7. What term describes what is occurring when a computer is simultaneously running two or more programs at the same time?
   a. job management
   b. multitasking
   c. device management
   d. file management
   e. ROM BIOS
8. Which of the following describes a distinct level of the Windows operating system, with major changes to the core components, as well as a distinctive and unifying look to the GUI?
   a. application
   b. version
   c. client
   d. firmware
   e. server
9. In Windows, what is the name for the graphic object that you move around with your mouse and use to select other graphic objects?
   a. focus
   b. Live tile
   c. partition
   d. window
   e. pointer
10. Which of the following shortcut key combinations will open the Windows 8 Settings bar?
    a. CTRL-ESC
    b. ALT-TAB
    c. ALT-F4
    d. Windows key+I
    e. Lock+S

Essay Quiz

1. Write a few sentences describing every interaction you have had with computing devices in the past 24 hours, and list the types of computing devices.
2. If you use more than one operating system on a regular basis, describe some of the similarities and differences you have noticed between two of those operating systems. If you do not work with more than one operating system, find someone who has (classmate or other) and interview that person to answer this question.
3. Consider the possibility of working with the same OS with the same GUI on all your computing devices. In your opinion, would there be an advantage to this? Disadvantage? Write a few sentences to describe your thoughts.

Lab Projects

LAB PROJECT 1.1

Examine the operating system on your class lab computer, and answer questions related to the operating system functions described in this section. If you're not familiar with the operating system on your lab computer, you may need to do some research to answer some of these questions. If so, you can search several places. First, look for a Help program in the OS, or read any documentation that is available to you for this OS. If you cannot find the answers in one of these sources, use a search engine on the Internet to find another source of information for your OS.

For this Lab Project, you will need the following:

- A computer with a working OS that you can log on to
- Internet access and an Internet browser, such as Internet Explorer, Firefox, or Chrome

1. Start your computer and log in, if necessary.
2. In your own words, describe the user interface.
3. Can you see an indication that this operating system provides a job management function? If so, provide a description.
4. If your operating system supports task management, explain how you can demonstrate the task management functions to someone else.
5. Look for tools used to manage files. Then describe how you can copy a file from one location on your hard drive to another.
6. Did you see any evidence that this OS provides security? If so, describe why you believe this is so.

LAB PROJECT 1.2

Explore an important feature of Windows 8 on your own. When you have a problem or a question about using Windows 8, help is at hand. For this lab, you will search for Windows 8 Help and Support, launch it, and find answers to questions.

1. From the Start screen type "help" (without the quotes). From the results on the left, click or tap Help and Support.
2. The initial Windows Help and Support screen contains three areas: Getting Started; Internet & Network; and Security, Privacy & Accounts. Explore each one and find the answer for the following questions:
   a. You are unable to connect to the Internet. Where will you find help for this problem in Windows Help and Support?
   b. You have an older application program that ran well in Windows XP, but, although you installed it into Windows 8, and it launches in a Windows Explorer window, it does not run well. What does Windows Help and Support suggest for this problem, and where did you find the answer?
   c. You are concerned about keeping your data and your identity secure while using a Windows 8 computer. Where in Windows Help and Support will you find the information you need?

LAB PROJECT 1.3

Microsoft designed Windows 8 to run on a variety of computer devices, as well as on traditional PCs and laptops. One of their targets is the growing market for touch-enabled tablet PCs. Use an Internet browser to determine how successful they have been in capturing this market, based on the number of tablet PCs sold with Windows 8. Then write a few sentences on your findings, including the market share of Windows 8 tablet PCs and how this compares with the market share of the 400-pound gorilla of tablets, the Apple iPad.

chapter 2

Navigating and Customizing the Windows 8 GUI

"Technology is becoming more natural and intuitive. People already use gesture and speech to interact with their PCs and devices; such natural ways to interact with technologies make it easier to learn how to operate them. Our Natural User Interface (NUI) collaboration projects focus on facilitating the use of future computer paradigms by keeping the human user in mind."

—Microsoft Research on Natural User Interface
(research.microsoft.com/en-us/collaboration/focus/nui/default.aspx)

Until Windows 8, desktops and laptops had entirely different operating systems from popular mobile devices, such as tablets and smartphones. Each had a unique and different GUI, which meant that to use your tablet you used a different set of navigation skills than those you used on your PC or laptop. However, Microsoft decided to have one operating system that works on consumer devices across the computing spectrum from desktop PCs to mobile devices. They also concluded that they should not completely abandon the Windows Desktop because many thousands of applications are written for that GUI, and Windows 8 cannot leave them behind, at least not on desktops, laptops, and to some extent, on tablets. So, there are now two Windows GUIs, the new Windows 8 GUI (Metro) developed for people using touch-screen devices (but usable without a touch screen) and the legacy Windows Desktop GUI—simply called the Desktop—for those of us who cannot or will not abandon our desktops and laptops. It can be confusing to move between these two GUIs, but move you must if you are going to learn to use this new OS.

Learning Outcomes

In this chapter, you will learn to:

- LO **2.1** Navigate the Windows 8 GUI with a mouse and keyboard or with touch gestures.
- LO **2.2** Customize the Windows 8 Desktop.
- LO **2.3** Manage Windows 8 and Desktop apps.

While Windows 8 was in development, Microsoft referred to the new GUI as "Metro." Shortly before it was released they announced that the new GUI would simply be called "Windows 8." That makes it a bit difficult to separate the new GUI from the name of the OS, but we will try.

LO 2.1 | Navigating the Windows 8 GUI

Windows 8 reacts to the nuances of touch gestures on touch screens on tablets and gesture-aware touchpads on laptops and continues to support the traditional input devices that the majority of people continue to use: the keyboard and mouse. In this section we explore the various methods for navigating the Windows GUI. We begin with a brief description of the Natural User Interface, one of the goals of the Microsoft team who created the Windows 8 GUI, and then we examine the face of each of the two GUIs, and how to navigate them.

Windows 8: The Natural User Interface

You can learn more about other implementations of NUI by pointing your web browser to nuigroup.com, the website of the Natural User Interface Group, and learn about other Microsoft NUI projects by connecting to Microsoft's Research site at research.microsoft.com/ and searching on "nui."

Microsoft put a great deal of research, development, and testing into creating a new user interface for today's consumer, and one of the goals they set was to create a **Natural User Interface (NUI)**, which is any computing device interface that allows a user to use speech or gestures rather than the conventional keyboard and mouse. To this end, they developed the Windows 8 GUI. This simple user interface hides a great deal of complexity and still manages to keep what you need handy.

Mouse-Keyboard Actions

The most common input devices for PCs are a mouse and keyboard, often used in combination to accomplish tasks. This is also true on laptops, although a built-in touchpad often replaces the mouse, and on newer models, the touchpad may support multiple simultaneous gestures, responding to the same gestures that Windows 8 supports on touch screens.

Throughout the book you'll find instructions covering the keyboard and mouse for various actions. We list them all in Appendix A where you'll find helpful Windows 8 keyboard shortcuts as well as a list of mouse and mouse+key actions.

Over the years, Microsoft has added many mouse actions, as well as mouse-keystroke combinations. Microsoft OSs and apps also use a long list of **keyboard shortcuts**, which are key combinations that will quickly perform an assigned action in Windows. For instance, for as long as we can recall, holding the Alt key while pressing the Tab key switches between open Windows apps. There are also keyboard shortcuts that combine the Windows key with another key to quickly perform an action, and Windows 8 has added new uses for these keyboard shortcuts. We will explore this and other keyboard shortcuts as we move through the book.

Touch Gestures

Windows 8 supports multitouch on both touch screens and on touchpads. A **multitouch device** is an input device that interprets multiple simultaneous touch gestures, such as the pinching gesture, in which fingers first touch the device at separate spots and then pinch together. This action is also interpreted when it is reversed by spreading the fingers. Whatever touch device you have, the device itself must support multitouch gestures. There are many important touch gestures, and most people figure out touch gestures simply by experimentation. However, it is also advantageous to know the actions and their meaning. They include tapping, swiping, panning, zooming, and several multitouch actions. If you have a touch-screen tablet or a compatible touchpad on your laptop, keep these actions in mind as you go through this book.

Touchpad versus Touch Screen

Although many of us do not have touch screens, you may be able to experience some of the touch-enabled features of Windows 8 if you have a new or recent laptop with a touchpad. A **touchpad**, or **trackpad**, is a small touch-sensitive device embedded into many laptops in front of the keyboard that usually takes the place of a two-button mouse, responding to fairly simple

TABLE 2-1 Windows 8 Touch Gestures

Gesture Name	Finger Movement
Multitouch	Actions using two (or more) fingers, such as pinching, which involves touching with two fingers spaced apart and pinching them together.
Panning	Place finger on an object and drag it, usually horizontally.
Semantic Zoom	Two-finger pinch in (compress the view) or out (expand) or Double-tap an image or portion of a document to expand it or to have it return to its original size.
Tapping	Briefly and purposefully touching an object on the screen.
Swiping	Touching the screen and flicking the finger left or right to move a page or on object.

gestures, such as tapping and dragging. Synaptics, a company that supplies the touchpads for many laptop manufacturers, has Windows 8 drivers to bring multitouch capabilities to touchpads, as well as other touch devices. If a touchpad has the right hardware under the hood, you will be able to use the types of gestures on your laptop that you use on a touch screen.

Keyboard Shortcuts!
As with previous versions of Windows, you can open Windows Help and Support with the following keyboard shortcut: Windows key+F1. You can search for answers and watch tutorial videos that will help you learn to navigate and customize the Windows 8 GUI.

Anatomy of the Start Screen

The Start screen, Figure 2-1, is not just a starting point, but the launching pad for everything you do in Windows 8, regardless of which GUI you prefer. The Start screen is the place you return to repeatedly when using Windows 8. It is the heart of the new Windows 8 GUI and it consists of a mosaic of live tiles that you can click or tap to open programs or folders during your Windows 8 session. A **live tile** is a small graphical object on the Start screen that behaves in part like a gadget, and yet it opens into a full screen application. A **gadget** is a program that performs some simple function, such as tracking the weather in a city and keeping information generated by the app handy in a tiny screen object. Each installed Windows 8 program has its own live tile on the multipage Start screen. A live tile has no border, and apps that open from these tiles are full screen without borders, thus saving the screen real estate that is so important on the small screens of portable devices. In Figure 2-1, you'll notice that the green Store tile at the upper left is a 1 × 1 tile, whereas the Mail tile below it is a 2 × 1 tile. Either size tile can display active content, similar to a gadget in Windows Vista and Windows 7. Thus, in active live tiles you may see weather information, stock quotes, news feeds, or social networking alerts

Aside from the live tiles, the Start screen has a User tile in the top-right corner with the username of the currently logged on user and a picture. In Figure 2-1 the default "picture" displays, begging you to replace it with a picture or graphic with more character. We will do that later when we customize the User tile in Step-by-Step 2.3. Another feature of the Start screen is the **horizontal scroll bar** along the bottom to allow for (What else?) horizontal scrolling when the screen content extends horizontally beyond the physical limits of the screen. Drag the scroll bar with your mouse or use a swiping motion to scroll through the Start screen on a touch screen. When using a keyboard, press the End key to jump to the end of the Start screen, and press Home to jump to the beginning.

FIGURE 2-1 The Windows 8 Start screen and the magnified zoom button

FIGURE 2-2 Shrink the tiles (zoom out) by clicking the Zoom button or by using a pinching motion on a touch screen.

without needing to open the app. Windows 8 Live Tiles differ from gadgets in that a tile opens an application, whereas the small screen space of a gadget contains all of a gadget program's screen output.

At the far right on the horizontal scroll bar is a Zoom button that you can click to shrink the Start screen, as Figure 2-2 shows. Or use two fingers, positioned a few inches apart, and touch the screen while using a pinching motion to shrink the tiles. This gives you a quick look at all the tiles on the Start screen, and while the tiles are "shrunk," you can do something you cannot normally do in the Start screen: move groups of tiles around by dragging with your mouse or finger. This is very handy and necessary, because the group of apps you use the most may sit off the screen to the right. Move them to the left so that you don't need to scroll to them to open the apps you want. To return the tiles to full size, click or tap anywhere on the screen.

They call this operation **semantic zoom**, and this example of semantic zoom in the Start screen demonstrates its value for navigating the GUI. This is also a great tool for understanding data better, zooming in on one area of a large relational database to look at the data in different views. Or an app might let you look more closely, even at another layer of data. Using a map program with semantic zoom allows you to zoom in from a satellite view with major roads, and then zoom close enough to view a single building.

> **Keyboard Shortcuts!**
> Anytime you want to return to the Start Screen, simply press the Windows key.

> **Keyboard Shortcuts!**
> Alternatively, use the Ctrl key+"−" (the minus key) to zoom out and Ctrl Key+"+" (the plus key) to zoom in.

try this!

Zoom the Start Screen

Use the mouse or touch actions to zoom the Start screen.

1. From the Start screen, move the mouse to the bottom-right corner, and click the Zoom button or use a pinching action.
2. While the Start screen tiles are small, use your mouse or touch actions to rearrange the groups.
3. Click or tap the screen when you are ready to return the Start screen to full size.

Windows 8 Search

Windows 8 has an improved Search function for finding files and programs, based in a **Search bar** that slides out on the right side of the screen. You can access it from the Start screen by starting to type a search string. Or you can open the **Charms bar**, containing **charms** labeled Search, Share, Start, Devices, and Settings. Charms are shortcuts that open Windows features. Select the Search charm to open the Search bar. The Search bar opens with a list of search types, and the focus will be on whatever makes sense to Windows 8

> **Keyboard Shortcuts!**
> Open Windows 8 Search with the Windows key+Q (think "q" for query).

when you open the Search bar. The Search screen opens focused on Apps, and the left side of the screen shows the Apps page. You will have many opportunities to work with the Windows 8 Search feature as you move through this chapter and do the Step-by-Step and Try This! exercises.

The Charms Bar
The Charms bar and the features it represents are all available from anywhere in Windows 8, including within apps. Remember, to open the Charms bar, swipe in from the right edge of the screen or point your mouse to the bottom-right corner and move it up.

Corners and Edges

What you cannot see at first glance in both the Start screen and the Windows Desktop is also significant and discoverable, such as screen corners and edges, which make it easier to switch between apps. Mouse gestures activate the corners, and the edges respond to **edge gestures**, which are touch motions that begin close to the bezel of the screen. Step-by-Step Exercise 2.1 walks you through some common navigation tasks in Windows 8.

Step-by-Step 2.1

Exploring the Start Screen

Take time to explore the Start screen and practice basic navigation skills with the mouse and keyboard or with your fingers on a touch screen.

Step 1

To horizontally scroll the Start screen and display more tiles, slide your finger from the edge toward the center of the screen, or use a mouse to drag the horizontal scroll bar.

Step 2

To rearrange an individual tile, drag it with your mouse or slide it with your finger to move it around. Windows rearranges tiles depending on the size of the tile. If you move a small tile, the empty space remains.

Step 3

Click or tap a tile to open its app.

Step 4

Move your mouse to the bottom-left corner to see the **Start Tip**, a **thumbnail** (a small graphic image) of the most recent active app.

Start Tip

Step 5

Click or tap the Start Tip to quickly open the app.

Step 6

Use a swipe or the Windows key to return to the Start screen and open a second app. Repeat until you open five or six apps.

Step 7

Drag your finger in from the left, and without lifting it pull it back to see the **Start Tip bar** with thumbnails to all open apps—both Windows 8 and Desktop apps. Or drag your mouse from the bottom-left corner up (or top-left corner down) to open it. Clicking or tapping any thumbnail switches to that app, making this a handy task switcher.

Step 8

Now drag your mouse from the bottom-right corner up (or top-right corner down) or swipe from the right to open the Charms bar.

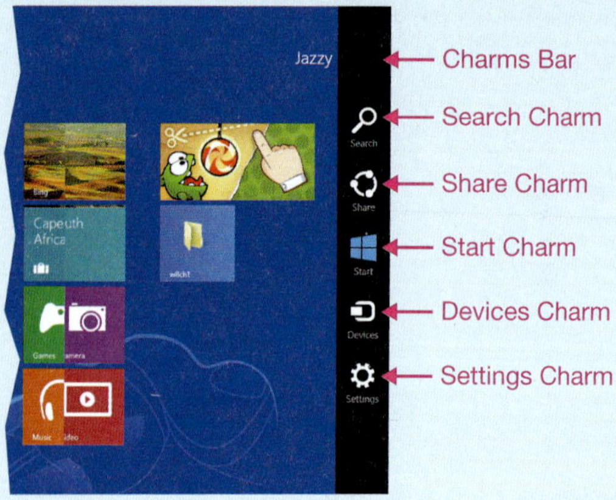

Keyboard Shortcuts!
Open the Start Tip bar and switch between the apps with Windows key+Tab. Or, to switch among apps in the style of Windows 7 with thumbnails across the middle of the screen, press and hold Alt while repeatedly pressing Tab.

Keyboard Shortcuts!
Open the Charms bar with this keyboard shortcut: Windows key+C.

Switching between Two GUIs

You will spend your time between the Windows 8 and traditional Desktop GUIs unless you are working with the Windows RT edition for ARM computers, which supports only the Windows 8 interface. We will explore the ease of moving between these two GUIs and the use of the on-screen keyboard in both GUIs.

Keyboard Shortcuts!
Windows key+D opens the Desktop.

Keyboard Shortcuts!
Windows key+E opens a new File Explorer window on the desktop.

Keyboard Shortcuts!
Any time you want to return to the Start screen from any app or the Desktop, press the Windows key.

Opening the Desktop

Tap or click the Desktop tile (or press Windows key+D) to open the Desktop, returning you to the familiar look of previous versions of Windows—almost. Gone is the Windows Orb or Start button that previously opened the Start menu. Gone is the Start menu. As you learned in Chapter 1, you can still sign off or shut down without the Start menu, and we will show you how to get to other former Start menu options a little later.

Windows' main file management tool has long been called Windows Explorer, but it has been renamed in Windows 8 to File Explorer. To open File Explorer first open the Desktop, and then tap or click the File Explorer icon on the taskbar. Figure 2-3 shows the File Explorer window open on the desktop. A quick way to switch from Desktop view back to the Start screen is to press the Windows key.

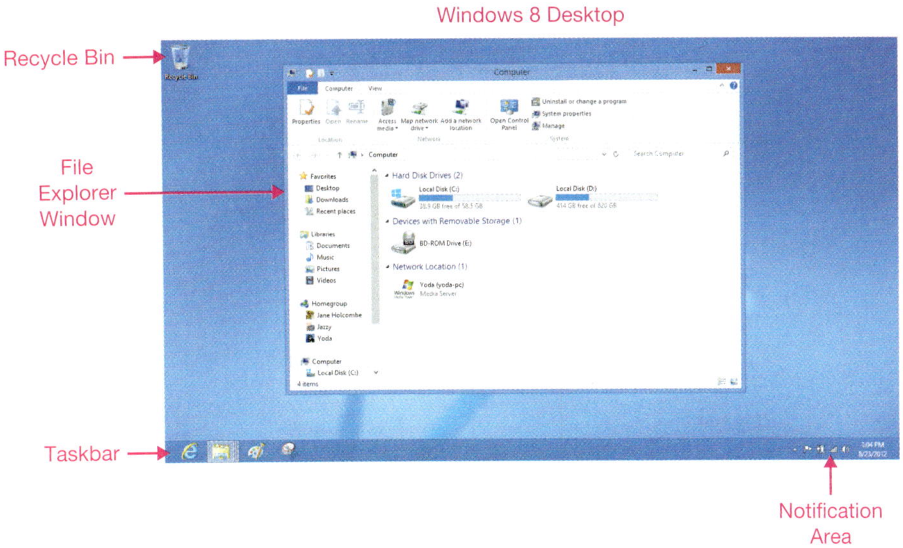

FIGURE 2-3 The desktop with a File Explorer folder window open

LO 2.2 | Customizing Windows 8

In this section we demonstrate a few of the many ways to customize Windows 8. We begin by showing you where to find accessibility features. After that we will locate some subtly hidden customization tools and show how to use some of these tools for customization, beginning with disabling the Lock screen (for a system with a keyboard and mouse). Then we show how to change the user account picture that appears on your User tile at the Sign-In screen and the Start screen. You'll learn about the screen resolution required by Windows 8 apps, customize your Start screen, and change the Desktop background.

Ease of Access

You can use several features to make your computer more accessible; the most widely used ones are available from the Ease of Access button on the lower-left corner of the Sign-In screen, as shown in Figure 2-4. When you click or tap the Ease of Access button, a menu appears, shown in Figure 2-5, and the Narrator begins reading aloud the items in the menu and other screen contents, a necessary aid to someone with low vision. You can select among these options (Narrator, Magnifier, On-Screen Keyboard, High Contrast, Sticky Keys, and Filter Keys) to aid in logging in, or you can open the Ease of Access page in PC Settings after you sign in.

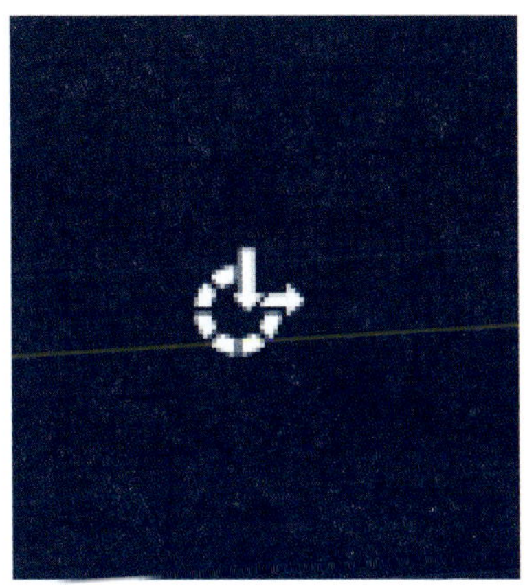

FIGURE 2-4 The Ease of Access button on the bottom left of Sign-In screen.

Ease of Access Settings

After you sign in, you can access more Ease of Access settings using the Ease of Access page in PC Settings. To do this, first open the Charms bar (swipe in from the right edge of the screen or point your mouse to the bottom-right corner and move it up) and select Search. Enter "ease of access" into the Search box, select Settings, and then select Ease of Access from the results, as shown in Figure 2-6. If you want to make a computer more accessible for yourself or someone else, experiment with the Ease of Access settings.

The On-screen Keyboard

As with previous versions, Windows 8 has an on-screen keyboard, but it is even more important now that Windows 8 supports touch screens. In previous

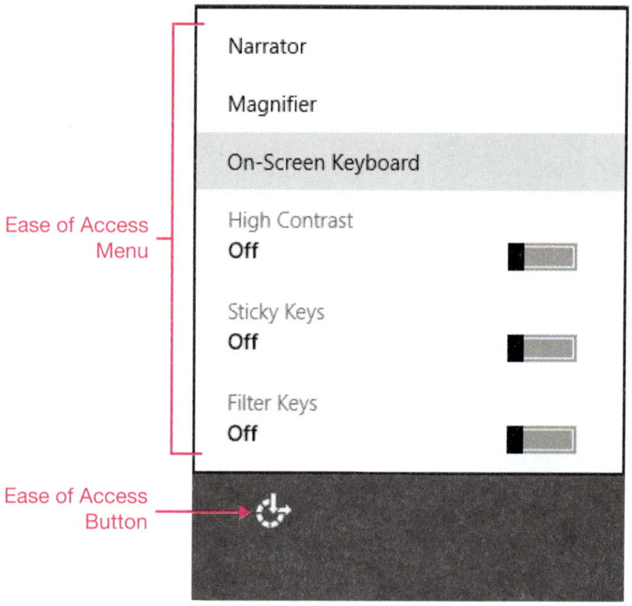

FIGURE 2-5 The Ease of Access button and menu on the Sign-In screen

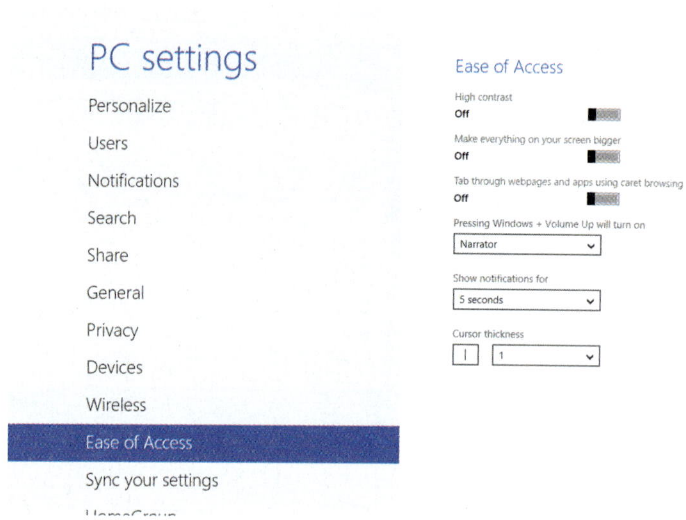

FIGURE 2-6 The Ease of Access page in PC Settings

versions of Windows, the on-screen keyboard was part of the accessibility options. At this point, Windows 8 has two on-screen keyboards, a Windows 8 version that works in both GUIs and a Desktop-only version, with several ways to open them. We will look at just a few of the ways. To open the Windows 8 version of the on-screen keyboard for use at the Sign-In screen, tap or click the Ease of Access button, the small clocklike button at the bottom left on the Sign-In screen and select the On-screen Keyboard option, shown in Figure 2-7. You can use this to type in a password.

On a touch-screen computer, it will open in context, or it opens when you touch an empty area of the screen or an area requiring typing. You can also open both keyboards on a nontouch-screen PC. Open the Windows 8 version from the Start screen by using the Search function, which you enable when you begin typing at the Start screen. Display it in the Results list by typing "k" (Figure 2-5) or by typing "osk." Select it from the results, and it will then

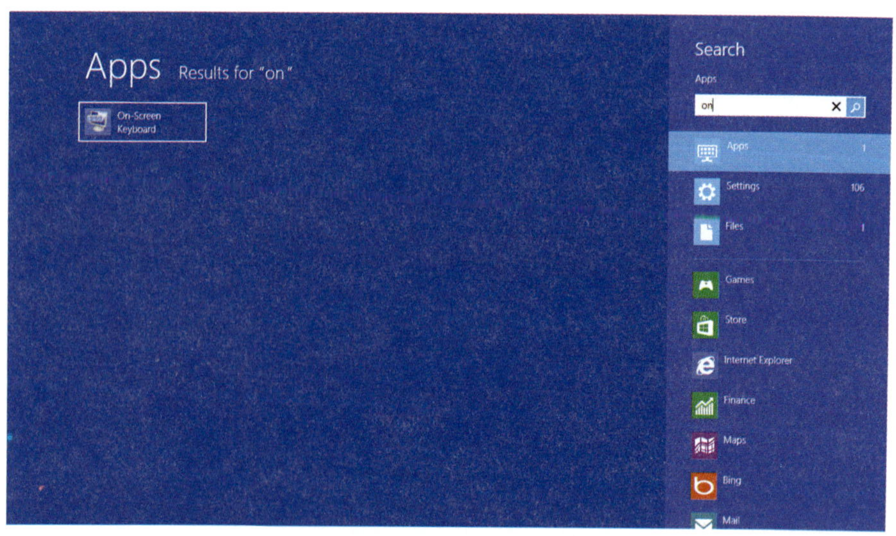

FIGURE 2-7 Use Search to locate the On-Screen Keyboard.

FIGURE 2-8 The On-Screen Keyboard

display on the Desktop. However, it remains on the screen as you switch between the Desktop, Start screen, and open apps. To close it, click the Close button on the upper-right of the On-screen Keyboard. Figure 2-8 shows the On-screen Keyboard with the Windows key depressed because on the physical keyboard, the Windows key was depressed at the time of grabbing this screenshot with Windows key+PrtScr.

Another on-screen keyboard that runs only with Desktop and windowed apps is the Touch Keyboard. Create a taskbar shortcut to open and close this keyboard by right-clicking the desktop taskbar, expanding Toolbars, and then selecting Touch Keyboard. The Touch Keyboard has a different look than the Windows 8-enabled On-Screen Keyboard. If you click or tap the key with a tiny keyboard icon on the bottom right, four keys light up, representing various keyboard configurations, as shown in white in Figure 2-9. The key on the left selects the current view, which is the QWERTY keyboard, and the next one changes the Touch Keyboard to a split view, convenient for using your thumbs on a touch screen. The third one brings up pen view, where you can enter data in script. The last button minimizes the keyboard.

try this!

Experiment with the Touch Keyboard

Open the Touch Keyboard on the desktop and experiment with the different keyboard views.

1. From the Desktop, right-click the taskbar, expand Toolbars, and then select Touch Keyboard. This pins the Touch Keyboard icon to the taskbar.
2. Click the Keyboard icon.
3. In the Touch Keyboard, click the keyboard icon on the bottom right to open the configuration choices and experiment with each keyboard view. When you are done, click the Close button on the upper right to close the Touch Keyboard.

Keyboard Shortcuts!
Do you need to take screenshots of your desktop? Capture the screen and save it as a PNG file in the Pictures folder using Windows key+PrtScr. The files will be automatically named and numbered (screenshot (1), screenshot (2), and so on).

FIGURE 2-9 The Touch Keyboard keyboard in QWERTY view

The functions previously available on the Windows Start button are scattered here and there in Windows 8. You now launch programs from the Start screen, and begin a search, access shares, and sign out and work with devices and settings from the Charms bar. At the end of the day, you access the Shut Down menu from the Power button on the Settings bar. But how do you customize Windows 8?

Power Tools

You'll find the functions for customization in several locations. In fact, there are at least two ways to access each. For instance, a group of tools is available from a special context menu, and many of these tools are also in Control Panel and/or in Administrative Tools. Therefore, we will look at how to access these three locations in Windows 8.

The Start Context Menu

> **Keyboard Shortcuts!**
> Open the Start context menu with the Windows key+X. For this reason, some people call it the Win-X menu.

Power users and IT professionals immediately look for their favorite tools for customizing and troubleshooting Windows. These are functions the casual user has little or no interest in until a need arises. You will find them on the Start context menu that opens when you right-click the bottom-left corner in either Desktop view or Windows 8 view, as shown in Figure 2-10. These tools include individual Control Panel applets, such as Programs and Features, Network Connections, Power Options (power saving settings), System Properties, or the top-level Control Panel window. Power users also need the Run box to launch one of several special programs using the executable name. For example: msinfo32 is the executable that opens the System Information utility. Other favorites include Device Manager, Disk Management, Computer Management, Task Manager, and the good old Command Prompt.

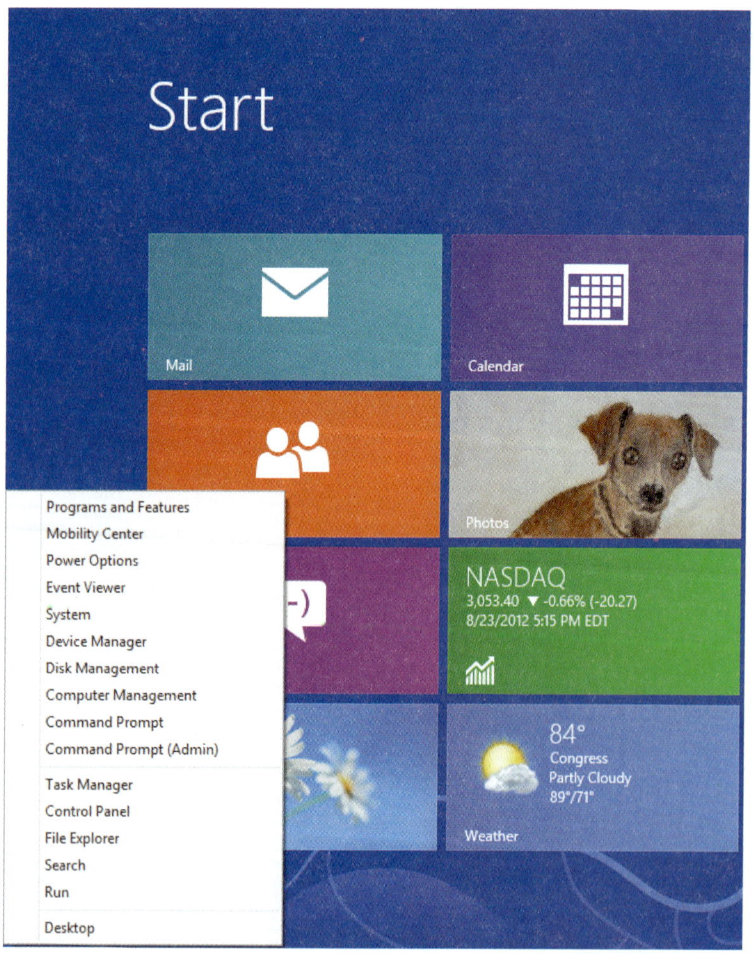

FIGURE 2-10 The Start context menu contains tools for power users and IT professionals.

Control Panel

Control Panel, which you can open from the Start context menu, contains several dozen tools. Poking around in Control Panel is probably the slowest way to locate and launch one of them, but doing just that is a great way to become familiar with the tools. Control Panel has three views—category, small icons, and large icons—selectable from the drop-down menu, shown open on the top right of the Control Panel home page in Figure 2-11. Category view does not clearly show the individual tools but arranges them under links organized in categories, as Figure 2-11 shows. This is a logical arrangement, requiring that you think about what you want to do first, and then click the links in a likely category until you locate the correct task.

The other two views—small icons and large icons—each contain the same complete alphabetized list of more than four dozen applets, each with an icon. The only difference between the two is in the size of icons. Figure 2-12

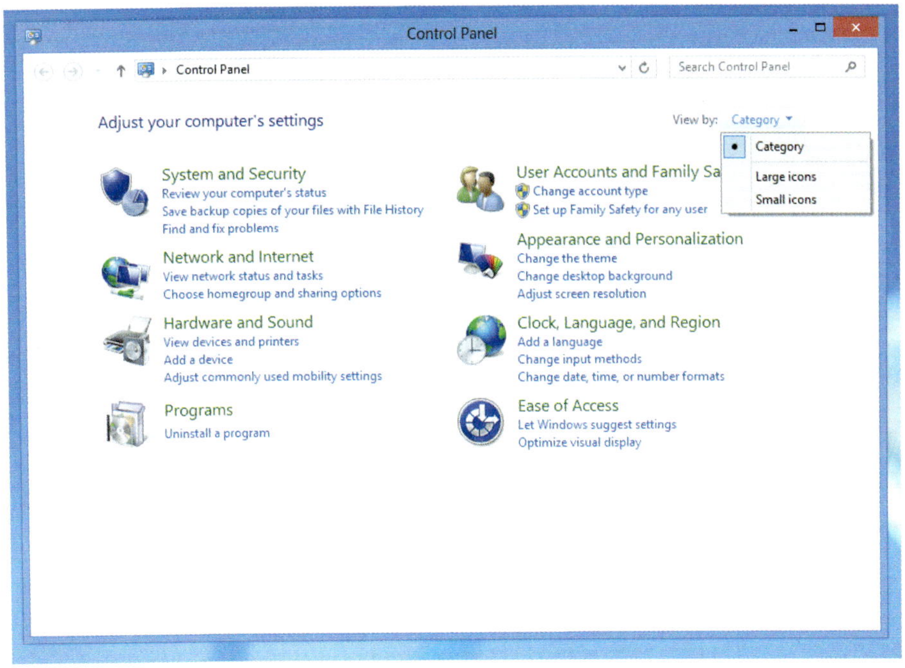

FIGURE 2-11 Control Panel in category view

shows small icon view. We counted 48 icons, but that will vary, based on the edition of Windows 8 and how many installed devices have added icons to Control Panel.

Administrative Tools

Yet another way to access tools is through a grouping of utilities called Administrative Tools. Administrative Tools appears as a single icon in Control Panel. In previous versions of Windows, you could add Administrative Tools to the right column of the Start menu through the Start menu tab on the taskbar and Start Menu Properties dialog box. If you find you use these tools frequently, you might want to add them as a group to the Start screen, as described in the Try This! exercise. They will then appear as shown in Figure 2-13. Several of these tools are more advanced than most power users and IT professionals require; if you find that is the case for you, remove all the tiles at once by reversing the process, or remove only the tiles of the ones you never use. In the next section of this book we explore how to remove tiles from the Start screen.

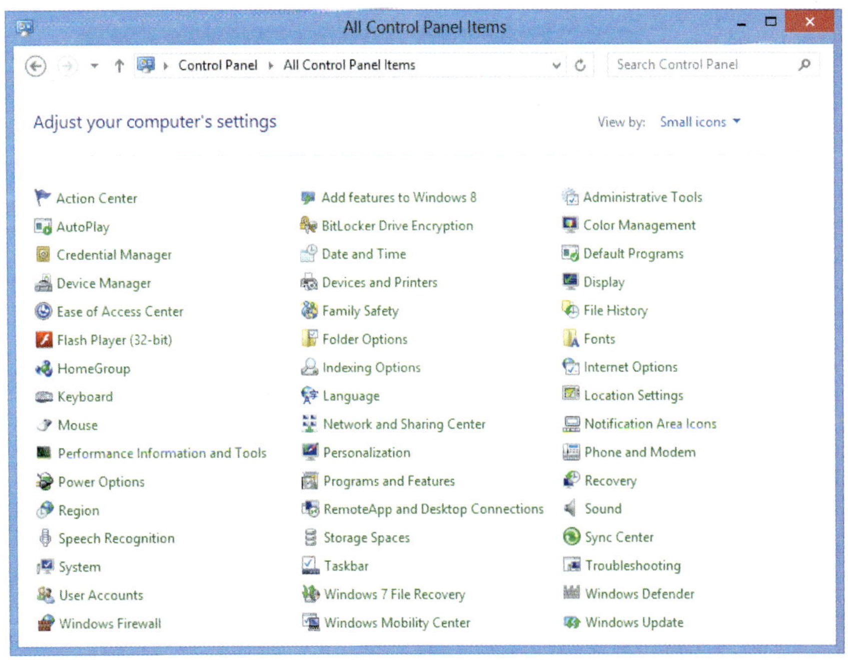

FIGURE 2-12 Control Panel in small icon view

The Windows 8 Command Prompt

Windows 8 arguably has a third user interface, in addition to Windows 8 and the Desktop. This user interface is

FIGURE 2-13 You can add administrative tools to the Start screen.

a command-line interface (CLI) known as the Command Prompt, and it is how advanced users and administrators enter useful commands for managing their systems. Its use has diminished as Microsoft has added more powerful GUI tools, but it at least deserves a brief mention here.

The Command Prompt in Windows 8 can be called up from the Start context menu (Windows key+X) and it has two versions, Command Prompt and Command Prompt (Admin), shown in Figure 2-14. The first one, when open, can run only programs that do not require administrative rights, whereas the second one can run privileged programs. First, to start the Administrator Command Prompt you must get past the User Account Control dialog box that pops up before opening the Command Prompt (Admin). Learn more about Windows 8 user accounts and User Account Control in Chapter 4. Once in the Administrator Command Prompt, notice that it is focused on the C:\Windows\system32 folder. That is because this is the location of many Windows CLI utilities.

A cursor in a CLI is merely a marker for the current position where what you type on the keyboard appears. Further, only a limited set of characters fits on the screen; each in its own little equal-sized grid of space. How do you call up a program? You type the

Keyboard Shortcuts!
Open the Setting bar with the Windows key+I.

try this!

Add the Administrative Tools to the Start Screen

Add tiles for the Administrative Tools to your Start screen.

1. From the Start screen, use a swiping motion from the bottom-right corner up with your finger or mouse to open the Charms bar. Then tap or click Settings to open the Start Settings bar. Alternatively, from the Start screen directly open the Start Settings bar with the Windows key+I.
2. Click the Tiles link directly under the title Start to access the Show Administrative Tools slider, shown here.

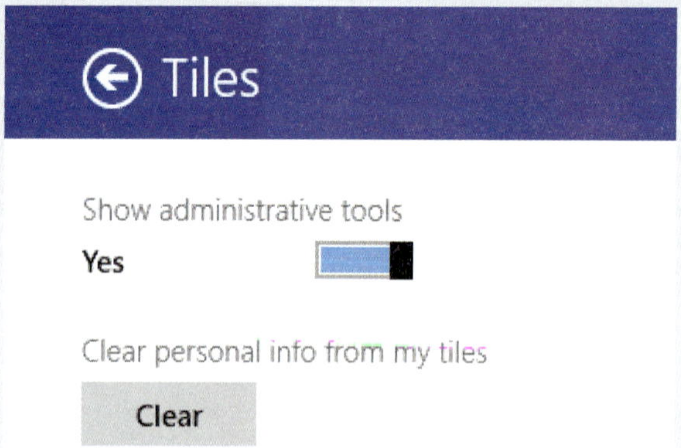

3. With mouse or finger, move the slider to Yes, or simply click to turn to Yes.
4. Click or tap the Start screen to close the bar, and scroll the screen to see the new tiles.
5. Some of these tools are available from Start context menu, and the entire Administrative Tools set is available in Control Panel. To remove them from your Start screen, repeat steps 1 and 2 above and move the slider to No.

FIGURE 2-14 The Windows 8 Command Prompt with Admin privileges

command (e.g.: `notepad` to call up the Notepad text editor) and press Enter. You must either memorize commands or keep a cheat sheet handy. If a command has variations, you must enter the correct modifiers and subcommands. There's no clicking around to find what you want. Everyone should experience the Command Prompt at least once in a lifetime, so if you haven't yet, spend a minute or two with the Try This! exercise.

> try this!
>
> **Use the Windows 8 Command Prompt**
>
> Let's open the Windows 8 Command Prompt and enter a few commands. We will use the Command Prompt without administrative privileges.
>
> 1. Open the Start context menu by right-clicking the bottom-left corner of the screen and select Command Prompt. It will open focused on the location of your personal folders, although it is not very obvious. The prompt—the string of characters preceding the blinking cursor—will look something like this: C:\Users*yourname*>.
> 2. Use the DIR command to list directories and files. Type: `dir` and press Enter. The result will be a list of the directories (folders) containing your personal files.
> 3. The Change Directory command (CD) lets you change the current directory. Type: `cd documents` and press Enter. Your changed directory and the prompt will now read C:\Users*yourname*\Documents>.
> 4. Use the DIR command to list the contents of the Documents directory. It may be empty if this is a new installation.
> 5. Type: `cd ..` and press Enter to move back up to the *yourname* directory.
> 6. Type: `exit` to close the Command Prompt.

Disabling the Lock Screen

The Lock screen is a great thing to have on a touch-screen tablet or smartphone. Without the Lock screen on such a device, you might accidentally start a program, delete something, or dial someone. Some call this last action "pocket dialing." But you don't need a lock screen on a computer without a touch screen, so consider disabling it on your desktop or laptop PC. To do this you must edit your computer's local computer policy using a utility called Local Group Policy Editor with an executable name of gpedit.msc. You will see the importance of knowing this name in Step-by-Step 2.2, which will walk you through disabling your lock screen.

Editing the group policy is a rather advanced task; group policy is a bit complex as a topic. In short, a computer has a great number of configuration settings called policies. If your computer is part of a Microsoft Domain at school or work, two sets of policies affect it: local group policies stored on the computer and domain group policies stored in the domain database. We further separate each of these group policies into those that affect the computer and are applied every time Windows starts up, and those that affect a user and are applied every time that user logs on. The domain group policies override the local group policies.

When you select the Lock options from the User tile context menu after you disable the Lock screen, rather than displaying the Lock screen, the Log-In/Sign-In screen displays.

You should disable the Lock screen only on a device without a touch screen. With those caveats in mind, Step-by-Step 2.2 will walk you through disabling your Lock screen.

If you have administrative rights to your computer, you can change the local group policy and change settings, such as the one that controls the Lock screen. We discuss the issue of administrative rights in Chapter 4, but for now, understand that you may not have administrative rights to a computer belonging to your school or work and should attempt to disable the Lock screen only on your own personal PC or laptop. Also, if your computer is part of a Microsoft Domain at work or school, even if you do have administrative rights to the computer, any changes you make may be undone when the domain's group policies are applied to your computer at the next restart or sign in.

Step-by-Step 2.2

Disable the Lock Screen

The tool you need to disable your Lock screen is not easily available unless you know the executable name for it. The executable name for the Local Group Policy Editor is gpedit.msc. Follow these steps to run this advanced tool and disable the Lock screen.

Step 1

From either GUI, open the Start context menu by right-clicking in the lower-left corner of the screen, then click Run.

Step 2

In the Run box, enter `gpedit.msc` and click OK. If you see an error message stating that Windows could not find the file, click the OK button to close the message and the Run box will open again, displaying what you last typed in. Recheck and reenter *`gpedit.msc`*, being sure to type in the period and the extension (msc).

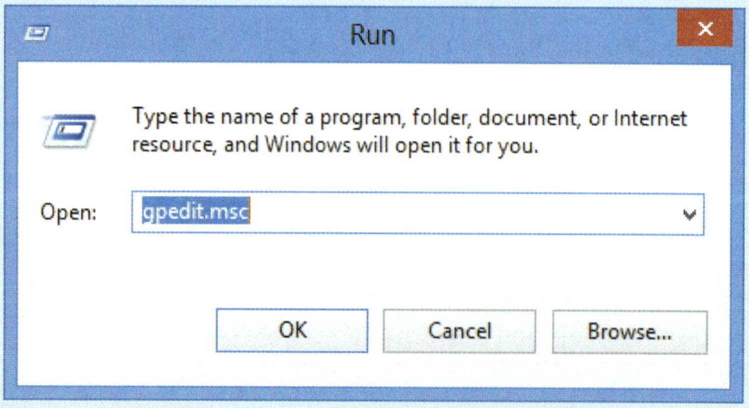

Step 3

When the Local Group Policy Editor opens, use the folder view pane on the left. Select the triangle in front of each folder to expand the folder hierarchy and move down to Computer Configuration | Administrative Templates | Control Panel | Personalization. In the right pane, double-click the setting titled Do Not Display the Lock Screen.

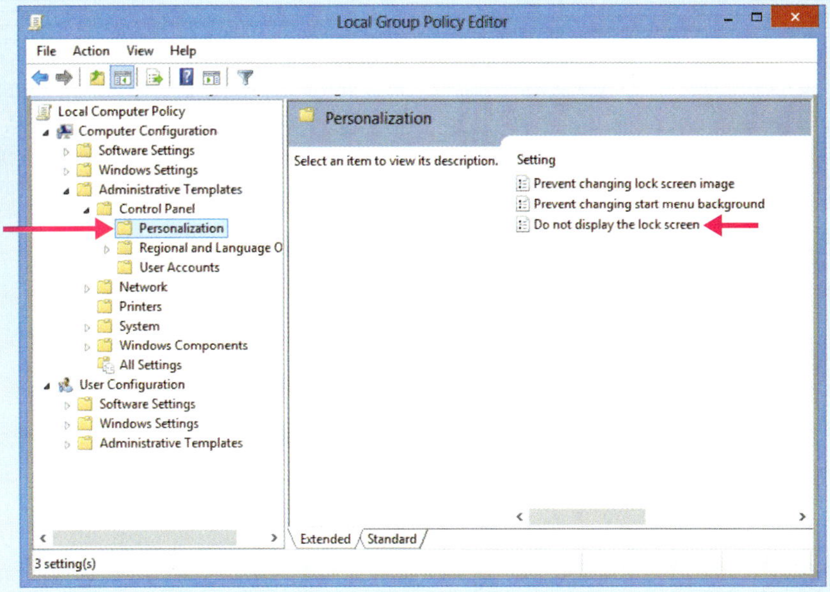

Step 4

In the dialog box for the setting, select Enabled. This actually disables the Lock screen, because you are enabling Do Not Display the Lock Screen. (Talk about a double negative!) Click the OK button and then close the Local Group Policy Editor.

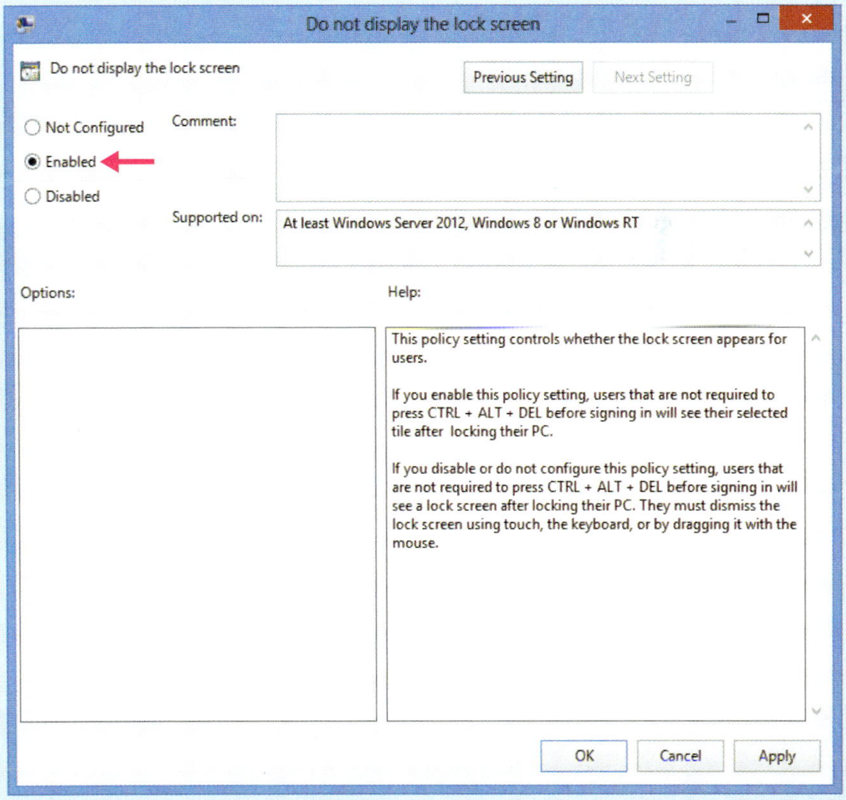

Step 5

Restart Windows and you will be greeted by the Sign-In screen, bypassing the Lock screen.

FIGURE 2-15 The Default User Account picture

Customizing the User Account Picture

The user account picture displays on the Sign-In screen, as well as on the User tile in the upper right of the Start screen, along with the name of the currently logged-on user. When you first sign in, the default picture is used, shown in Figure 2-15. You can change it to something more meaningful by following the instructions in Step-by-Step 2.3 if you have a file containing the picture you want to use or a webcam to take a self-portrait using the Camera.

Step-by-Step 2.3

Changing the User Account Picture

Change the account picture in Windows 8 to an image of yourself, or one that reflects your personality.

Step 1

On the Start screen, click or tap the User tile to open its context menu.

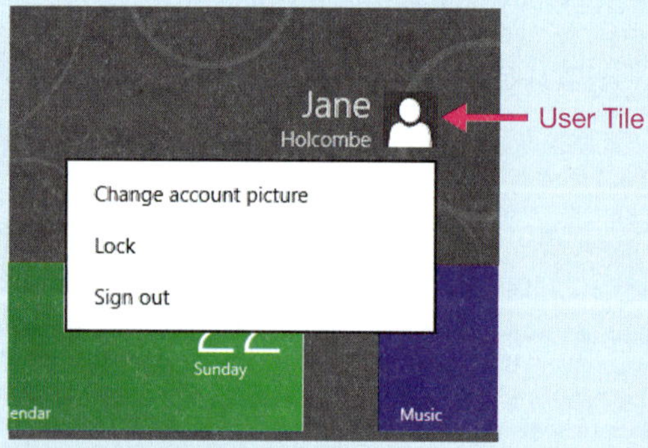

Step 2

Click or tap Change Account Picture to open the PC settings page showing the Windows 8 Control Panel for Account Picture Settings. Click the Browse button.

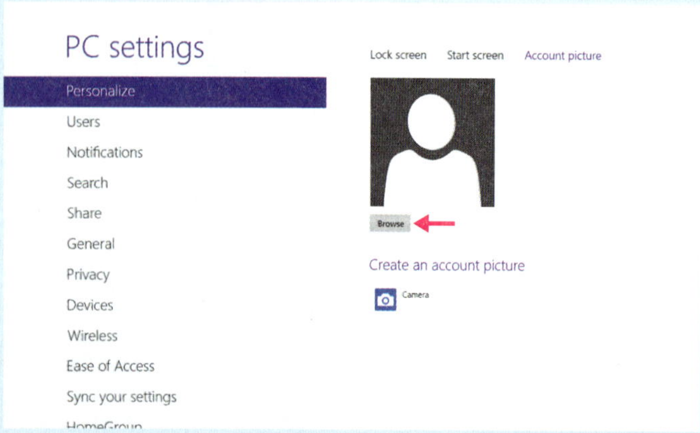

Step 3

On the Files page select a location to browse. If you have saved pictures on your computer, click or tap Pictures to open the pictures folder.

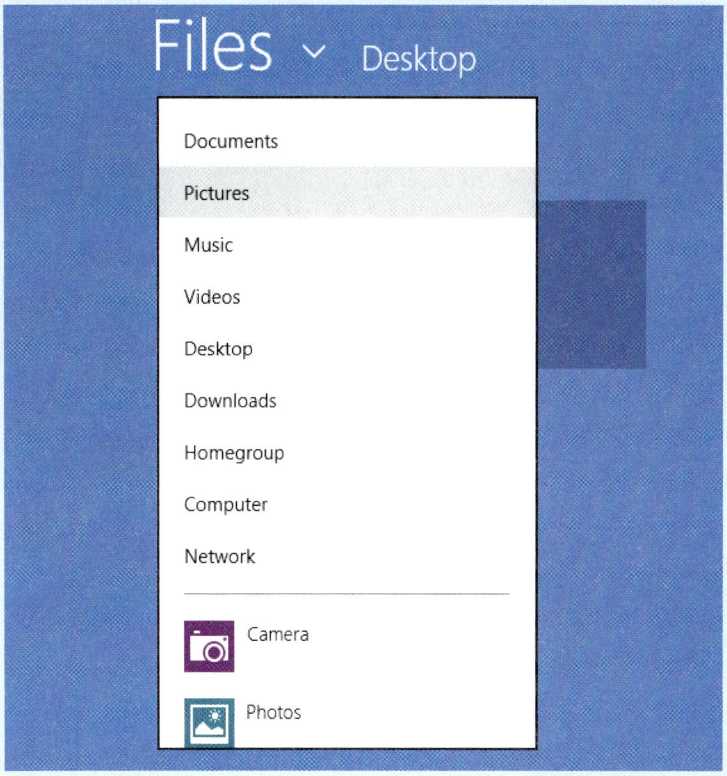

Step 4

We show only three pictures here, but you may have more than one screen to scroll through. When you locate a picture you want to use, click or tap it, and then click or tap the Choose Image button on the bottom right.

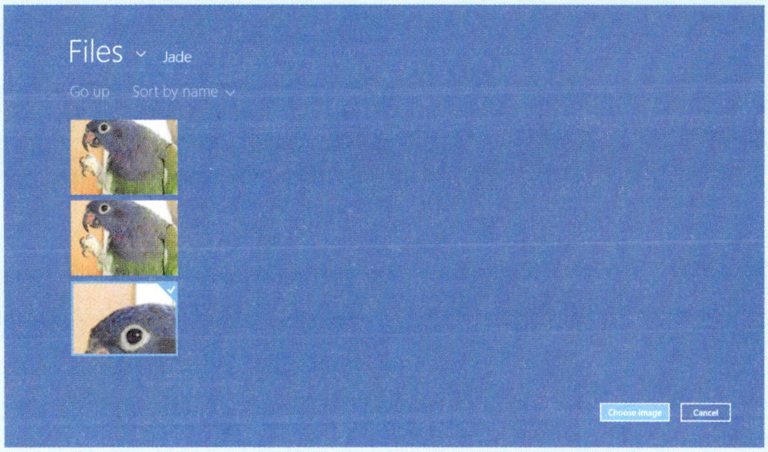

Step 5

The Account Picture Settings page will display with your new picture. Return to the Start screen where the new picture will be in your User tile. You will also see this same image on your Sign-In screen.

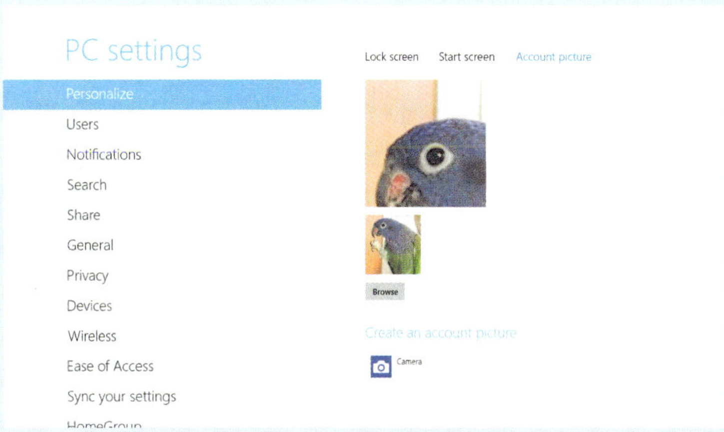

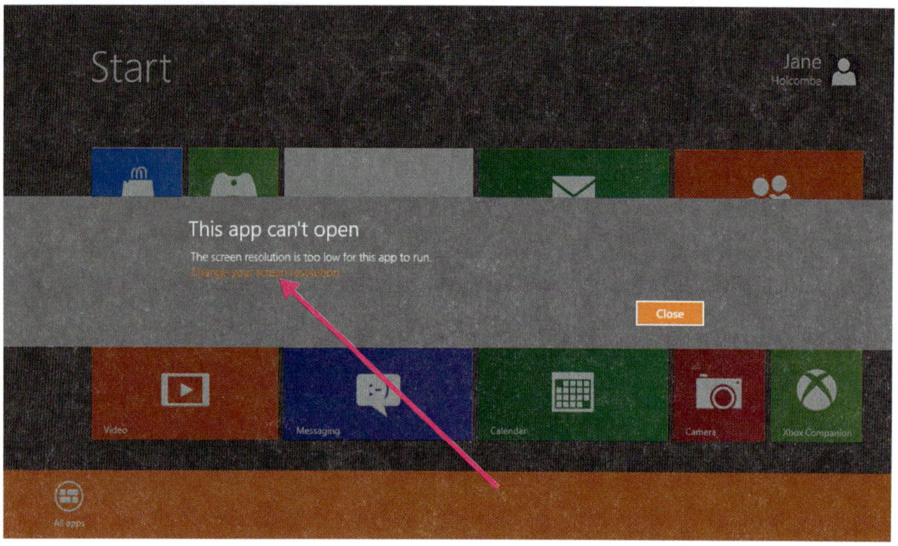

FIGURE 2-16 Windows 8 apps cannot run at a resolution lower than 1,024 × 768. You will see this message if you attempt to open a Windows 8 app at a lower resolution.

Windows 8 and Screen Resolution

Windows 8 apps require a minimum screen resolution of 1,024 × 768. If your screen resolution is less, the Start screen will display, but when you try to open a Windows 8 app you will see the message Figure 2-16 shows. Click Change Your Screen Resolution to open the Screen Resolution applet and make the necessary changes. If you do not use this link to open Screen Resolution, you can open it by first opening the Charms bar, selecting Search, then selecting Settings, and in the Search box start typing `screen resolution` until one of the search results is Adjust Screen Resolution.

The 1,024 x 768 resolution is a bare minimum; for the best visual experience, you will need a resolution of 1,366 × 768 to support features like Snap, which we explore later in this chapter.

The various screenshots in this book are in three resolutions: we created the wider ones (with a screen ratio of 16 × 9) at a screen resolution of 1,366 × 768, and the others (at a 5 × 4.5 ratio) we created at a resolution of 1,152 × 864 or 1,024 × 768. Any computer technician will tell you that you don't always have a choice when it comes to screen resolution because an LCD or similar technology flat-screen display has only one physical screen resolution, and you must use that. It will either be the only option available, or it will be the option labeled "recommended," as shown in Figure 2-17, which shows the Screen Resolution applet with a range of resolutions between 1,024 × 768 and 1,366 × 768. What does not show is that there are only two other choices within that range that are selectable: 1,280 × 768 and 1,360 × 768.

try this!

Change the Start Screen Background

Change the Start screen to suit your tastes. Try This!

1. From the Start screen, open the Charms bar and select the Settings charm. This brings up the Settings sidebar.
2. In the Settings sidebar, locate the Change PC Settings link at the bottom and click it to bring up the PC Settings Control Panel.
3. Select Personalize from the list of tasks on the left, and select Start screen on the right.
4. Select the background preference and then move the slide control to select a color.
5. Swipe the bottom left until the Start Tip appears and tap it or use the Windows key to return to the Start screen.

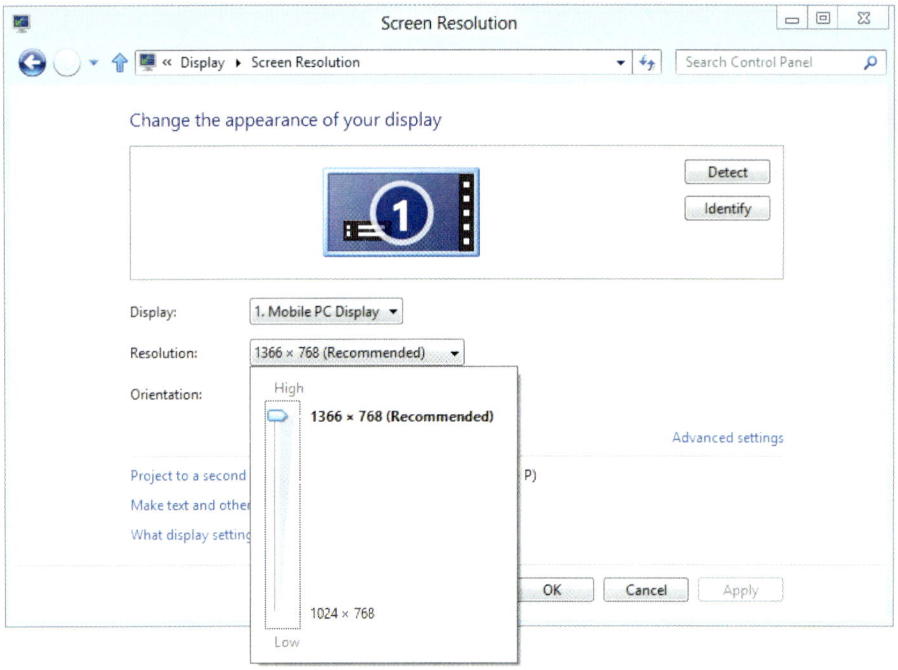

FIGURE 2-17 This display has a range of screen resolutions between 1,024 × 768 and 1,366 × 768.

Customizing the Start Screen Background

You can change the background on the Start screen, controlling both the pattern and the color displayed behind the tiles. Do this from the PC Settings Control Panel, a Windows 8 full screen tool for making changes to your system that affect Windows 8 in general. See Figure 2-18.

Personalizing the Desktop Background

You must configure the Desktop separately from the Start screen. If you have changed the background and screen savers in previous versions, you will be

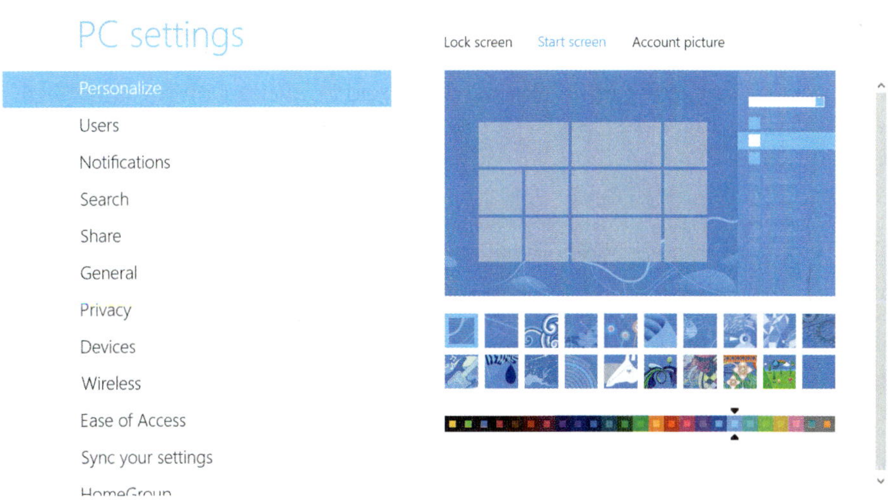

FIGURE 2-18 The PC Settings Control Panel

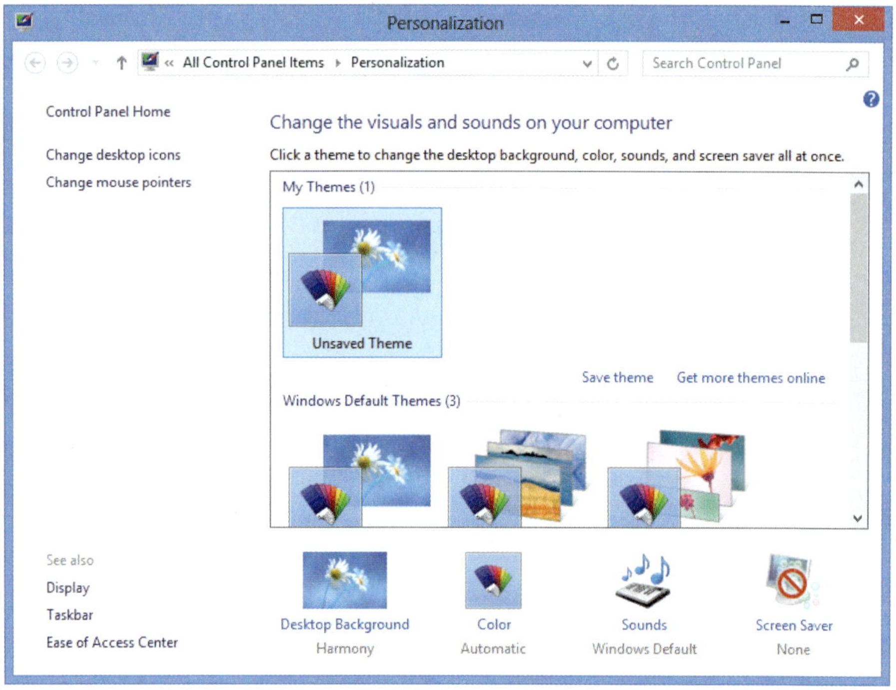

FIGURE 2-19 The Personalization applet for the Windows 8 Desktop

familiar with the process. In fact, you will use the same Control Panel applet you used in Windows 7: Personalization, shown in Figure 2-19. As with previous versions of Windows, you right-click an empty area of the Desktop and select Personalize from the context menu. Here you can select the desktop background, window color, sounds, and screen saver separately. Or you can select a preconfigured theme with coordinated background, windows color, and sounds. The screen saver will work for both GUIs, bringing up an animated screen when a preconfigured amount of time passes without activity (keyboard, mouse, and now, touch).

Adding the Hibernate Option to the Power Button

Recall the discussion of the Shut Down, Restart, Sleep, and Hibernate options in Chapter 1 under the topic "Logging Off and Shutting Down Windows 8." Windows 8 unmodified, right-out-of-the-box, is configured to have three options from the on-screen Power button: Sleep, Shut down, and Restart. Suppose you are in the middle of some project on your laptop, and you need to carry your computer elsewhere—perhaps to board a plane, or to leave the library and go to a class. There are two modes you can use to save the state of your computer with all your apps and data files open as you left them: Sleep and Hibernate, which we described in Chapter 1. However, of these two, only Sleep is available on a new Windows 8 computer; you will need to make a change in Windows 8 to enable Hibernate on the on-screen Power button.

Step-by-Step 2.4 walks you through the process of adding the Hibernate option to your computer's on-screen Power button and the Shut Down Windows dialog box. Do this only on a computer with a conventional hard drive because there is some question about the effect of repeatedly saving hibernation files on an SSD device.

> As stated in Chapter 1, Hibernate may not be a good choice on a computer using SSD storage because you can write to these devices only a limited number of times in the same location. This is not usually a problem with normal usage, but the hibernation file adds additional usage, and some experts question the wisdom of using Hibernate because it may shorten the life of an SSD device. Maybe this is why it is optional in Windows.

Step-by-Step 2.4

Enabling the Hibernate Option

To enable Hibernate as a choice on the on-screen Power button and the Shut Down Windows dialog, you need to use the Power Options Control Panel applet.

Step 1

From either GUI, open the Charms bar and select Search.

Step 2

In the Search bar, click Settings to move the focus to Settings and then enter po into the Search box. In the results list, click or tap Power Options.

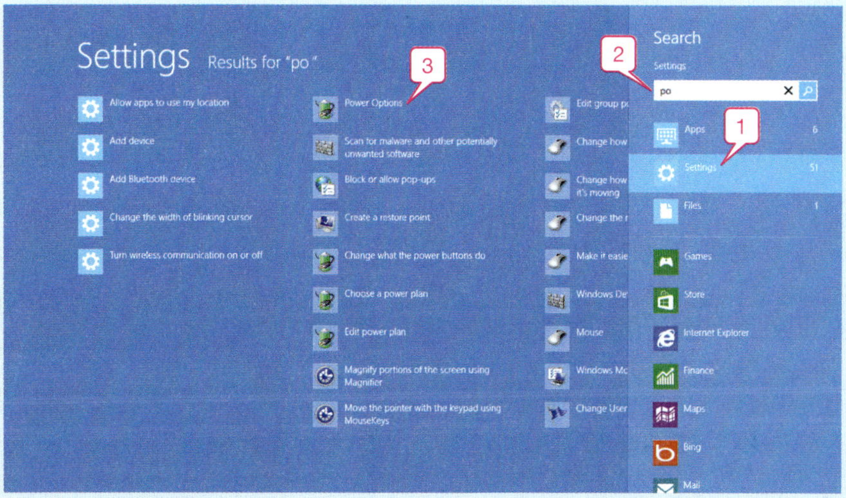

Step 3

In the task pane (on left) of the Power Options applet, select Choose What the Power Buttons Do.

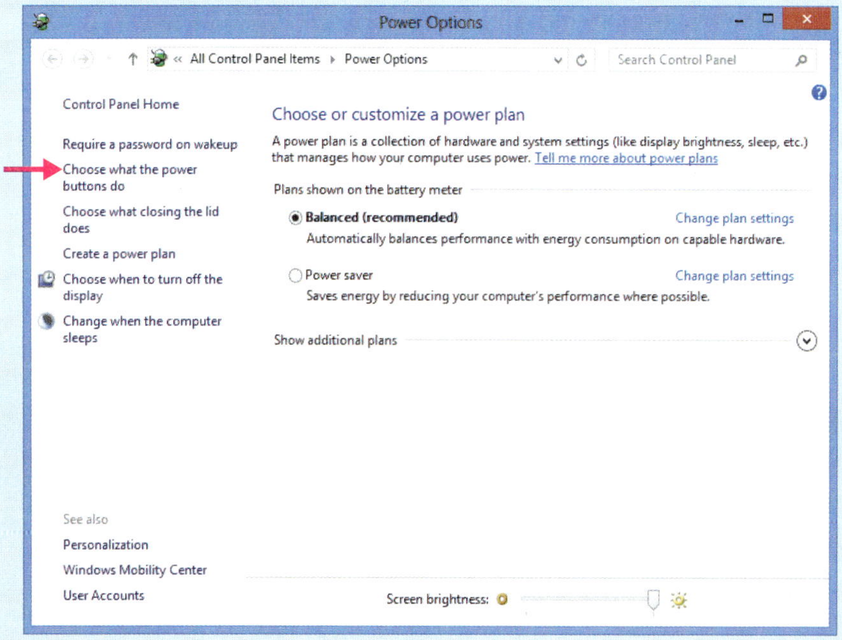

Step 4

In the System Settings applet, first scroll down and notice that many settings are grayed out, indicating that they are not available. Scroll back to the top of the box and select Change Settings That Are Currently Unavailable.

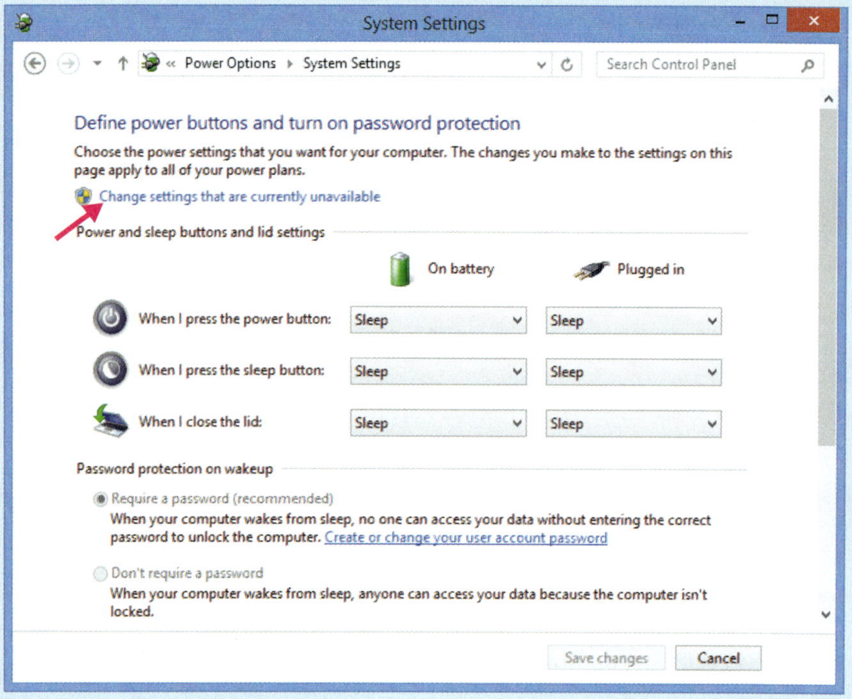

Step 5

Scroll down in System Settings to the Shutdown Settings section. Click or tap to place a check in the Hibernate box. Then click Save Changes.

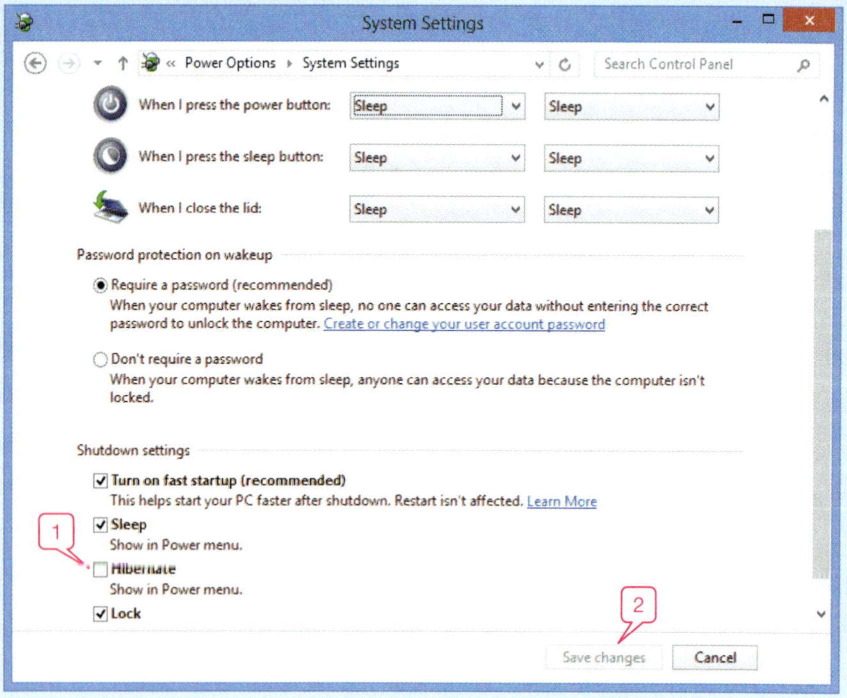

Step 6

You are back at the Power Options applet. Close the applet by clicking the red X in the upper-right corner.

Step 7

Access the on-screen Power button. Do this by first opening the Charms bar and then selecting Settings, or open the Settings bar with the Windows key+I and then select Power. The Power menu should now show Hibernate as an option.

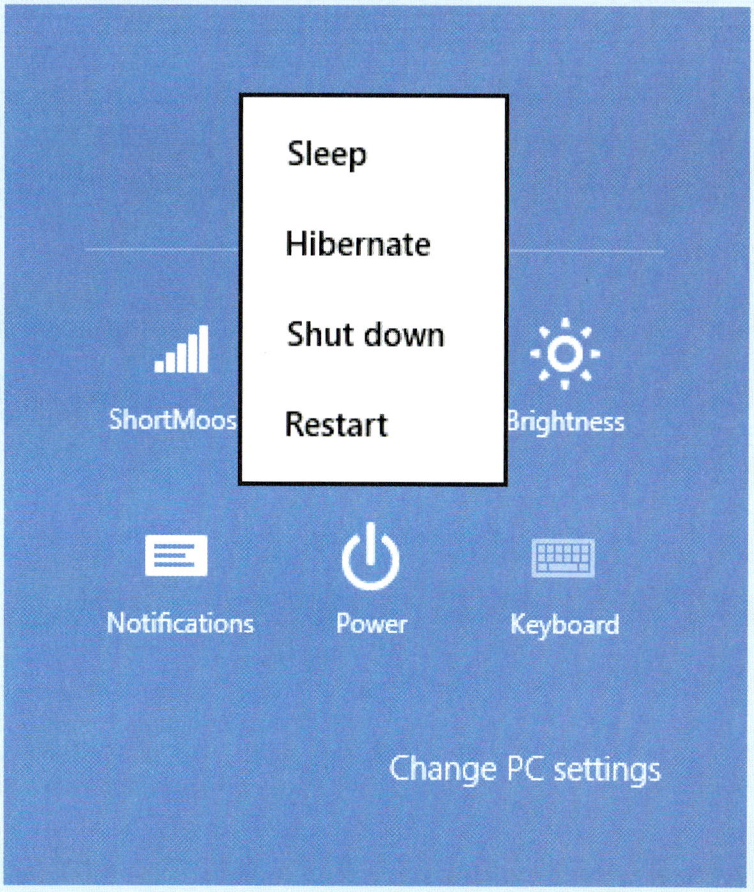

Keyboard Shortcuts!
Quickly bring up the Power button by pressing the old standby: Ctrl+Alt+Delete, which will display a screen with a list of choices in the top center (Lock, Switch User, Sign Out, Task Manager) and two buttons: the Ease of Access Button (left) and the Power button on the right. Now you can choose to shut down or select one of the other Power menu options.

Assigning Hibernate to a Laptop's Power Button

If you have a laptop, you might want to assign Hibernate mode to your physical Power button so that when you need to quickly Hibernate your Windows 8 session, you can do it by pressing the Power button. You can do this in the System Settings applet shown in Step 4 in Step-by-Step 2.4. Notice that you can configure a different group of settings—one for when your laptop is on battery power and one for when it is plugged into a power outlet. We prefer to assign Shut Down to the Power button when the laptop is plugged in and Hibernate to the Power button when the laptop is on battery, because that is when we are most likely to need to use Hibernate. See Figure 2-20.

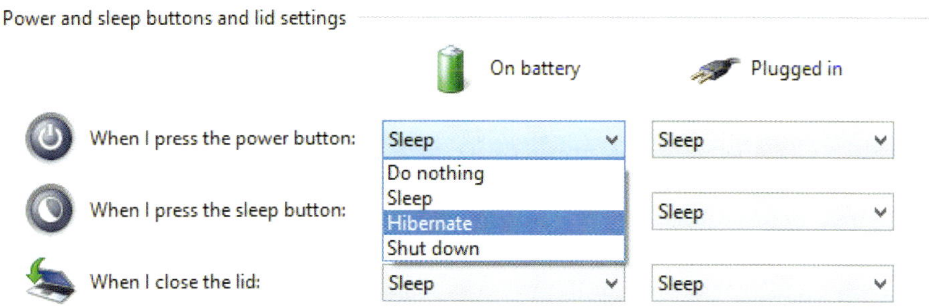

FIGURE 2-20 Assign the Hibernate function to the computer's Power button.

FIGURE 2-21 The Windows Store

LO 2.3 | Managing Apps in Windows 8

Microsoft now calls all applications in Windows 8 "apps." As you have seen, opening an app in Windows 8 is as simple as clicking or tapping its tile, but how do you add apps to Windows 8? How do you remove apps? How are your apps updated? And what is the only way that you can have two Windows 8 apps display on-screen simultaneously? (Hint: it's a Snap.) These all have to do with managing apps in Windows 8, and we'll answer those questions in this section.

The Windows Store

The online Windows Store, available through the Store tile, is your source for Microsoft-certified Windows 8 apps, although you can continue to buy old-style Desktop apps from other sources. When you connect from the Store tile in Windows 8, it opens to the Windows 8 page. You will need a Microsoft Account, which you may already have if you use Hotmail, Microsoft Messenger, or Xbox Live. If you do not have an account, point your browser to live.com and, on the Sign-in page, click the Sign Up button and follow the instructions to create an account. After you sign in to the store, you will notice that some apps in the Microsoft Store are free, others require a fee, and some offer a limited-time free trial. See Figure 2-21. If you have a Windows 8 computer with an Internet connection, follow the instructions in the Try This!

When in Doubt, Right-Click!
In many cases, right-clicking brings up a context menu. When you right-click on the Start screen, it brings up the App bar at the bottom of the screen. Right-click within some apps, and in addition to the App bar you will see a bar of options slide down from the top of the screen.

Updating Windows 8 Apps

Windows Update updates the Windows operating system program code, but Windows 8 apps are updated through the Windows Store. If the Store tile has its live tile turned on, the tile will display a number on the bottom right, indicating that updates are available and how many are available. This is very subtle, and easy to miss. If you see a number on the Store tile and open the app, you will see a link on the top right of the page. For instance, if there are six updates, the link will read "Updates (6)" as Figure 2-22 shows. Click this link, and a list of App updates displays, along with the App bar for the Windows Store. Click Install from the App bar to install all

try this!

Find Free Apps for the Windows 8 GUI

Connect to the Microsoft Store and browse for free apps. Try This!

1. Tap or click the Windows Store tile. If you have an Internet connection, this will connect to the Windows Store site. Notice that the groupings resemble the tiles on your Start screen and are arranged in groups by categories.
2. Scroll through the selections and click those that interest you. Look for a free or free-trial app.
3. Follow the on-screen instructions to download and install the app to your computer.

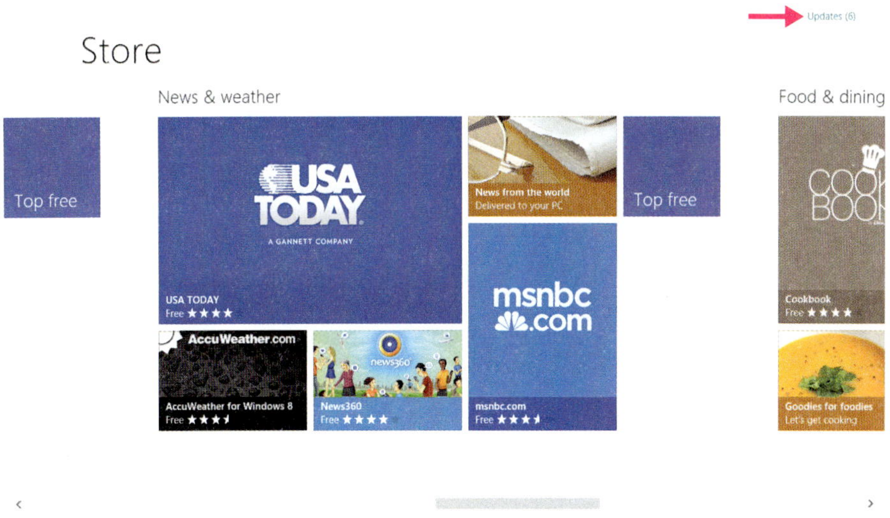

FIGURE 2-22 The Windows Store indicates the number of updates available.

updates, or right-click to clear the check from the apps you do not want to update first. You can also choose to update each app individually.

The App Bar!
Swipe from the bottom or right-click any tile on the Start screen or in the Apps screen to open the App bar, which has a different assortment of options, depending on the selected app or apps. Open it within an app to access features of an app.

The Apps Screen

To see a complete list of all installed apps, open the Apps screen by opening Search, and if it is not selected, select Apps. You can also open it with Windows key+Q. The apps are organized in groups, including by software suite, making it easier to locate programs within a suite. See Figure 2-23.

Keyboard Shortcuts!
Open the App bar with Windows key+Z.

Unpinning an App from the Start Screen

Are you a clean desk person? Or do you work best with piles of papers all over your desk and nearby surfaces? Of course, there are many variations on how we keep our desks where we work, study, or play. The same is true of both the Desktop and the Start screen. Most apps install a tile on the Start screen, and eventually you will need to scroll through several pages to find an app. Even with the ability to move tiles and

try this!

Unpin an App from the Start Screen

Try unpinning an app from the Start screen. Try This!

1. Open the Start screen and select an app to unpin.
2. Right-click the app to open the App bar for that app.
3. On the App bar select Unpin from Start.

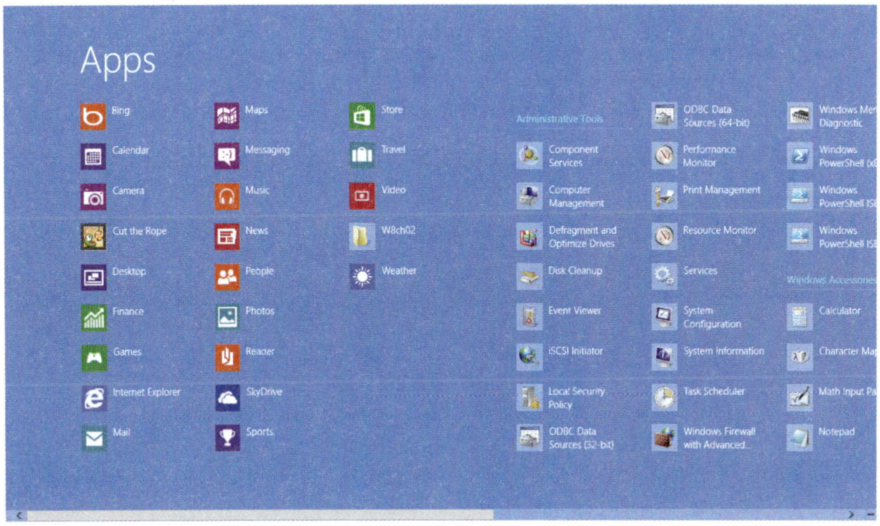

FIGURE 2-23 The Apps screen showing dozens of installed apps at a glance

FIGURE 2-24 Select Unpin from Start to remove the app's tile from the Start screen.

groups around, you may decide to clean house and unpin some apps from the Start screen. This doesn't uninstall the app, and you can still find it on the Apps screen anytime you need it. Figure 2-24 shows the open Apps bar for the selected app, Photos. The tile for the selected app has a small border with a check mark in the upper right.

Pinning an App to the Start Screen

To pin an app to the Start screen, you need to locate the app in the Apps screen (shown back in Figure 2-23), right-click it to open the Apps bar, and if the app does not have a tile on the Start screen it will have a button labeled Pin to Start. Select Pin to Start, and when you return to the Start screen, the app will be there, but it may be on the last page. You may want to move it to the desired group by dragging the tile. To open the Apps bar on a touch screen, touch the app's live tile or entry on the Apps screen and swipe down. The Try This! walks you through pinning an app to the Start screen.

Pinning Apps to the Taskbar

You can customize the Taskbar in the Desktop GUI, much as you did in Windows 7, by pinning applications for fast startup. When you run an older app, or Windows components created for older versions of Windows, it will run in a window on the desktop. While the app is open, right-click the app's icon in the taskbar and select Pin This Program to Taskbar, shown in Figure 2-25.

Closing Open Apps

Once launched, Windows 8 apps remain open until you sign off or shut down. Until then, those you are not presently using go temporarily into suspension so that they do not take up processing power and tax your battery-based devices. Windows 8 apps also release most of the memory they use, but Desktop apps do not. Yet a Windows 8 app will still come up quickly when you switch to it. This is by design, and, just like on your smartphone, you don't worry

try this!

Pin an App to the Start Screen

Pin an app to the Start screen. Try This!

1. Open the Apps screen.
2. Right-click an app to open the App bar.
3. Select Pin to Start.
4. Return to the Start screen, locate the app's tile, and move it to a convenient location.

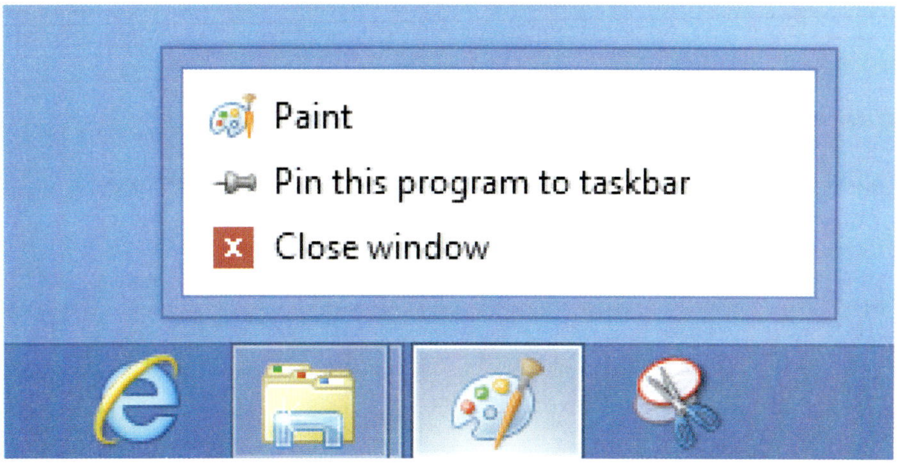

FIGURE 2-25 Right-click a windowed app's icon and select Pin This Program to Taskbar.

about what is or is not open; your Windows 8 apps are available to you whenever you select them.

You can close traditional windowed apps and Windows component applets and dialogs by using the Close button on the top right of the app's window, and the old standby, Alt+F4, still works to close the current app—Windows 8 or Desktop.

Either type of app can also be closed in Task Manager, which is a bit more trouble. It is also worth knowing how to open Task Manager in case you believe an app is a problem and want to see its status. If an app is stalled, its status may be "Unresponsive." To open the Task Manager, open the Search bar and enter `task` into the search box. Then select Task Manager from the results. By default, it opens in a very simplified view, but if you click More Details on the bottom left, it expands with the Processes tab open. This page gives you quite a bit of information, with the Status column normally empty except when an app has failed, in which case you will see a message such as "Not Responding." To see even more information, click the Details tab and you will see the status for all running programs (Figure 2-26). "Running" and "Suspended" are normal statuses for programs, but if you see a status of "Not Responding," then you have found a problem program. Select that program and click the End Task button at the bottom.

Keyboard Shortcuts!
Press Alt+F4 to close the currently open app. Press Ctrl+Shift+Esc to quickly open the Task Manager.

Uninstalling Apps and Removing Windows Components

You can uninstall most apps from Windows 8 through the App bar in the Start screen or Apps screen, including some Desktop apps. For instance, the Microsoft Office 2010 Suite is a group of Desktop apps, but they install into Windows 8 with tiles on the Start screen and are listed in the Apps screen. Therefore, to uninstall most apps, open the App bar for the app and select Uninstall. For those apps that do not have tiles in the Start screen but are listed in the Apps screen, open Programs and Features from the Start context menu, locate the app in the list of programs, and uninstall it.

Similarly, the Start screen or the Apps screen lists some Windows components, and you can uninstall them from the app's App bar, but you must uninstall many other Windows components from the Programs and Features applet. In the task list on the left select Turn Windows Features On or Off. This opens the Windows Features dialog box shown in Figure 2-27. Then locate the feature and click or tap to remove the check in the check box. You can also turn on individual Windows features here.

FIGURE 2-26 The Details pane in Task Manager shows the status of all running programs.

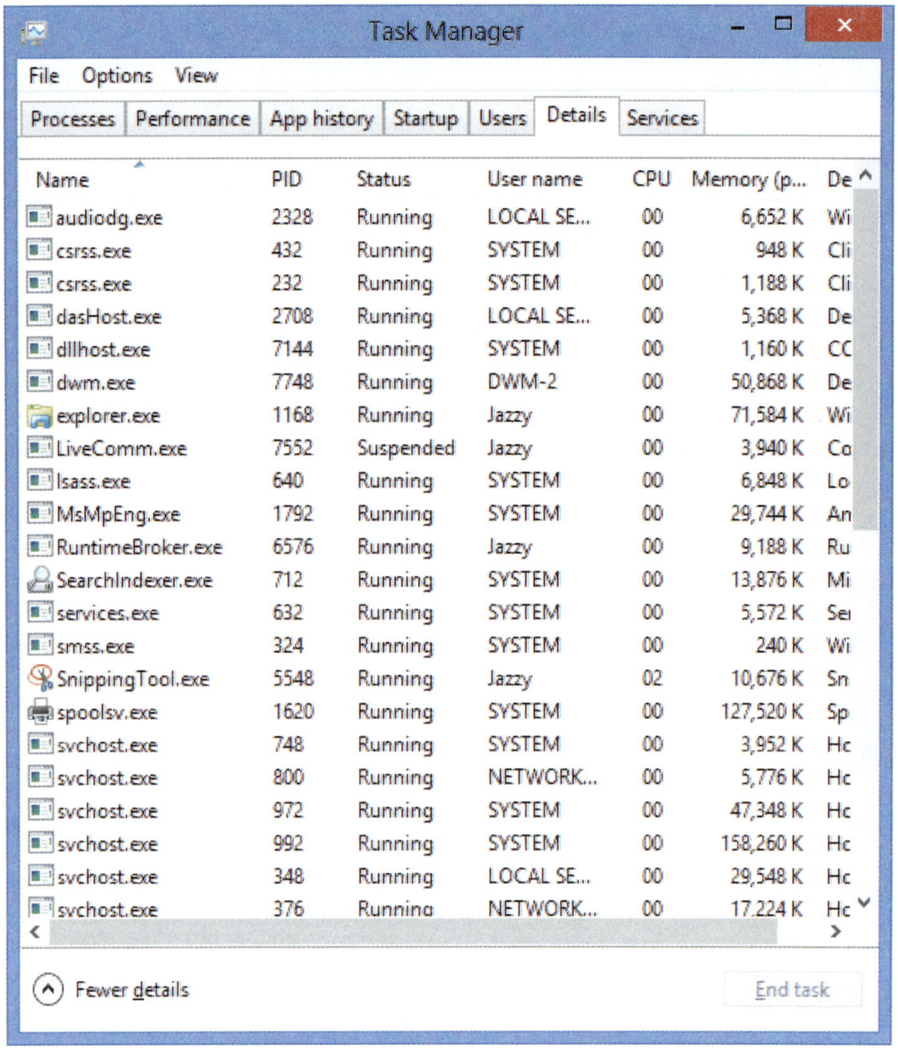

FIGURE 2-27 Turn Windows features on and off using the Windows Features applet.

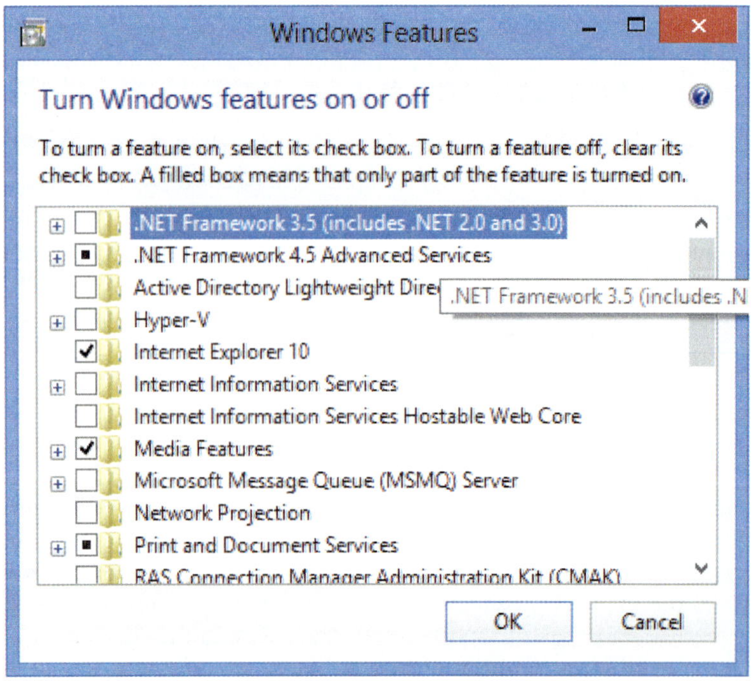

FIGURE 2-28 Using Snap, you can display two Windows 8 apps side-by-side.

Windows 8 Snap

Although Windows 8 apps are all full screen by default, you can display two Windows 8 apps at once using a feature called **Snap**. Here's how it works. After opening at least two Windows 8 apps, on a touch screen, swipe from the left or right edge of the screen, but stop before bringing the new app completely in and pause, moving your finger down to snap it into place next to the app that presently has the screen. When using a mouse, hover at the left side of the screen until a tiny tile image of the other app shows by the edge. Then gently drag the tile a very short distance from the edge and release. It should snap into a small vertical portion of the screen, as shown in Figure 2-28. The main app is the one occupying the majority of the screen—a space that is 1,024 pixels wide, while the snapped app is 320 pixels wide, for a total width of 1,366. This explains the need for a resolution of 1,366 × 768 for the best Windows 8 visual experience. To switch the main app with the snapped app, drag by touch or mouse the three dots on the bar between the apps. Alternatively, use the Windows key+. (period) keyboard shortcut to snap the current Windows 8 app to the right (repeat to snap to the left, and again to return the app to full screen). It hardly seems necessary, but Windows key+Shift+. (period) snaps the open app to the left, repeating cycles it right, and repeating again goes to full screen.

Keyboard Shortcuts!
Use the Windows key+. (period) keyboard shortcut to snap the current app to the right (repeat to snap to the left, and again to return the app to full screen).

Chapter 2 REVIEW

Chapter Summary

After reading this chapter and completing the exercises, you should understand the following facts about navigating and customizing Windows 8.

Navigating the Windows 8 GUI

- The Windows 8 GUI for Windows 8 is an example of a Natural User Interface (NUI).
- In Windows 8 you can use a mouse and keyboard or touch gestures on a touch screen and on some laptop touchpads.
- When you are using Windows 8, you return to the Start screen to access programs. The Start screen contains live tiles that you use to launch full-screen Windows 8 apps. Live tiles can display live content for the app.

- A User tile in the top-right corner of the Start screen displays the username of the currently logged-on user and a picture, which the user can customize.
- Use the Windows 8 semantic zoom feature to see all the Start screen tiles in miniature. In this view you can move the groups around.
- If you start typing at the Start screen, the Search bar opens and you can search through apps, settings, and files.
- The Charms bar and the features it represents are all Windows features available from anywhere in Windows 8, including within apps.
- Screen corners are activated with mouse actions, and edges are activated with edge gestures, which are touch gestures that begin close to the bezel of the screen.
- The Start tip appears at the bottom left of the screen and is a thumbnail of the most recent active app. The Start Tip bar displays along the left of the screen, showing thumbnails of all open apps.
- Open the Desktop from the Desktop tile on the Start screen. The Start button and Start menu are gone, but the Start screen and the Charms bar mostly replace their functions.
- The File Explorer tile will open a File Explorer window on the Desktop.

Customizing Windows 8

- Use the Ease of Access button on the Sign-In screen to enable some of the Windows 8 Ease of Access features including Narrator, Magnifier, On-screen Keyboard, High Contrast, Sticky Keys, and Filter Keys. When you are signed in, you can open the Ease of Access page in PC Settings for more such features.
- Right-click the bottom-left corner of the screen to access the Start context menu containing a list of handy Windows tools.
- Some Windows tools are grouped as Administrative Tools, which you can access through Control Panel, or you can add their tiles to your Start screen.
- If you need to use the Windows Command Prompt, call it up from the Start context menu, then select one version with ordinary privileges or another with administrative privileges.
- If you do not have a touch screen, consider disabling the Lock screen through a more advanced tool called the Local Group Policy Editor.
- Windows 8 requires a minimum screen resolution of 1,024 × 768, but 1,366 × 768 is required to use some features, such as Snap.
- Change the Start screen background through the Windows 8 Control Panel for PC Settings.
- Use the Control Panel's Personalization applet to configure the Desktop to suit your tastes. The screen saver settings will apply to both GUIs.
- Add the Hibernate option to the Power button and assign it to your physical Power button through the Power Options Control Panel applet.

Working with Applications

- Add apps to Windows 8 through the Windows Store, accessible via the Store tile. This is the only source of Windows 8 apps, although you will still find Desktop apps through other channels.
- Windows 8 apps are updated through the Windows Store.
- See a complete list of installed apps in the Apps screen.
- Unpin an app from the Start screen through that app's App bar.
- Pin an app to the Start screen by locating it in the Apps screen, opening its App bar, and selecting Pin to Start.
- Pin Desktop apps to the Taskbar by right-clicking its taskbar icon and selecting Pin This Program to Taskbar.
- Whereas Windows 8 apps release most of their memory while in background, Desktop apps do not. Close traditional windowed apps by clicking the Close button on its window. Close Windows 8 apps through the Task Manager.
- Uninstall most apps—both Windows 8 and Desktop—from the App bar for the app on either the Start screen or the App screen.
- Remove Windows components through the Windows Features applet.
- Windows 8 Snap is the exception to displaying only one Windows 8 app at a time. With Snap you can display two apps, but the snapped app will only be partially visible in a bar on the side of the screen.

Key Terms List

charms (28)
Charms bar (28)
edge gestures (29)
gadget (27)
horizontal scroll bar (27)
keyboard shortcuts (26)
live tile (27)
multitouch device (26)
Natural User Interface (NUI) (26)
Search bar (28)
semantic zoom (28)
Snap (53)
Start Tip (29)
Start Tip bar (30)
thumbnail (29)
touchpad (26)
trackpad (26)

Key Terms Quiz

Use the Key Terms List to complete the sentences that follow. Not all terms will be used.

1. Using the ______________ feature of Windows 8, you can temporarily reduce the size of the tiles on the Start screen for a better overall view, and you can then rearrange the tile groups.
2. Open the ______________ to access shortcuts to Search, Share, Start, Devices, and Settings.
3. ______________ are touch actions that begin very close to a computer's screen bezel.
4. Move your mouse to the bottom-left corner to see the ______________, a thumbnail of the most recent active app.
5. One way to open the ______________ is to begin typing on the Start screen.
6. A/an ______________ is any computing device interface that allows a user to use speech or gestures rather than the conventional keyboard and mouse
7. A/an ______________ is a small graphical object on the Start screen used to launch a program, but it also displays active content for the app when the app is not on-screen.
8. Use the ______________ at the bottom of the Start screen to move through the multiple pages of live tiles.
9. A/an ______________ is an input device that interprets multiple simultaneous touch gestures.
10. Use the ______________ feature to display two Windows 8 apps at a time, with one occupying most of the screen, and the other in a bar on either side.

Multiple-Choice Quiz

1. The old *Star Trek* TV show and movies depicted Scotty talking to the starship's engineering computer, an example of the application of this type of computer interface.
   a. GUI
   b. CLI
   c. Narrator
   d. NUI
   e. ARM
2. This feature in Windows will read aloud the contents of the screen to the user.
   a. GUI
   b. CLI
   c. Narrator
   d. NUI
   e. ARM
3. This is a term used to describe a combination of key presses, such as Windows key+Q, which will quickly produce an assigned action in Windows.
   a. Windows key
   b. gadgets
   c. Charms
   d. Zoom
   e. Keyboard shortcuts
4. Which of the following will open the Windows Help and Support?
   a. Ctrl key+"+" (the plus key)
   b. Windows key+F1
   c. Windows key+Q
   d. Windows key+Tab
   e. Windows key+C

5. Which of the following opens Windows Search?
   a. Ctrl key++
   b. Windows key+F1
   c. Windows key+Q
   d. Windows key+Tab
   e. Windows key+C
6. Which of the following is a group of shortcuts that sit on a bar that opens on the right side of the Windows 8 screen?
   a. gadgets
   b. Start Tip
   c. gestures
   d. live tiles
   e. charms
7. Which of the following opens at the bottom left of the Windows 8 screen and is a thumbnail of the most recent active app?
   a. gadgets
   b. Start Tip
   c. gestures
   d. User tile
   e. charms
8. What is the name for the area on the Start screen that displays your sign-in name and a picture?
   a. gadget
   b. taskbar
   c. User tile
   d. Windows Orb
   e. Ease of Access button
9. Which of these is necessary on a touch-screen device, but inconvenient on an ordinary laptop or desktop?
   a. Apps screen
   b. Lock screen
   c. Sign-In screen
   d. Search bar
   e. Charms bar
10. Which of the following is your source of updates for Windows 8 Windows 8 apps?
    a. Windows Update
    b. Windows Store
    c. Programs and Features
    d. Windows 8 Search
    e. Snap

Essay Quiz

1. In your own words, describe the Windows Start screen, describing both its appearance, including features, and its purpose.
2. You need to take screenshots of Windows 8 to send to a fellow student who is curious about Windows 8. Describe how you would take the screenshot, where it will be saved, and how it will be named.
3. Describe the Windows 8 Snap feature, including the required screen resolution for using it and how you enable it.

Lab Projects

LAB PROJECT 2.1

Experiment with the Windows 8 Search feature. Search apps using a keyword, such as "game" or "word." Search Settings using the keyword "share." Search files using your logged-on name as the keyword. The search of files will search the contents of files, the file authors' names, and the file name.

LAB PROJECT 2.2

Use Windows Help and Support to learn how to open and close the Magnifier and practice using it in the following ways: on the Start screen, opening Windows 8 Apps, on the Desktop, and within Desktop apps. After you have closed it, discuss why the following statement is (or isn't) true: "The Magnifier appears to be a windowed app that can run anywhere in Windows 8, including the Start screen."

LAB PROJECT 2.3

Test how well you can manage a Windows 8 app. If you have Internet access connect to the Windows Store, select an app that is free; then download and install it. Locate the app on the Start screen and move its live tile to the first page of the Start screen. Resize the tile. If it has live content, experiment with turning the live tile off and on. Finally, uninstall the app.

chapter 3

Windows 8 File Management and Printing

"Our life is frittered away by detail. Simplify, simplify."

—Henry David Thoreau, *Walden and Other Writings*

One thing that has not changed over the decades of computer usage is that your most valuable computer asset is your data. You should know how to perform basic data management tasks, connect to printers, and print your data. You'll first learn basic file management tasks in Windows 8, then certain intermediate file management tasks and how to use the new File History feature to recover from accidental deletions of important files. You'll also learn how to connect to and use local and network printers in Windows 8.

Learning Outcomes

In this chapter, you will learn how to:

LO **3.1** Perform basic file management operations such as create, copy, move, delete, and save from within apps as well as from File Explorer.

LO **3.2** Perform intermediate file management tasks, such as managing libraries; searching for apps, files, and folders; managing AutoPlay options for connected devices; and following safe procedures for disconnecting external storage devices.

LO **3.3** Use the new File History option to keep versions of your data files so that you can easily recover from accidental deletions of important files.

LO **3.4** Connect and use local and network printers.

LO 3.1 | Basic File Management in Windows 8

In this section you will learn how to manage your files and folders in Windows 8. The primary tool for creating and saving files is any app you use to create and modify files. Each app can create and edit certain types of files—a word processor can create and edit one or more word processing file formats, a spreadsheet app can create and edit spreadsheet format files, and a photo-editing program can usually create and edit many graphic types. Each is a tool for creating, editing, and saving, but after you have created and saved your data files, the best tool for copying, moving, renaming, and deleting files is File Explorer. Even so, you can do many other file management tasks from within an app; it just isn't the best tool for most of those tasks compared to File Explorer. We'll explore methods of file management using both your apps and File Explorer. But first, we will consider the basics of files and folders.

A File and Folder Primer

You have probably used a PC or some form of computing device since preschool, and you may be a very intuitive and proficient user. Even so, you may take some things for granted, such as the files you create and how you organize them, until you see a strange error message about an illegal character (nothing personal) or you have a problem finding an important file. If you have experienced any issues or confusion concerning files on your Windows computer, it is time to review the basics of files and folders. The good news is that most of this applies to other operating systems too—not just to Windows 8.

Files and File Names

A **file** is a container for data (whether program code or some type of user data such as a Word document, picture, or sound file) organized as a unit, saved on mass storage, and identified with a special name, called a file name. The author/creator of a file determines how much information to save in a single file. For instance, the chapter you are reading right now is a single file. We could have chosen to save all the chapters of this book in a single file, but instead, we chose to save them in individual files because it breaks the information up into more workable "chunks." That's the key to working with information in general—using chunks that you can manage well.

A file name consists of a base file name followed by an extension, the two parts separated by a period. The **extension** is usually three or four characters long and identifies the type of file, although an extension can be longer or shorter. Office files have four characters in the extension. Of course, it takes more than an extension to make a file a certain type. For instance, a file with an `exe` extension must contain within it code that can be executed by the operating system. A file with one of the many graphic file extensions (`GIF`, `JPG`, `PNG`, `TIF`, and so on) must contain within it data that is correctly coded and organized for use by any program that can edit that type of file. In other words, you can't just put an extension on a file and expect it to be the type of file the extension indicates. But extensions are still very important, and to protect them, Windows hides file name extensions in the GUI. You can change this default setting using an option in File Explorer, as you will see later in this chapter.

When naming a file, the best tactic is to keep it simple and meaningful. Beyond that, you can create a file name and extension of up to 255 characters, including spaces and other legal characters. Legal file name characters include upper- and lower-case alphabet characters, numerals (0–9) and many other characters. The operating system reserves certain characters for special purposes. Therefore, if you attempt to create a file name containing these characters, you will see an error message that may call them "illegal" characters. They include the following:

\ / : * ? " < >|

Rather than memorize the illegal file name characters, stick to alphanumeric characters and one or two special characters, such as the hyphen ( ) or underscore (_). And, as for that 255-character limit, the complete path to the file is also included. For instance, a file named `meeting_minutes.docx` saved in the Documents folder for a user named Chuck could have a complete file specification of `C:\users\chuck\My Documents\meeting_minutes.docx`. The file specification includes the entire path through the file system hierarchy to the file, as well as the file name and extension. The **path** to a file includes the drive letter and each folder leading to the file, with a backslash (\) separating each component. Therefore, although you have plenty of leeway in creating a long file name, it still pays to keep it short and simple.

Folders

A **folder** is a logical container used to organize files in a file system on a storage device. The original name, **directory**, is also frequently used. The name "folder" came about when operating systems adopted the image of a paper file folder to represent a directory.

When you are working in an application, such as a word processor, it will usually have a default folder into which it saves your files, but you can choose to save a file in other folders—you can even create additional folders. You have choices like these when you are working with data files.

Typically, you organize your files by separating them into folders containing related files—perhaps all the files for a single project. It's important to understand how to organize files and folders properly so you can easily access important files. Then, because even the best file organization won't guarantee that you'll always remember the name of that very important file or even where you saved it, you should practice searching for files, which you will do later in this chapter.

Any filing system needs a level of organization if it is to be useful. If you use a filing cabinet to hold a number of important documents, most likely you organize those documents into separate file folders and use some sort of alphabetical arrangement of the folders so you can locate the documents quickly when you need them. Imagine what a difficult time you would have finding your tax-related documents if all year you simply threw everything into a large box and then had to sort through each piece of paper to find the few important ones.

In Windows, you do not need to alphabetize your folders; Windows will sort them for you in the GUI, and you can change how File Explorer sorts and displays them. As for naming files and folders, use names that make sense to you. You might name a folder for a department, such as "accounting," or for a project or customer name.

As your data files grow in number, you will want to make more folders to organize them more logically. You will soon find that you have created an entire logical hierarchy of folders consisting of folders and subfolders; the outermost folder is considered the top folder. Having them organized by how you work will make them easier to back up. You can select the top folder and have the backup program back up all subfolders and files. As you work with Windows, you will develop your own filing system.

As part of managing your files, you'll perform different actions—such as opening, closing, copying, renaming, deleting, and moving files and folders. File management in the Windows GUI is easy and relatively safe, because you can see exactly what files and folders you have selected for a file management operation.

File Management from a Windows App

You may spend your entire day in one or two Windows apps, such as a word processor or spreadsheet program. You may work at a job where the computer is configured to start up a single app, and you work within that app and never leave it all day. It may even automatically save the data created without your intervention. In that case, you need no real file management skills. At the other extreme, whether on your work or home computer, you may use several apps throughout the day, frequently creating and saving new files. Or you may use the computers in a lab at school and be required to save assignments to network locations and create your own personal copies on your own flash drive so that you can take them with you. If you fit somewhere within this end of the file management spectrum, you need file management skills—using both your Windows apps and File Explorer.

For our examples, we'll use a very simple word processing app, Microsoft WordPad, that comes with Windows and is so easy to use that we can focus on creating, saving, and opening documents without having to teach the finer points of a more advanced app. If you have a Windows 8 computer you will be able to complete this Step-by-Step.

Step-by-Step 3.1

Creating and Managing Documents in a Windows App

Learn how to create a new document, save the document with a meaningful file name, close the document, and then locate and open the document again.

Step 1

From the Start screen type `wordpad`. Click or tap WordPad in the results list to launch the WordPad App. The app opens on the desktop with a blank, unnamed document.

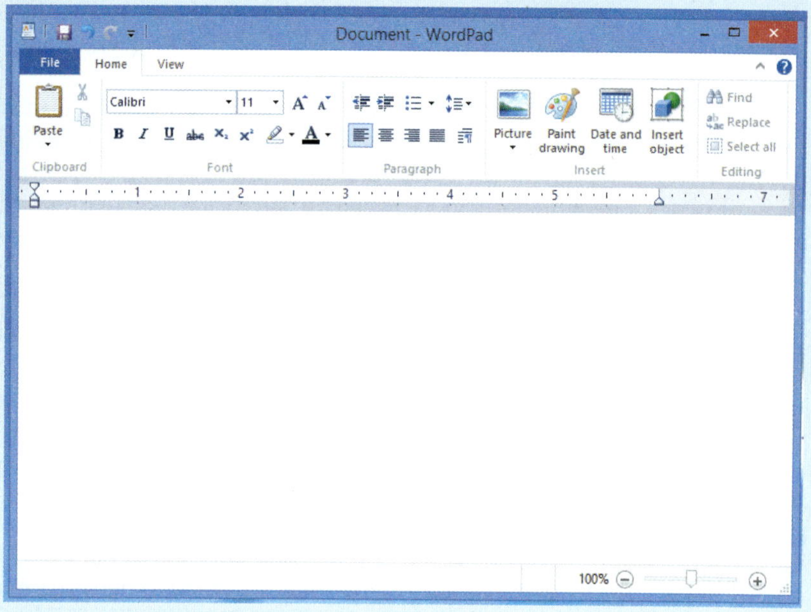

Step 2

Type a short paragraph describing a book you read recently, explaining the topic or time and place and why you like or don't like the book.

Step 3

Click File to open the file menu. Notice all the file operations you can choose from. You will find similar options in most apps in Windows 8. Because this is a Windows desktop app, you accessed it through the ribbon, but in Windows 8 apps, you find such options by opening the Apps bar. Notice the tooltip (not visible in this image) that pops up when you hover the mouse over the Save option. Such tips are plentiful in File Explorer and in Windows Apps.

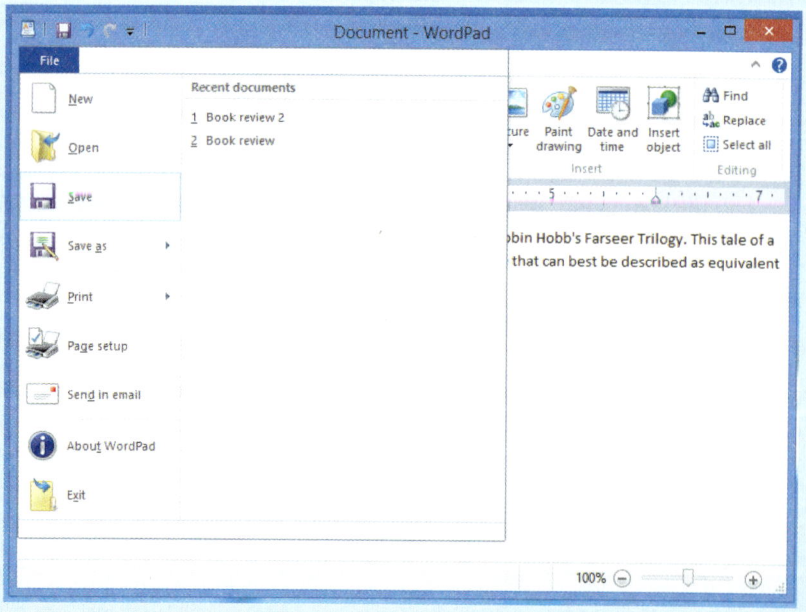

Step 4

From the File menu select Save. Because this is a new document, the Save As dialog box, which typically points to your Documents Library, opens. Verify the Save As location by checking the path displayed in the Save As window shown in the illustration. We'll look more closely at Libraries in the next section. Type a name for the file, such as MyLatestRead. Notice that you can choose among several file types. This is also common among various apps. The top file type, Rich Text Format (RTF), is the default file type for WordPad. Select it and click or tap the Save button that is hidden in this illustration, but which will appear when the Save As Type box is closed. After you have saved a document, when you select Save (or press Ctrl+S) the document will save in the folder in which you last saved it, and it will not open a dialog box. If you want to save the file using a different file name or location, you must select Save As.

Keyboard Shortcuts!
To save a document in a Windows app, press Ctrl+S.

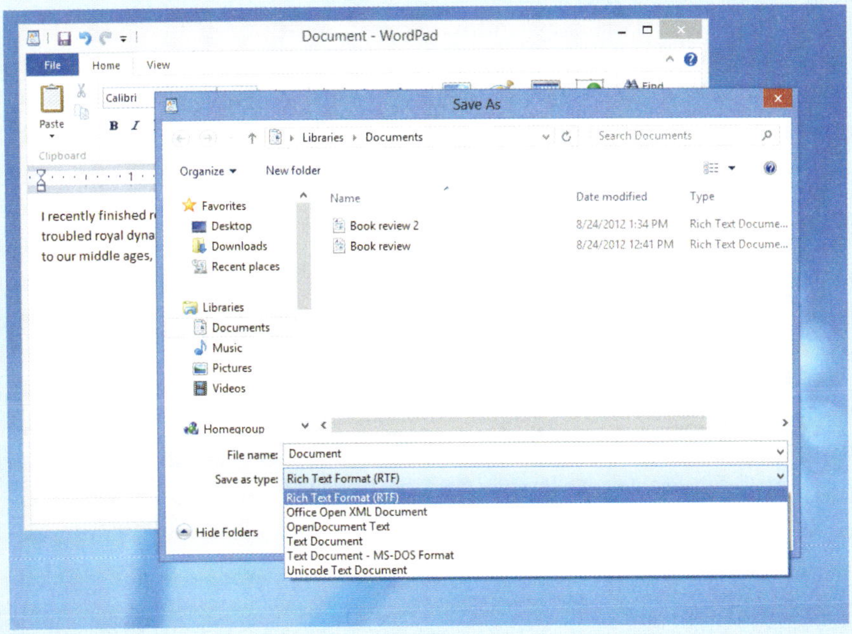

Step 5

After you save a document, the file name will appear at the top of the window, as shown here.

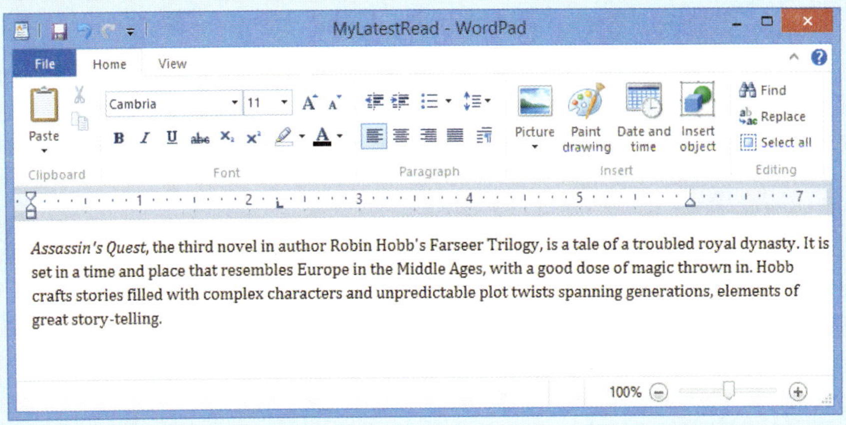

Step 6

Now create three more files and save them so that with the one you created earlier you have saved four files to the Documents folder. We named ours Test1, Test2, and Test3 and saved them as TXT files. This will give us some files to work with later in the chapter.

Step 7

Open the File menu and tap or click Exit to close WordPad.

Just as you saved a file in a Windows app in Step-by-Step 3.1, you can also perform many other file and folder operations, such as creating, copying, moving, renaming, or deleting files or folders. Open a Windows app, such as WordPad, and select Save As from the File menu. In the Save As dialog box (Figure 3-1) you can do several file management tasks. For instance, by default, WordPad saves all files to the Documents folder, but if that is the only place you save WordPad files, it could soon become a long list, especially if you are doing the same with other apps. Some apps will create a folder within the Documents folder, but even then, a single folder for all the files created by an app may not be the best way to proceed.

We recommend that you create a folder within Documents for each related group of files. For instance, we create a folder for each new book project, and then within that folder, we have separate folders for each chapter. Within each

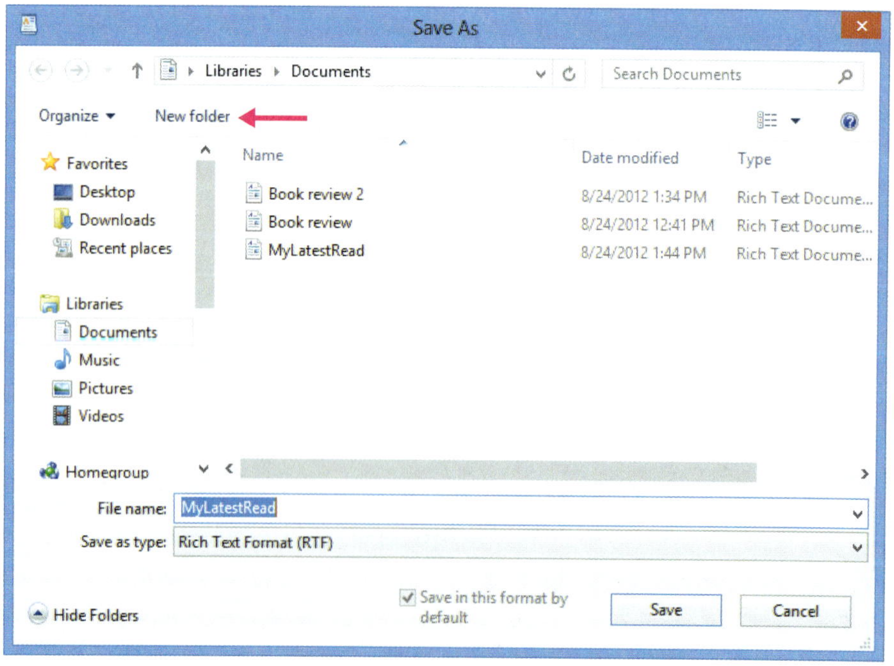

FIGURE 3-1 You can do file management from the Save As dialog box in a Windows app.

chapter folder we save the Microsoft Word document containing the chapter text and all photos and graphic files that we create for that chapter. Then, when we finish a chapter, it is easy to gather up all the related files and send them to the publisher.

Practice doing file and folder management within a Windows app. The Try This! will get you started.

try this!

Creating a Folder and Moving a File in WordPad

Use WordPad to create a folder within the Documents folder. Try This!

1. Open WordPad using the method described in Step-by-Step 3.1.
2. Open the File menu and select Save As.
3. Do not save right now, but click the New Folder button (see Figure 3-1) and type `Books` to name the folder and press Enter.
4. Now move a file from the Documents folder into the Books folder by dragging it to the folder and releasing it. Figure 3-2 shows the MyLatestRead file moving into the Books folder.
5. When finished, click Cancel and close WordPad.

A **drag-and-drop** operation involves pressing the active mouse button (usually left) without releasing while holding the pointer on a file or folder object and moving to another location where you release it. These operations work from within the Save As dialog box and also within File Explorer. A simple drag-and-drop from one location to another on the same drive volume will move the file or folder, as done in the Try This! When you **move** a file or folder, Windows copies it from the source location to a target location and then deletes the source file so the file or folder exists only in the new location. If you drag a file or folder between two separate drive volumes (for instance, between drive C and drive D), you perform a **copy** operation because the item will be copied, leaving the source file or folder intact and creating a copy at the target location. Alternatively, you can access the copy or move functions by dragging while holding the right mouse button, and then releasing it at the target location (see Figure 3-3). In the resulting pop-up menu Move here is the default action, but you can select Copy here if you want to copy the file to the target location and leave it in the source location, even if the two locations are on the same drive volume.

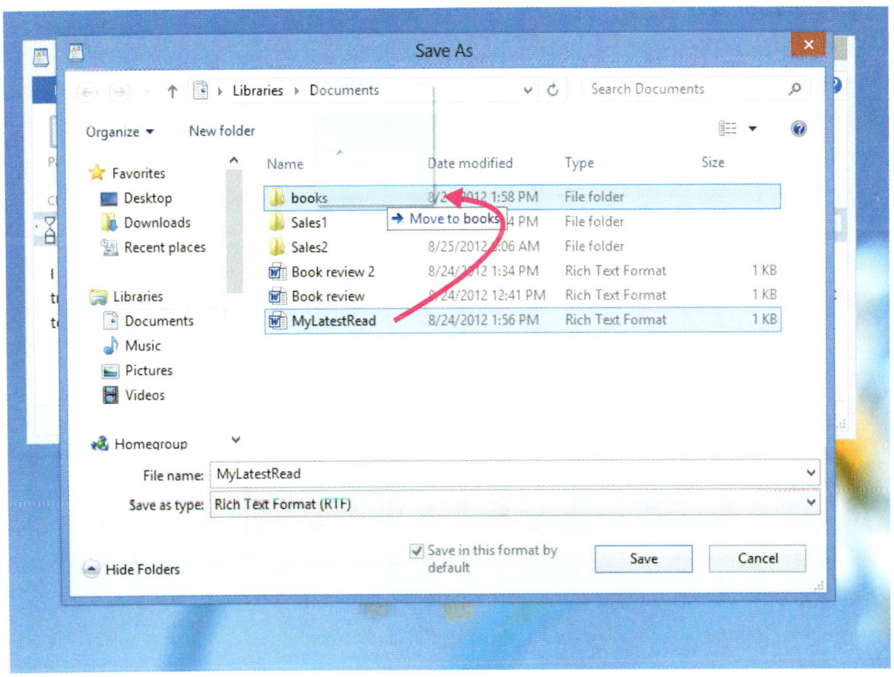

FIGURE 3-2 Moving a file to a new folder using Save As.

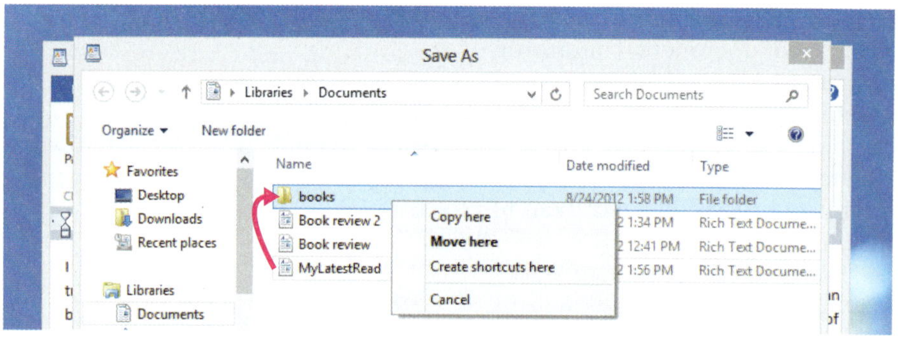

FIGURE 3-3 Right-click while dragging; then release the mouse button to display a pop-up menu.

> Think of Cut as an incomplete Move. If you do not complete it with a Paste, it is rolled back and the cut file remains in the source location.

You can also delete a file in the Save As dialog box. Select the file and either press the Delete key or right-click and select Delete from the file's context menu (Figure 3-4), which has many other file management options. Delete moves a file into the **Recycle Bin** folder.

The **Cut** option first saves a file in the Windows **Clipboard**, an area in memory for temporarily saving data. Then you can position the cursor in a new location and move it to the target location by selecting **Paste**. Or use

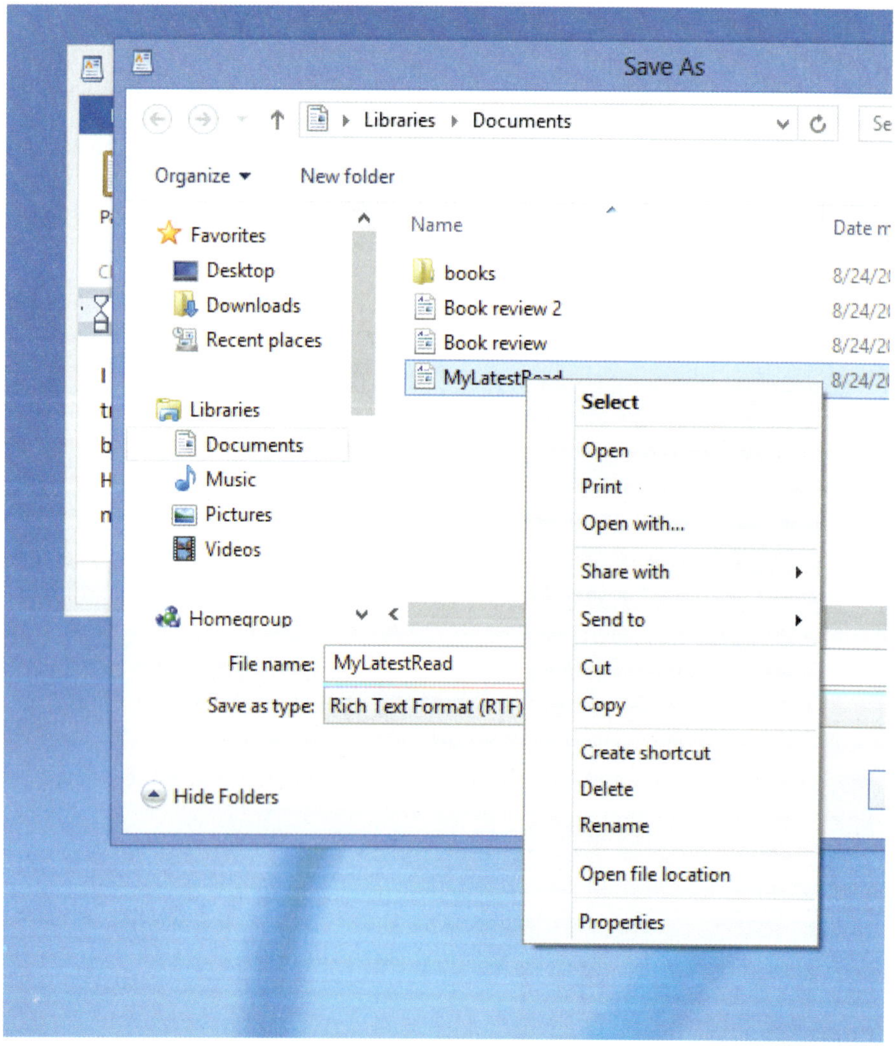

FIGURE 3-4 The context menu for a file includes many file management options.

shortcut keys (see sidebar). If you do not complete a cut by doing a paste, Windows will not delete the selected file or folder at the source.

You can also rename a file from the Save As dialog box, but we recommend that you do only basic file operations, such as create and save, from within your apps, because it is easy to become confused and overwrite an existing file with the current document. It seems like a "beginner's" problem, but trust us, it isn't. For instance, normally when you open the Save As dialog box, you have a document open within the app. Because the main purpose of Save As is to save the current document, it is very easy to accidentally overwrite one of your existing files while trying to do other file functions, as we have painfully learned. That is why we suggest that you leave most file management tasks for File Explorer.

Basic File Management in File Explorer

Although you can do many file management tasks from within a Windows app, the File Explorer utility was designed especially for file management and offers you a host of tasks, which we will explore here.

The File Explorer folder window in Windows 8 (Figure 3-5) has many of the same features found in Windows Explorer in Windows 7. The Quick Access toolbar at the left of the Title bar shows the return of the Control button (the folder icon on the far left) that disappeared in Windows 7. Clicking the Control button opens a menu of options to control the window itself: Restore, Move, Size, Minimize, Maximize, and Close. You can still close any windowed app with the Alt+F4 shortcut. To the right of the Control button is the Properties button (Alt+Enter) that opens the Properties dialog for the selected item in File Explorer. Next is the New Folder button (Ctrl+Shift+N) that creates a new folder in the current location. The last default item on the Quick Access toolbar is a button that opens the Customize Quick Access Toolbar drop-down menu for adding or removing buttons on this toolbar. See Figure 3-6.

Windows 8 has inherited a feature found in recent versions of Microsoft Office: the **ribbon**, a horizontal area below the title bar containing links to tools and options. If the ribbon is not visible, click the Minimize/Maximize Ribbon button on the right just below the Title bar.

Keyboard Shortcuts!

Use keyboard shortcuts in the Save As dialog box and in File Explorer to copy, cut (delete), and paste. To move a file or folder, select it and then press Ctrl+X to cut; navigate to the target location and press Ctrl+V to paste the deleted file or folder from the clipboard. If you change your mind before pasting, press Esc to cancel the operation and the file or folder will remain at the source location. To copy, use Ctrl+C on the selected object, position the cursor in the target location, and then press Ctrl+V. The file will then exist in both locations. This also works on many types of data within an application, letting you copy or paste data from and to applications.

Keyboard Shortcuts!

Alt+F4 has no effect at the Start screen or within a Windows 8 app, but if you use it while in a windowed app, it will close the window. If you use it at the Windows 8 Desktop with no other windows open, it will bring up the Shut Down Windows dialog box.

Alt+Enter, when used within File Explorer, opens the Properties dialog box for the selected item.

Ctrl+Shift+N, when used within File Explorer, creates a new folder.

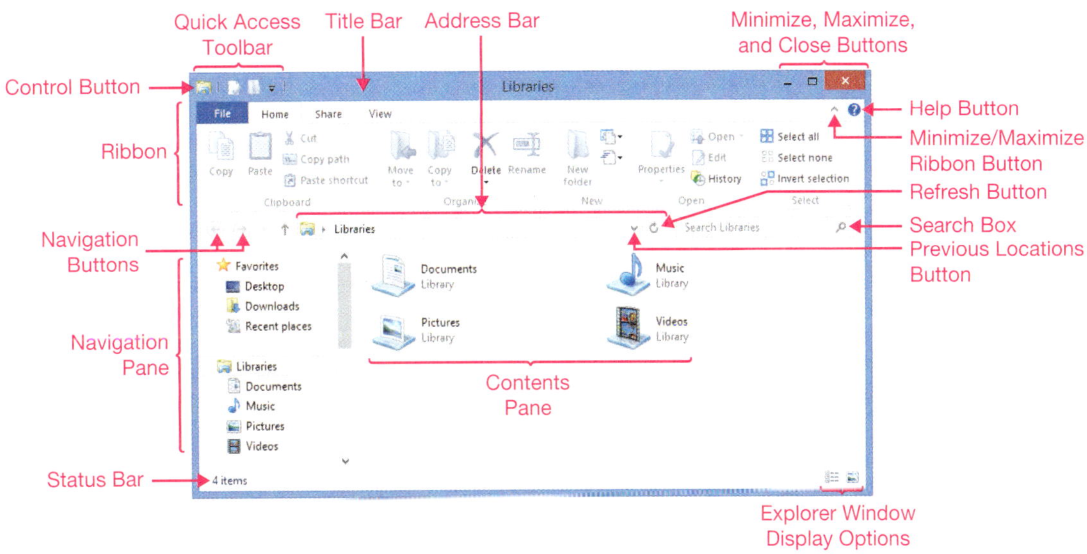

FIGURE 3-5 The File Explorer window default ribbon tabs are File, Home, Share, and View.

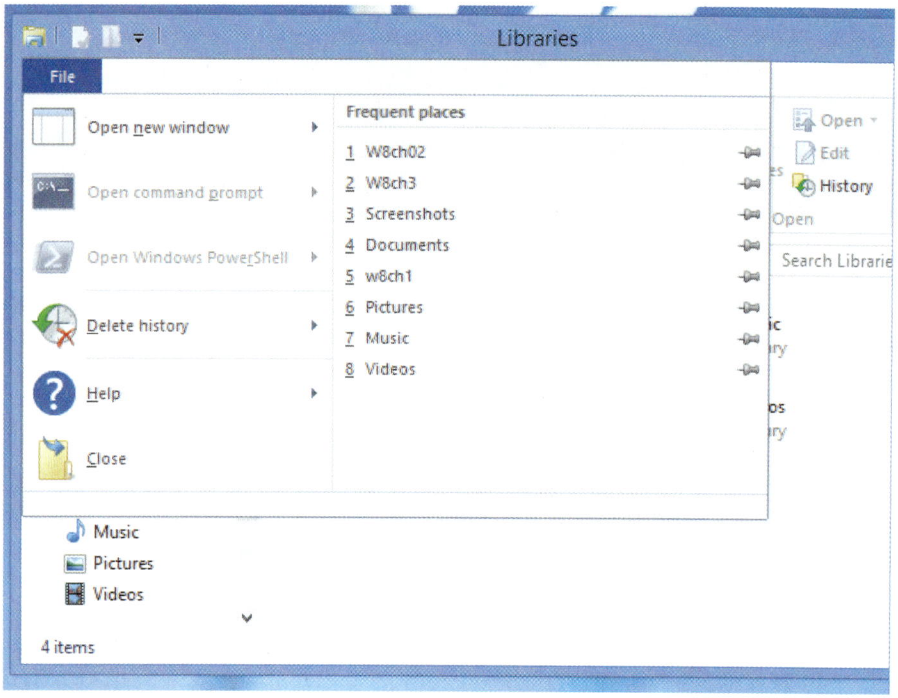

FIGURE 3-6 The File Explorer File menu.

The ribbon changes based on the focus within the File Explorer window, bringing up tools and features you might need and sparing you the task of digging around in multilevel menus for those same features. When the ribbon first appeared in Microsoft Office 2007, many people were frustrated because they couldn't find options where they once resided, but the authors of this book eventually realized that almost anything they needed appeared on the ribbon just in time. So, while navigating in File Explorer, take a few minutes to notice all that is available on the ribbon as it changes with the file and folder location selected.

When you first open File Explorer it is focused on the Libraries folder, as shown in previously in Figure 3-5. Notice that at this point the only tabs on the ribbon are File, Home, Share, and View. That will change as you navigate folders and files in File Explorer; the options available vary based on what is selected in the File Explorer folder.

File Explorer File Tab

Clicking the File tab brings up a two-column drop box with a menu of options on the left (Figure 3-6), as well as a list of Frequent Places on the right. These places may be folders, drive volumes, and network locations. Some choices in the menu on the left may be grayed out, depending on the focus of File Explorer when you open the File menu. File Explorer was focused on the Desktop object when we opened the File menu seen in Figure 3-6. Here is a brief survey of the File menu options:

- **Open New Window** opens a new Explorer window with the current location selected.
- **Open Command Prompt** opens the Windows Command Prompt with the current focus of File Explorer as the current location in Command Prompt. It will not open if the focus is on a library because Command Prompt must point to an actual location, such as the desktop, a drive, or a file folder. See Figure 3-7. The Windows Command Prompt is a special window in which you can enter commands in a simple command-line

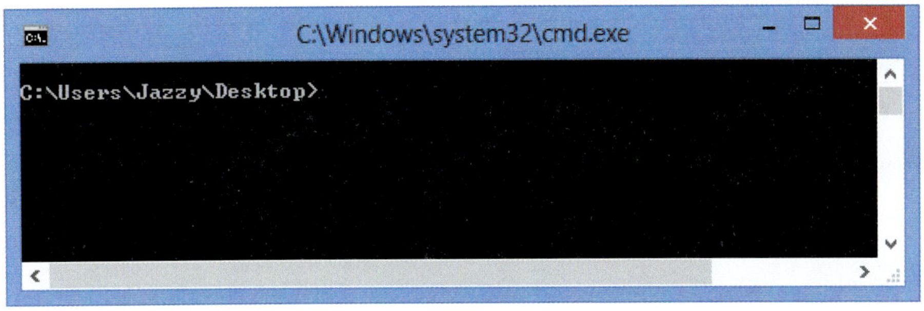

FIGURE 3-7 The Windows Command Prompt focused on the Desktop folder.

interface (CLI). If you run a GUI program from the Command Prompt, it will load into a separate Window, but if you run a character-mode program, it will run within the Command Prompt, displaying any output or messages within the Command Prompt. We strongly suggest that under normal circumstances you not do file management from the Command Prompt because you can use only text-mode commands that give you very little feedback, and a minor typo can result in disaster.

- **Open Windows PowerShell** launches the Windows PowerShell, yet another CLI designed for administrators who need to create and run custom scripts for advanced tasks.
- **Delete History** lets you delete the contents of the recent places list and the Address bar history.
- **Help** opens Windows Help and Support where you can search the local Help database, as well as Microsoft's online Help and Support sources.
- **Close** closes the File Explorer window—something you can also do by clicking or tapping the red Close button (top right) or using the Alt+F4 keyboard shortcut.

Keyboard Shortcuts!
The Alt+F4 keyboard shortcut quickly closes a windowed app.

What Is Missing from the File Menu?
Curiously, anything that has a direct effect on files is missing from the File menu. File-related commands are found on the Home and Share tabs.

File Explorer Home Tab

The File Explorer Home tab gives you access to many file management tools, depending on the object selected in the window. For instance, previously in Figure 3-5 the Libraries folder was selected, and many of the Home options were grayed out to show that they were unavailable. However, in Figure 3-8 a file is selected, and so most of the Home tab buttons are available. Like other

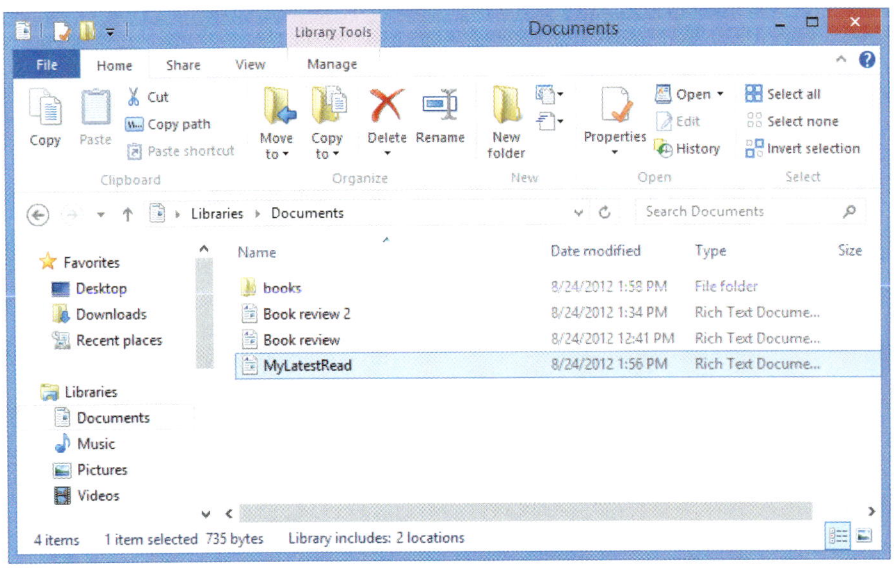

FIGURE 3-8 The File Explorer Home tab.

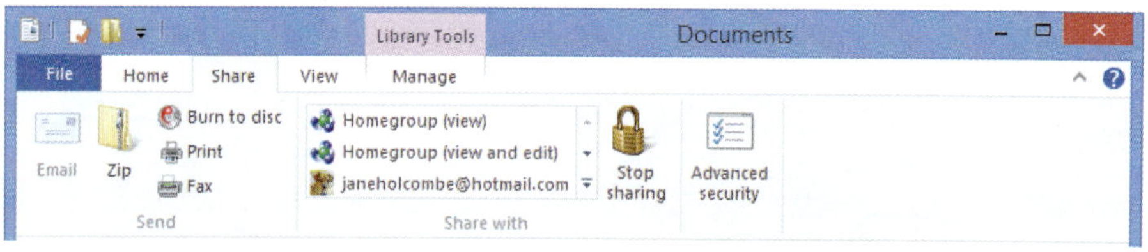

FIGURE 3-9 The File Explorer Share tab.

tabs on the ribbon, the Home tab organizes the options into groups of related functions, each with its own section of the ribbon. The Home ribbon groups include Clipboard, Organize, New, Open, and Select. Notice all the file management tasks, such as Copy, Paste, Cut, Move To, Copy To, Delete, Rename, New Folder, and much more. Copy Path copies the path of the selected file (e.g.: C:\users\Chuck\Documents\filename) to the Clipboard, and Paste Shortcut pastes a copied shortcut to the current window.

File Explorer Share Tab

When you select an appropriate object, such as a folder or file, the File Explorer Share tab (Figure 3-9) allows you to do a number of tasks related to sharing your selected file. You can choose to e-mail it, zip it (one or several files together) to create a smaller file for e-mailing, burn it to disc, print it, and/or fax it. Further, if you are part of a network HomeGroup, the options on the Share With section allow you to share files and folders via the HomeGroup, or you can share with specific people. Advanced Security allows you to assign specific permissions to files and folders. You can also turn sharing off for the selected item with the Stop Sharing button.

File Explorer View Tab

The options on the View tab of the ribbon control the layout of the current File Explorer window. Figure 3-10 shows the View tab for a folder within the Pictures library. The Panes section of the View ribbon has buttons for the Navigation pane, the Preview pane, and the Details pane. The last two occupy the same pane (the one on the right in Figure 3-10), so you can either display details of an item selected in the Contents pane (at center), or you can display a preview of the item, provided Windows has the appropriate software to preview the file.

The Layout section of the View ribbon tab controls the appearance of items in the Contents pane, such as small, medium, large, and extra large icons, or options to list with or without details.

The Sort By button in the Current view section opens a drop-down menu (Figure 3-11) that lets you sort the items listed by eleven characteristics (Name, Date, Tags, Size, Rating, Type, Date Created, Date Modified, Date Taken, Folder Path, and Dimensions) and in ascending or descending order. Also at the bottom of the Sort By drop box is a Choose Column option that lets you add columns to the Contents pane, visible when it is in Details view.

To the right of the Sort By button are three buttons. At the top is the Group By button (a square icon within brackets) that opens a drop-down menu that allows you to

try this!

Unhide File Name Extensions

File name extensions are, by default, hidden in File Explorer, but you can unhide them. Try This!

1. Launch File Explorer and navigate to a folder containing data files, such as the My Documents folder under the Documents library.
2. Click the View tab to display the View options in the ribbon.
3. In the Show/Hide selection, click to place a check in the box labeled File Name Extensions.
4. Notice that the file name extensions now display in the File Explorer Contents pane, as shown in Figure 3-12.

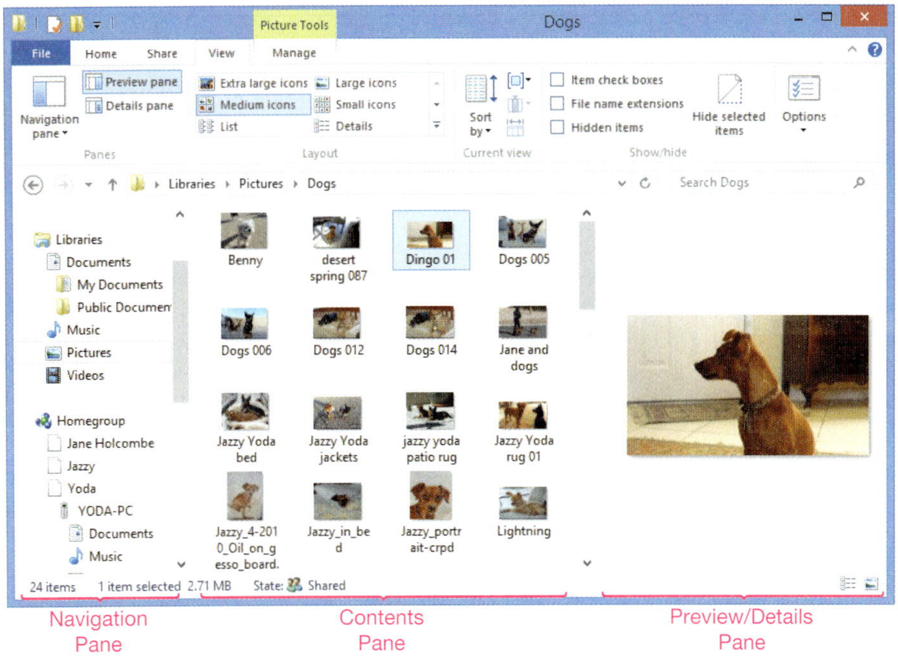

FIGURE 3-10 The File Explorer View tab with the My Documents folder selected.

group items based on the column headings. The second button opens the Add Columns drop-down menu, a shortened version of the Choose Columns option in Sort By. The bottom one of these three buttons sizes all the columns to fit their contents.

The Show/Hide section of the View tab lets you either show or hide file names, file name extensions, and hidden items. This is a handy tool for when you want to make a normally hidden file visible or when you want to show the file name extensions.

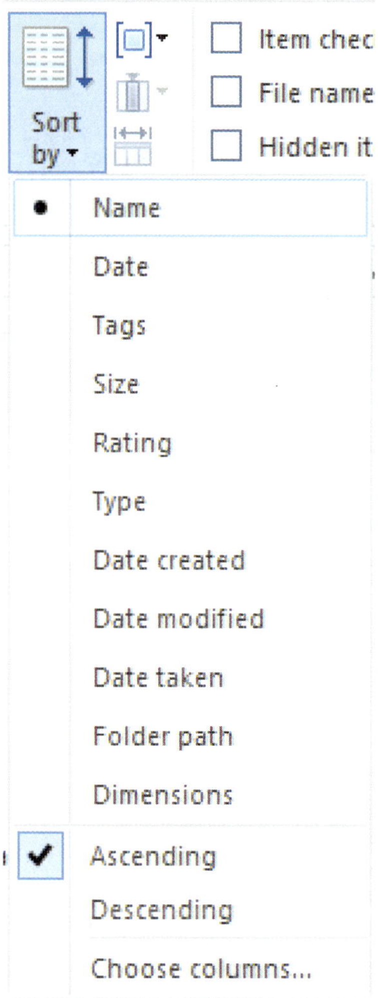

FIGURE 3-11 The Sort By list.

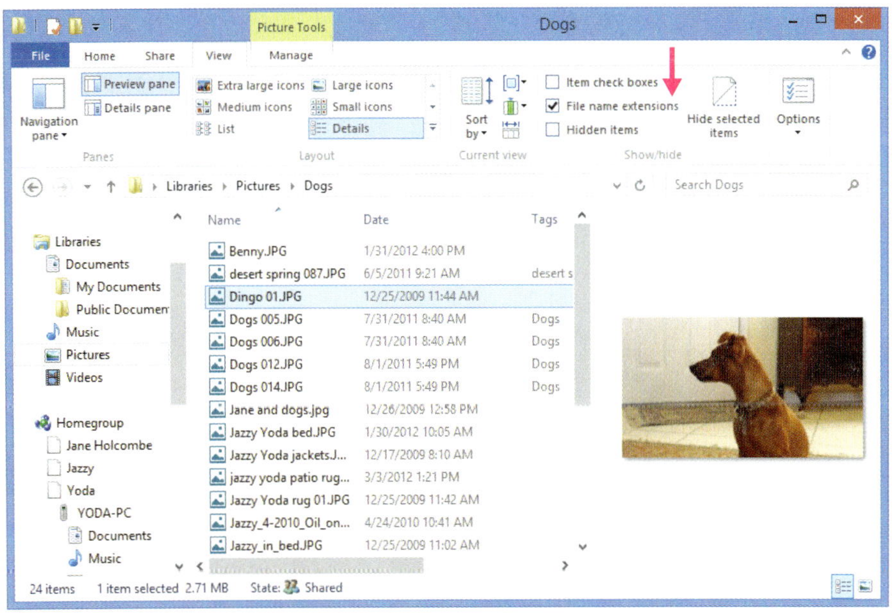

FIGURE 3-12 Place a check in the File Name Extensions box to display file extensions in File Explorer.

Preserve File Name Extensions
File extensions are very important because each extension, such as DOC or JPG, is associated with a certain type of program. When file extensions are hidden, they are also protected and less likely to be deleted when you rename a file.

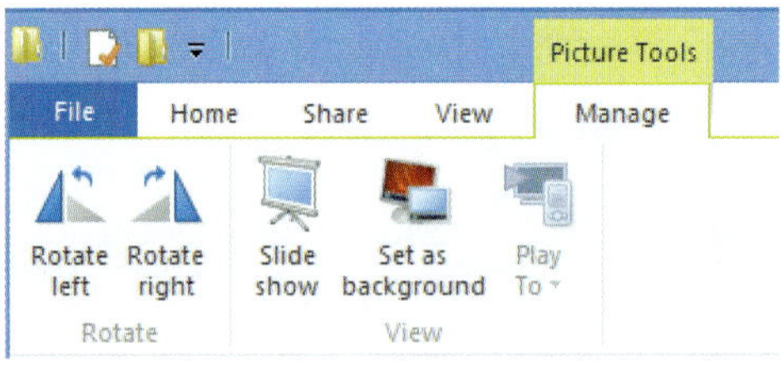

FIGURE 3-13 The File Explorer Picture Tools tab.

File Explorer Contextual Tabs

File Explorer in Windows 8 also opens context-sensitive tabs for certain types of files. Each of these contextual tabs is a colorful "super tab" in the Title bar, connected to a new tab in the ribbon, which, in turn, contains menus and buttons for actions that apply to the types of files that are the current focus of File Explorer. For instance, anytime the Pictures folder, a subfolder of Pictures, or any picture or graphic file is selected, the Picture Tools tab (Figure 3-13) appears in the Title bar attached to the Manage tab. Click it and it displays tool buttons for options to manage pictures. These include rotating the image left or right 90 degrees, displaying images in a slide show, setting the current image as the desktop background, and playing the selected item or items on another device. This last item depends on a device, such as a projector or TV, being connected and available for use.

Similarly, the Music Tools tab appears when you select the My Music folder or a music file. See Figure 3-14. The Disk Tools tab displays when you browse to the Computer folder or to one of the local drives, as shown in Figure 3-15. The Shortcut Tools tab displays if you select a shortcut, and the Application Tools tab displays when you select an executable file, such as the AmazonMP3Downloader.exe file selected in Figure 3-16. Another context tab is Library Tools, which appears when you select a library folder. When one of these tabs appears, you still need to click the new tab to see the available options. We will look more closely at Libraries in the next section.

Multiple contextual tabs can also appear, as when the Pictures library folder is selected and both the Library Tools and Picture Tools tabs display.

FIGURE 3-14 The File Explorer Music Tools tab.

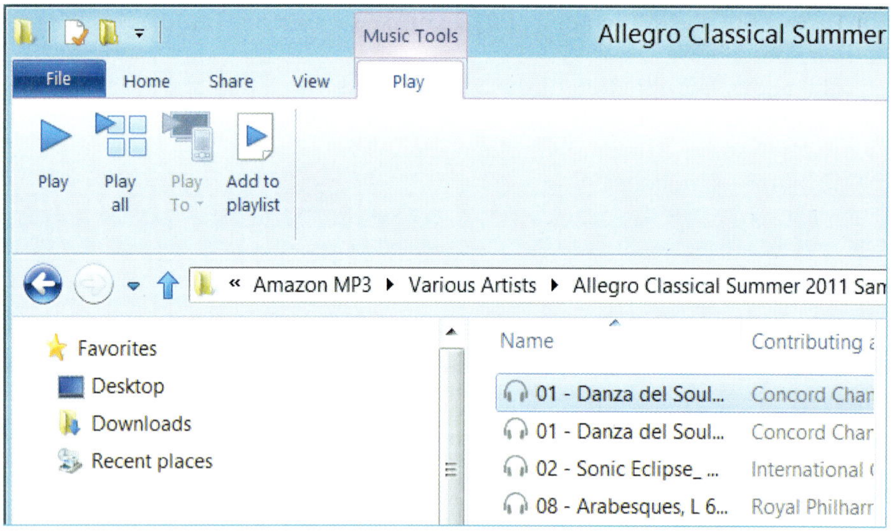

FIGURE 3-15 The File Explorer Disk Tools tab.

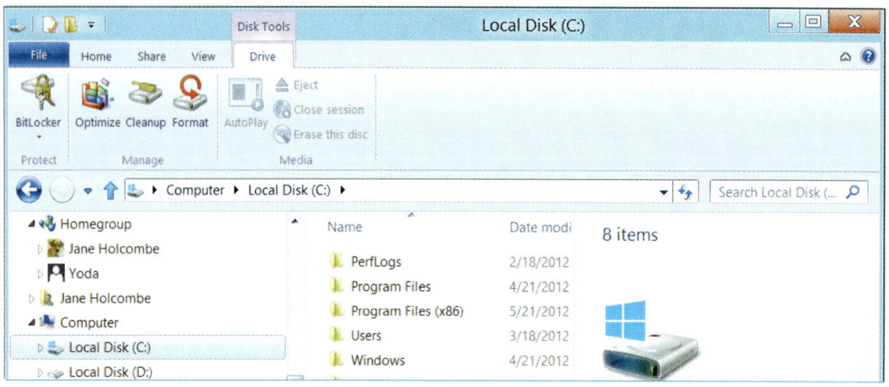

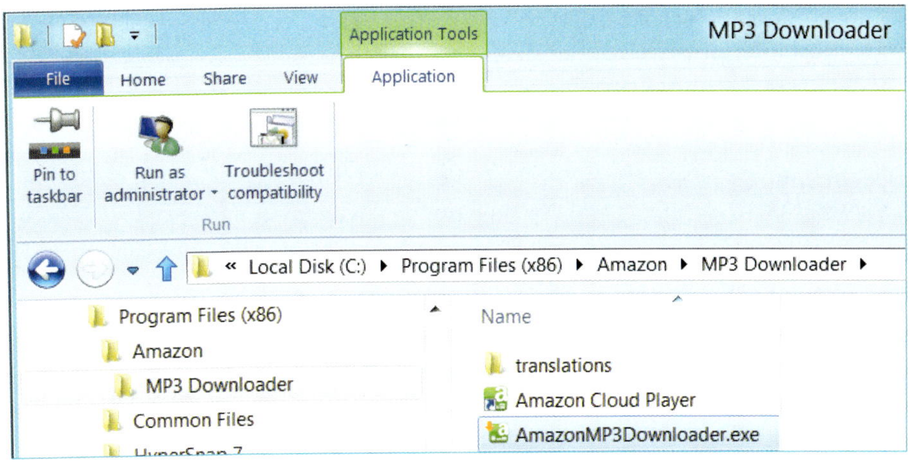

FIGURE 3-16 The File Explorer Application Tools tab.

Step-by-Step 3.2

Using File Explorer for File Management

Practice creating folders and moving, copying, renaming, and deleting files in File Explorer.

Step 1

From the Desktop open the File Explorer shortcut on the taskbar. In File Explorer ensure that the ribbon is open. If it is not, click or tap the Expand the Ribbon button (or press Ctrl+F1) to open the ribbon. Select Documents.

Step 2

On the Home tab of the ribbon, click or tap New Folder. Name the folder Sales1. Repeat this step and create a folder named Sales2.

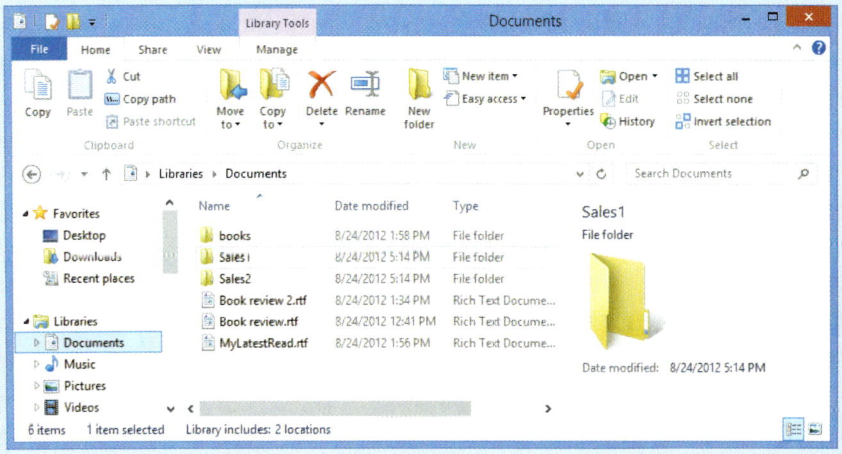

Step 3

Open the Sales1 folder in the Contents pane and then select New Item on the ribbon. On the New Item menu select Text Document. Name the document report1.txt. Note: Be sure to preserve the TXT file extension. If file name extensions are visible, you are more at risk of overwriting the extension. If they are not visible, you will not see the TXT file extension, but it will be present as long as you choose Text Document.

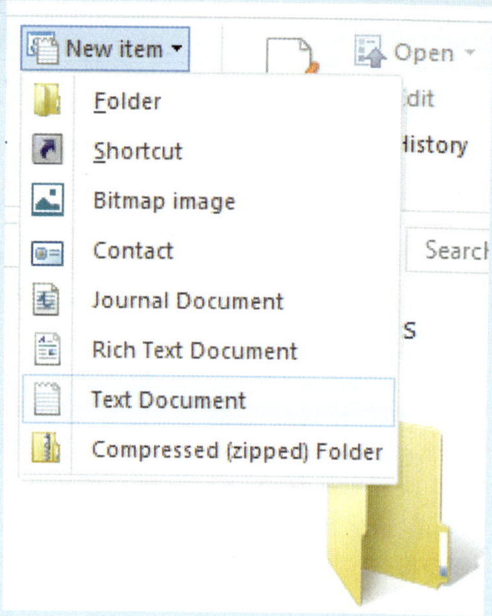

Step 4

In the Folder pane, click or tap to expand (open) the folders Libraries\Documents\My Documents\ so that both the Sales1 and Sales2 folders are visible. Then drag the file report1.txt from the Contents pane, and drop it on the Sales2 folder in the Folders pane. This moves the file, so it no longer exists in the Sales1 folder. Note that Sales1 is empty when you complete the move.

Keyboard Shortcuts!
Alternatively, select the report1 file and press Ctrl+X (Cut), then navigate to the Sales2 folder and press Ctrl+V (Paste).

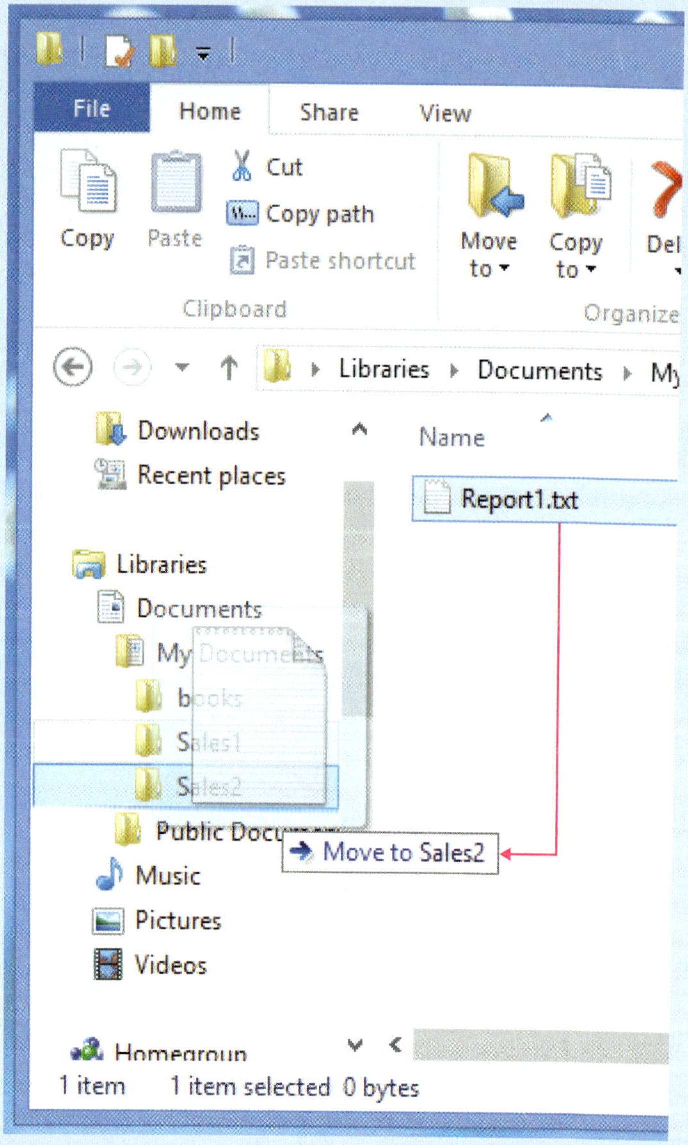

Step 5

Open the Sales2 folder and confirm that report1 moved to this folder.

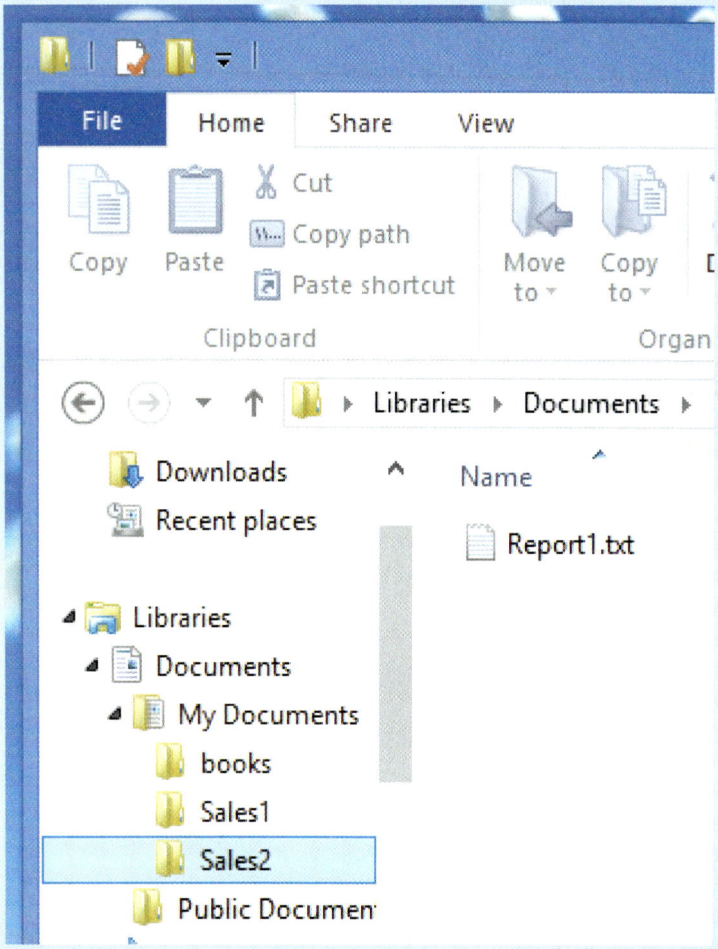

Step 6

Select the Report1.txt file again and then select the Copy To button in the Home tab of the ribbon. In the open Copy menu, select Choose Location.

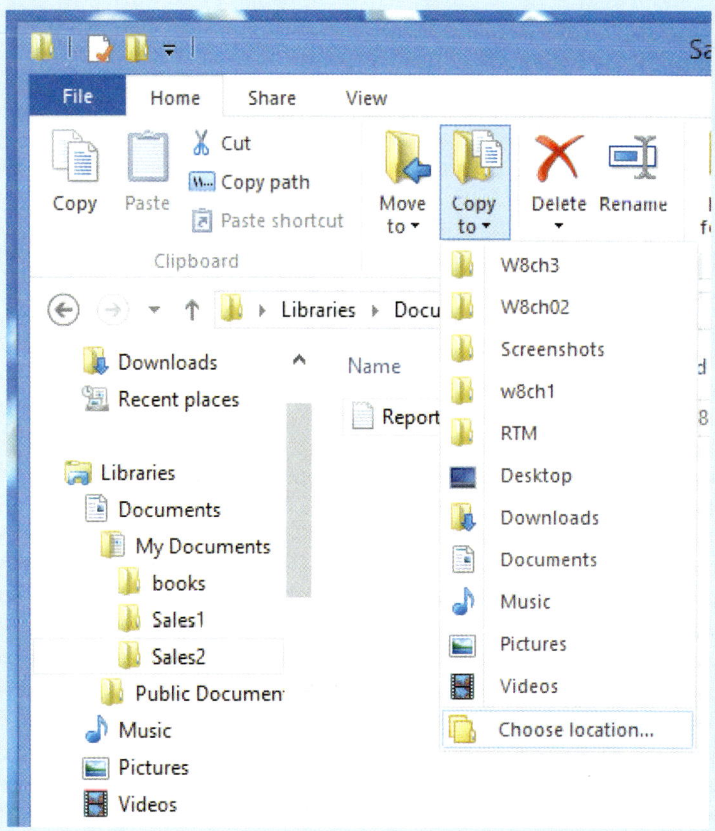

In the Copy Items menu, navigate to the Sales1 folder by starting in Desktop\Libraries\Documents\My Document; then select Sales1 and click the Copy button.

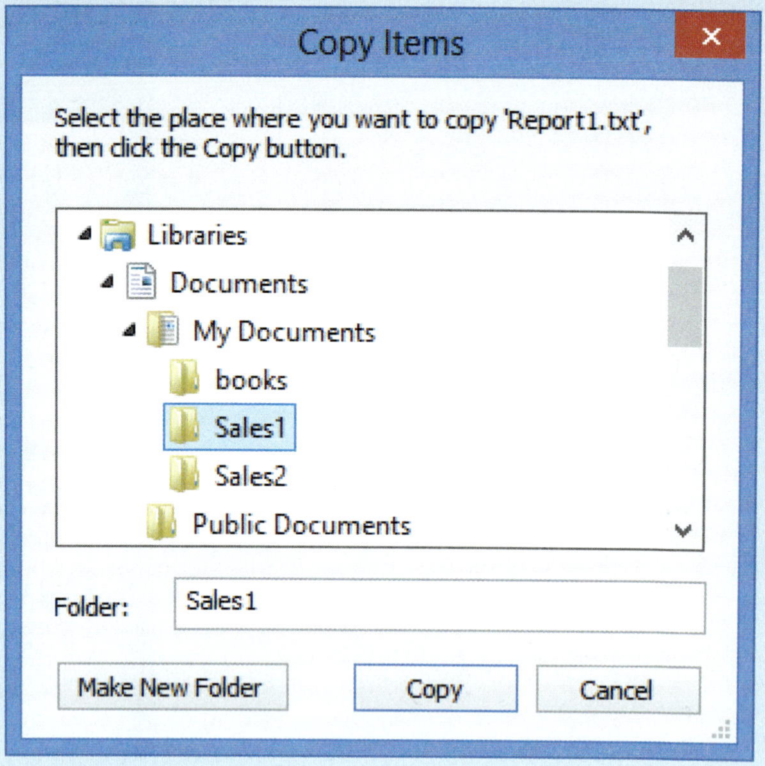

Step 7

Verify that the file Report1.txt exists in both the Sales1 and Sales2 folders. Open the Sales2 folder and right-click the file name Report1.txt and select Rename. Change the file name to Report2.txt. Then close the File Explorer window.

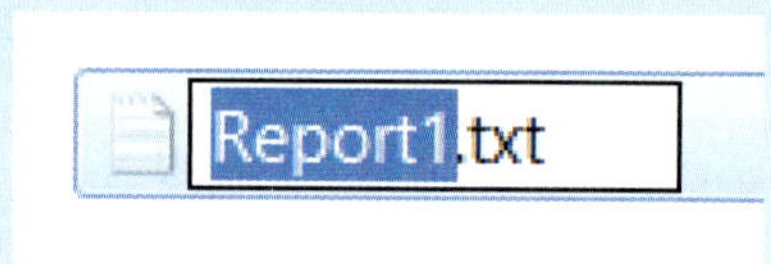

Improved Copy and Move

The file copy and move tasks you experimented with in Step-by-Step 3.2 were very simple tasks. What happens if there is a name conflict when you attempt to copy or move a file into a folder that already contains a file by the same name? First, you will see the Replace or Skip Files dialog box, shown in Figure 3-17. If you are certain that all the source files are newer than all the target files, you can select Replace the Files in the Destination Folder. However, if you are not certain, you can select Skip These Files, which will proceed with the copy, but skip files with conflicts. Or you can select Choose the Files to Keep in the Destination Folder, which will result in dialog boxes similar to Figure 3-18. This allows you to compare the file size and date and make a decision about each file. If you choose to keep both versions, the incoming (source) file will have a number appended to the file name.

Windows 8 also gives you more options when you need to copy or move large quantities of data and/or have two or more simultaneous large copy functions running. You can now have multiple copy or move jobs running at once, and Windows will let you manage them separately, even to the point of allowing you to pause one to let another complete sooner. This is something you might want to do when you copy data to a jump drive before leaving the office. Figure 3-19 shows a dialog box monitoring two separate, large file copy operations. When they first started, the box was titled "2 Running Actions." By clicking the Pause button, we stopped the top job, and the title changes to "1 Running Action." To resume that paused action, click the Pause button again. To stop one altogether, press its Close button (the small "x"). This dialog box gives you lots of information, including the number of items being copied, the names of the source and destination folders, the name of the current file, estimated time remaining, and number of items remaining.

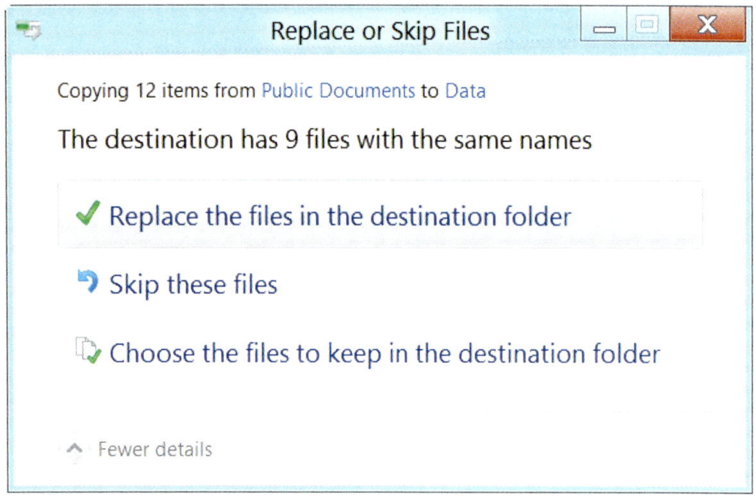

FIGURE 3-17 Decide how to treat files with file name conflicts.

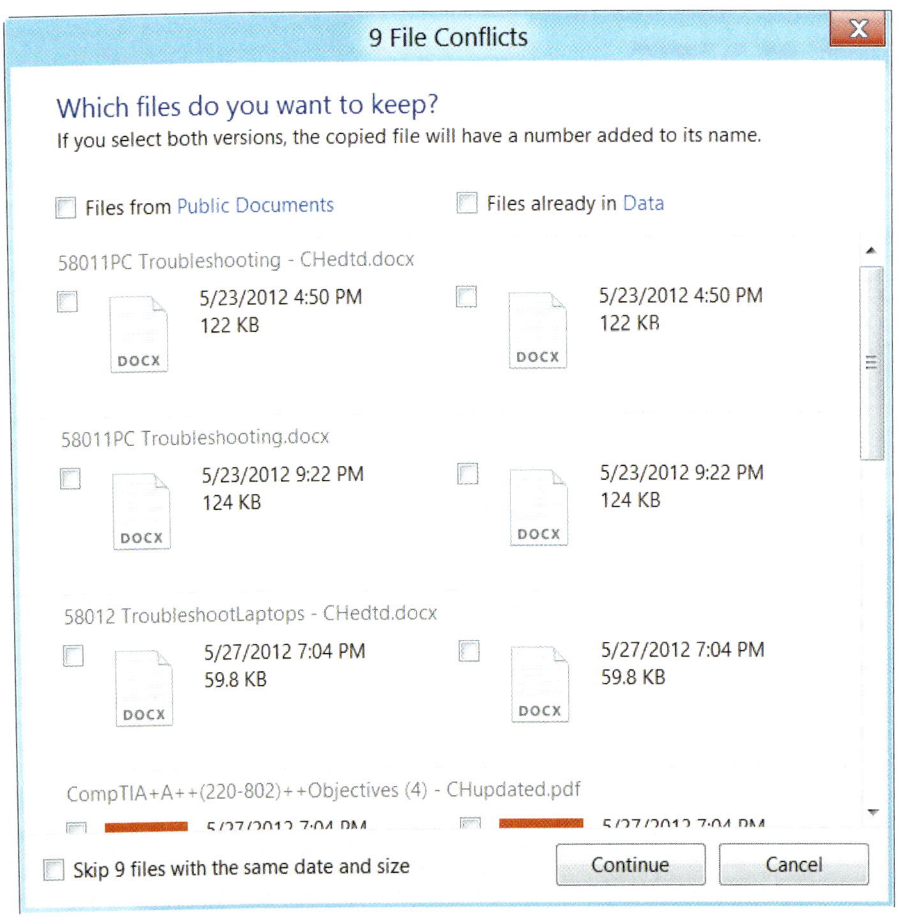

FIGURE 3-18 Select the action for each file.

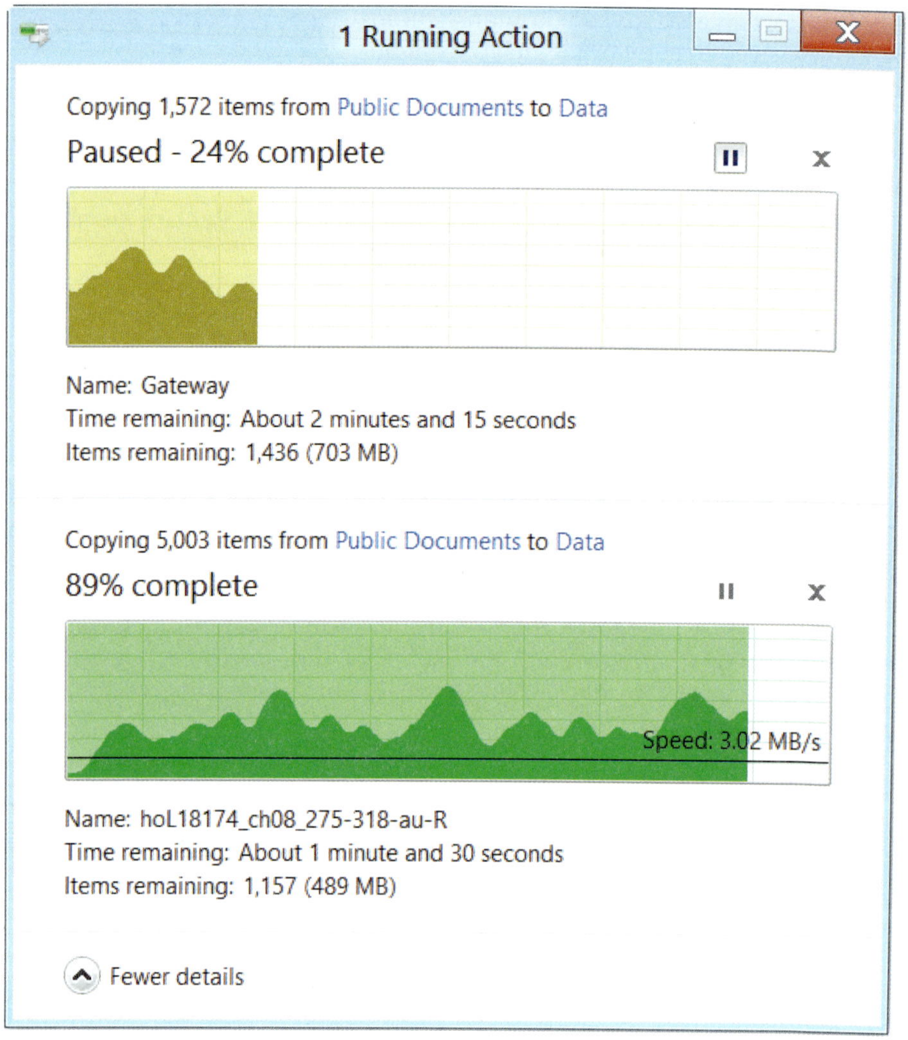

FIGURE 3–19 Two copy operations were started, but one is paused.

LO 3.2 | Just Beyond Basic File Management in Windows 8

It is difficult to separate file management tasks into levels of complexity, because we believe that the more you understand about Windows 8 file management, the better your experience will be. But we needed to draw the line somewhere to break down the knowledge and skills. Although we will not go into advanced disk and file management topics, we will extend the discussion beyond the basic concepts and tasks introduced in the previous section to describe libraries and how to manage them. We'll give you practice using Windows 8 Search, take a look at jump lists, and describe how you can customize Windows 8 so that it takes certain actions when you insert various types of media. Finally, we would like to instill a good habit that will save you from losing files when you disconnect those flash drives or external hard drives from your computer.

Introduction to Windows 8 Libraries

In Step-by-Step 3.1 you saved your file in the Documents library, which may elicit the question: What is a library? A **library** looks like a folder that contains other folders and files, but it is not a conventional storage folder. A library

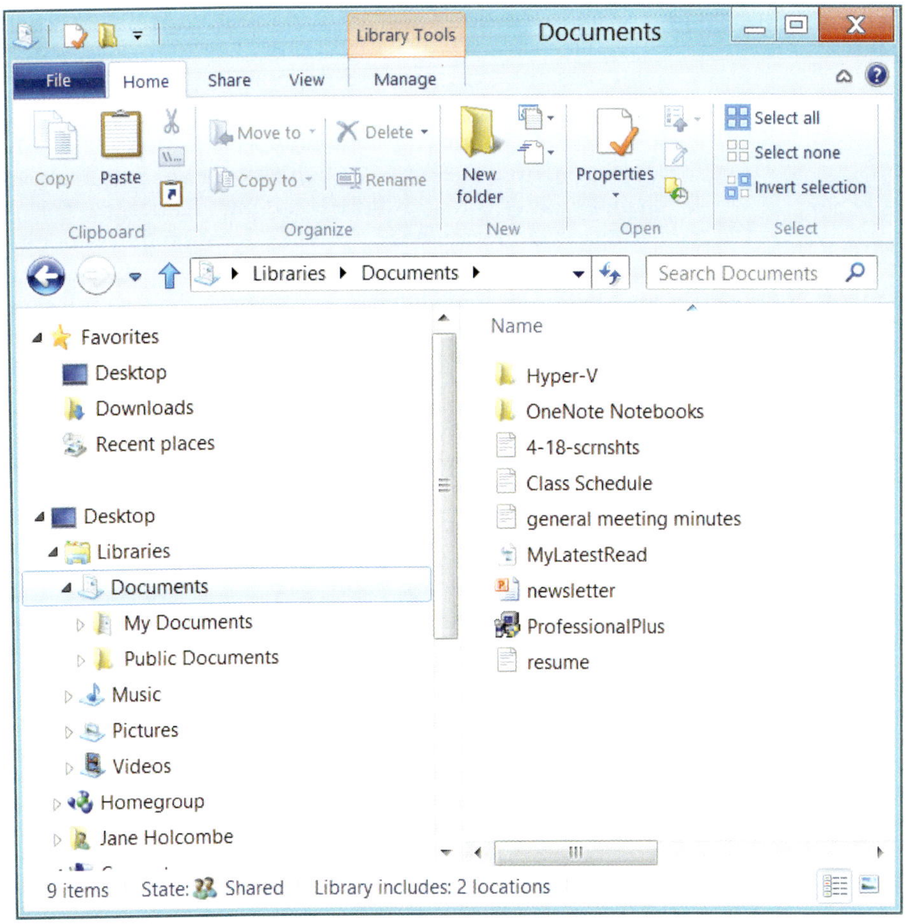

FIGURE 3-20 The Documents library displaying the contents of two locations, My Documents and Public Documents.

gathers files from multiple locations and displays them as a single folder independently of their location. Rather than actually storing the contents that you see listed within a library, a library stores only information about the locations of those folders and files, displaying them as if they were all in one location. A single library can point to various locations on local storage or network storage. Libraries make it easier for you to find related information or types of files. Libraries also make it easier to back up related files because you can point to one library and back up files from all locations.

Windows starts out with several libraries, and you can create new ones. The four default libraries in Windows 8 are Documents, Music, Pictures, and Videos. If you click or tap one of these libraries, the Status bar at the bottom of the window reveals information about that library, such as how many items it contains, the number of locations it links to, and its state, which for the documents library in Figure 3-20 is Shared. Another change to the window when you select a library is the appearance of the Library Tools Manage tab at the top above the ribbon. Click the tab to access the library tools, as shown in Figure 3-21.

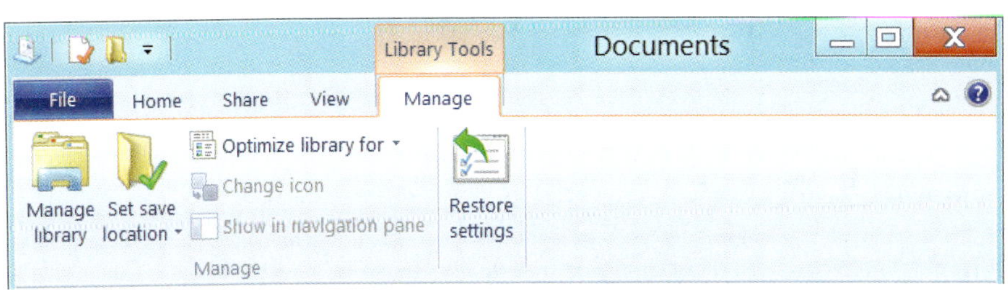

FIGURE 3-21 The Library Tools ribbon.

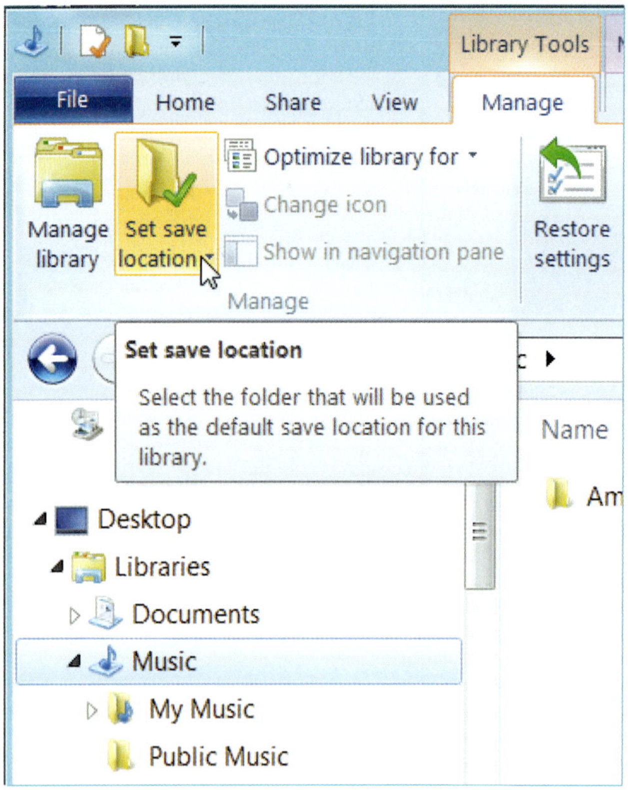

FIGURE 3-22 Each library has a save location.

Another important feature of Libraries is that you can save into a library, which might cause you to wonder where your files are actually saved or copied or moved. The answer is that all these operations send files to a default save location. Each library has a default save location (e.g., My Documents for Documents), which you are not likely to change unless you add more locations to a library. This is because each library has a "private" location that is not intended to be shared with users over the network, and each has a Public location, intended for sharing. The default save location is the private location, so until you add a location to one of the libraries, you should not need to change the default save location. See Figure 3-22.

There are also rules about what happens when you delete libraries and folders and files within libraries. A deleted library is moved to the Recycle Bin, but the files and folders that appeared within the library remain untouched at their actual locations. If you change your mind about deleting a library, open Recycle Bin and recover the library, as shown in Figure 3-23. When you delete, copy, or move individual files and folders in a library, these actions occur to the actual files and folders, and the rules for deleting and recovering files applies, as described later in this chapter when we talk about deleting and restoring files.

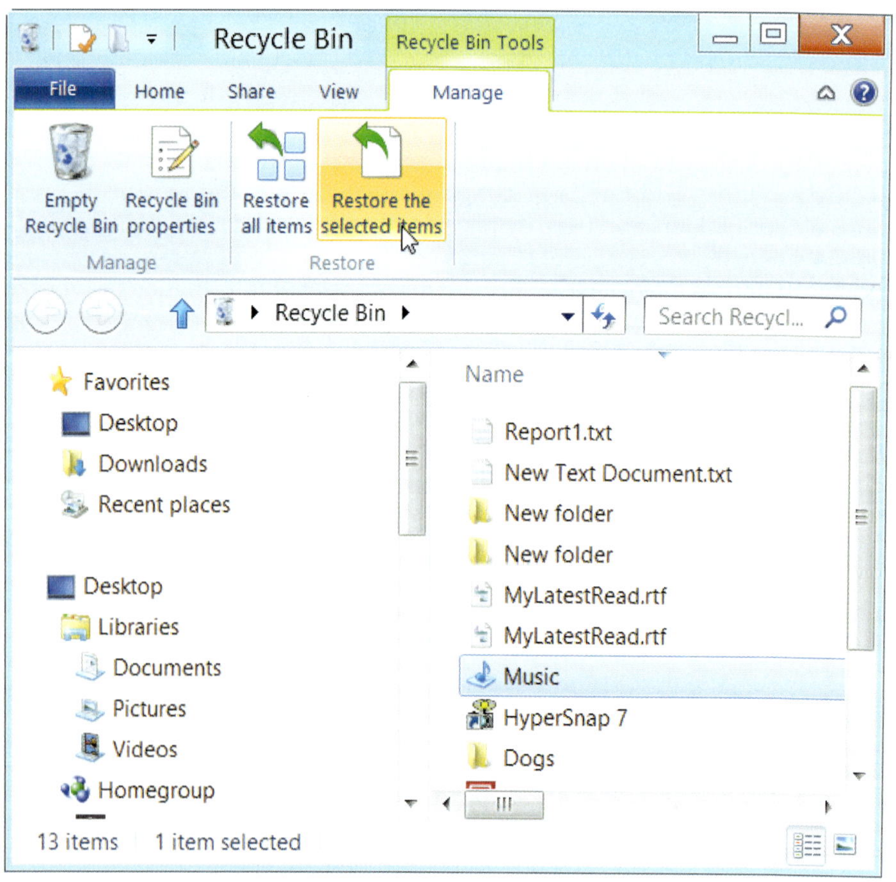

FIGURE 3-23 Recovering the deleted Music library from the Recycle Bin.

Step-by-Step 3.3

Managing Libraries

Learn how to add locations to Libraries and change the default save location.

Step 1

If a File Explorer window is not currently open, either open one from the File Explorer tile on the Start screen or from its shortcut on the Windows Desktop. Then, if the Library Tools tab does not display in the Title bar, click or tap the Documents library and then click or tap the Libraries tab in the Title bar to open the Library Tools Manage tab on the ribbon. Click a folder in the Contents pane to highlight it.

Step 2

On the Library Tools tab, select the Manage Library button to open the Documents Library Locations dialog box. Notice the two locations—My Documents and Public Documents. The path My Documents points to is the currently logged on user's Documents folder, and the path to the Public Documents location is C:\Users\Public\Documents.

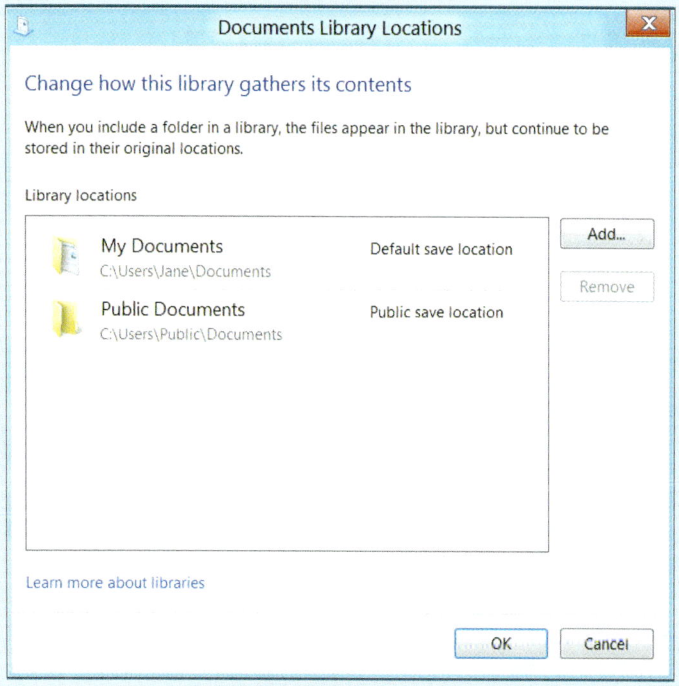

Step 3

Click the Add button to open the Include Folder in Documents dialog box. If you have additional locations you would like to add to a library, this dialog box allows you to navigate to that location and then click or tap the Include Folder to add the new location to the library. Another location can be an additional internal or external drive or a network location.

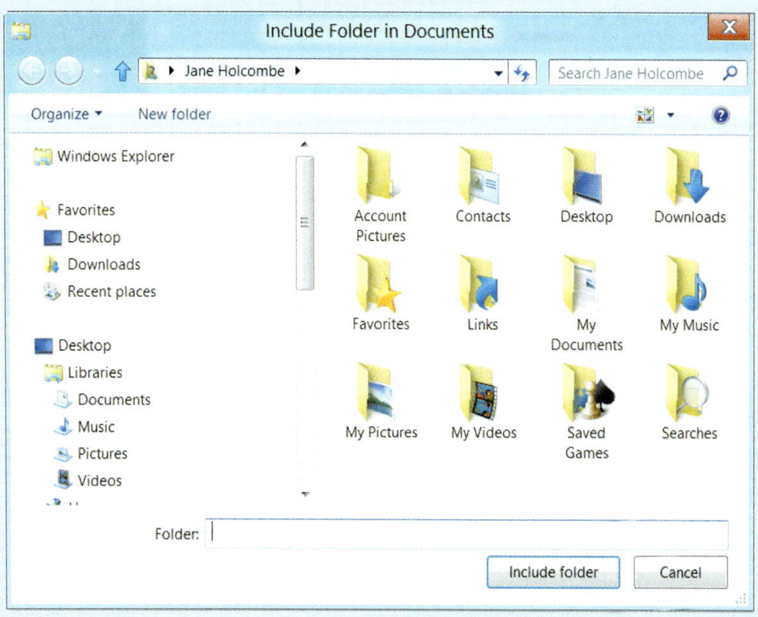

Step 4

If you have a location you would like to add, do so now. We added the Data folder on our second hard drive volume. This opened the Document Library Locations dialog box showing all locations for our Documents library. When you are finished, click OK to close the dialog box.

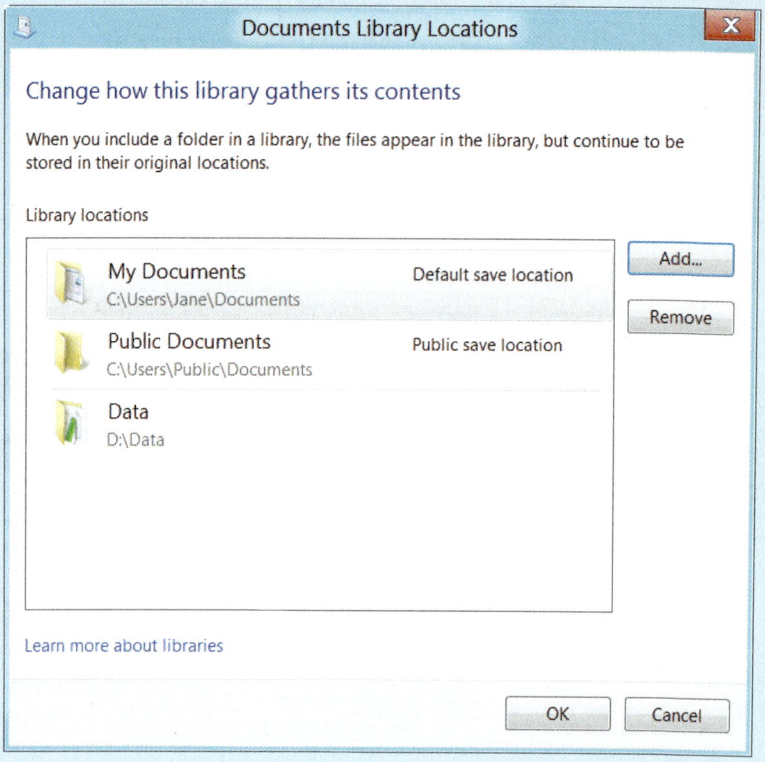

Step 5

The File Sharing dialog opens after you add a new location to a library. Select No, Don't Share This Folder. (We work with file sharing in Chapter 5.)

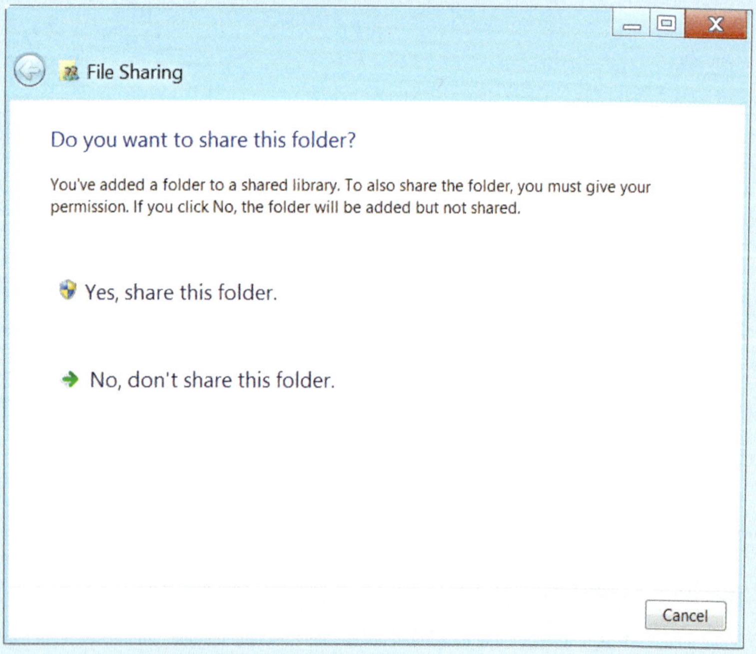

Step 6

Back in File Explorer, notice the locations in the Documents library. Leave File Explorer open.

FIGURE 3-24 Apps Search bar and screen.

Searching for Apps, Files, or Folders

You can search for files, folders, and apps using the Windows 8 search utility or by using the Search box in File Explorer.

Keyboard Shortcuts!
Windows key+F opens File Search. Windows key+Q opens Apps Search.

Searching in the Windows 8 GUI

Open the Search bar from either Start screen or the Desktop by moving your mouse or swiping from the bottom right and selecting the Search charm. This opens the Apps Search bar (Figure 3-24) with a list of all apps in the main screen. This list includes all installed apps, regardless of the type and regardless of whether the app has a Start screen tile. Enter the name of an app here to begin a search of apps. For instance, entering `word` narrowed down the results to Microsoft Word 2010 and WordPad. Click or tap one of the results to call up the app.

To search for files, after opening the Apps search, move the selection to Files. Or use the Windows key+F to directly open Windows 8 Search focused on Files. Figure 3-25 shows the result from entering **re**. Click or tap one of the results in the bar, and it will appear in the results list on the left. Clicking or tapping one of the results will open it in an app, if the file type is supported by one of the installed apps.

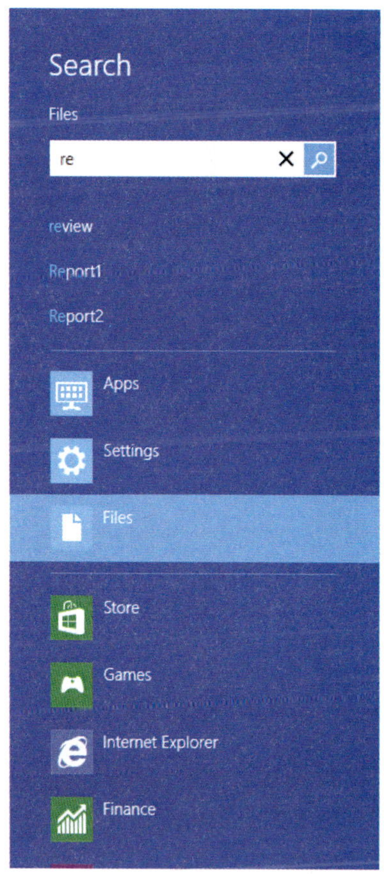

FIGURE 3-25 The Files Search bar with a list of results under the Search box.

Searching with File Explorer

Search within File Explorer using the Search box, which will use the selected drive, library, or folder as a starting point and search the contents of that location and all the folders within it. Search starts as you enter characters into the box, and the results are displayed in the Contents pane with a Search Tools tab active, as shown in Figure 3-26.

Jump Lists

When you open a desktop app, it has a shortcut icon on the taskbar that will normally disappear when you close the app. You can attach that shortcut to the taskbar to make it easier to launch the app. This action is called **pinning**. Whether an app is pinned or not, right-clicking its icon will open a jump list,

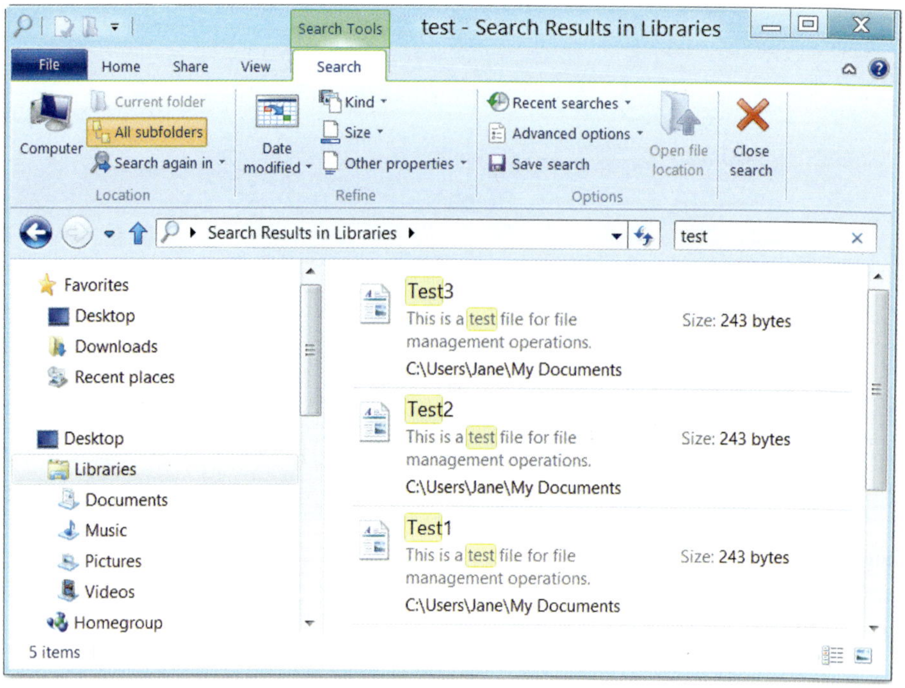

FIGURE 3-26 Select one of the results.

as shown in Figure 3-27. A **jump list** contains links to recently opened items and desktop apps that give you quick access to these and other items you may choose to add (pin) to the jump list. You can pin a program or file to the taskbar, and then, in turn, each one has a jump list of recently opened items and optional items that you have pinned to the jump list.

The jump list feature was introduced in Windows 7 and has been improved on in Windows 8. The jump list in Figure 3-27 shows a list of recent items automatically added, and one item that the user pinned to the taskbar by right-clicking it when it was in the Recent list and selecting Pin To This List. Windows 8 jump lists can include programs and links to any type of content, such as an RSS feed, an album, or a person's profile. Jump lists now have privacy controls.

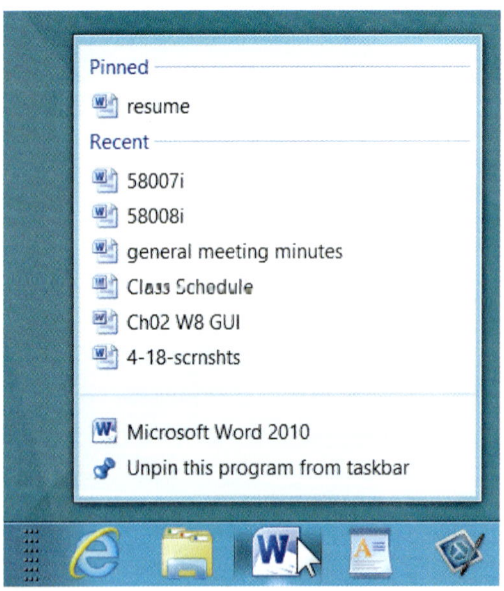

FIGURE 3-27 A jump list pinned to the taskbar with Microsoft Word.

You can modify settings for your entire jump list by right-clicking an empty place on the taskbar and selecting Properties. Then select the Jump Lists tab (Figure 3-28) to control the number of items displayed, and to control listing opened programs and/or recently opened items. These last two are considered privacy settings if you work on confidential information or have any reason for not wanting observers to see what you have recently opened. These settings protect you only from the automatic display of programs and files; they do not protect you from yourself. For instance, the pinned item, résumé (shown without the accents in Figure 3-27) would reveal that an employee is working on his or her résumé and maybe should not have selected this file to pin to the jump list.

Inserting a Disc or Connecting an External Drive

When you insert a CD or DVD disc or connect an external flash drive or hard drive to your system, it will automatically be recognized. What happens at the moment of recognition depends on the **AutoPlay** settings. If AutoPlay is turned off, you will need to go looking for the disk or drive—usually from within an app or from File Explorer. If AutoPlay is turned on, the action Windows takes depends on the settings.

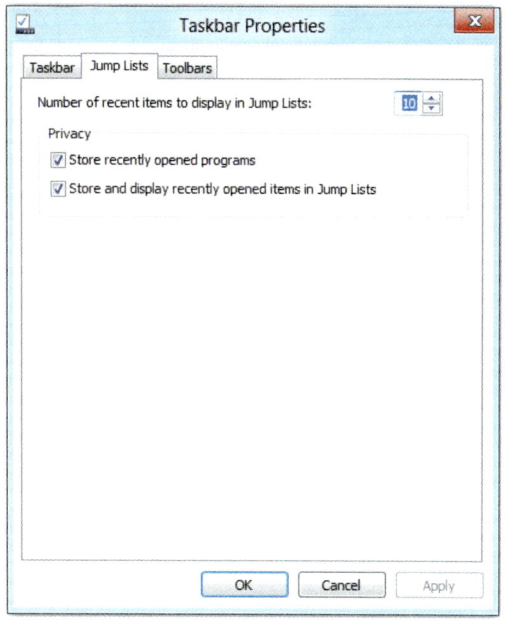

FIGURE 3-28 Configure jump list settings.

What to Do about AutoPlay

You see and change these settings in the AutoPlay control panel. To do so, open Settings Search by moving your mouse or swiping from the bottom right and selecting the Search charm and then moving the selection highlight to Settings. Or use Windows key+W to directly open Settings Search. Enter `autoplay` and select AutoPlay from the results.

In the AutoPlay control panel, scroll down to see the entire list of media and devices you can configure for AutoPlay. These include removable drives, camera storage, DVDs, Blu-ray discs, CDs, software (when a program is configured to automatically run on removable media), and devices connected to the computer. Each item in the list has several settings you can configure. Figure 3-29 shows the options for removable drives, with the added feature of letting you choose what to do with each type of media (pictures, video files, audio files, and mixed content).

On your own, view the entire list and create settings that work for you. Because we are very much hands-on, using our work computers for research and writing, we usually deselect the first check box and call it good. Then we can choose what to do for each instance. But if you use your computer to view lots of photos or watch videos, keep the check in the first check box, and place a check in the second box so that you can choose what to do for each media type. Then configure pictures to open a File Explorer folder to view files and configure video files to play automatically.

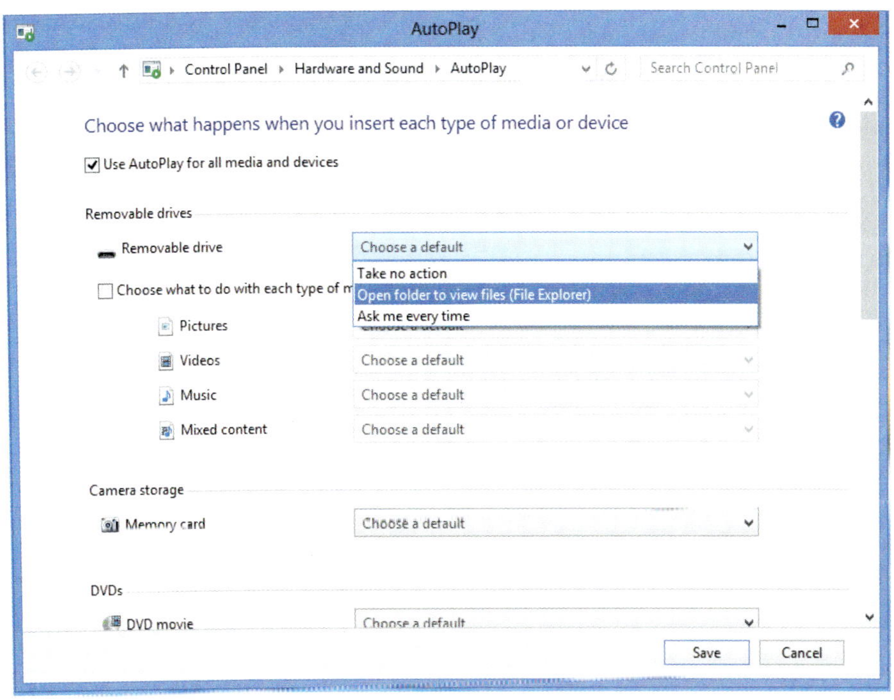

FIGURE 3-29 Autoplay settings.

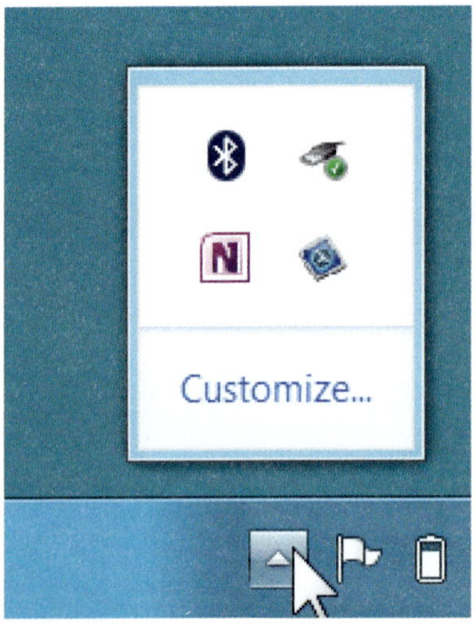

FIGURE 3-30 Click the Show Hidden Icons button to reveal the notification shortcuts.

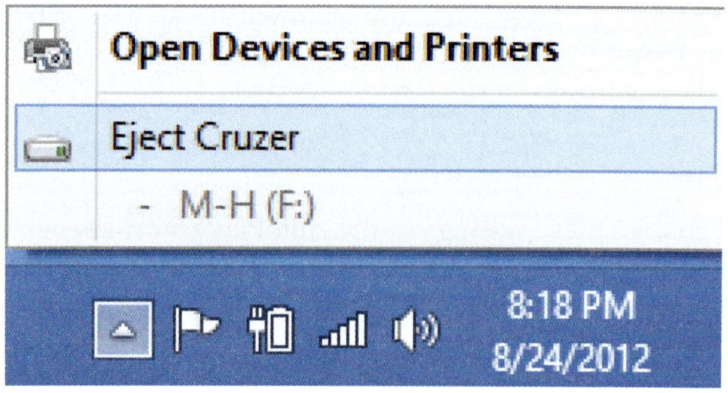

FIGURE 3-31 Eject removable drive.

Disconnecting an External Drive

When it comes time to disconnect an external storage device, simply disconnecting it leaves you vulnerable to damaging the files on the device. Therefore, you need to take one precaution before disconnecting so Windows can close any open files on the device. To do so, click or tap the Show Hidden Icons button on the notification area (far right) of the desktop taskbar (Figure 3-30). Then tap or click the Safely Remove Hardware and Eject Media button shown here at the top right of the open box. This opens a list of removable items, shown in Figure 3-31. Locate the device you want to disconnect and select Eject <device name>. When the Safe to Remove Hardware message balloon pops up, remove the device. If an application has a file open on the device, a balloon will display with a warning. In that case, close out any application that may have a file open on the device and try again.

LO 3.3 | Backing Up and Restoring Files in Windows 8

Windows 8 has a file backup program that is not easy to find because it is no longer called "Backup" but **File History**. It takes advantage of a file versioning feature that has been a nearly hidden part of Windows since Windows XP, but has evolved into a very useful backup tool. It does have its limits, but if you save your data files in certain special folders, Windows File History will back up your files on a predefined schedule, saving versions that you can restore, if needed. After you turn on File History, as long as the location you specify is available, you will not have to think about scheduling backups—they will happen as necessary. The folders that File History backs up are Libraries, Desktop, Contacts, and Favorites.

Configuring File History for Backups

File History can only back up to either an external drive or a network location. We like this because that is how we have backed up our data for many years, using network servers whenever they were available to us and then using external hard drives when a dedicated network server was not, as in the three years we lived and traveled full time in an RV. And a network location can be on your local network or on the Internet.

Whatever location you choose, it must always be available when File History performs the backups. If you plan to use an external drive, connect it to your computer before configuring File History. If you plan to use a network location, make sure it exists beforehand and that your user account has full read and write access to that location. If you are using a location at school or

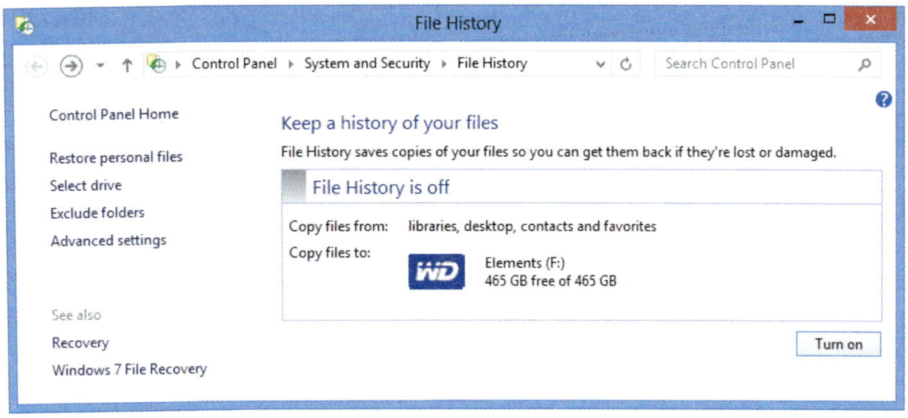

FIGURE 3-32 File History detected an external drive.

work, a network administrator will take care of the details and give you instructions for connecting. If you are at home and have a Windows HomeGroup, you can use one of the default locations or create a new one. Learn about working with HomeGroups in Chapter 5.

When you have arranged for a location to use, open the File History control panel. One way to do that is to open the Settings Search, enter `file history`, and select File History from the results. File History first looks for an external hard drive; if it finds none, it will include a message prompting you to connect a drive or use a network location.

Figure 3-32 shows the File History control panel after it found an external drive. Click the Turn On button. After the new location appears in the Change Drive list, click the OK button, which brings you back to the first screen, with location listed, and with the Turn On button now active. Click the Turn On button.

Keyboard Shortcuts!
Windows key+W opens the Search bar focused on Settings.

If your computer is a member of a Microsoft HomeGroup, you will be prompted to recommend the location to others in your HomeGroup. A HomeGroup is something we'll describe in Chapter 5. However, if you already have a HomeGroup and want to make the HomeGroup location the default File History backup location for other computers in the HomeGroup, select Yes.

Changing File History Settings

After you turn on File History, it will quietly make backups of the files in your Libraries, Desktop, Contacts, and Favorites folders. Open File History to check the status, restore files, change the drive or network location, exclude folders (to save backup disk space), and make other changes through Advanced settings.

We recommend that you click the Advanced Settings button and check out these important settings shown in Figure 3-33 and consider what works best for you. The frequency is set to every hour, but you can change that to a

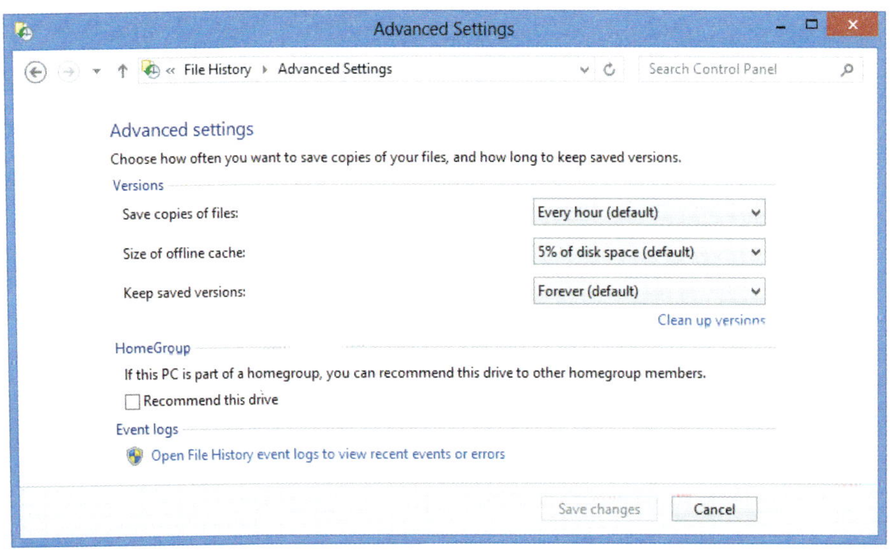

FIGURE 3-33 File History Advanced Settings.

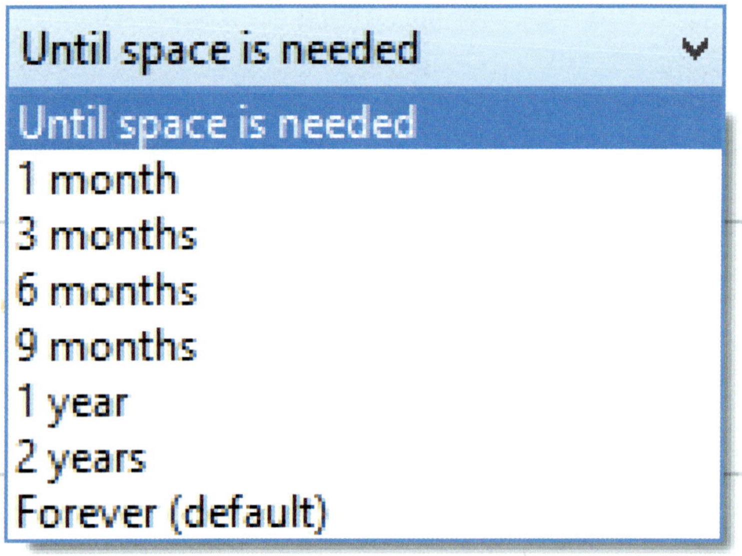

FIGURE 3-34 Choose how long saved versions are kept.

range of settings from every 10 minutes to daily. Keep the default size of the offline cache setting unless you see a File History error message concerning cache space. An important setting, Keep Saved Versions, controls when, if ever, backed-up files are deleted, as shown in Figure 3-34. If this is for your personal files, consider changing the setting to Until Space Is Needed so that you will not run out of disk space.

Restoring a Deleted File

What happens when you delete a file? It depends on where the file is when you delete it and how you delete it. If you delete a file that is on a network drive, it is permanently deleted. If you delete a file that is saved on your local hard drive, Windows moves it to the Recycle Bin, giving you a second chance to recover the file unless you permanently delete it. If you select a file in File Explorer and either press the Delete key or select Delete from the GUI (from a menu or the ribbon), it moves to the Recycle Bin and is easily recoverable as long as you don't wait too long, because depending on the Recycle Bin settings, it will eventually permanently delete the file. The Recycle Bin receives deleted files from locations protected by File History, as well as locations that File History does not protect, so this is your tool for restoring less-than-permanently deleted files from anywhere on your local hard drive.

However, if you press the Shift key while pressing the Delete key, you permanently delete the file. That's when you need to restore a file from your latest backup. Windows File History makes this possible, as you will see in Step-by-Step 3.4 where you will compare using the Recycle Bin with recovering a file from File History.

Keyboard Shortcuts!
Select a file, and then press Shift+Delete to permanently delete the file.

Step-by-Step 3.4

Restoring Deleted Files

Practice restoring files from both the Recycle Bin and File History. To complete this exercise, you need the Test1 and Test2 files created in Step-by-Step 3.1, and you will need File History turned on long enough to have backed up the Test1 and Test2 files.

Step 1

Open File Explorer, navigate to your Documents library, and select the Test1 file you created earlier. Delete the file by pressing the Delete key. The file disappears from File Explorer.

Step 2

Locate the Test2 file and delete it by pressing the Shift+Delete key combination. When the Delete File box appears, click the Yes button to permanently delete the file.

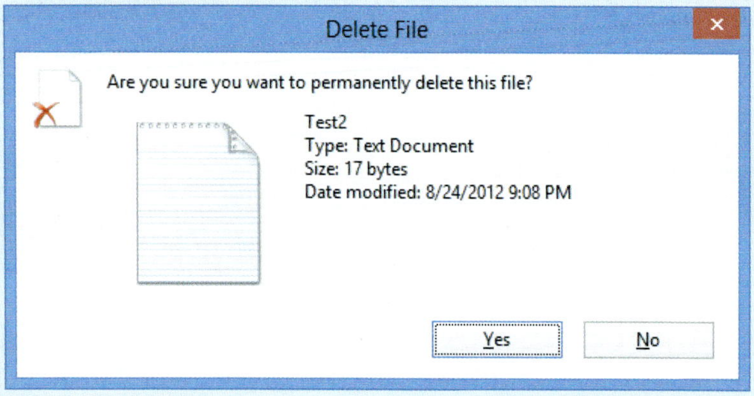

Step 3

Now locate the Recycle Bin shortcut on the Desktop and open it. Recycle Bin opens in a File Explorer window. Navigate to the folder containing the deleted files. Notice that of the two files you just deleted, only Test1 displays because Test2 was permanently deleted and not sent to the Recycle Bin.

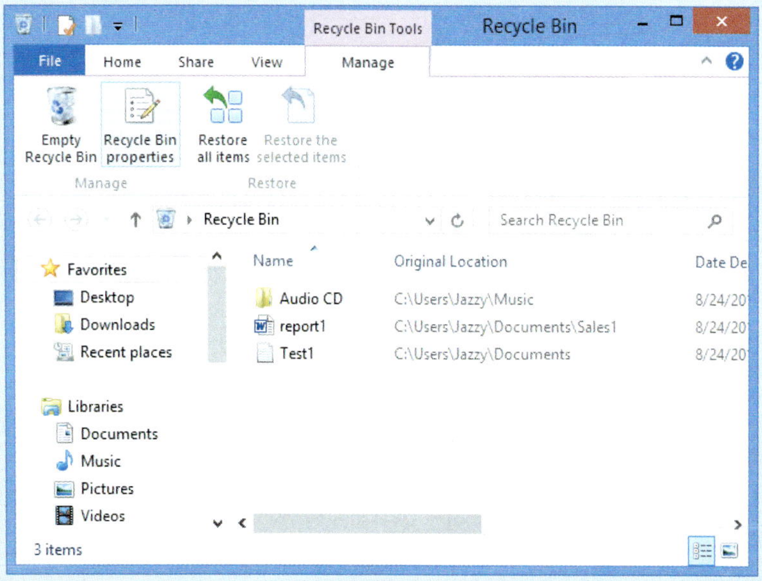

Step 4

Select Test1 and click the Restore the Selected Items button in the ribbon. The file will disappear from the Recycle Bin and show in the original folder. Return to the Documents library and verify that the file was restored.

Step 5

To restore Test2, open File Explorer and navigate to the Documents library. On the Home tab, click or tap the History button near the right end of the ribbon.

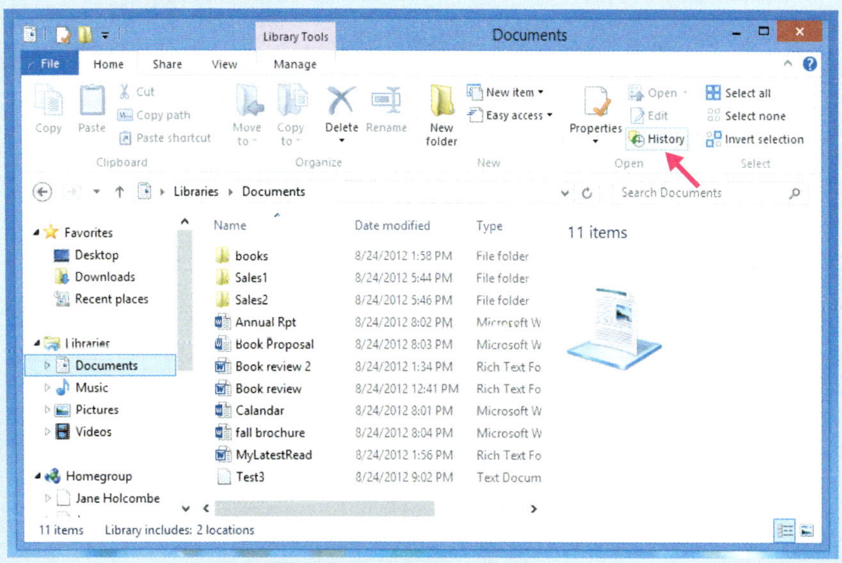

Step 6

In the File History window, notice that you can view the previous versions of File History using the arrows on the bottom of the window to scroll back and forth through the various versions. The button between the arrows restores the selected files.

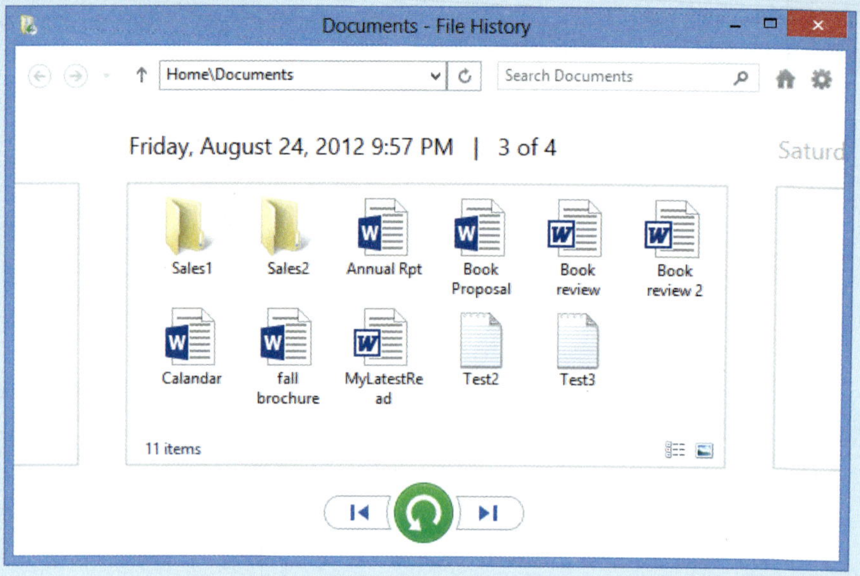

Step 7

Locate the latest version of the deleted file and select it. To find the latest version, use the horizontal scroll buttons near the center bottom. Then select the file and click or tap the green Restore button. If a file of that name still exists in the same location, this will bring up the Replace or Skip Files dialog box, which lets you replace the file, skip the file, or compare the two versions. Once you complete the operation, File Explorer will display the folder with the restored file.

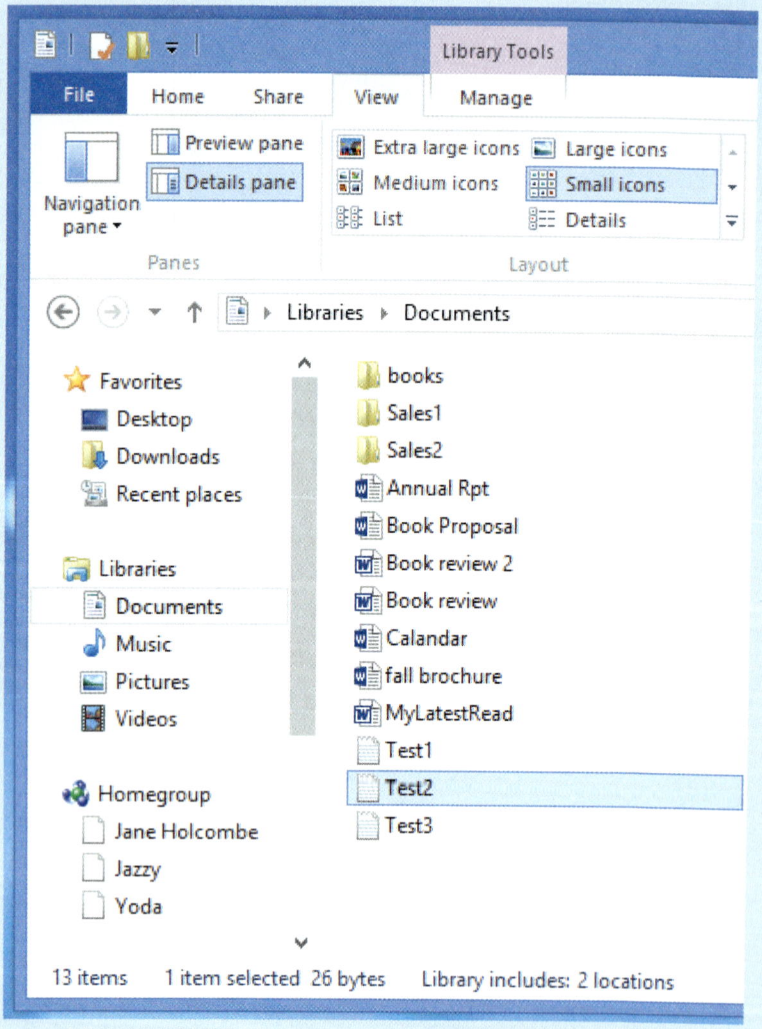

LO 3.4 | Working with Printers in Windows 8

Each version of Windows has improved the handling of printers. With Windows 8, once you install a printer, much of the work is done for you.

Installing a Local Printer

Installing a printer in Windows 8 is very automated. If it is a **local printer**, one that connects directly to a computer, connect it to a power outlet, connect it to your computer, and then turn it on. Windows will recognize the printer and install the driver. In most cases, the next time you attempt to print from an app, you will be able to print to your new printer. If it is the first printer installed in Windows 8, it becomes the **default printer**—the printer Windows uses if you do not select a different printer. Figure 3-35 shows the Print menu from WordPad. If you want to verify which printer it will use, click the Print option in the right side of the drop-down menu. This brings up the Print dialog box shown in Figure 3-36. From here you can select a printer, make choices to control the print job, and when ready, select Print to send the job to the printer.

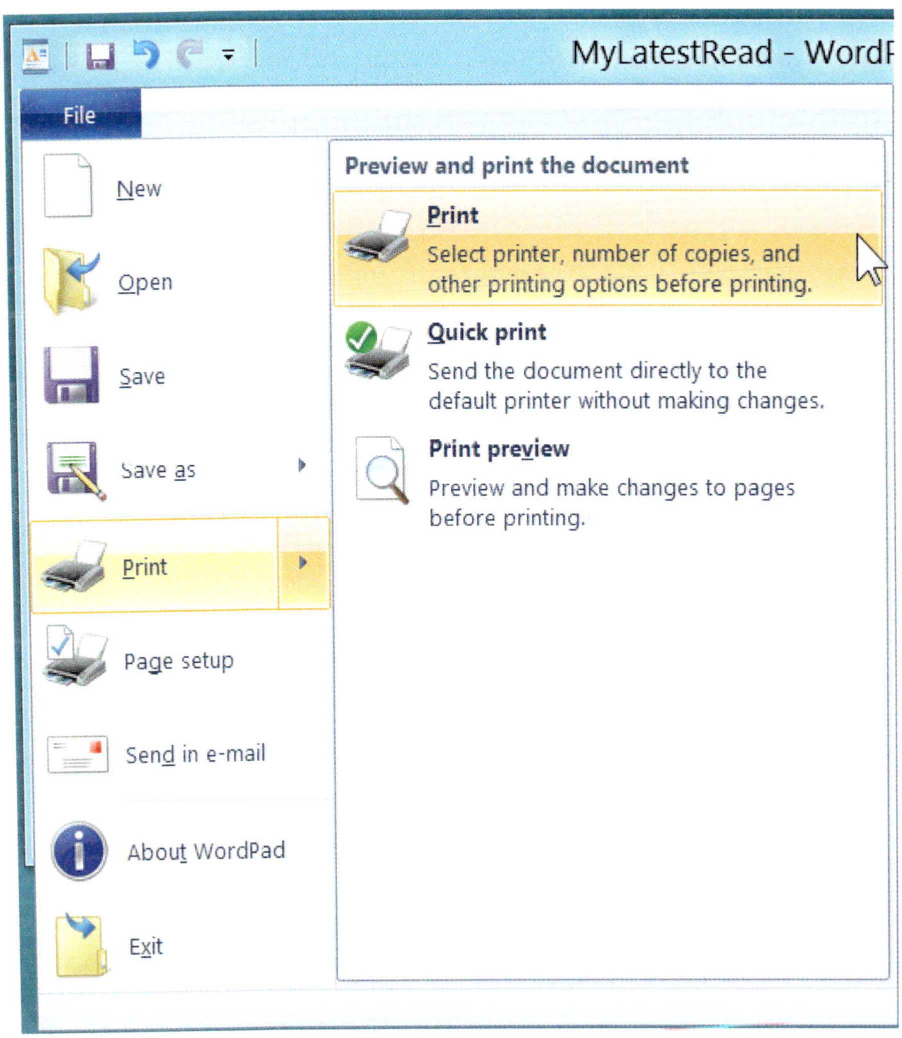

FIGURE 3-35 The Print selection menu in a Desktop app.

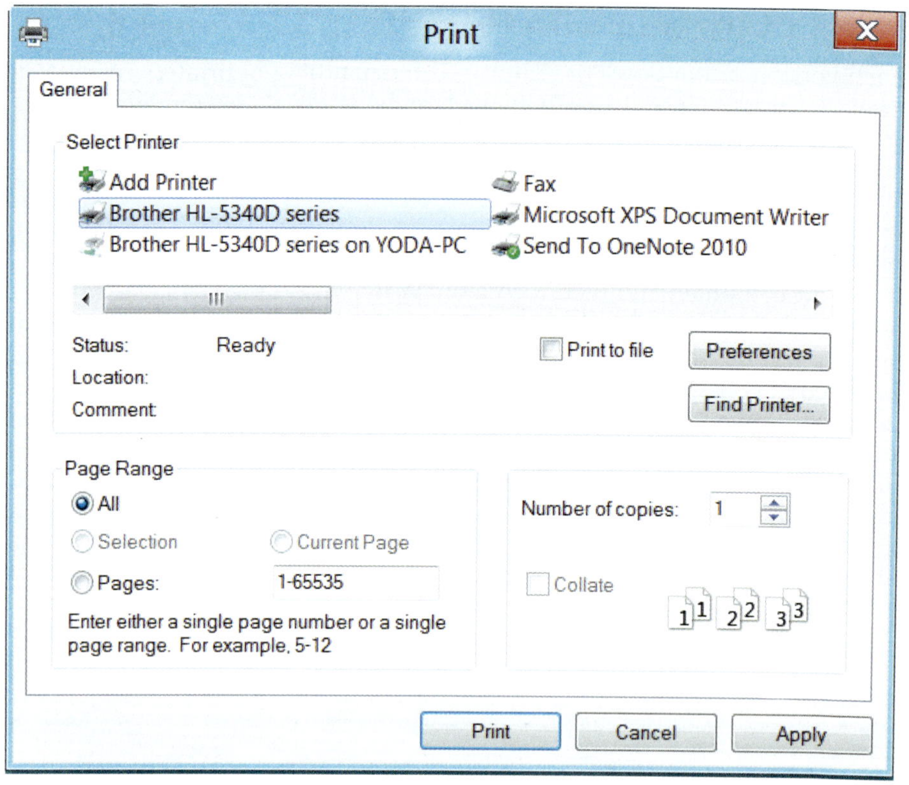

FIGURE 3-36 The Print menu in a Desktop app.

The print options are available for local printers, as well as network printers.

If you need more control over a print job, use the Preferences button to open a larger list of options where you can control the paper size and orientation, the number of copies, resolution, specify single-sided versus double-sided (duplex) printing, and the paper source. Most printers support at least two paper sources: one or more trays and manual feed. If you have multiple trays, you can load letterhead into one tray and plain paper into the others, and select the letterhead tray when required. You can even print out a multiple-page letter, designating one tray for the first page and the other tray for subsequent pages.

Another way to see if a printer has been installed is to open the Settings Search bar by swiping in from the bottom right and selecting Search, or open it by pressing Windows key+W. In the Settings Search box type `printers`. Select Device and Printers from the results list. This opens the **Devices and Printers** control panel (Figure 3-37) where you can see all connected devices and manage their settings.

If a local printer is not installed, check to see that it is turned on and connected to your computer. If it is connected and powered up, you may need to check with the manufacturer to see if Windows 8 supports the printer. It should at least recognize the printer when you click Add Devices and Printers or Advanced Printer Setup, both of which look for a connected local or network printer.

Installing a Network Printer

A **network printer** is a printer that is shared over a network—whether through a computer acting as a print server or directly connected to the network, in which case the printer contains within it circuitry that lets it

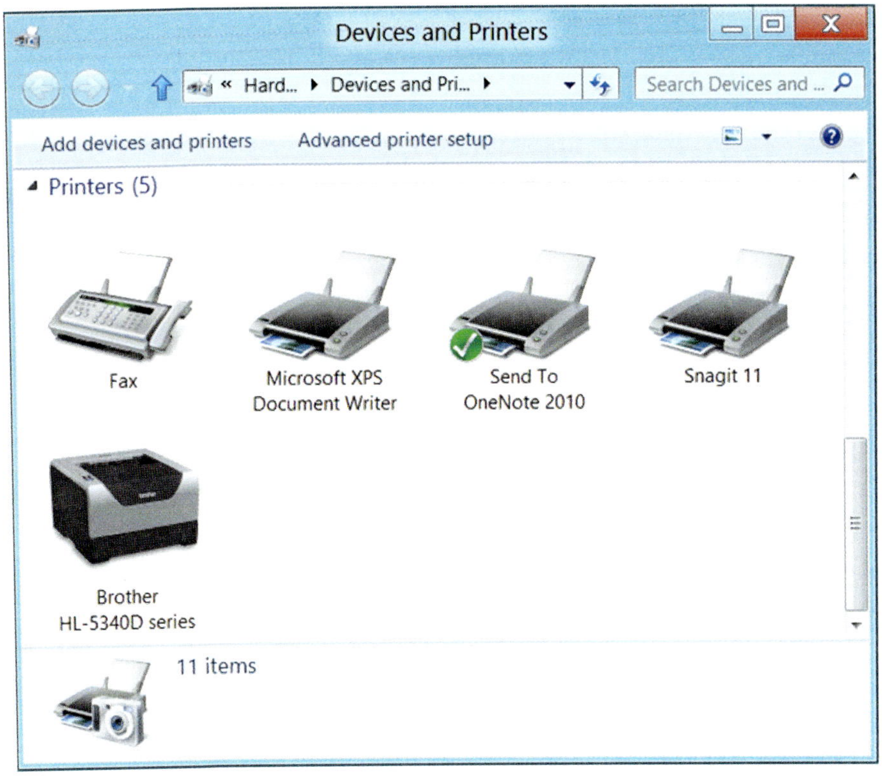

FIGURE 3-37 Devices and Printers shows the installed printers.

act as a print server. A **print server** is either a computer or circuitry within a printer—both with specialized software—that intercepts incoming print jobs and sends them to be printed, returning status messages to the correct client computers for each print job. If network printers are on your network, or if your computer is part of a HomeGroup or otherwise connects to a Microsoft workgroup or domain, you should see the printers that are shared from an Apps Print menu as well as in Devices and Printers, as Figures 3-38 and 3-39 show.

Setting a Default Printer

In Devices and Printers shown in Figure 3-38, the default printer is one of the three "soft" printers installed. They include Microsoft XPS Document Writer, Send To OneNote 2010, and Snagit 11. If you print to one of these printers the so-called printer creates a special file. In the case of the Microsoft XPS Document Writer, it creates a document that is readable by anyone with the free Microsoft XPS Reader, but it is not editable. Microsoft's XPS file format serves the same purpose as Adobe's PDF file format. Many free programs install as printers and let you create a PDF file out of almost any document you have. These are then readable by the free Adobe Reader or many other programs.

The question now is which printer will best serve you as the default printer. In most cases, it will be a locally installed printer or a network printer. To change the default printer, locate the printer either in your app's Print dialog box or in Devices and Printers. Right-click your choice for default printer and select Set As Default Printer from the context menu, shown in Figure 3-39.

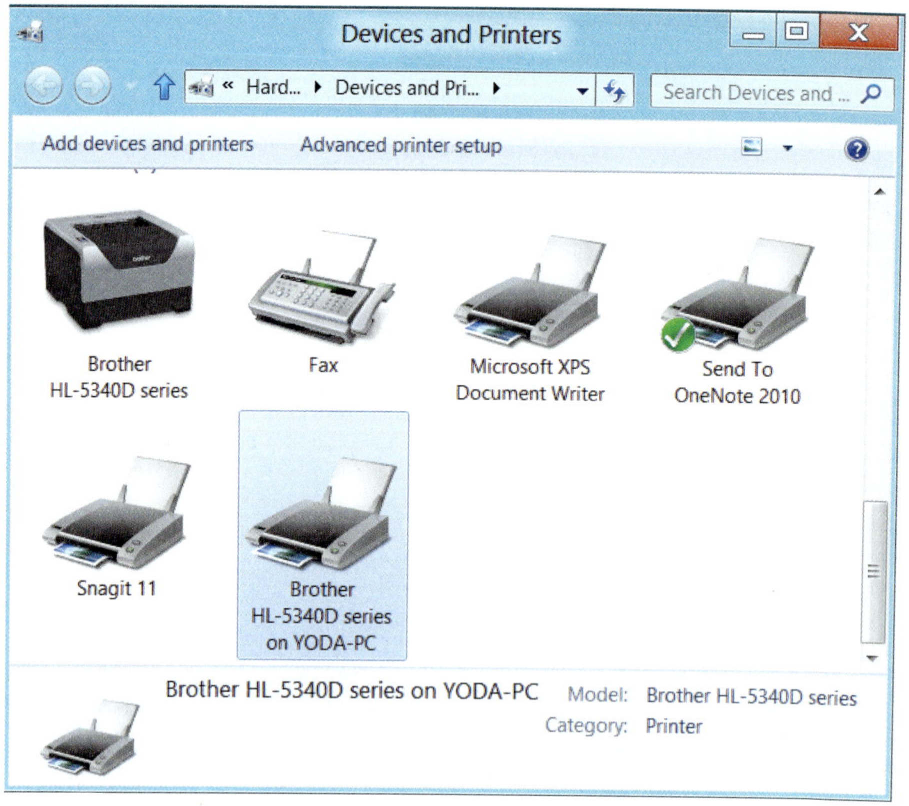

FIGURE 3–38 The selected printer is a network printer shared from the computer YODA-PC.

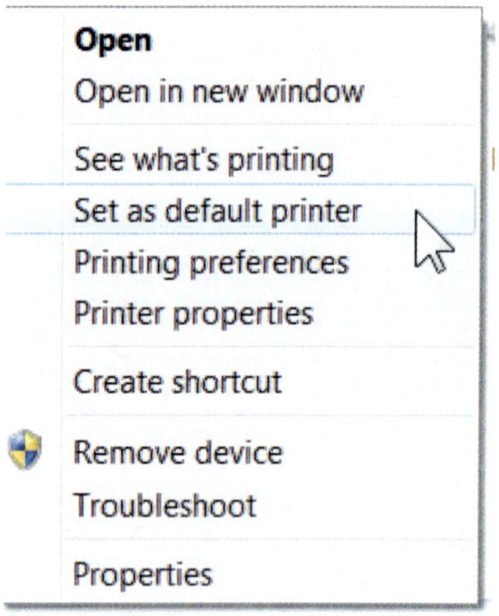

FIGURE 3–39 Set the default printer.

Chapter 3 REVIEW

Chapter Summary

After reading this chapter and completing the Step-by-Step tutorials and Try This! exercises, you should understand the following facts about file management and printing in Windows 8:

Basic File Management in Windows 8

- A file is a container for data (whether program code or some type of user data) organized as a unit, saved on mass storage, and identified with a special name, called a file name.
- A file name consists of the file name and extension, separated by a period.
- Keep file names simple, even though Windows allows very long file names.
- A folder is a logical container used to organize files and folders on a storage device. The original name, directory, is also frequently used.
- Create and save files from Desktop apps. Copy, move, rename, and delete files in File Explorer.
- File Explorer in Windows 8 opens context-sensitive tabs for certain types of files; each of these contextual tabs is a colorful "super tab" in the Title bar, connected to a new tab in the ribbon, which, in turn, contains menus and buttons for actions that apply to the type of files that are the current focus of File Explorer.
- File Explorer contextual tabs mentioned in the chapter include Picture Tools, Music Tools, Disk Tools, Shortcut Tools, Application Tools, and Library Tools.
- File and folder Copy and Move have improved to let you manage multiple large copy operations and give you more tools to resolve file name conflicts. You can even pause one copy operation to allow another one to complete faster.

Just Beyond Basic File Management in Windows 8

- A library looks like a folder, but it stores only information about the locations of the folders and files it displays. A single library can point to various locations on local storage or network storage. Libraries make it easier for you to find related information and it allows you to easily backup related files stored in multiple locations.
- The four default libraries in Windows 8 are Documents, Music, Pictures, and Videos. Each of these has two locations: one folder to store personal files that are not shared, and another folder that is a public folder available to others over the network when sharing is turned on.
- Library Tools include various library management functions such as adding locations or changing the default save location of files saved to the library.
- A deleted library is moved to the Recycle Bin, but the files and folders that appeared within the library remain untouched at their actual locations.
- If you change your mind about deleting a library, open Recycle Bin and recover the library.
- You can search for files, folders, and apps in Windows 8 using the Windows 8 search utility or using the Search box in File Explorer.
- A jump list, associated with a taskbar program icon, contains links to recently opened files and programs that give you quick access to these and other items you may choose to pin to the jump list. Windows 8 added privacy controls to jump lists, so that you can stop a jump list from automatically showing recently opened programs and/or other items.
- Use the AutoPlay control panel to control the automated actions that occur when you connect external media. You can turn off AutoPlay altogether or control actions for each type of media.
- Use the Safely Remove Hardware and Eject Media button on the Hidden Icons box from the taskbar to safely close all open files on external storage before disconnecting it.

Backing Up and Restoring Files in Windows 8

- File History is a feature of Windows 8 that will back up your files on a predefined schedule, saving versions that you can restore, if needed. The folders that File History backs up are Libraries, Desktop, Contacts, and Favorites.
- To use File History, you must designate either an external drive or a network location for the backup. This location must always be available to File History.
- You can configure how often File History backs up, the size of the offline cache, and how long it keeps versions. You can also share a location for other members of your HomeGroup to use for File History.
- If you delete a file from a location backed up by File History, open File History and scroll through the versions to select the version of the file you want to restore.
- Local files that have *not* been permanently deleted are saved in the Recycle Bin. You can restore them from Recycle Bin or from File History, depending on their location, because File History backs up only certain locations and Recycle Bin works on all local hard drive locations.

Working with Printers in Windows 8

- A local printer is one that connects directly to a computer.
- When you connect a local printer to a Windows 8 computer and turn on the printer, Windows will recognize and install a driver for it.
- The first printer installed is the default printer, meaning that when you do not specify a printer, that is the one that will receive print jobs. You can change the default printer through the Print dialog box.
- A network printer is a printer that is shared over a network—whether through a computer acting as a print server or directly connected to the network, in which case, the printer contains within it circuitry that acts as a print server.
- A print server is either a computer or circuitry within a printer that intercepts incoming print jobs and sends them to be printed, sending out status messages to the correct client computers for each print job.
- If network printers are on your network, or if your computer is part of a HomeGroup or otherwise connects to a Microsoft workgroup or domain, you should see the printers that are shared from an app's Print menu as well as in Devices and Printers.
- If several printers are available, use Devices and Printers to select a default printer that you will use most frequently.

Key Terms List

AutoPlay (82)
Clipboard (64)
copy (63)
cut (64)
default printer (89)
Devices and Printers (90)
directory (58)
drag-and-drop (63)
extension (58)
file (58)
File History (84)
folder (58)
jump list (82)
library (76)
local printer (89)
move (63)
network printer (90)
paste (64)
path (58)
pinning (81)
print server (91)
Recycle Bin (64)
ribbon (65)

Key Terms Quiz

Use the Key Terms List to complete the sentences that follow. Not all terms will be used.

1. When you perform a/an ______________ operation, you click or hold the cursor on a file or folder object and move it to another location where you release it.
2. When a file or folder is ______________ it is removed from the source location and saved into the Windows Clipboard until you paste it into another location.
3. During a/an ______________ operation, Windows copies a file or folder from the source location to a target location and then deletes the source copy so that it exists only in the target location.
4. A/an ______________ to a file includes the drive letter and each folder leading to the file, with a backslash (\) separating each component.
5. A/an ______________, originally called a directory, is a logical container used to organize files on a storage device.
6. A/an ______________ looks like a folder containing other folders and files, but it is not a conventional storage folder. It contains only pointers to multiple locations.
7. ______________ settings control what happens at the moment Windows recognizes a new CD, DVD, or when an external storage device is connected.
8. A/an ______________ is a container for data (whether program code or some type of user data) organized as a unit, saved on mass storage, and identified with a special name.
9. A/an ______________ identifies a file type and is usually three characters separated from the file name by a period.
10. ______________ is the Windows 8 file backup service that regularly saves versions of your files located in just four folders: Libraries, Desktop, Contacts, and Favorites.

Multiple-Choice Quiz

1. Of the following, which is designed to be your primary Windows tool for file management?
   a. Start screen
   b. Search Files
   c. File Explorer
   d. WordPad
   e. Microsoft Word
2. An ordinary delete operation anywhere on a local hard disk can be reversed with this Windows tool.
   a. File History
   b. Clipboard
   c. Jump list
   d. Recycle Bin
   e. Library
3. This file backup option lets you restore from various versions of a file.
   a. File History
   b. Clipboard
   c. Jump list
   d. Recycle Bin
   e. Library
4. A drag-and-drop of a file between two separate drives will default to which of the following operations?
   a. move
   b. delete
   c. copy
   d. rename
   e. cut

5. Which of the following pastes files or data from the Clipboard to a location or into a data file?
   a. Ctrl+X
   b. Ctrl+C
   c. Windows key+F
   d. Windows key+Q
   e. Ctrl+V
6. Which of the following shortcut keys, when used at the Windows desktop, will close an open window on the desktop or (when all open windows are closed) bring up the Shut Down Windows dialog box?
   a. Ctrl+X
   b. Ctrl+C
   c. Alt+F4
   d. Ctrl+Shift1N
   e. Ctrl+V
7. Which of the following shortcut keys opens the Windows 8 Search Files screen?
   a. Ctrl+X
   b. Ctrl+C
   c. Windows key+F
   d. Windows key+Q
   e. Ctrl+V
8. Right-clicking the icon for a program on the taskbar brings up a box containing which of the following?
   a. File History
   b. Jump list
   c. Libraries
   d. AutoPlay
   e. Ribbon
9. Whether it is a physical printer or specialized software, this is where print jobs are sent if you do not specify another location.
   a. Local printer
   b. Network printer
   c. Print server
   d. Default printer
   e. Devices and printers
10. Which of the following is not a default library in Windows 8?
   a. Documents
   b. Games
   c. Videos
   d. Pictures
   e. Music

Essay Quiz

1. Explain contextual tabs in File Explorer, including why they exist and how you use them; give three examples of contextual tabs.
2. Explain the need for a default save location for a library and how you can change it.
3. You have been asked to print 50 copies of a multiple-page letter with the first page printed on letterhead and subsequent pages printed on plain paper. Explain what feature the printer must have to let you automate this, how you will load the paper, and where in Windows you would configure this.

Lab Projects

LAB PROJECT 3.1

Practicing running multiple copy jobs.

For this Lab Project, you will need the two folders in My Documents named Sales1 and Sales2, which you created in Step-by-Step 3.2. In addition, you will need a flash drive with at least a few dozen files on it. The file types do not matter.

1. Use one of the methods you learned in the chapter to copy the entire contents of the flash drive into the Sales1 folder.
2. Copy the contents of the flash drive into the Sales2 folder. When the copying is finished, remove the flash drive using the method described in the chapter.
3. Now, select both folders (Sales1 and Sales2) in My Documents folder and move them into the Pictures library.
4. If you have many files, a dialog box will open showing how many running actions (jobs) are active, as shown in Figure 3-19. Try to pause one of the move operations by clicking or tapping the Pause button.
5. When the remaining action is complete, click the button for the paused job to resume.
6. When the copying is complete, open the Sales1 folder and select all the files, and then copy them into the Sales2 folder.

7. Because both folders have files with the same names, the File Conflict dialog box should open. Experiment with the options, and then click Cancel when you are finished.
8. If you need to clean up the computer, delete the Sales1 and Sales2 folders.

LAB PROJECT 3.2

Work with Windows 8 libraries. If you have a collection of personal data files, organize them into the Windows 8 libraries by type, and practice with the tools for each type.

For this project, you will need a Windows 8 computer and access to a collection of your own data files. Access these either by plugging in an external drive or by connecting over a network, if available, between you and the source location of your files.

1. Copy your document files into the Documents library.
2. Copy music files into the Music library.
3. Copy picture and other graphic files into the Pictures library.
4. Copy videos into the Videos library.
5. In the Documents library, create folders for your documents based on some criteria, such as hobbies or projects.
6. In the Music library, select the Music Tools tab and play one of your music files.
7. In the Pictures library, create a slide show of selected pictures using the Slide Show button, or select a picture and set it as the background for the desktop.
8. In the Videos library, select the Music Tools tab and play one of your music files.

LAB PROJECT 3.3

Use the Windows Help and Support app to research how to do a complete system backup in Windows 8. Then, if you have an external drive or network location, perform a system backup.

chapter

4 Windows 8 Security

"If you reveal your secrets to the wind, you should not blame the wind for revealing them to the trees."

—Kahlil Gibran (1883–1931), *poet and author*

No form of computing is safe from threats as long as computers connect to networks leaving them exposed to threats. And although networks are how most threats find our computers, malicious code on flash drives, floppy disks, and even optical disks can still infect those few that do not connect to networks. Even our mobile computing devices are under attack. The McAfee company released a report by McAfee Labs titled "McAfee Threats Report: First Quarter 2012," which revealed the state of computer security based on their research of threats worldwide. Whereas in 2011, they saw declines in malware threats in several areas, in the first quarter of 2012 they saw increases in malware targeted at PCs as well as at mobile devices.

Windows and other modern operating systems have a long list of security features. In addition, vendors update each OS as they discover new vulnerabilities. An entire multibillion-dollar industry has grown up to provide security products for home and business computers worldwide. It is a dangerous world out there, and today "out there" is everywhere. In this chapter, learn what the threats to your data, to your identity, and even to your hardware are. Then explore the fundamentals for protecting yourself and your computer.

Learning Outcomes

In this chapter, you will learn how to:

- LO **4.1** Identify common threats to privacy and data for computer users.
- LO **4.2** Install and configure security software in Windows 8.
- LO **4.3** Describe how you would recover from a malware attack.

LO 4.1 | Threats to Privacy and Data

Your computing devices are necessary for much of what you do now and in the future at work, school, and home. However, in our massively connected world, those same computers and smartphones put you at risk, and the threats are growing. You don't need to be a government agency, utility company, or multinational enterprise to be a target of threats to your privacy, your data, even to your financial security. New threats appear every day, and the more you understand about the types of threats, the better you will be prepared to protect yourself.

Computer Hardware Theft

Computer security begins with physical security: locking doors, keeping hardware locked away from prying eyes and sticky fingers, and being extra vigilant when traveling with a laptop or other computing device. People steal a huge number of computers, especially laptops and tablets, each year from businesses, homes, and automobiles. When this happens, you lose important tools and valuable data files—and perhaps even your identity. Many years ago, when a modest IBM PC cost several thousand dollars, hardware theft was only about the hardware, but today's thief is savvy enough to know that your computer will give them easy access to personal financial information and just about any data you have privileged access to over a network. So take steps to keep your computer physically secure and learn how to protect the data contained on your Windows 8 computer.

Disasters, Big and Small

Disasters come in many forms and sizes. Only the victims can define some disasters. For instance, each of us has at one time or another accidentally erased an important file, pressed the wrong key and deleted a file, or created a file and then forgotten its name and location. To the person who made the error, this is a disaster.

More obvious to the rest of the world are disasters in the form of fires, earthquakes, or disasters resulting from tornados, lightning strikes, or floods. There is, of course, the possibility of a disaster of an even greater magnitude, such as a Katrina-like storm, with the obvious consequences and the resulting

Guard against computer theft.

damage to the people, the environment, and the economy. Whatever the scale of the disaster, your best protection from the loss of equipment and data is to make frequent, comprehensive backups.

Social Engineering

Social engineering is the use of persuasion techniques to gain the confidence of individuals for both good and bad purposes. People with malicious intent use social engineering to persuade targeted people to reveal confidential information or to obtain something else of value. Social engineering is as old as human interaction, so there are countless techniques. Following are just a few categories of computer threats that qualify as social engineering.

Fraud

Fraud is the use of deceit and trickery to persuade someone to hand over money or valuables. Fraud is often associated with identity theft, because the perpetrator will falsely pose as the owner of the victim's credit cards and other personal and financial information.

Phishing

Phishing is a method of obtaining personal financial information through web page pop-ups, email, and even paper letters mailed via the postal service. Think of the metaphor of a fisherman preparing and casting his bait in an ocean full of fish. Even if only one in a hundred fish take the bait, he is statistically likely to have many successes. We'll concentrate our discussion on web page pop-ups and email. A phishing message ("bait") often purports to be from a legitimate organization, such as a bank, credit card company, retailer, and so on. In a typical phishing scenario, the email or web page may contain authentic-looking logos, and even links to the actual site, but the link specified for supplying personal financial information will take recipients (the "phish") to a "spoofed" web page that asks them to enter their personal data. The web page may look exactly like the company's legitimate web page, but it's not at the company's site. A common practice is for a phisher to use the credit information to make purchases over the Internet, choosing items that are easy to resell and having them delivered to a destination address to which the phisher has access, such as a vacant house.

Be very suspicious of email requesting personal financial information. Legitimate businesses will never contact you by email and ask you for your access code, Social Security number, or password. Phishing is just an old-fashioned scam in high-tech dress.

Phone Phishing

Phone phishing (sometimes called "vishing" using "v" for "voice") is another form of phishing. To gain the intended victim's confidence, a phishing email will urge the reader to call a phone number to verify information, at which point the person on the phone will ask the victim to reveal the valuable information.

What makes this so compelling to the user is that phone phishing often involves a very authentic-sounding professional Interactive

try this!

Take a Phishing Test

It is often difficult to discern which emails are legitimate and which are "phish." Try This!

1. Use your web browser to connect to the phishing test at **www.sonicwall.com/furl/phishing/.** If this URL no longer works, use a search engine to find a phishing test.
2. After reading the instructions and helpful hints, start the test.
3. You will be presented with 10 emails, and you must decide whether each is legitimate or phish.
4. When you finish you will get the correct answers. Each email also has a detailed explanation as to why it is either legitimate or phish. Read these explanations carefully.

Voice Response (IVR) menu system, just like a legitimate financial institute would have. It may ask the user to enter his password or personal identification number (PIN). To ensure that the system captures the correct password or PIN, the system may even ask the victim to repeat it. Some systems then have the victim talk to a "representative" who gathers more information.

Hoax

A **hoax** is a deception intended either for amusement or for some gain with malicious intent. Hoaxes take many forms. One example is an email message from someone you know claiming she took an unplanned trip to London where she was mugged in the subway. The email address looks legitimate, but when you respond, you receive a message from someone else stating that your friend is now in jail and needs bail money. Sounds outlandish? We received such a message, but we were suspicious and called our friend who reported that she was safe at home and that several of her friends had responded to the message and received the plea for money.

Identity Theft

Identify theft occurs when someone collects personal information belonging to another person and uses that information to fraudulently make purchases, open new credit accounts, and even obtain new driver's licenses and other forms of identification in the victim's name. They may not even be interested in actual financial information; obtaining your Social Security number and other key personal information may be enough to steal your identity. Amazingly, medical identity theft is growing rapidly, with perpetrators stealing someone's identity in order to obtain health care.

There are many ways not directly involved with computers for thieves to steal your identity. Identity theft is a huge business involved in the theft of large numbers of persons' data from large databases. These criminals sell

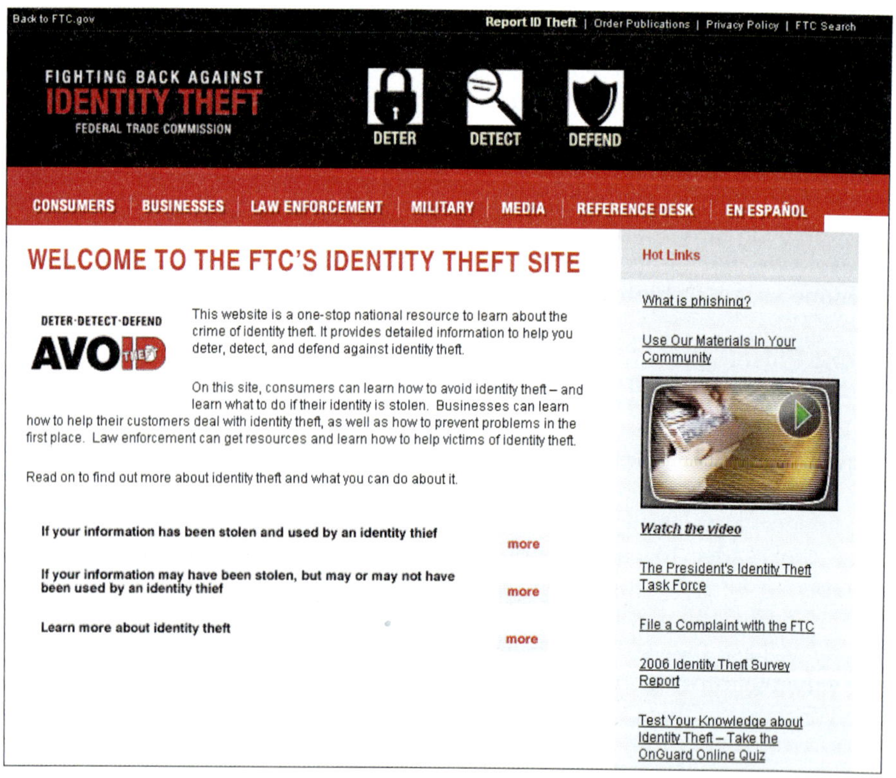

The Federal Trade Commission's ID Theft web page.

such identity information for pennies per record. Several websites maintained by the U.S. government offer valuable information for consumers who want to protect themselves from identify theft.

> **try this!**
>
> **Learn More about Identity Theft**
>
> Learn more about identity theft in general, how to protect yourself, and how to report suspected identity theft. Try This!
>
> 1. Open your browser and use a search engine to search on "FTC id theft." (Omit the quotation marks.)
> 2. In the search results, select the site identified as the U.S. government's central website for information about identity theft.
> 3. At the Federal Trade Commission's ID theft website, explore the various links from this page to learn more about identity theft and related topics.
> 4. If it is available, watch the video on identity theft. You may be surprised at how easy it is to be a victim of identity theft.

Exposure to Inappropriate or Distasteful Content

The Internet, and especially the World Wide Web, is a treasure trove of information. It is hard to imagine a subject that cannot be found somewhere on the Internet. However, some of this content may be inappropriate or distasteful. To some extent, only an individual can judge what is inappropriate and distasteful; however, circumstances in which certain content is harmful to some individuals—such as young children—is considered a threat and therefore inappropriate.

Invasion of Privacy

One can also view many of the threats discussed so far as invasions of privacy. Protecting against privacy invasion includes protecting your personal information at your bank, credit union, online, and at bricks-and-mortar retail stores, athletic clubs, or almost any organization in which you are a customer, member, or employee. All steps you take to make your computer more secure also contribute to the protection of your privacy.

Misuse of Cookies

A more subtle form of privacy invasion involves the misuse of something called cookies. **Cookies** are very small files an Internet browser saves on the local hard drive at the request of a website. The next time you connect to that

Invasion of privacy

same website, it requests the cookies saved on previous visits—often giving you the convenience of automated logins to each site. Cookies are text files, so they cannot contain viruses, which are executable code, but what they may contain includes the following:

- User preferences when visiting a specific site.
- Information you may have entered into a form at the website, including personal information.
- Browsing activity.
- Shopping selections on a website.

The use of cookies is a convenience to a user who does not have to reenter preferences and pertinent information on every visit to a favorite website. In fact, users are not overtly aware of the saving and retrieving of cookies from their local hard disk, although most good websites clearly detail whether they use cookies and what they use them for. You can find this information in the privacy statement or policy of the site. Cookies are accessible only by the website that created them, or through some subterfuge of the website creator. A **first-party cookie** is one that originates with the domain name of the URL to which you directly connect. The domain name portion of a URL is the string of characters separated by a period, followed by a top-level domain name, such as com, biz, net, edu, etc. Therefore the domain name in the URL http://www.msn.com/?ocid=iehp is msn.com. If you trust the domain, you may not mind that it places cookies on your computer to remember your preferences the next time you connect to the domain.

A **third-party cookie** is one that originates with a domain name other than the one shown in your URL. An ad embedded in a web page—called a banner ad—can use cookies to track your web surfing habits. This would place a cookie on your computer from a domain you did not visit and were not even aware of, so you really have no choice in this behavior. All popular Internet browsers let you configure how cookies are treated, and you will learn how to do that in Chapter 5.

Stealing Passwords

We first considered calling this section "Discovering Passwords," but that phrase is far too innocent sounding—as if the perpetrator was innocently walking along and "discovered" your password lying on the sidewalk. What really happens is theft with intent to break into computers and networks. It is stealing, so let's call it that! There are many methods of stealing passwords.

Stealing Passwords through Websites

People use a huge number of programs and techniques to steal passwords. One commonly used technique is to invade an unsecured website to access information unwitting users provide to the site, such as usernames and passwords, and such personal information as account numbers, Social Security number, birth date and place, and much more.

WARNING!

If you enter the words *password cracker* into your favorite search engine, you will discover that there are password crackers for every operating system, every type of computing device, and all the social networking services in use today.

Stealing Passwords with Password Crackers

Another technique people use for discovering password is a **password cracker**, a program used to discover a password. Some password crackers fall into the category of "brute-force" password crackers, which means the program tries a huge number of permutations of possible passwords. Often, because people tend to use simple passwords such as their initials, birth dates, addresses, etc., the brute-force method works. Other password crackers use more sophisticated statistical or mathematical methods to discover passwords.

Stealing Passwords with Keystroke Loggers

Another method for discovering passwords, as well as lots of other information, is by using a **keystroke logger**, also called a **keylogger**. These are either a hardware device or a program that monitors and records every keystroke, usually without the user's knowledge. In the case of a hardware logger, the person desiring the keystroke log must physically install it before recording and then remove it afterward to collect the stored log of keystrokes. For example, the Spytech keystroke logger is a USB device, the size of a flash drive that installs between the keyboard cable and a USB connector on the computer. There are also hardware keystroke loggers for PS/2 keyboard connectors. They are all very unobtrusive when connected to the back of a PC; one keystroke logger can hold a year's worth of keystroke data in flash memory and comes with special software for reading the specially formatted data files.

A software keystroke logger program may not require physical access to the target computer, but simply a method for downloading and installing it on the computer. This could occur through such routes as spyware, a pop-up downloader, or a drive-by downloader. Once installed, such a program can send the logged information over the Internet via email or other methods to the person desiring the log.

Some parents install keystroke loggers to monitor their children's Internet activity, but such programs have the potential for abuse by people with malicious intent including stalking, identity theft, and more. A simple Internet search of "keystroke logger" will yield many sources of both hardware and software keystroke loggers. The latter are now the more common.

Malicious Software

Malware, a shortened form of "malicious software," is a term that covers a large and growing list of threats, including many that you no doubt know about, such as viruses, worms, Trojan horses, or spam. But have you heard of pop-up downloads, drive-by downloads, war driving, bluesnarfing, adware, spyware, back doors, spim, or hoaxes? Do you know the difference between a vector and malware? Read on and learn about the many vectors and then learn about the various types of malware that are delivered by vectors.

Vectors

A **vector** is a mode of malware infection. Although some malware may use a single vector, multivector malware uses an array of methods to infect computers and networks. Let's look at a few well-known vectors.

Email Vectors

Some malware infects computers via email. You may have believed it was always safe to open email as long as you didn't open attachments, but the simple act of opening an email containing the Nimda virus can infect computers, depending on the software you are using to read the message. Although most recent email programs have protections against that particular virus and other known viruses, email is still a potential vector, as long as people open attachments and click links.

Code on Websites

Some malware infects computers by lurking in hidden code on websites. When an unsuspecting user browses to that site and clicks a link that, without her knowledge, takes her to this malware, the code launches and installs itself on her computer. Clicking the link gives the program permission to run.

Trojan Horse image

Trojan Horses

A **Trojan horse**, often simply called a Trojan, is both a type of malware and a vector. The modern day Trojan horse program gains access to computers much like the ancient Greek warriors who, in Homer's famous tale, gained access to the city of Troy by hiding in a large wooden horse, presented as a gift to the city (a Trojan horse). A Trojan horse program installs and activates on a computer by appearing to be something harmless, which the user innocently installs. It may appear as a useful free program that a user downloads and installs, but it is a common way for malware to infect your system.

Searching for Unprotected Computers

An unprotected computer becomes a vector when discovered by malware that searches for computers with security flaws, takes advantage of the flaws to install itself on the computer, and then uses that computer to gain access throughout a private network.

Sneakernet—The Oldest Vector

Yet another vector is as old as PCs. In the days when it was uncommon for computers to connect to any network, the mode of sharing data between computers was to carry a floppy disk containing data or programs from one computer to another. The slang for this practice is **sneakernet**. Sometimes, the floppy disk contained malware, making sneakernet the oldest vector. Sneakernet still exists today, but the storage device of choice is the flash drive, and the computers are usually also on a real network, which extends the risk when malware infects a single computer via a flash drive. In August 2010, the U.S. Deputy Defense Secretary revealed that a flash drive inserted into a U.S. military laptop in 2008 on a military post in the Middle East was the vector for malicious code that caused a significant breach of military computers. News outlets reported the breach and cited anonymous Defense Department officials as stating that this attack originated from outside the United States.

Back Doors

In computing, a **back door** is a way in which someone can gain access to a computer, bypassing authentication security. Sometimes a program's author installs a back door into a single program for easy access later for administering and/or for troubleshooting the program code. Or an attacker may create a back door by taking advantage of a discovered weakness in a program. Then any program using the back door can run in the security context of the invaded program and infect a computer with malware. In one well-known situation, the Code Red worm took advantage of a specific vulnerability in Microsoft's Internet Information Server (IIS) to install a back door. The result was that the worm displayed a message on every web page on the IIS server. The message included the phrase "Hacked by Chinese." Then the Nimda worm took advantage of the back door left by the Code Red worm to infect computers.

Rootkits

A **rootkit** is malware that hides itself from detection by anti-malware programs by concealing itself within the OS code or any other program running on the computer. A rootkit is first installed by someone with administrator (root) access to the computer; then the rootkit is used as a vector to install any type of malware to quietly carry out its mission. "Rootkit" also refers to the software components of a rootkit.

Pop-Up Downloads

A **pop-up** is a separate window that displays (pops up) uninvited from a web page. The purpose of a pop-up may be as simple as an advertisement, but some pop-ups can be a vector for malware. A **pop-up download** is a program downloaded to a user's computer through a pop-up page. It requires an action on the part of a user, such as clicking a button that implies acceptance of something, such as free information, although what that something may actually be is not usually clear. The program that downloads may be a virus or a worm.

Drive-by Downloads

A **drive-by download** is a program downloaded to a user's computer without consent. Often the act of browsing to a website, or opening an HTML email message, may result in a surreptitious download. A drive-by download may also occur when the user installs another application. This is particularly true of certain file-sharing programs that users install to allow sharing of music, data, or photo files over the Internet. Some drive-by downloads may alter your Internet Explorer home page and/or redirect all your browser searches to one site. Any drive-by download may also install a virus, a worm, or even more likely, adware or spyware (described later in this chapter).

War Driving

War driving is the name given to the act of moving through a neighborhood looking for open Wi-Fi networks—those connected to the Internet without using security to keep out intruders. Today, someone can do this with a Wi-Fi-enabled smartphone or tablet computer running one of several specialized apps. The more traditional equipment is a laptop equipped with Wi-Fi wireless network capability or a simple Wi-Fi sensor available for a few dollars from many sources. People who do this are called war drivers, and they often mark a building where a hotspot exists so people "in the know" can later use that hotspot to access the Internet, a practice called **war chalking**.

Not only are they using Internet access illegally, riding on the subscription of the hotspot owner, but they also can capture keystrokes, email, passwords, and usernames. If the individual computers on the wireless network, or other networks connected to it, are unprotected, unauthorized people may access those computers, making this a vector for malware.

Some people create hotspots intentionally—more and more hotspots are available for free or for a small charge by various businesses, such as coffee shops, bookstores, restaurants, hotels, truck stops, and even campgrounds. Using an unsecured hotspot can expose you to threats unless your computer is secure. If you need to be inspired to secure your Wi-Fi network, check out the Internet where many websites describe how to war drive, as well as how to protect your data from theft. There are even many war driving videos on YouTube.

Bluesnarfing

Similar to war driving, **Bluesnarfing** is the act of covertly obtaining information broadcast from wireless devices using the Bluetooth, a short-range wireless standard used for data exchange between desktop computers and mobile devices such as smartphones or tablets. Bluetooth devices have a range of from 10 centimeters to 100 meters, depending on the power class of the device. Using a smartphone, a bluesnarfer can eavesdrop to acquire information, or even use the synchronizing feature of the device to pick up the user's information—all without detection by the victim.

Spam and Spim

Spam is unsolicited email. This includes email from a legitimate source selling a real service or product, but if you did not give the source permission to send such information to you, it is spam. Too often, spam involves some form of scam—a bogus offer to sell a service or product that does not exist or that tries to include you in a complicated moneymaking deal. If it sounds too good to be true, it is! We call spam perpetrators spammers, and spam is illegal. Some corporate network administrators report that as much as 60 percent of the incoming email traffic is spam. Spam is most often considered a vector for social engineering, but it can also be

try this!

Research Spam Statistics

Find out the latest bad news on the amount of Internet email identified as spam. Try This!

1. Open your browser and connect to your favorite search engine, such as Google, Bing, or Chrome.
2. Search on the words "spam statistics." For a more targeted search, include the current year in your search string.
3. In the results list, many of the links will be for antispam programs that provide individual statistics. Review the results and select a link that appears to give actual statistics on spam occurrences for Internet email users. Discuss the results with your classmates.

used to deliver malware to your computer. Spam accounts for a huge amount of traffic on the Internet and private networks, and a great loss in productivity as administrators work to protect their users from spam, and as individuals sort through and eliminate spam.

Spim is an acronym for *sp*am over *i*nstant *m*essaging, and the perpetrators are spimmers. Small programs, called bots (short for robot, a program that runs automatically), sent out over the Internet to collect information often collect instant messaging screen names. The spimbot then sends unsolicited instant messages to the screen names. A typical spim message may contain a link to a website, where, like spam, the recipient will find products or services for sale, legitimate or otherwise.

Web Browser Hijacking

We received a call the other day from Dave, a finance officer at a large farm implement company. Every time he opened Internet Explorer, the home page pointed to a site advertising adware removal software. This is an example of web **browser hijacking**, a practice that has been growing. Some unscrupulous people do this so that their website will register more visitors, and then they can raise their rates to advertisers.

Dave was able to reverse this by changing the default page in Internet Options, but it was very annoying. He was lucky; sometimes hijackers make it very difficult to defeat the hijack because they modify the registry so that every time you restart Windows or Internet Explorer the hijack reinstates. Or you may even find that a registry change makes Internet Options unavailable.

Malware

Malware is as diverse as the methods for delivering it. Malware sources range from the mischievous or malevolent individual to nation states using covert malware attacks on enemy infrastructure and industries. Details continue to trickle out about Stuxnet and the more recent Flame virus—both likely examples of international cyber warfare—waged over computer networks rather than on geographic battlefields.

A huge industry has grown up around detecting and fighting malware attacks, and an equally large unofficial industry is out there creating malware. As evidenced by the long list of vectors, malware can access computer systems through many pathways. After it gains access to your system, it may use your local administrative authority to invade, and/or it may exploit a vulnerability in your operating system or apps. As software publishers discover vulnerabilities, they attempt to plug the security hole with updates, as described earlier. However, malware can take advantage of vulnerabilities as yet unknown to the software company and exploit them before an update is available.

An undiscovered vulnerability is called a **zero-day vulnerability**, and malware that takes advantage of such a vulnerability is a **zero-day exploit**. The famed Stuxnet virus, targeted at a country's nuclear development industry, reportedly took advantage of four zero-day vulnerabilities, and the more recent Flame virus that appears to have the same target also takes advantage of zero-day vulnerabilities.

Viruses

In the broadest sense, "virus" is a term used for all malware; technically, however, a **virus** is one class of malware: a program installed and activated on a computer without the knowledge or permission of the user. A virus may hide in a file, and replicate and spread as you copy or share the infected file. At the least, the intent is mischief, but most often it is intended to be genuinely damaging.

In the wild is a term frequently used to describe the overall computing environment—most notably including the Internet.

Like a living virus that infects humans and animals, a computer virus can result in a wide range of symptoms and outcomes. Loss of data, damage to or complete failure of an operating system, or theft of personal and financial information are just a few of the potential results of viruses infecting an individual computer. If you extend the range of a virus to a corporate or government network, the results can be far reaching and even tragic. Thousands of viruses exist "in the wild" today.

Worms

Like a virus, a **worm** is a program installed and activated on a computer without the knowledge or permission of the user. But a worm replicates itself on the computer or throughout a network. In other words, a worm is a network-aware virus that does not require action from the unwitting user to replicate, and it can have a similar range of outcomes. In recent years the Netsky and MyDoom worms caused chaos and loss of productivity just in the amount of network traffic they generated. The typical worm resides in a single file that it replicates onto multiple machines. However, the Nimda worm changed all that by inserting its code into other executable files on the local drive of each machine to which it replicates itself, making it hard to locate and remove the worm.

Botnets and Zombies

A **botnet** is a group of networked computers that, usually unbeknownst to their owners, are infected with programs that forward information to other computers over a network (usually the Internet). A **bot**, short for robot, is a program that acts as an agent for a user or master program, performing a variety of functions—both for good and evil. An individual computer in a botnet is a **zombie** because it mindlessly serves the person who originated the botnet code. Most often affecting home computers, botnets have grown to be one of the biggest threats on the Internet. While a botnet is arguably a vector as much as malware, the fact that a botnet takes over systems puts at least one foot in the malware territory.

Spyware

Spyware is a category of software that runs surreptitiously on a computer, gathers information without the user's permission, and then sends that information to the people or organizations that requested it. A virus may install Internet-based spyware—also called a **spybot**—on a computer, as can many other means of secretly installing software. Spyware is used for a full spectrum of purposes—some good, some evil, and some in a gray area between the two extremes. Spyware can be used by companies to trace users' surfing patterns to improve the company's marketing efforts; it can be used for industrial espionage; it can be used by law enforcement to find sexual predators or criminals (with appropriate legal permissions); and it can be used by governments to investigate terrorism.

Adware

Adware is a form of spyware software downloaded to a computer without permission. It collects information about the user in order to display targeted advertisements, either in the form of inline banners or pop-ups. Inline banners are advertisements that run within the context of the current page, taking up screen real estate. Pop-ups are a greater annoyance because they are ads that run in separate browser windows that you must close before you can continue with your present task. Clicking to accept an offer presented on an inline banner or a pop-up may trigger a pop-up download that can install a virus or worm.

LO 4.2 | Protecting Yourself

No simple solutions exist for protecting yourself from the damaging and mischievous threats that lurk on the Internet and on private networks, but doing nothing is not an option. We need to make our best efforts to thwart these threats, and even implementing basic security will keep many threats out. Here are some recommended defensive practices that you can apply both in Windows 8 and in your computing life in general to avoid being a victim.

Education

This chapter may be just the beginning of your education about how threats, such as viruses, get access to computers and networks and how our own behavior can make us vulnerable to such threats as identity theft. Beyond understanding how these things can happen, also be alert to signs of a virus or that someone is using your credit.

Any unusual computer event may indicate that a virus, some sort of browser hijack, or other form of spyware, adware, and so on infects your computer. Signs to look for include the following:

- Strange screen messages
- A sudden computer slowdown
- Missing data
- Inability to access the hard drive

Similarly, unusual activity in any of your credit or savings accounts can indicate that you are a victim of identity theft, including the following:

- Charges on credit accounts that you are sure you or your family did not make.
- Calls from creditors about overdue payments on accounts you never opened.
- Being rejected when applying for new credit for reasons you know are not true.
- A credit bureau reports existing credit accounts you never opened.

Along with education about threats comes paranoia. However, if you use a computer at home, work, or school, and are on a network and/or the Internet, a touch of paranoia is healthy. Just don't let it distract you from your day-to-day tasks. Take proactive, responsible steps, as we outline here.

Keeping Windows 8 Updated

The software threats to computers are increasing, and software products are targets. Therefore, software companies like Microsoft work to discover where vulnerabilities lie, to plug all security holes as soon as they can, and to create updates to their products and make them available to their customers. For a long time, this was not a formal process, but for the past several years Microsoft has issued updates to all their software—desktop and server Windows systems, Office, Visual Basic, and more on a regular basis—usually the second Tuesday of each month. This is known as Patch Tuesday. Occasionally, Microsoft issues an additional urgent out-of-cycle update, as occurred recently when the Flame virus was using Windows Update to infect computers. However, Microsoft updates its own security products and components, such as Windows Defender, more often than that.

You can update Windows and other Microsoft software without your direct intervention if you keep the default setting for Windows Update set to Automatic. Then the system checks regularly, and when it discovers updates it downloads them and updates your computer.

Using Strong Passwords

A **password** is a string of characters that you enter, along with an identifier such as a username, to authenticate you. A password is an important piece of the security puzzle. Don't take your password for granted. In fact, that should be plural, because you should not use the same password every time you create a new account, and you should put a great deal of thought into creating passwords that truly help you protect yourself. This is important because, unless you deal strictly in cash and do all your transactions in person at the bank, secure authentication is your basic defense against an invasion of your privacy. Your password is central to having secure authentication and so is a very important part of any security system. Most experts recommend using a password that is at least ten characters long and contains at least two words. It's easy to guess a password that contains a single common word, such as the name of a pet; therefore, they offer little in the way of real security.

Establish a method for creating strong passwords—whether it is some scheme that you think up or software that helps you create these passwords. Begin by thinking of a phrase that is easy to remember (a passphrase), such as, "I love the Boston Red Sox." Then take the first letter of each word in that phrase and string the letters together. In our example, the result is: iltbrs. Now turn it into a more complex password by capitalizing some of the alpha characters and inserting numbers and other symbols between the letters: i-l,T.b+r-s. If this meets the minimum password requirements, you have a password. Now, the trick is to remember this password without the use of sticky notes!

WARNING!

Blank passwords or those written on a sticky note and kept handy near a computer provide little security. Always insist on nonblank passwords that are not sitting out in the open.

You may have habits that make you vulnerable to identity theft or another type of attack on your computer, data, or personal information. Consider these questions:

- Do you have too many passwords to remember?
- When you have an opportunity to create a new password, do you use your favorite password—the one that you use everywhere?
- At school or work, do you have your password written on sticky notes or your desk calendar?
- Have you used the same password for more than a few months?

WARNING!

Even people with staff dedicated to keeping them safe have problems with creating strong passwords. Recently, a hacker claimed that he gained access to a presidential candidate's Hotmail and Drop Box accounts by using the name of the candidate's family pet.

If you've done any of these things, you are at risk! And the risk is not only with your password. Because many websites allow you to provide a username when you log in, you may also be reusing the same username and password combination. Now a hacker doesn't even have to guess your account name.

Authentication and Authorization

Windows supports authentication and authorization as a core security component. Your most visible defense against threats is authentication via a sign-in. Recall from Chapter 1 that authentication is the verification of who you are. Authentication depends on security accounts, which we will discuss as the next topic. Authentication goes hand-in-hand with authorization. Recall that authorization determines the level of access to a computer, file, folder, printer, or other resource granted to an authenticated user. You have varying levels of access to files on your local computer. For instance, you have full control (read, write, and delete) of files and folders within your document, music, picture, and video folders, but if your computer includes another user account, that other user has his or her set of folders (again, document, music, picture, and video) that you cannot access. Every time you access a new file or folder on your computer, authentication occurs behind the scenes. You are aware of it only if you see a message.

For instance, even if your account is a member of a special group on your computer called Administrators, when you try to run an administrative program or access a folder that contains critical operating system files, you will see the User Account Control dialog box, and you will need to take some action to continue. This is authentication at work.

Authentication may be one-factor, two-factor, or even three-factor. An example of **one-factor authentication** is the common use of a username and password for sign-in to a computer. When you do this, you are authenticated based on something you know: your username and password. We will focus on this type of authentication in this chapter.

However, for your general knowledge, we'll briefly explain two-factor and three-factor authentication. **Two-factor authentication** involves the use of something you know, plus something you have, referred to as a **token**. If you use a cash card at an ATM, you are familiar with the use of two-factor authentication, because the something you know is your **PIN (personal identification number)**, and your cash card is the token. For even more security, look to **three-factor authentication**, adding biometric data, such as a retinal scan, voice print, or fingerprint to the token and password or PIN. Now or in the future you may work in a facility that requires three-factor authentication.

Security Account Basics

Windows 8 has robust security that begins with user and group accounts and the requirement to log in to the computer with a user account, which is a type of security account. A **security account** is an account that can be assigned **permission** to take action on an object (such as a file, folder, or printer) or the right to take some action on an entire system, such as install device drivers into an operating system on a computer. A security account may identify a single entity (individual or computer) or a group of entities. Security accounts exist in security databases, such as those maintained by network servers and by Windows desktop operating systems. We will limit our discussion to Windows 8 local accounts and Microsoft Accounts.

Computer Accounts

Computers (and sometimes devices) may also have security accounts within a security accounts database maintained by a network server, such as in a Microsoft Windows Active Directory domain. This means your computer joins a domain before you, as a user, can log on to the network. When this occurs, new group accounts appear in the accounts database on your desktop Windows computer as it integrates into the domain. The details of this relationship are beyond the scope of this book, but be aware that this is the case if your computer is part of a Windows Active Directory Domain. How could this affect you? If you bring your personal laptop to the office, you will not be able to log on to the corporate network in the same way that you do from your desktop until an administrator makes your computer a member of the domain. If joining your personal laptop to the network is undesirable, there are other methods to give you access to the corporate network. Computer accounts do not exist within a Windows 8 security database.

Group Accounts

A **group account** is a security account that contains one or more individual accounts and may contain other groups. Some groups are built in and administrators can create others. Windows 8 has local user and group accounts. The **built-in local groups** in Windows 8 include Administrators, Users, Guests,

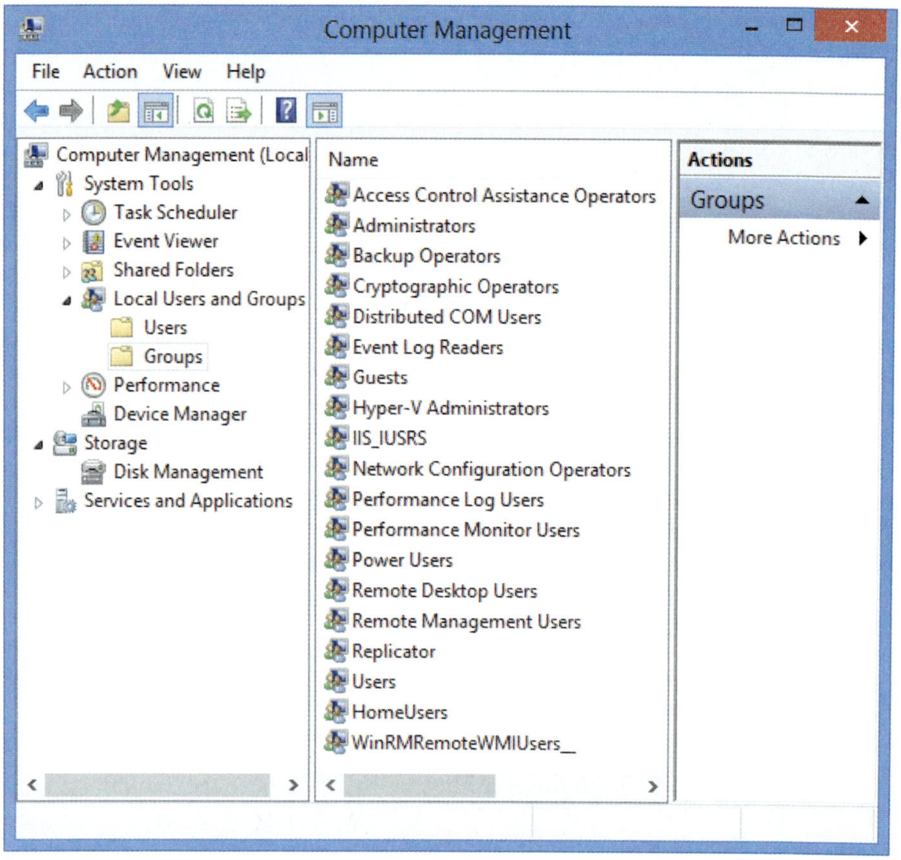

FIGURE 4-1 The Groups node in Computer Management showing the local groups.

and many others that the system creates for various Windows services and programs (see Figure 4-1). An administrator can create additional group accounts.

Local User Accounts

A **user account** is a security account assigned to a single person. In the security database, a user account contains, at minimum, a username and password used to authenticate a user. Depending on the structure of the security accounts database, a user account may contain additional identifying information. Typically, a user account will include the user's full name, a description, and a variety of other fields, including email address, department, phone numbers, and so on. User accounts exist in all Windows security accounts databases. The first user account created as you install Windows 8 is granted membership in the Administrators local group so that this account can install apps and drivers and change system settings.

Built-in Local User Accounts Windows 8 has a special, very privileged built-in account—a super user—that can perform virtually all tasks on a computer, from installing a device driver to creating other security accounts. In Windows this very privileged **built-in local user** is **Administrator**. It is a member of the Administrators group, and Windows 8 disables it by default. At the other end of the privilege spectrum, we have **Guest**. This built-in local user account is the least privileged, and Windows also disables it by default. If this account is enabled, a stranger can log in with the account (usually with no password) but cannot see anyone else's files and cannot make changes to the system.

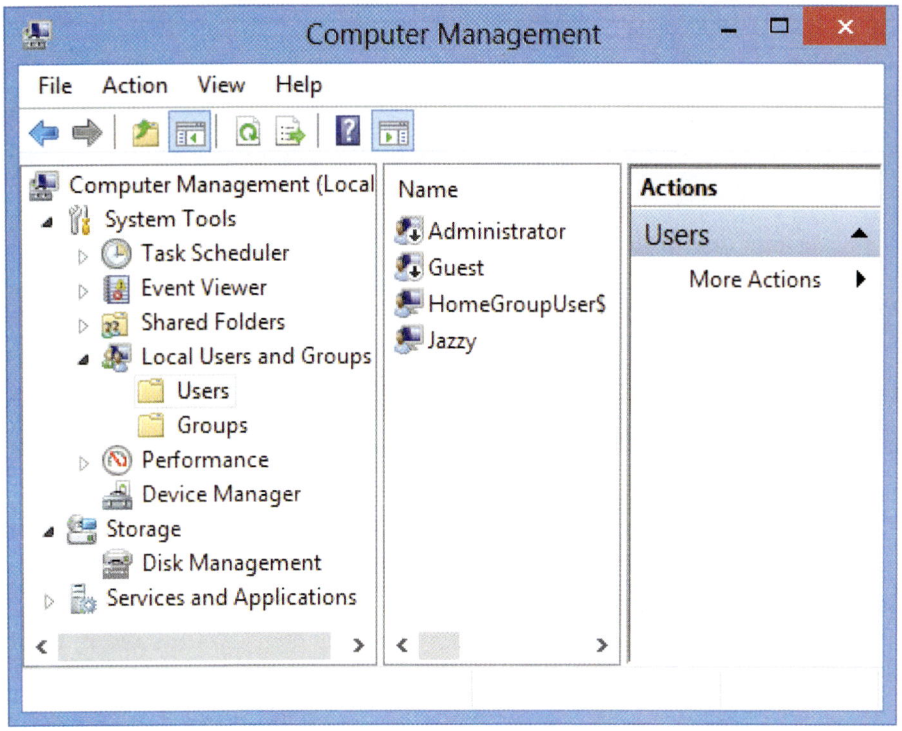

FIGURE 4-2 The Local Users and Groups node in Computer Management showing the local users.

Then Windows creates special accounts for use with certain services that are not available or intended for human users. Figure 4-2 shows the Computer Management console opened to the Local Users and Groups node, which shows four individual users: Administrator, Guest, HomeGroupUser$ (the $ shows that this is one of those system-created accounts), and Jazzy (the account created by Windows for a user during Setup). Note that Local Users and Groups is an advanced tool for user and group management and not one that most people will need to use on a Windows 8 computer. We use it here simply because more accounts are visible than you will see in the Users page of PC Settings—the tool you will normally use to create and modify user accounts.

Local Account Types: Standard versus Administrator Accounts The account created during the installation of Windows 8 uses the name and password you provide to the Setup program to create a local account that is a member of both the HomeUsers and the Administrators local groups. The HomeUsers and Users groups are the default local users groups for standard users. Membership in the Users group gives the standard user limited access to the local computer, whereas the HomeUsers group gives members access to the HomeGroup that the local computer belongs to. We will discuss HomeGroups in Chapter 5.

Windows has simplified terms for the types of local user accounts you can create and manage through the Users page of the PC Settings control panel. A **standard user account** is for an "ordinary" user without administrator status and is a member of the Users group, but not of the Administrators or Power Users group. Users logged on with a standard account can change their passwords and other personal settings, but cannot change computer settings, install or remove software and hardware, or perform other systemwide tasks. In contrast, a user logged on with an **administrator account type** can perform systemwide tasks.

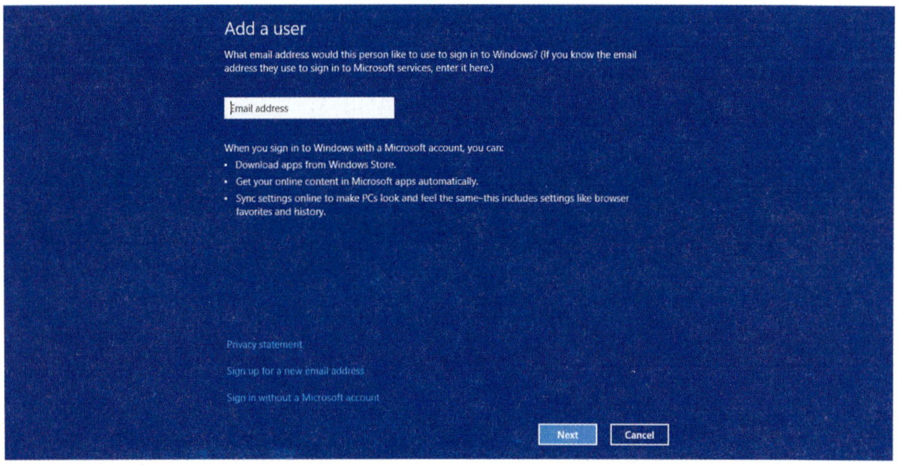

FIGURE 4–3 The Add a User page in PC Settings.

The first user account created for your use in Windows 8 is an administrator account type, meaning that it is a member of the Administrators local group. When logged on with this account, you can create additional accounts. You can use the Users page of the PC Settings control panel to create local accounts or a **Microsoft account** that gives you access to Microsoft Internet services, described later. If you choose to use a Microsoft account when installing Windows 8 or the first time you turned on your new Windows 8 computer, it creates a local user account associated with the Microsoft account. If you started out with a local user account as the first account and then switched your sign-in to a Microsoft account, the local account is associated with the Microsoft account. In both cases, the Microsoft account has the privileges of the local user account plus access to all the online resources available to the Microsoft account.

When you select Add a User, from the Users page of PC Settings, the Add a User page opens, as shown in Figure 4-3, and you can choose to create a Microsoft account or Local account for signing in to Windows 8. If this is a child's account, you can turn on a feature called Family Safety, which will send reports to your Microsoft account concerning your child's online activity. If you are signed in to a Windows 8 computer as the first user account, create a new account using the Try This!

try this!

Creating a Standard User Account

Sign in with a user account that is a member of the Administrators group. The first account created on the computer will do. Then create a new local account that is not a Microsoft Account. Try This!

1. Open the PC Settings control panel. To do this on a touch screen, first swipe from the bottom right to open the Charms bar, select Settings to open the Settings bar, and then select Change PC Settings. On a keyboard, use Windows key+I to open the Settings bar, and then select Change PC Settings.
2. In PC Settings, select Users. In the bottom of the Users panel, select Add a User.
3. On the first page labeled Add a User, do NOT enter an email address, but click the link at the bottom of the screen labeled Sign In Without a Microsoft Account.
4. The next page will explain the differences between a Microsoft Account and a Local Account. Read about these two account options, and then click the Local Account button at the bottom of the screen.
5. On the next page provide a username and password (enter twice) and a password hint. Then click or tap Next.
6. On the next page (Figure 4-4) verify that the account information is correct. If this account is for a child, you can select the check box under the user picture to turn on Family Safety. Click or tap Finish to create the account.

Microsoft Accounts

A Microsoft Account is a **Windows Live ID** account that you use with Microsoft's Windows Live services, such as Hotmail, Skydrive, Xbox Live, and Messenger. If you do not already have a Windows Live ID,

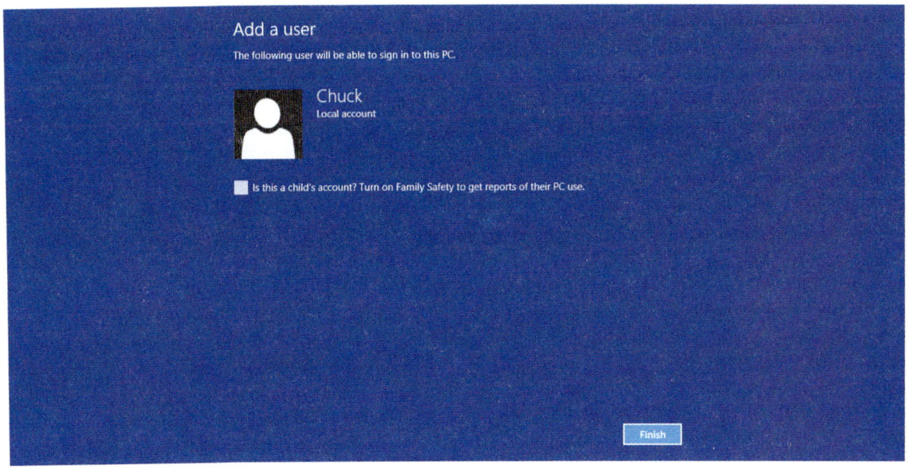

FIGURE 4-4 Click to place a check in the box to turn on Family Safety for a child's account.

sign up for an account at the Microsoft Windows Live website or through the Users page of the PC Settings control panel. When you sign in using a Windows Account, you can synchronize your settings on other Windows 8 PCs that use the same sign-in. Soon after you sign in to a computer using your Windows Account, you will receive, via email, a message with a number to use to confirm that the computer you added is trusted. Use the link, which presently is a URL that includes account.live.com, and locate the new computer in the list (if it is your first, there will be only one), and click or tap the Confirm button. Then enter the seven-digit code from the message.

User Account Control

Before Windows Vista, if you wanted to make changes to your system, such as installing a new device or program, you had to log on as an administrator. This meant, if you were already logged on with an account that did not have administrative access, you would have to log off and log on again with an administrator account before you could perform a major system task. To avoid this annoyance, many people stayed logged on all day every day using an account with administrator access. This meant that if malware infected your computer, which it could do without your knowledge, it would have full control over your computer because it used your administrative access. Windows 8 uses **User Account Control (UAC)** (introduced in Windows Vista), and Microsoft continues to improve it in each version of Windows. This effective security feature prevents unauthorized changes to Windows. Enabling UAC protects your system, even if you are logged on as an administrator, as long as you make good decisions. There are two scenarios. In the first, a user logged on with a privileged account with administrative rights has only the privileges of a standard account, until the user (or a malicious program) attempts to do something that requires higher privileges. At that point, UAC makes itself known, graying out (dimming) the desktop and displaying the **Consent Prompt** shown in Figure 4-5. In this case, we attempted to run the Command Prompt as an administrator. You must click Yes or No. If you click Yes, the program runs with your administrative privileges, and you return to working with standard privileges in other programs.

In the second scenario, a user logs on with the privileges of a standard user and attempts to do something that requires administrative privileges. In

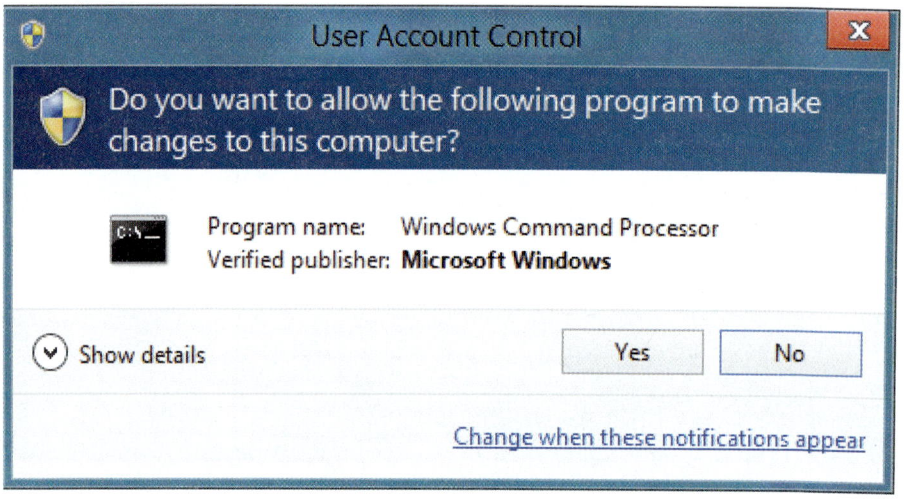

FIGURE 4-5 User Account Control Consent Prompt displays when a logged-on member of the Administrators group tries to run a program requiring administrative privileges.

this case, UAC displays the **Credentials Prompt**, requiring the username and password of an account with administrative privileges, as shown in Figure 4-6. If you provide these, the program or task will run with these elevated privileges, but you will return to the standard user privileges for all other activities. In either case, if you do not respond in a short time, UAC will time out, cancel the operation, and return the desktop to you.

Although it is possible to disable User Account Control, we do not recommend it.

Even with UAC turned off, you may still not be allowed to perform all tasks and will see a message such as, "The requested operation requires elevation" when you attempt to perform certain functions.

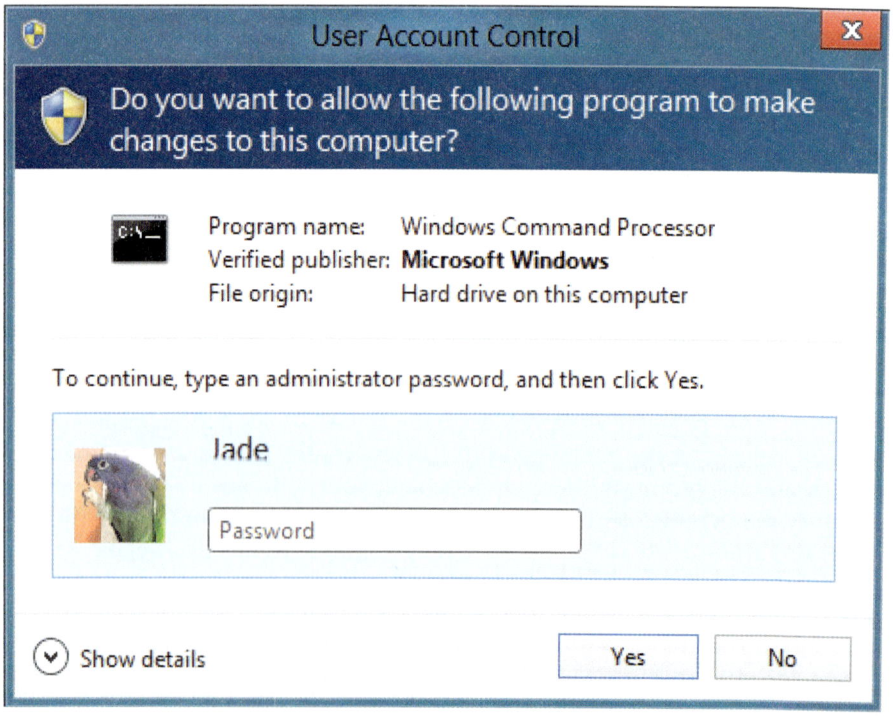

FIGURE 4-6 User Account Control Credentials Prompt displays when a standard user is logged on and tries to run a program requiring administrative privileges.

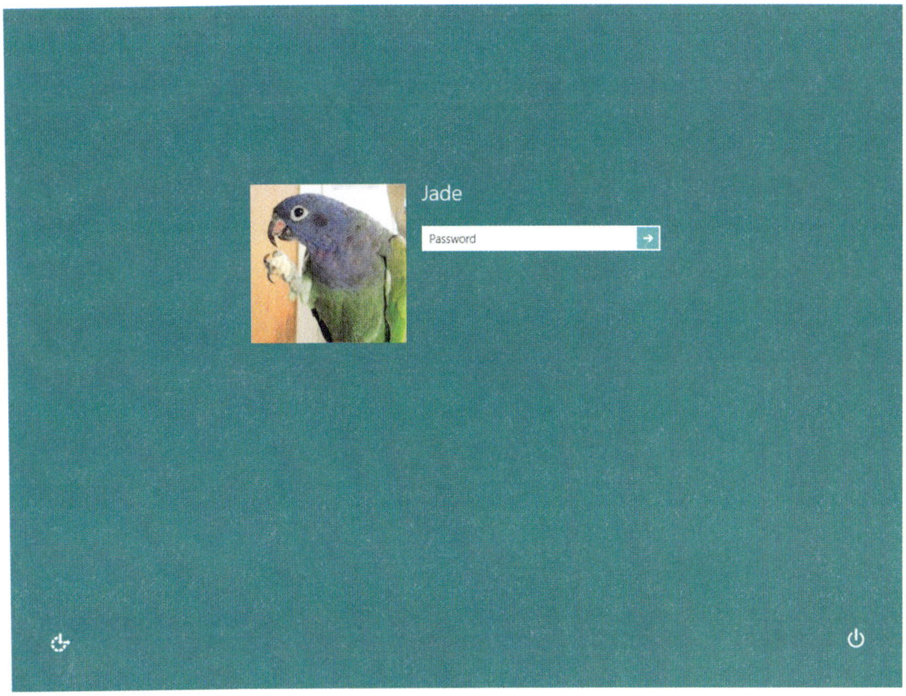

FIGURE 4-7 The sign-in screen for a local user account on a single-user computer.

Windows 8 Sign-in Options

To sign in to Windows 8, you must have an account. The account you log on with may be a local user account, existing only in your Windows 8 installation, or it can be a Windows domain user account if you are logging on to a corporate network, or (new in Windows 8) it can be a Microsoft account.

The appearance of the Sign-In page can vary based on how your computer is configured for signing in. Windows 8 offers three options: the conventional typing of a password, using a four-character PIN, or using screen gestures on a photo of your choice—a touch-screen-friendly option. All of these methods still are associated with whatever account you have chosen for sign-in.

Figure 4-7 shows the conventional Windows 8 sign-in screen. In this example there is only one user account on the computer, so the username for that account is displayed, and you need to enter only the password and click or touch the arrow button or press the Enter key to be authenticated. The Administrator account does not appear here, nor do the special accounts for services and programs. However, if you create additional accounts for co-workers or family members, the Sign-In page will display the name of the last logged-on user, with a small circle with an arrow just to the left.

The **Picture Password sign-in** option ties your username and password to a picture of your choice, on which you register three gestures as part of your Picture Password sign-in. This option is best for touch-screen devices.

We are all familiar with the use of a **personal identification number (PIN)** tied to our bank cards. You must provide this unique numeric code every time you swipe your cash card in a cash machine before you can withdraw or deposit money. Using the PIN sign-in option, you can associate a PIN to your user account and use this rather than a password when you sign in. Step-by-Step 4.1 walks you through changing to the Picture Sign-In option.

Step-by-Step 4.1

Configuring Picture Sign-In

Explore the Windows 8 Picture Sign-In option.

Step 1

Open the Settings sidebar. Do that on a touch screen by swiping the bottom-right corner to open the Charms bar, and then selecting Settings. If using a keyboard, go directly to the Settings bar with Windows key+I. In the Settings bar select Change PC Settings.

Keyboard Shortcuts!
Windows key+I opens the Settings bar.

Step 2

In the PC Settings control panel, select Users, which will display settings for your account. The first example is what you will see if you have signed in with a local account, and the second example is what you will see if you are signed in with a Microsoft account.

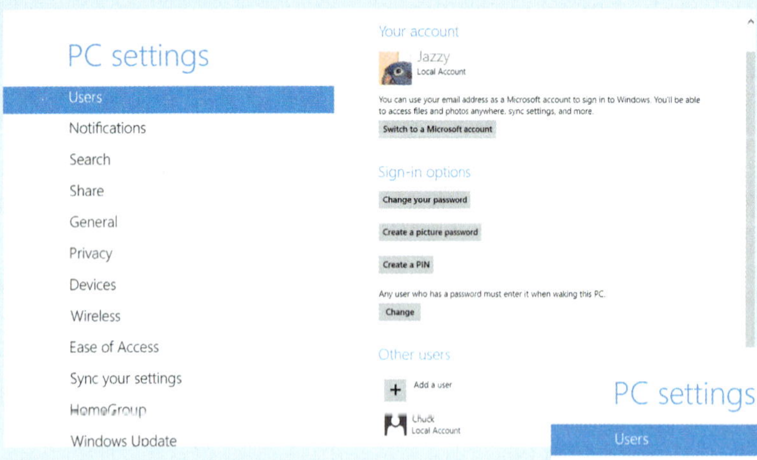

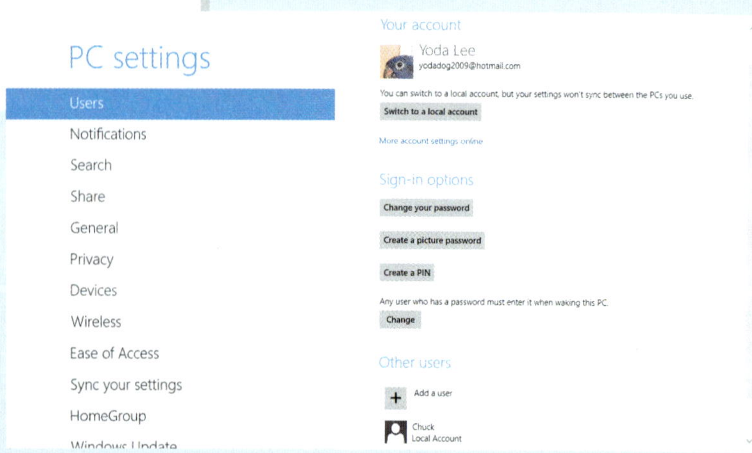

Step 3

The Picture Password option is for touch-screen displays, but it is possible to do on a keyboard, if you desire. When you select it, your first prompt will be to enter your current password, as shown here.

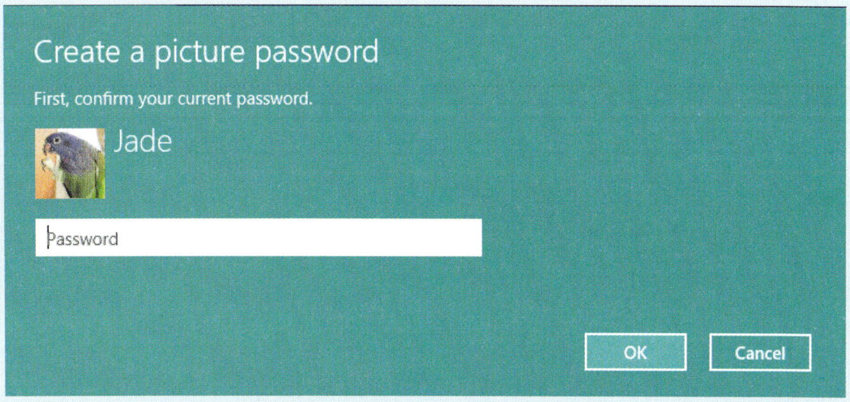

Step 4

After you enter your password, the Welcome to Picture Password page opens. This page has animation that demonstrates gestures you can use on a picture as your password. Use the Choose Picture button to select a picture. This opens the Files page displaying pictures from your Pictures folder. You can also go to other locations, beginning with the Go Up button.

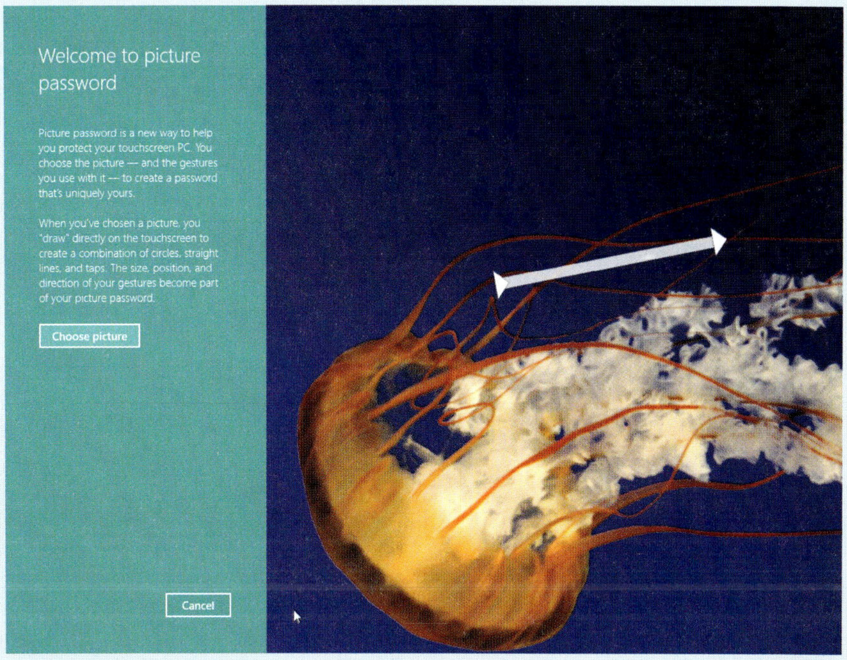

Step 5

When you select a picture, it will appear in the How's This Look? Page, where you can drag it around to fit better in the space, if needed. When you decide to use the picture, click the Use This Picture button.

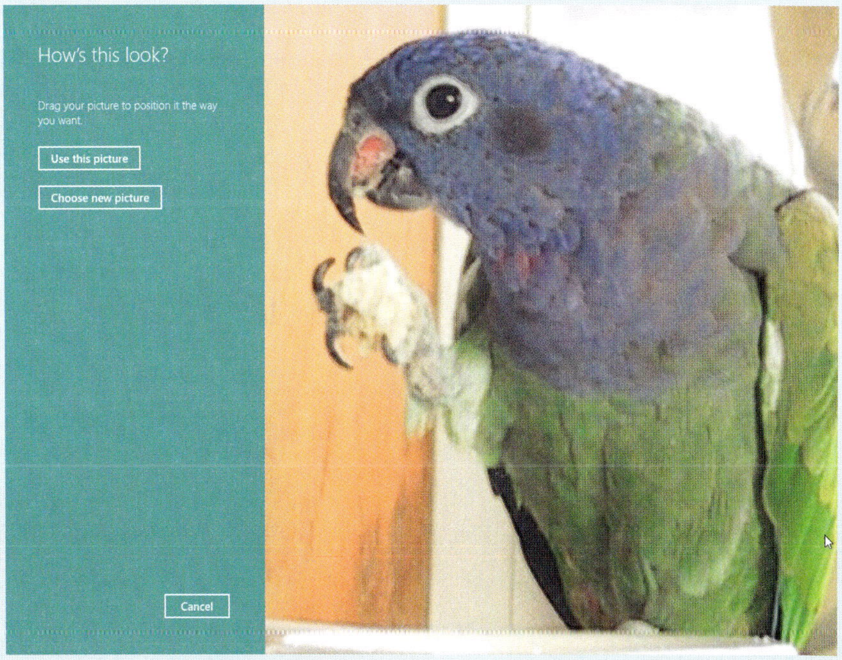

Step 6

Following the instructions on the bar to the left of your picture, enter a set of three gestures, using circles, straight lines, and taps. You must do this twice to confirm the gestures, just as you need to enter a password twice when you create or change it. If you cannot duplicate the gestures, the Try Again button will display under a "Something's not right" message, and you can click the button and try again to match the gestures.

Step 7

After you have successfully entered and duplicated the three gestures, the Congratulations message will display in the left bar, and after you click the Finish button, your Picture sign-in is ready to use. The Users page now shows a Remove button next to the Change Picture Password button so that you can revert to the password sign-in or choose a PIN sign-in.

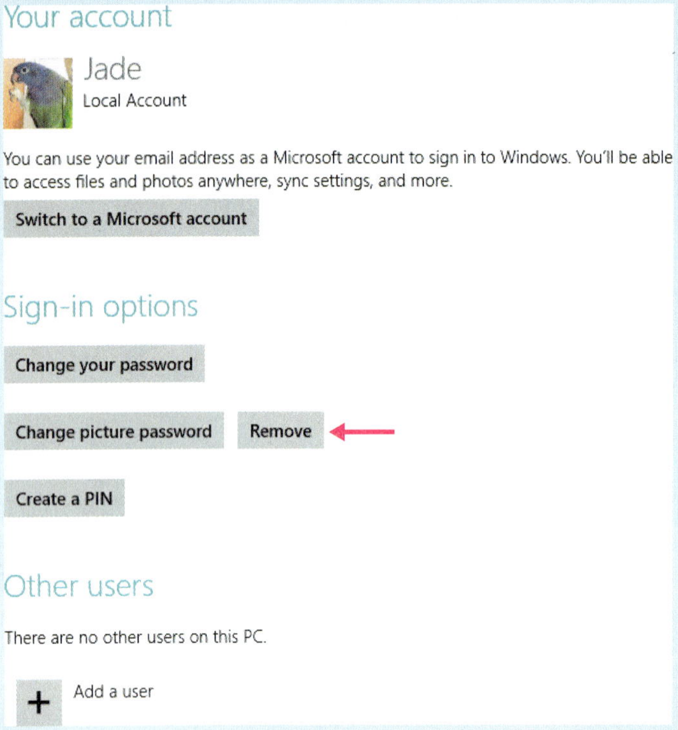

Step 8

The next time you sign in, the Sign-In page will look something like this, and you sign in by making the preset gestures on the picture. Notice that if you suddenly find yourself unable to duplicate the gesture, you can click or tap the Switch To Password button and enter the password.

Antivirus/Antispyware: Windows Defender

An **antivirus** is software that detects and removes viruses and other malware, and **antispyware** is software that detects and removes spyware. In Windows 8, Microsoft has combined their two free security packages, Microsoft Security Essentials (antivirus and more) and Windows Defender (antispyware), into **Windows Defender**, which now offers broad protection against malware. It comes with Windows 8 and is updated as needed, unless you disable the update function. Windows Defender protects against spyware, viruses, worms, bots, and rootkits. The default settings are sufficient for most circumstances, so all you need to do is to open Windows Defender and check out the settings in case you want to make changes.

Step-by-Step 4.2

Exploring Windows Defender Settings

Check out the Windows Defender settings.

Step 1

From the Start screen, begin typing "defender," which will open the Search bar focused on apps. Select Windows Defender from the results on the left, and Windows Defender will open on the Windows 8 Desktop with the Home page current. This page gives you a brief summary. In the example, Windows Defender real-time protection is on, monitoring for any suspicious activity, performing scheduled scans of your computer, and ensuring virus and spyware definitions are up to date. These definitions are a database of identifying characteristics and behavior of viruses and spyware that Windows Defender automatically checks for and updates so that it will detect known malware activity. The scan options are set to Quick, but you can modify that, and you can also choose to scan immediately, rather than wait for the next scheduled scan.

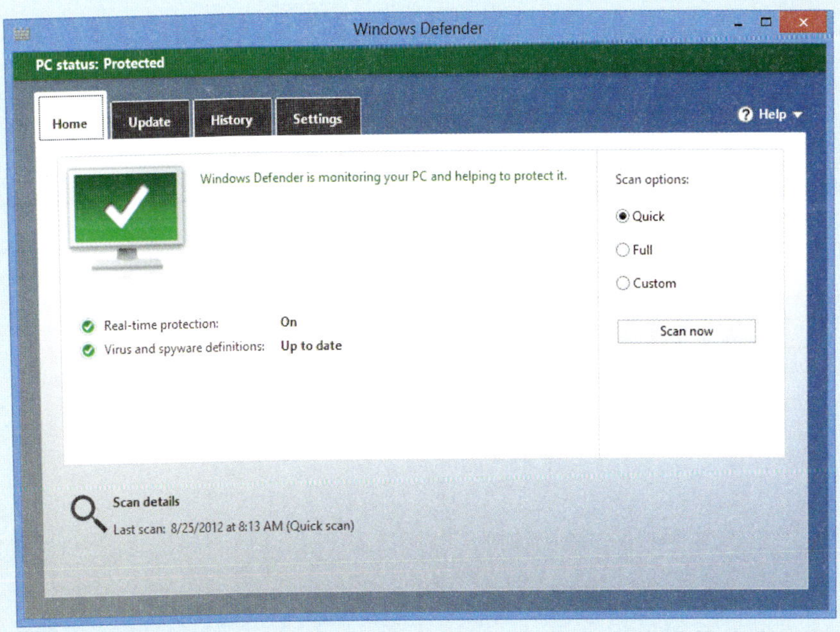

Step 2

To double-check, click the Update tab. This page informs you that malware definitions are up to date. You can choose to update immediately by tapping or clicking the Update button.

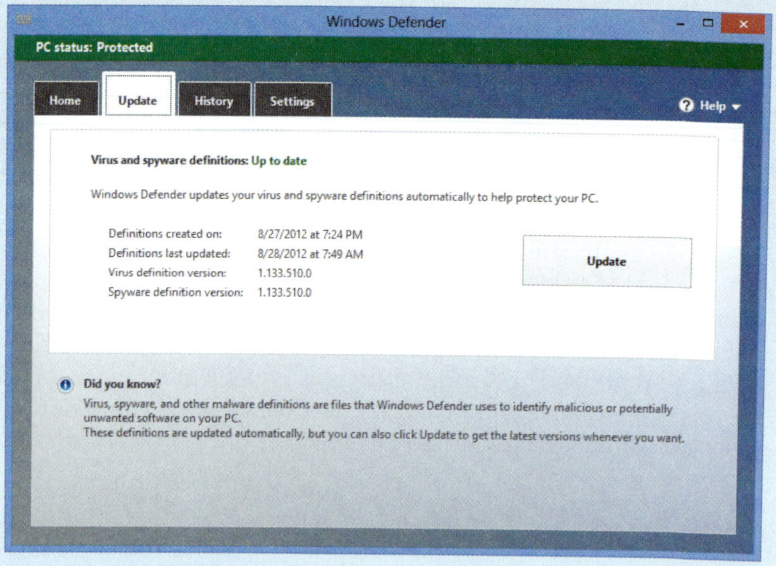

Step 3

Click or tap the History tab. From here, if you have signed on as an administrator, you can view the quarantined items that Windows Defender identified as potential malware and placed in a location where they cannot be active. To view them, click the View Details button. In the resulting list box, you can remove items (permanently deleting them), and you can select an item to restore if you know that it is not malware and was identified in error. Similarly, when you select Allowed Items and then click View Details, you will see a list of items that are allowed, even if Windows Defender identifies them as malware. From here you can remove items from the Allowed Items list. Finally, you may select All Detected Items and click the View Details button to see the history of all detected items. In the resulting list box, you can select an item to allow, which will move it to the Allowed Items list.

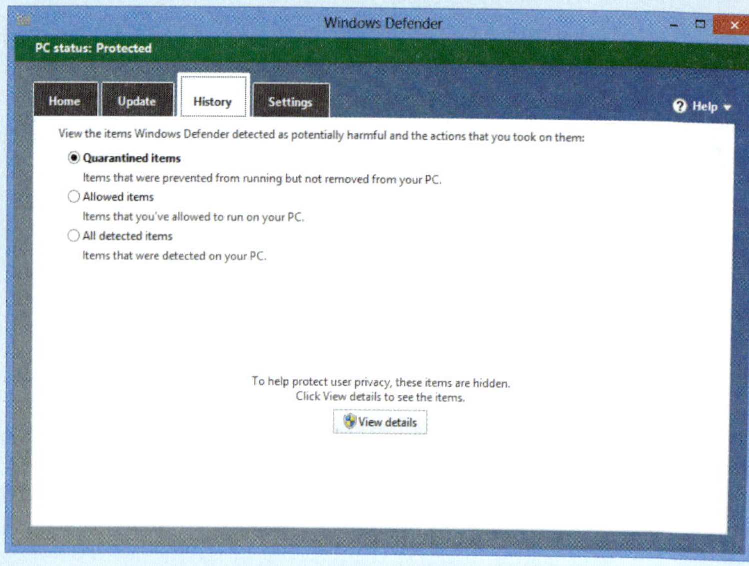

Step 4

Select the Settings tab, which has several pages that you select by choosing one of the options on the left. You configure Windows Defender from this tab. The Real-Time Protection watches for malware activity and will alert you with a warning message when it detects such activity. This is on by default, and you should leave it on.

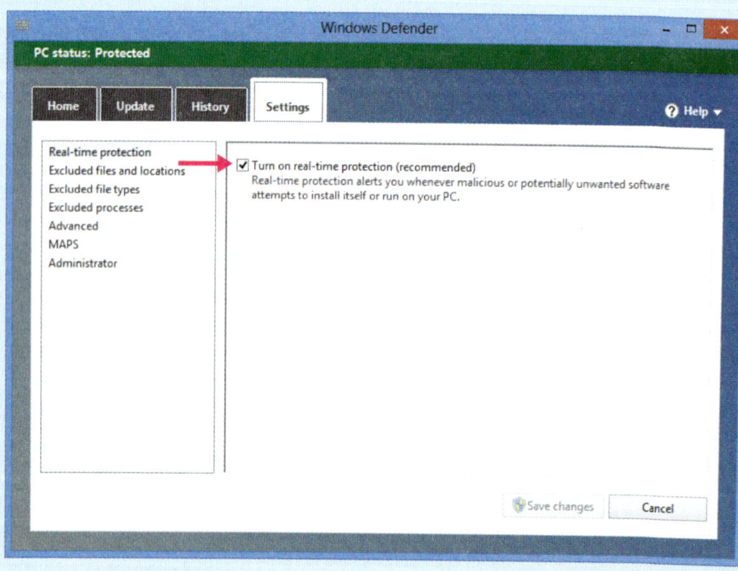

Step 5

The Excluded Files and Locations page allows you to select files and locations to exclude from Windows Defender's malware scans. We suggest that you do not exclude any files or locations for the sake of security. The next two pages are similar in that they allow you to add exclusions for file types and processes. Again, we do not recommend doing that.

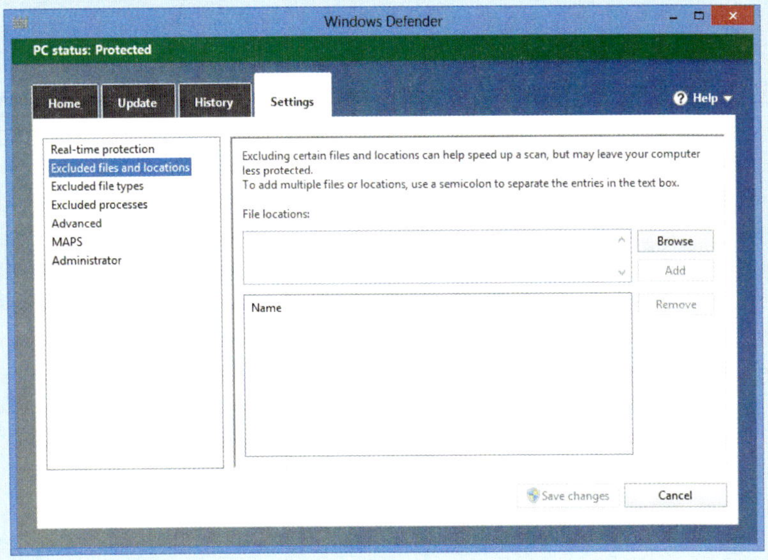

Step 6

The Advanced page has several settings. The default settings are Scan Archive Files and Remove Quarantined Files After 3 Months. We selected Scan Removable Drives and Create a System Restore Point for additional security and recoverability. Recall that, by default, only an administrator can view the details of the history. The fourth setting on this page, if selected, makes that history viewable to anyone. If multiple people use a computer, that option has the potential of allowing them to see each others' personal data, if a data file is infected and quarantined. If you make changes on this page, select the Save Changes button.

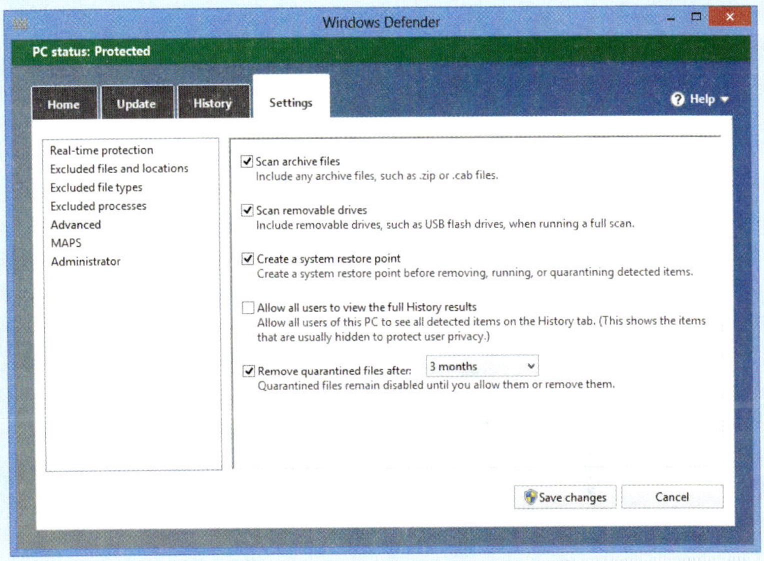

Step 7

The MAPS page lets you choose to either change your level of participation or opt out of Microsoft Active Protection Service (MAPS). This program takes information gathered, sends it to Microsoft who uses it to update definitions, and aggregates the information to improve overall malware detection. If you participate, the service may download the latest information to help Windows Defender remove the threat. We believe it is worth participating in this as either a Basic (default) or Advanced member.

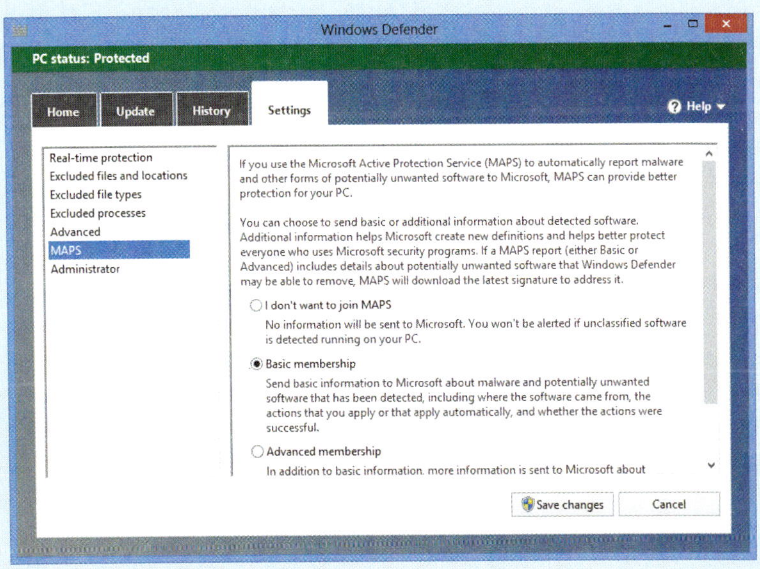

Step 8

The final page, having just one setting, is a bit underwhelming, but it is the all-important Windows Defender on/off switch. The default is On, and we strongly suggest that you keep it that way.

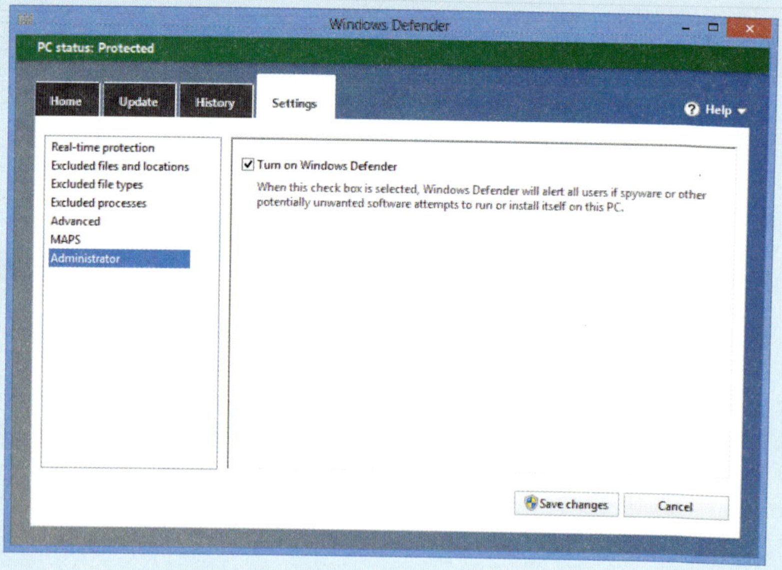

Step 9

When you are finished, click the Cancel button on the Windows Defender window.

Using a Secure PDF Reader

Why consider a reader as a protection against threats? It can be a protection if it behaves differently from older readers. In the past, the bad guys could use PDF files as vectors for malware. The programs used to open these files—such as Adobe Acrobat—could not catch these threats. Windows 8 includes **Reader**, a Windows 8 app for securely reading PDF and XPS files. Before the release of Windows 8, this program was described as Modern Reader and may continue to be called that by the early reviewers, but in the final release this app is simply named Reader. The Reader program is associated with PDF and XPS files, which means that when you activate a PDF of XPS file with a double-click or a tap, it opens in Reader.

Action Center

The **Action Center** (Figure 4-8) is a control panel that gives you access to important security and maintenance tools. If Windows detects a security or maintenance problem, it alerts you and shows a red icon on the Action Center flag icon on the desktop taskbar. There are at least two ways to open Action Center. One is by clicking the flag on the taskbar and selecting Open Action Center. Another is by opening the Settings Search bar (Windows key+W), entering "action" in the search box, and selecting Action Center from the results. If Action Center has detected a problem, it highlights the problem area in Action Center. In Figure 4-8, Action Center has not detected any problems.

The first time you sign-in from a computer using a Microsoft Account, Action Center will include a Trust This PC message under the Security category. You will not be able to synchronize your passwords for apps, websites, and networks until you complete the Trust This PC process. Therefore, if you see that message, click the Trust This PC button to connect to your online Microsoft Account and confirm that you trust the PC. Microsoft will send you a confirmation number that you will need to enter from the PC before your settings will synchronize. Your Microsoft Account will maintain a list of trusted PCs.

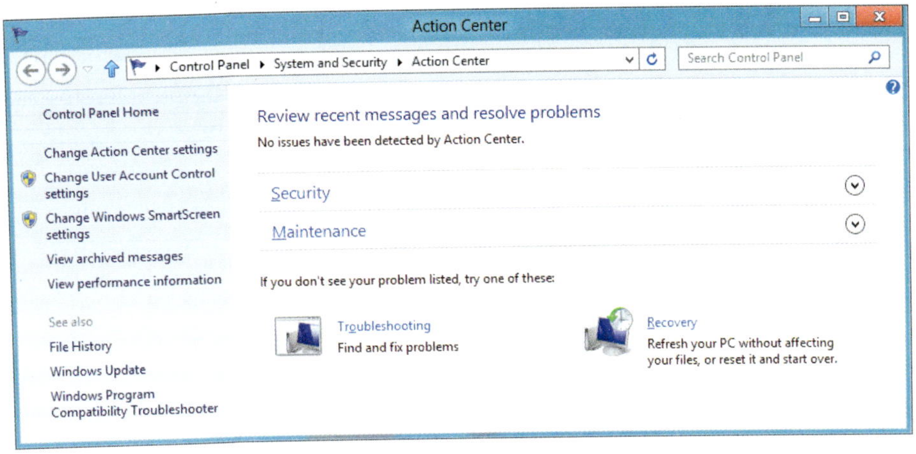

FIGURE 4-8 Action Center has not detected any problems.

Change Action Center Settings

The Change Action Center Settings option opens a page where you can control what security and maintenance warning and status messages display. The settings are all on by default, and when there is a change of status for any item, a warning displays on the notification area of the desktop taskbar. We recommend that you keep these items selected. The security messages include the following:

- Windows Update
- Internet security settings
- Network firewall
- Microsoft account
- Windows activation
- Spyware and unwanted software protection
- User Account Control
- Virus protection
- SmartScreen

The maintenance messages include the following:

- Windows Backup
- Automatic Maintenance
- Drive status
- Device software
- Startup apps
- Windows Troubleshooting
- HomeGroup
- File History
- Storage Spaces

Change User Account Control Settings

If you select Change User Account from the Action Center, the dialog box shown in Figure 4-9 displays. The default setting is Notify Me Only When Apps Try to Make Changes to My Computer, but you can make it more secure (or annoying) by moving the slider up the bar, or make it less secure by moving the slider down.

Change Windows SmartScreen Settings

SmartScreen is a Microsoft security feature enabled by default in Windows 8. It prevents you from opening links, website content, and even apps, based on the reputation of the source. How exactly Microsoft determines the reputation is not entirely clear. And it is no longer limited to what happens in your browser, as it was in previous versions of Windows. It will now prevent you from running an app it doesn't recognize (as in apps not purchased through the Store). When SmartScreen identifies such a threat, it darkens the screen, and the middle third of the screen displays a horizontal message bar titled Windows Protected Your PC, with a short message identifying the type of threat. You can click OK to allow it. You can also open the More Info link in the message box and you can

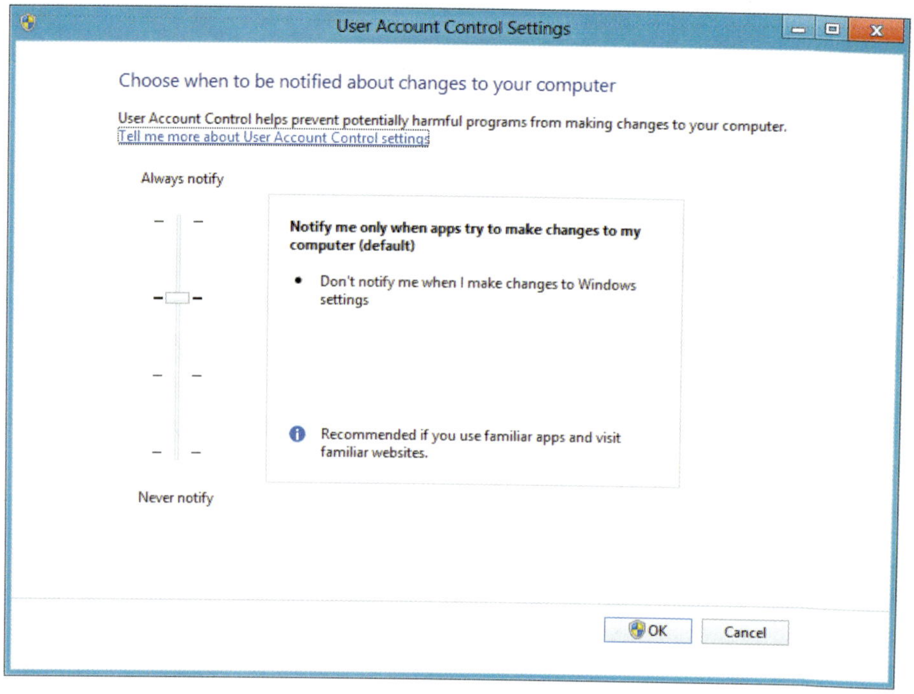

FIGURE 4-9 Use the slide control on the left to change User Account Control Settings.

override the protection for that instance. If you would like to change how SmartScreen works, select Change Windows SmartScreen Settings in the Action Center, as shown in Figure 4-10. The default is Get Administrator Approval Before Running a Recognized App from the Internet. You can choose the second option, which will simply warn you, but after you accept the app, it will not require administrator approval. The third option turns off SmartScreen.

View Archived Messages

Whenever Windows displays a security or maintenance status message, it also saves that message. Through the View Archived Messages option in Action Center, you can go back and read past messages. This may be important to do if you have a continuing problem and need to tell Help Desk personnel exactly what a past message said so that they can help resolve the problem.

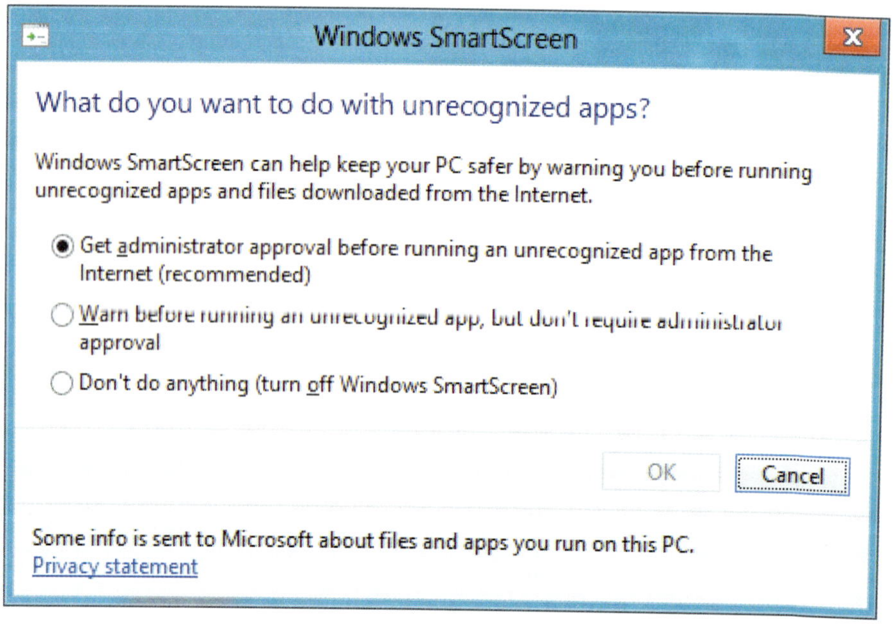

FIGURE 4-10 The default SmartScreen settings, shown here, are the most secure.

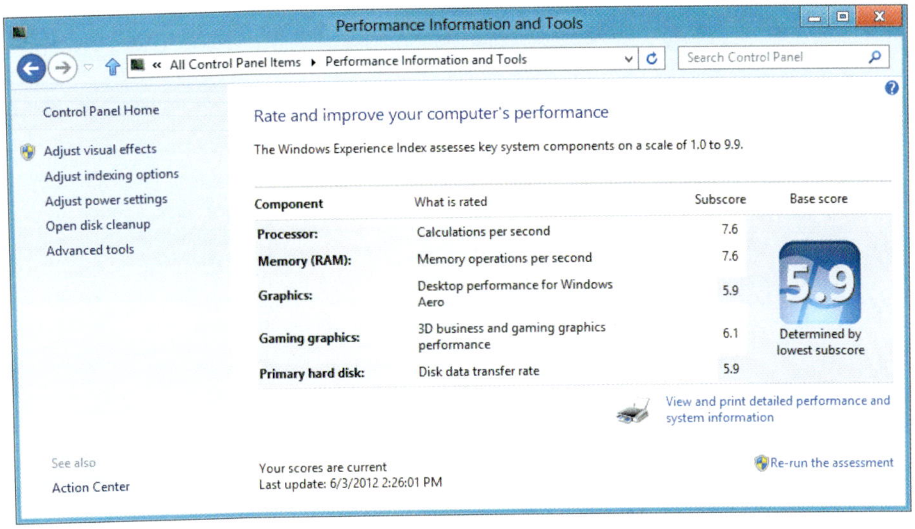

FIGURE 4-11 Performance Information and Tools lets you measure aspects of the computer.

View Performance Information

The View Performance Information option shown in Figure 4-11 is one of my favorite tools to use when I look at computers in a bricks-and-mortar store. Providing Windows isn't locked down too much, open this up to see how well a computer performs. It measures several aspects of the computer, including the processor, RAM, graphics system running ordinary desktop apps, graphics system running 3D apps, and disk data transfer rate. The first time you open this in Windows 8 it will not have performance information. There will be a message that reads "Your Windows Experience Index has not yet been established," and a button labeled Rate This Computer. Click the button to run a performance test. Once you run the test, the results will display, as shown in Figure 4-11.

Aside from checking out new computers, another reason for being aware of the Performance Information is that if you know what the base score is when you first get your computer, you can compare it with the base score after you perceive that your system has slowed down. Then, if Performance Information shows that one or more of the components seems too slow, there are a few things you can do about it through options on the left side of this control panel page, shown in Figure 4-11. If you cannot improve the performance to the "like-new" score, you might want to consider using the Refresh Your PC option described later in this chapter.

Create a Password Reset Disk

Windows allows the currently logged-on user to create a **Password Reset Disk** to use in case of a forgotten password. This is very important to have, because if you forget your password, and an administrator resets the password using User Accounts or Local Users and Groups, when you log on using the new password you will lose access to some items. These include files that you encrypted when logged on with the forgotten password. When you reset a password with a Password Reset Disk, you can log on using the new password and still have access to previously encrypted files.

> Encryption is a very advanced feature that you should use only after studying it carefully. It would take more than a chapter just to talk about encryption in depth!

You have this advantage only if you think to create a Password Reset Disk before you forget the password! If you need to create a Password Reset Disk for a computer on a network (domain), search the help system for Password Reset Disk and follow the instructions for a computer on a domain.

The Password Reset Disk is both a convenience and a threat. You have to create the password reset disk only once, regardless of how many times you may later change the password. It is a convenience in that you make it one

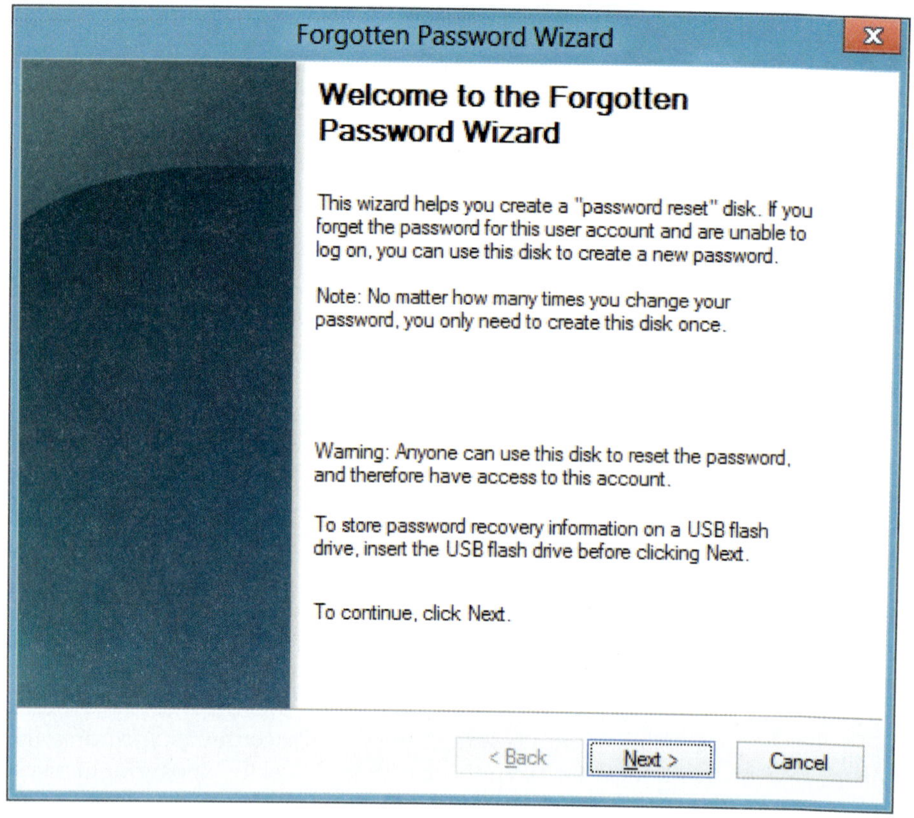

FIGURE 4-12 The Forgotten Password Wizard.

After you create a Password Reset Disk, you need to label it and put it in a safe place, dedicating it to this one task. However, a Password Reset Disk has a single file on it, userkey.psw, and it takes up less than 2,000 bytes of space. Therefore, use your smallest capacity flash drive.

time and it will always work. It is a threat in that it will always work on your machine, no matter who has it and uses it!

To create a Password Reset Disk, first connect a flash drive to your computer, open Settings search, and enter `password reset` in the search box. This opens the Forgotten Password Wizard seen in Figure 4-12. The first page explains the process and warns that others can use this to their advantage. Follow the instructions and click or tap the buttons to move to each next step. One page will allow you to select from a list of current removable or drives. Another page requires the current password.

Recovery Control Panel

The Recovery control panel, shown in Figure 4-13, contains advanced recovery tools for recovering from damage to the operating system files. To open the Recovery control panel, first open Settings search (Windows key+W) and

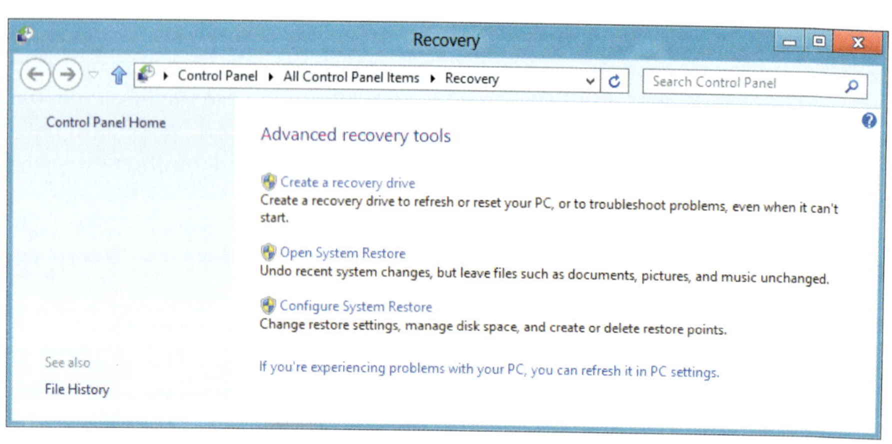

FIGURE 4-13 The Recovery control panel has advanced recovery tools.

enter "recover" into the search box. Select "Recovery." We will look at these advanced recovery tools.

Create a Recovery Drive

In the "Recovering from Damage to Windows" section later in this chapter, you will learn about the Refresh and Reset options. You can get to those options through Windows 8, as long as you can boot into it, but sometimes it is so unstable that you cannot do that. To prepare for those circumstances, you can create a **recovery drive** that you will use to boot up the system and give you access to those recovery options. If you have a flash drive that does not contain data you need, you can create a recovery drive, label it, and set it aside for an emergency, as described in the Try This!

try this!

Creating a Recovery Drive

You can use a flash drive or an external hard drive to create a recovery drive. However, you will lose all data previously stored on the drive. If you are willing to do that, try this:

1. Connect a flash drive.
2. Open the Recovery control panel.
3. Click or tap to Create a Recovery Disk and then respond to the User Account Control dialog box by click the Yes button (Consent Prompt) or by providing the password for an administrator account (Credentials Prompt).
4. In the Recovery Drive dialog box, choose to have the recovery partition (if it exists) on your computer copied, along with recovery information from the Windows system drive. Then click Next.
5. Wait while it searches for an appropriate drive to use. From the results, select your flash drive and click or tap Next.
6. A warning appears. If you are okay with deleting everything on the drive, click or tap Create.
7. A progress bar displays while it prepares the drive and copies the necessary files. When it is done, click or tap the Finish button. Label the flash drive and keep it in a safe place.

Configuring System Restore

For now, we will skip the second option in the Recovery control panel and look at the third option: Configure System Restore. **System Restore** is a feature that backs up your Windows configuration before Windows makes any significant changes, such as when it installed updates or installs a new program. These backups are **Restore Points**, and if your system is behaving abnormally, you can roll your system back to a restore point.

Normally you do not have to make changes to System Restore settings. If your computer has sufficient disk space, System Restore is on automatically; if there is not enough space, it will be off, in which case you should ensure that you create a recovery drive. The benefit of a recovery drive is that it uses an external drive. The disadvantage is that it is not as up to date as System Restore.

To see the status of System Restore, open Recovery and select Configure System Restore. This opens the System Properties dialog box on the desktop. Next, select the Configure button to open the System Protection dialog box shown in Figure 4-14. Notice that this example shows System Protection (System Restore) turned on and that it limits the amount of disk space used and allows you to delete all the restore points on the drive. Consider turning it on, if it is not.

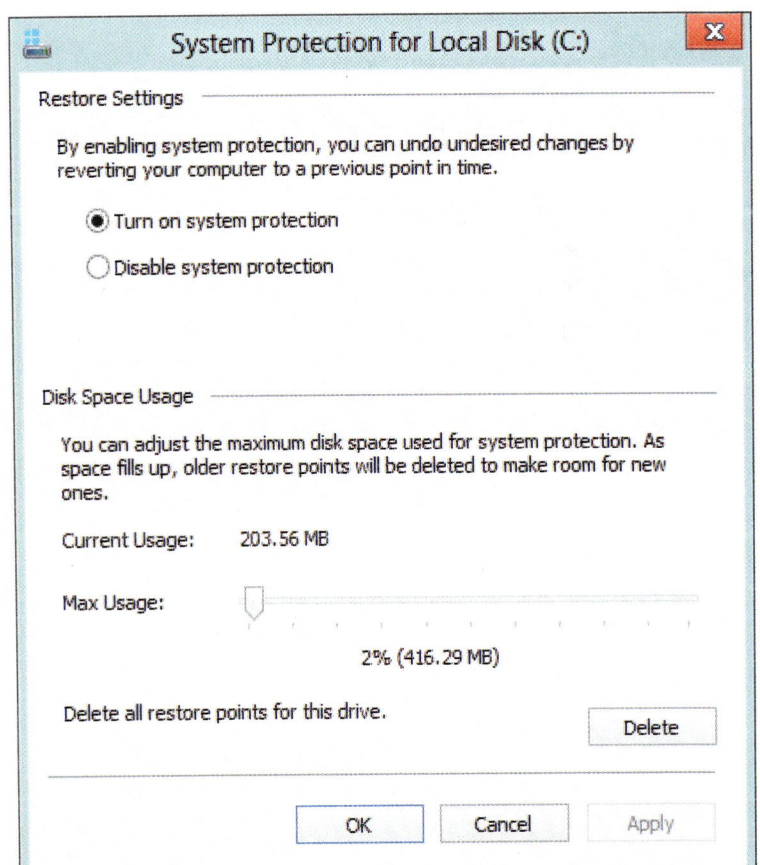

FIGURE 4-14 System Protection dialog box with System Protection turned on.

LO 4.3 | Recovering from Damage to Windows

Malware and other small-to-large disasters can cause damage to your system. When this happens, you need to return your computer to normal as quickly as possible to get back to work, schoolwork, or entertainment. The following describes your recovery options, beginning with the quickest and easiest possible fix and progressing to more advanced actions.

Restore System Files and Settings to a Point in Time

When you install a new app or a printer or other device, or whenever Windows or apps are updated, changes can be made to Windows system files and settings. If you notice an instability in Windows, think back to what has happened recently. If you recall one of these events, the easiest way to undo those changes is to restore the system files and settings that were preserved in restore points by System Restore. Before installing a Windows update, System Restore (also called System Protection) automatically creates a restore point. System Restore lists each restore point, along with the date and time and a description, such as "Windows Update." Figure 4-15 shows the System Restore dialog box with one restore point listed.

System Restore does not back up or restore data files—just the system state, which includes restoring any changed operating system files and settings.

We have used System Restore many times, and it has never damaged any data files; it leaves them intact. However, we still recommend that before you use System Restore, you make a backup of your data files.

We recommend that you try System Restore before trying Refresh Your PC (described next) because with System Restore, you lose only changes that occurred after the Restore Point was created. One of those changes may be what caused problems in Windows. That includes drivers, apps, and configuration changes. Refresh Your PC, although a great and easy solution, will remove any non-apps that were not obtained through the Windows App Store or those that are not part of a standard Windows installation.

try this!

Restoring from a Restore Point

Restore your system files and settings from a restore point.

1. Open the Recovery control panel.
2. Click or tap the middle option: Open System Restore.
3. The System Restore System Files and Settings dialog box opens with a page explaining System Restore. To begin, click or tap Next.
4. The page shown in Figure 4-15 displays. Although this one shows just one restore point, you may see many more. Select the most recent restore point and click or tap Next (which is not available until you select a restore point).
5. On the Confirm Your Restore Point page, confirm that the correct restore point is selected, and click or tap Finish.
6. A warning will display that once System Restore starts it cannot be interrupted. Click or tap Yes to continue.

Refresh Your PC

Windows 8 has a very quick solution to a scenario that previously required advanced tasks. Such a scenario would include very strange and erratic Windows behavior, such as unexpected fatal errors in which a blue screen appears, stating that your PC ran into a problem that it couldn't handle, and now it needs to restart. Believe it or not, this blue screen also has a sideways "frowny-face" similar to the emoticon ☹ without the eyes or circle. When this occurs, restart the system, and after (and if) Windows successfully restarts, sign in, open the PC Settings control panel, select the General page, and scroll down to the option to Refresh Your PC, as shown in Figure 4-16.

When you select the Refresh Your PC option, the computer boots into the **Windows Recovery Environment (Windows RE)**, which is a special operating system environment for installing Windows. Windows RE scans the hard drive for data settings and Windows 8 apps (Windows Store apps only), and saves them on the same drive, outside the folders where Windows is installed.

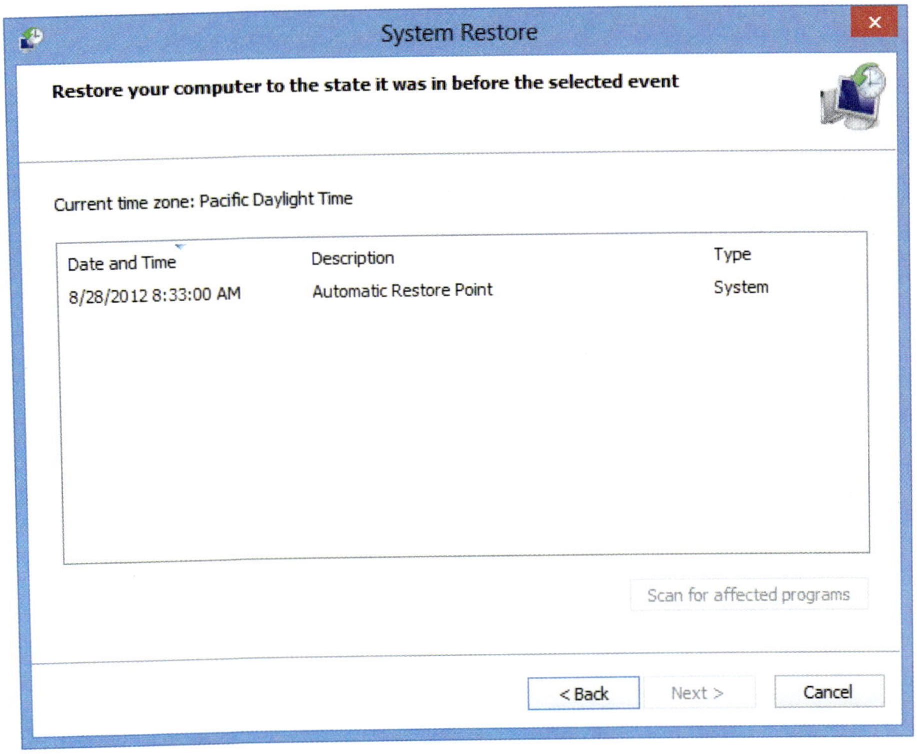

FIGURE 4-15 The System Restore dialog box with a single restore point listed.

Then it completely removes the existing installation of Windows 8 plus any apps that did not come with Windows or were not purchased through the Windows Store. That includes Desktop apps. It reinstalls Windows 8 and restores the data, settings, and apps that it saved.

When Windows restarts, you should have a cleaner, better running OS, with all your data as well as your previously installed Windows apps and apps from the Windows Store. Refresh will preserve data files and personal settings for all local users, but Windows System Settings will revert to the defaults. It preserves the apps from the Windows Store, but apps installed from other sources are re-

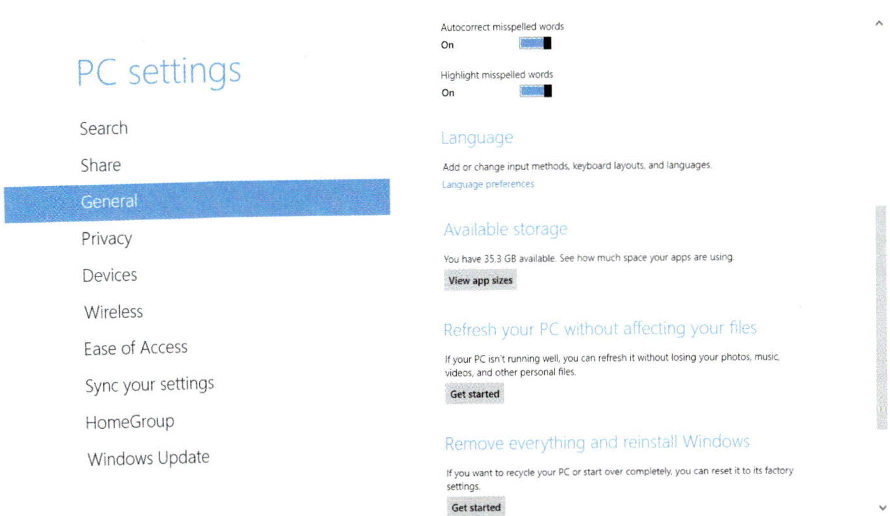

FIGURE 4-16 The option Refresh Your PC is a solution to serious instability problems.

moved and a list of all removed apps will be saved on your desktop. Do *not* choose this option unless your system has been very unstable, because although it preserves your data and refreshes your system with a clean installation of Windows, you will need to reinstall the apps that were not preserved. Of course, if one of those apps was the source of the problem, your system will run better.

Remove Everything and Reinstall Windows

The Remove Everything option, found immediately below the Refresh Your PC option on the General page of PC Settings, as shown in Figure 4-16, is a complete reset of your PC. In fact, in Microsoft documentation it is called Reset Your PC, and it will remove all your personal files and apps and change the system back to the defaults. This is much more extreme than Refresh Your PC and is something to consider if you want to give away or sell your computer because it removes all your personal data.

When you select the Remove Everything option, the computer boots into the Windows RE and erases and formats the hard drive partitions where Windows and your data were and then reinstalls Windows 8. You now have a factory fresh installation without any of the apps you installed, the changes you made, and without your data files. The computer is now ready to donate, give away, or sell.

Chapter 4 REVIEW

Chapter Summary

After reading this chapter and completing the Step-by-Step tutorials and Try This! exercises, you should understand the following facts about Windows 8:

Threats to Privacy and Data

- Threats include malware, phishing, social engineering, identify theft and fraud, exposure to inappropriate or distasteful content, invasion of privacy, misuse of cookies, hoaxes, and computer hardware theft. Other threats include accidents, mistakes, and natural and unnatural disasters.
- There are many methods used to steal passwords, such as capturing them from unsecured websites and using password crackers and keystroke loggers.
- A vector is a mode of malware infection, such as email, code on websites, Trojan horses, searching for unprotected computers, sneakernet, back doors, rootkits, pop up downloads, drive by downloads, war driving, and Bluesnarfing.
- Malware, or malicious software, includes viruses, worms, botnets, zombies, spyware, and adware.

Protecting Yourself

- Education is an important defense against threats. It includes knowing what the threats are and learning to recognize the signs of a threat or an infection.
- Keep Windows 8 and apps updated, because updating protects against discovered vulnerabilities.
- Use strong passwords on all your accounts. Do not use blank passwords and do not use the same password for multiple accounts. Do not write down passwords and leave them where others can discover them.
- Windows 8 supports authentication and authorization based on security accounts. Windows 8 maintains a database of local security accounts that include group accounts and user accounts.
- A group account is a security account that contains users and can contain other groups. Windows 8 contains local group accounts; it has many built-in local groups.
- A user account is a security account assigned to a single person, and it can be a member in one or more groups. Windows 8 contains local user accounts. The first local user account in Windows 8 is a member of the Administrators and HomeUsers local groups. A standard user in Windows 8 is a member only of the HomeUsers group.
- The local user Administrator is the most privileged account, but it is disabled by default. The local user Guest is the least privileged account, and it is also disabled by default.

- Windows 8 allows a user to sign in to the computer with one of the following: a local user account, Microsoft Domain user account, or a Windows Account (Microsoft Live ID).
- User Account Control (UAC) is a security feature of Windows that warns when a program attempts to launch that requires administrative access.
- Windows now includes three sign-in options: conventional password entry, picture password, and Personal Identification Number (PIN).
- Windows 8 now includes Windows Defender, which is a free antivirus and antispyware program that protects against various types of malware.
- The Action Center is a control panel that gives you access to security maintenance tools.
- Use the Forgotten Password Wizard to Create a Password Reset Disk to guard against being locked out of your computer if you forget your password.
- The Recovery Control Panel contains advanced operating system recovery tools, such as Recovery Drive and System Restore.

Recovering from Damage to Windows

- Use System Restore to restore the system to a point in time before an event, such as the installation of a new driver or program or a software update.
- If you have a recovery drive created before a problem occurs, you can refresh your PC.
- If you need to remove everything from your computer and return to the original installation, use the Remove Everything option on the General page of PC Settings.

Key Terms List

Action Center (124)
Administrator (112)
administrator account type (113)
adware (108)
antispyware (121)
antivirus (121)
back door (105)
Bluesnarfing (106)
bot (108)
botnet (108)
browser hijacking (107)
built-in local group (111)
built-in local user (112)
Consent Prompt (115)
cookies (101)
Credentials Prompt (116)
drive-by download (105)
first-party cookie (102)
fraud (99)
group account (111)
Guest (112)
hoax (100)
identity theft (100)
keystroke logger (103)
keylogger (103)
malware (103)
Microsoft account (114)
one-factor authentication (111)
password (110)
password cracker (102)
Password Reset Disk (127)
permission (111)
personal identification number (PIN) (117)
phishing (99)
phone phishing (99)
Picture Password sign-in (117)
personal identification number (PIN) (111)
pop-up (105)
pop-up download (105)
Reader (124)
recovery drive (129)
Restore Point (129)
rootkit (105)
security account (111)
SmartScreen (125)
sneakernet (105)
social engineering (99)
spam (106)
spim (107)
spybot (108)
spyware (108)
standard user account (113)
System Restore (129)
third-party cookie (102)
three-factor authentication (111)
token (111)
Trojan horse (104)
two-factor authentication (111)
user account (112)
User Account Control (UAC) (115)
vector (103)
virus (107)
war chalking (106)
war driving (106)
Windows Defender (121)
Windows Live ID (114)
Windows Recovery Environment (Windows RE) (130)
worm (108)
zero-day exploit (107)
zero-day vulnerability (107)
zombie (108)

Key Terms Quiz

Use the Key Terms List to complete the sentences that follow. Not all terms will be used.

1. A/An _______________ is a very small file an Internet browser saves on the local hard drive at the request of a website.
2. When you use a cash card at an ATM, you are using _______________.
3. When your browser home page changes without your knowledge, it is an example of _______________.
4. The _______________ security feature warns you if a program is attempting to run that requires administrative access.
5. A/An _______________ is the means by which malware infects computers.
6. An individual computer on a botnet is a/an _______________.
7. If you sign in to Windows 8 with a/an _______________, you use your Windows Live ID.
8. _______________ runs surreptitiously on a computer, gathers information without the user's permission, and then sends that information to the people or organization that requested the information.
9. The _______________ security feature prevents you from opening links, website content, and even apps, based on the reputation of the source.
10. The _______________ is the all-powerful super user account on a Windows computer.

Multiple-Choice Quiz

1. What term describes the use of persuasion to gain your confidence by various means?
   a. social engineering
   b. fraud
   c. phishing
   d. identify theft
   e. hoax
2. An ad embedded in a web page and originating from a domain other than that of the URL for the current web page can have your browser save this type of text file on your computer to track your web surfing habits.
   a. first-party cookie
   b. zombie
   c. third-party cookie
   d. spam
   e. spyware
3. An email that looks like an official communication from your bank but asks you to enter your Social Security number is an example of this type of threat.
   a. adware
   b. virus
   c. second party cookie
   d. phishing
   e. vector
4. The first local user account created for your use when installing Windows is this account type.
   a. standard user
   b. Microsoft account
   c. Guest
   d. Windows Live ID
   e. administrator
5. Administrator and Guest are both examples of what type of local account?
   a. Microsoft Account
   b. standard
   c. administrator
   d. group
   e. built-in
6. What type of malware vector requires administrative access to be installed into the operating system code where it is difficult to detect?
   a. rootkit
   b. Trojan horse
   c. botnet
   d. zombie
   e. spyware
7. This program acts as an agent for a user or master program, performing a variety of functions.
   a. virus
   b. spyware
   c. bot
   d. zombie
   e. cookie
8. What should you create as insurance so that you can sign in to your computer after forgetting your password?
   a. back door
   b. Password Reset Disk
   c. botnet
   d. administrator account
   e. keylogger

9. What free anti-malware software comes with Windows 8?
   a. Microsoft Security Essentials
   b. UAC
   c. Microsoft Account
   d. Windows Defender
   e. Picture Password

10. Which of the following options on the General page of the PC Settings control panel will reinstall Windows in a way that preserves all your data and any apps that you installed from the Windows Store?
   a. System Restore
   b. Refresh Your PC
   c. Remove Everything
   d. Windows RE
   e. Create a Recovery Drive

Essay Quiz

1. Explain the differences between first-party cookies and third-party cookies and why one is potentially more dangerous than the other.
2. Explain the latest sign-in account type that you can optionally use for Windows 8 and what the benefits are of this sign-in.
3. Explain the differences between using System Restore to return your computer to a point in time and using Refresh Your PC. Be sure to explain what happens to apps and settings in both cases.

Lab Projects

LAB PROJECT 4.1

Research identify theft on the Internet, as described in the following paragraphs, and write down your answers to the questions posed. Then share your results with classmates, comparing the information that each of you found.

1. Find a source that gives identity theft statistics over a period up to the previous year (if available). What is the estimated cost of identity theft in the United States in the past year (or most recent year provided)? What is the trend, compared to previous years? Is identity theft on the rise, stable, or decreasing?
2. Identity theft occurred before the proliferation of computers connected to the Internet. Find a recent news article about an identity theft ring and describe how the thieves operated. Did they use the Internet or computers in any way to steal individual identities?

LAB PROJECT 4.2

1. Recently the Flame virus made headlines and appears to a cyber warfare weapon, much like the previously discovered Stuxnet virus. Research these two viruses and search to see if any additional viruses exist that appear to be part of cyber warfare.

LAB PROJECT 4.3

Practice working with the Windows 8 recovery options. Because you may not have a computer on which you can do the first one, we have added a second activity to this project. Doing both would be very educational!

1. If you are permitted to do so, and if you do not have any non-Windows Store apps that you will miss when they are removed, run the Refresh Your Computer option on a Windows 8 computer.
2. If a test computer is available to you that you can wipe out, meaning removing all settings and data, install Windows 8 on it and test the use of the Windows 8 recovery option that wipes out everything on the computer (data, settings, additional installed apps) and reinstalls Windows 8.

chapter 5

Using Windows 8 on a Network

"One touch of nature makes the whole world kin."

—William Shakespeare

"A dream you dream alone is only a dream. A dream you dream together is reality."

—John Lennon

"Invisible threads are the strongest ties."

—Friedrich Nietzsche

"It is change, continuing change, inevitable change, that is the dominant factor in society today. No sensible decision can be made any longer without taking into account not only the world as it is, but the world as it will be."

—Isaac Asimov

Today, with the right devices and services, you can be connected anywhere. At work or school we connect to the corporate or school network and to the Internet, and at home, even TVs connect to the Internet. Desktop computers, tablets, laptops, and smartphones come with multiple options for connecting through wired or wireless networks. The biggest growth has been in the use of wireless, including Bluetooth for connecting to nearby wireless devices, Wi-Fi for connecting to wireless local area networks, and cellular for connecting to one of the major cellular phone/data networks. Whatever the mode, connections to these various networks have become automated and, for the most part, reliable.

This chapter prepares you for cloud computing by first presenting concepts you can practice in a small network. When connected, how do we use the features for working, researching, and living in a connected world? To answer this question, we look at how to share data from your Windows 8 computer on a small network, and then we expand our horizons and try out some of the features of Internet Explorer 10 in Windows 8, including

Learning Outcomes

In this chapter, you will learn how to:

- LO **5.1** Share files and printers in Windows 8.
- LO **5.2** Browse the Web in Windows 8 with Internet Explorer 10.
- LO **5.3** Configure Internet security settings.
- LO **5.4** Configure and use the Windows 8 Mail app.

navigation and security options. Finally, we'll practice using an email client in Windows 8 to send and receive email messages.

But shouldn't we be doing that new thing called **cloud computing**, which is based on accessing and sharing resources over a network (like the Internet)? In cloud computing, your data is stored on servers accessed through the Internet (which is commonly referred to as the cloud), and you may use apps from the Internet in place of locally installed apps.

It isn't all that new, but with fast and generally reliable Internet connections, more organizations and individuals are taking advantage of Internet-based services, such as Microsoft Hotmail, Skydrive, and Messenger. The difference between working with local network resources and working in the cloud is more about location than how you do it, and this chapter introduces you to skills for working with shared files and printers, navigating the Internet, and using email.

LO 5.1 | Sharing Files and Printers in Windows 8

Networks come in all sizes, from the small wired or Wi-Fi network you may have in your home for one or more computers to that world-spanning interconnected network of networks we call the **Internet**. There are many types of networks in between those two extremes, including private networks within government agencies and corporations. Like the Internet, these private networks are also interconnected networks, and they run the many protocols and services that compose the Internet. Such private networks using Internet technologies are **intranets**.

High-powered computers called servers are at the heart of all networks. They provide the services we, as clients, seek on a network. Special client-services software on our computers seek services from servers on our behalf. One of these services is file and print sharing, which allows users to share and access files and printers over a network. There are two sides to file and print sharing: the server side and the client side. On the server side, you create **shares**, which are folders or printers designated to be shared over a network. From the client side you connect to shares. Each side must have the appropriate software installed to participate. The client software lets you see computers on your network that have a compatible file-and-print-sharing service. The server side accepts your connections to shares and, depending on your permissions, you perform file operations, such as copying, moving, deleting, and opening data files, over the network in your locally installed applications.

Like previous versions, Windows 8 supports both sides, although its server side is meant to provide file and print sharing on a very small scale at home or in a small office. When hundreds or thousands of computers need to access files and printers over a network, those network servers use specialized software, such as Windows Server or Linux operating systems, which provide serious file-and-print sharing for large numbers of users at a time. Whether you are on a small network or a large corporate network, both sides of file and print sharing must use complementary file and print services that can talk to each other.

Each version of Windows has made sharing your local files and printers and connecting to shares over a network progressively easier, hiding more and more of the technical details from the user. In the following sections we'll explore two ways of sharing files in a small network: HomeGroups and Public Folders.

HomeGroups: Sharing Between Windows 7 and Windows 8 Computers

Windows 8 continues to support **HomeGroups**, which Microsoft introduced in Windows 7. This improved and easy way to share files and printers on small networks has a level of security that should be adequate for home use or in a small-office environment. It has an easy setup with just a few rules to remember:

1. A computer can belong to only one HomeGroup, no matter how many accounts exist on the computer.
2. A computer that belongs to a Microsoft Windows domain cannot create a HomeGroup.
3. A HomeGroup has a single password, used by all computers in the HomeGroup.

The first time the first user signs in to a new Windows 8 installation, Windows will either create a new HomeGroup or automatically join an existing HomeGroup. It all depends on your sign in. If the sign in is with a local account, Windows 8 will create a new HomeGroup. If it is with a Microsoft account, and if a local HomeGroup exists that is associated with that account, Windows will join the existing HomeGroup. Figure 5-1 shows a portion of the folder pane in File Explorer, including a HomeGroup with three member computers.

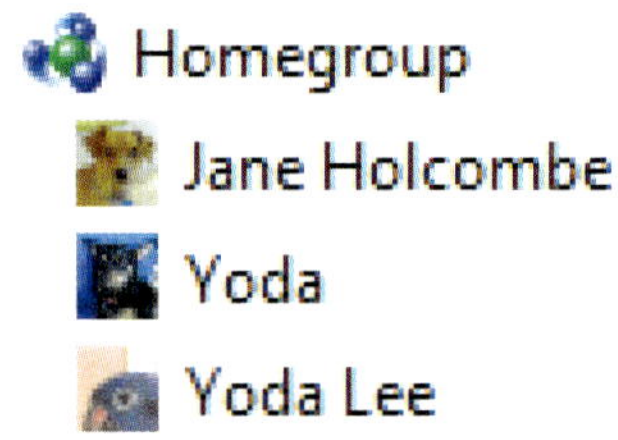

FIGURE 5-1 This HomeGroup has three members.

Configuring a HomeGroup

If you have a home network with other computers running either Windows 7 or Windows 8, you can easily let others join your HomeGroup. When it creates the HomeGroup, Windows also creates a password that each user on your network must use the first time they connect to your HomeGroup, but they will not need to enter it again. However, Windows does not turn on sharing. It leaves those decisions up to you, including whether you will share anything from your own computer, or just access shares on other computers in the HomeGroup.

Step-by-Step 5.1 walks you through a scenario for configuring what type of content on your computer you will share with others on your HomeGroup.

Step-by-Step 5.1

Sharing Content with a HomeGroup

You get to decide what type of content on your Windows 8 computer you share with a HomeGroup. You also get to decide if you will share all your local printers.

Step 1

Open the Charms bar, select the Settings charm, and from the Settings bar select Change PC Settings (at bottom). Then select HomeGroup. As you can see, this computer is a member of a HomeGroup, but it shares none of the user's content. Notice the membership password shown at the bottom of the screen.

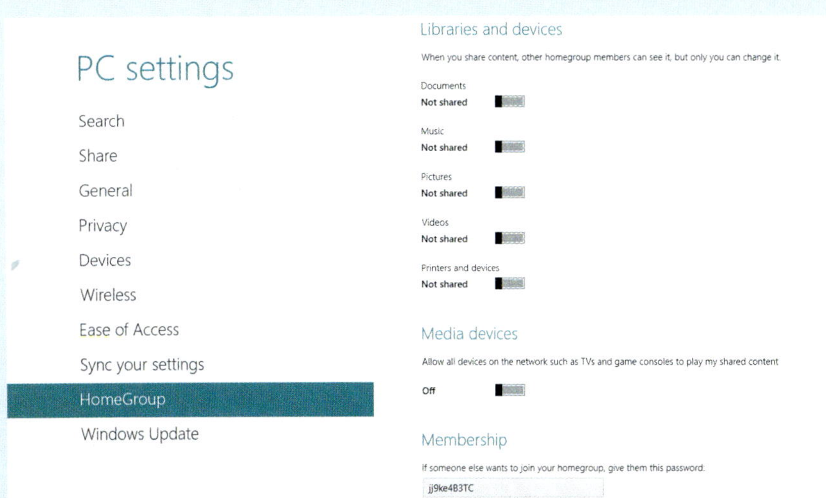

Step 2

Select content type to share and click or tap each type. In the example here we have shared all content in our public library folders except videos. And we did not open our shared content to media devices on the network, but we shared all locally connected printers and devices.

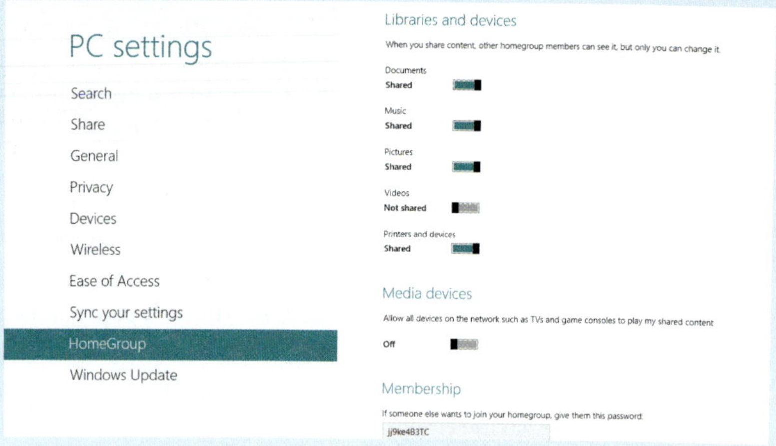

Step 3

You need to do one more thing to make content available: place files within the public folders that you shared and ensure that each shared printer is on when anyone wants to print to it. From the Start screen, open the desktop and then open File Explorer from its icon on the task bar. Browse to the public folders for each of the content types (documents, pictures, videos, or music) that you shared. If these folders are empty, which they are by default, you will need to place files into them when you want to share those files with others in the HomeGroup. If you copy files into the public folder you are sharing the copies of the files and will end up with two versions of a file.

Connecting to a HomeGroup

Our experience is that if you already have a HomeGroup on your network before you add your Windows 8 computer, you will need to remove the new HomeGroup on your computer before you can join the existing HomeGroup. However, you should test this theory by opening File Explorer and browsing to HomeGroup. If you know that a HomeGroup exists, and at least one other computer in the HomeGroup is powered on and connected to the network, but you only see your own computer, you are not a member of the existing HomeGroup and will not be able to share files with the other computers on the network. A computer can belong to only one HomeGroup at a time. You will need to either leave your new HomeGroup and join the other or ask the other members to leave theirs and join yours.

If you leave your HomeGroup, before you can join the other HomeGroup you will need the password for that HomeGroup. If a Windows 8 computer created that HomeGroup, you or the owner of that computer will need to locate the password on the HomeGroup page in PC Settings. If a Windows 7 computer created the existing HomeGroup, you will need to look elsewhere. Step-by-Step 5.2 describes the process of leaving your HomeGroup and joining another HomeGroup, including where to find the HomeGroup password on a Windows 7 computer.

Step-by-Step 5.2

Leaving a HomeGroup/Joining a New HomeGroup

Because a computer can belong to only one HomeGroup, you may need to leave a HomeGroup and join another HomeGroup in order to share files on a small network. To complete this exercise, you will need a Windows 8 computer that is a member of a HomeGroup and one other computer with either Windows 8 or Windows 7 running on it that is a member of another HomeGroup.

Step 1

Open PC Settings and select HomeGroup. Scroll to the very bottom of the HomeGroup page, and click the Leave button.

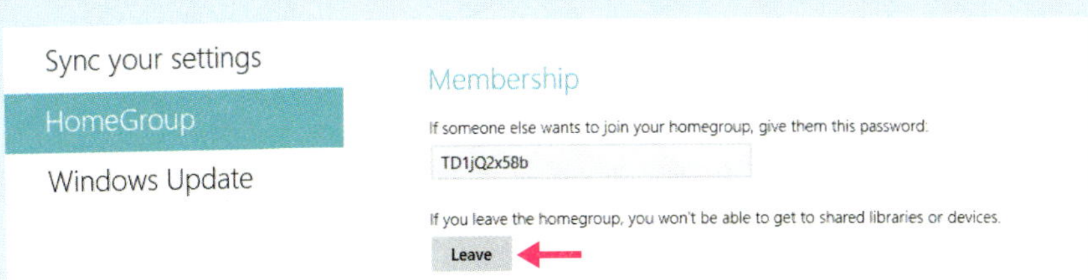

Step 2

If a HomeGroup is available, the right side of your HomeGroup page will display the name of the user and the computer that created the HomeGroup.

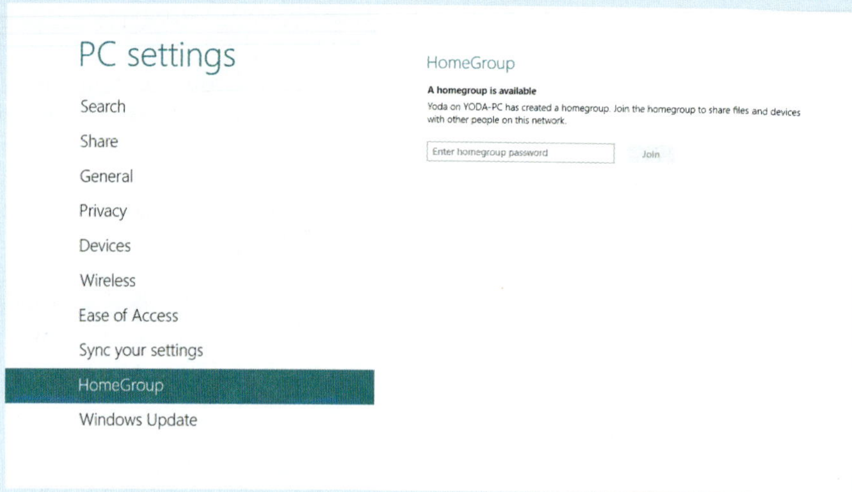

Step 3

You will need to obtain the password from a computer that has already joined the HomeGroup and enter it at the computer joining the HomeGroup. If the computer in the HomeGroup is running Windows 8, the password is on the HomeGroup page of PC Settings. Find the password and enter it on the computer you are joining to the HomeGroup. Then skip to Step 6. If the computer in the HomeGroup is running Windows 7, do Steps 4 and 5.

Step 4

At the Windows 7 computer, open the Start Search box, enter `HomeGroup`, and select HomeGroup from the results list. In Windows 7, the Change the HomeGroup Settings page opens (shown here), and you can click View or Print the HomeGroup Password.

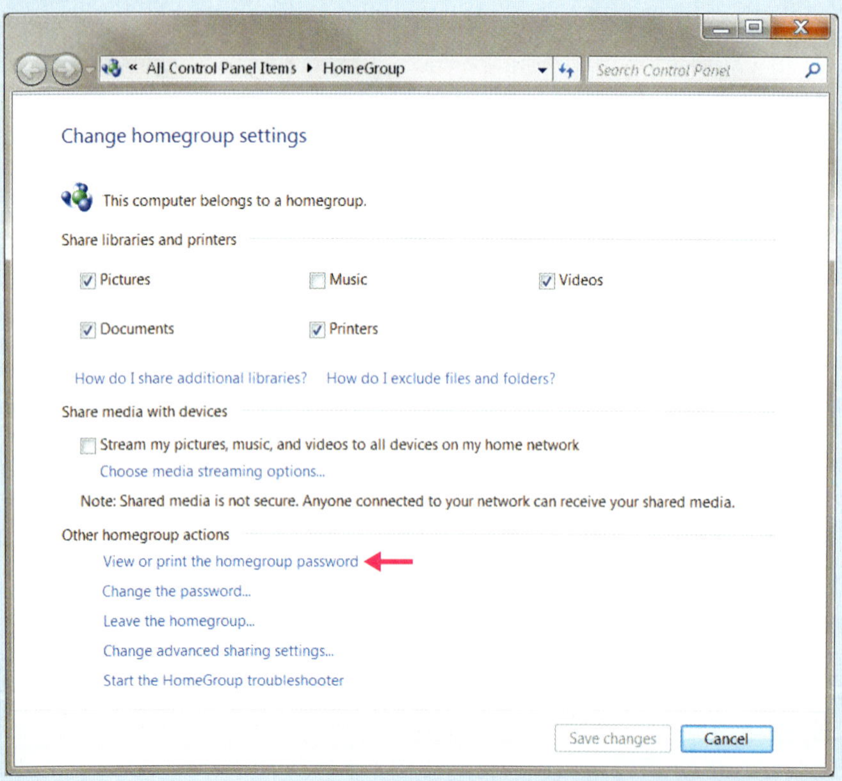

Step 5

On the Windows 7 computer you will see the password in a window like this, but it will not be the same password as you see here. Print or write down the password and take it back to your Windows 8 computer.

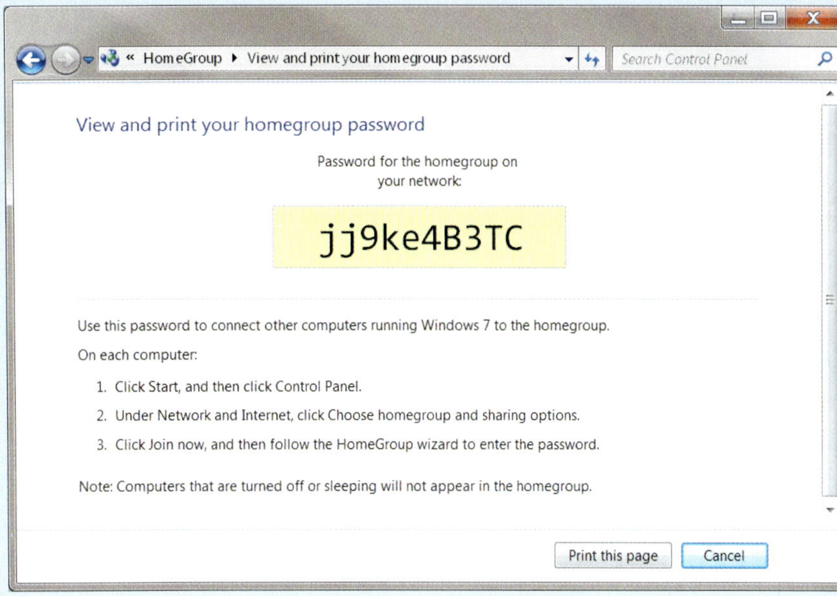

Step 6

Back at the Windows 8 computer, enter the password and click Join. After your computer joins the HomeGroup, the list of content to share displays, as shown in step 1, and you will need to decide what type of content to share, as you did back in step 2 of Step-by-Step 5.1. Any computer that is a member of a HomeGroup can display the HomeGroup password.

Multiple Accounts and HomeGroups
Each account (local and Microsoft) on a computer that is a member of a HomeGroup decides which of its own public folders to share.

Public Folders: Sharing Files Between Windows 8 and Windows XP and Windows Vista

HomeGroups are the easy way to share files among Windows 7 and Windows 8 computers. However, many of us have more than one Windows XP or Windows Vista computer in our homes or small offices, and those computers cannot join a Windows 7 or Windows 8 HomeGroup. If you have a mix of new and old Windows versions, you can continue to use a HomeGroup among Windows 8 and Windows 7 computers, and by adding users to your local accounts, give users on Windows XP and Windows Vista computers access to your Public folder. A Public folder is a folder usually located at C:\Users\Public. On Windows 7 and Windows 8 computers, the permissions on the Public folder allow anyone with a username and password on the local computer to access the Public folder and its contents. By default, the Public folder contains several folders named Public Documents, Public Downloads, Public Music, Public Pictures, Public Videos, and Recorded TV. This last folder is only on computers with Windows Media Center installed.

The one drawback to this method is that when you share your Public folder, you are sharing the entire folder—including all subfolders and their contents. Recall that when you share through a HomeGroup, you can control which folders within Public you share, although even then, you are sharing them with everyone on the HomeGroup.

To understand Public folder sharing, look at the Public folder and its subfolders on a Windows 8 computer. The master Public folder is located under the Users folder on the drive on which Windows 8 is installed. This folder is, by default, shared to anyone on the local computer or on the network who has an account in the local accounts database. In fact, if a user on the network is logged on to a Windows computer using an account that matches one on your computer (including the password), the user can connect to the Public share without going through a logon screen. Figure 5-2 shows the Windows 8 Public folder and its subfolders.

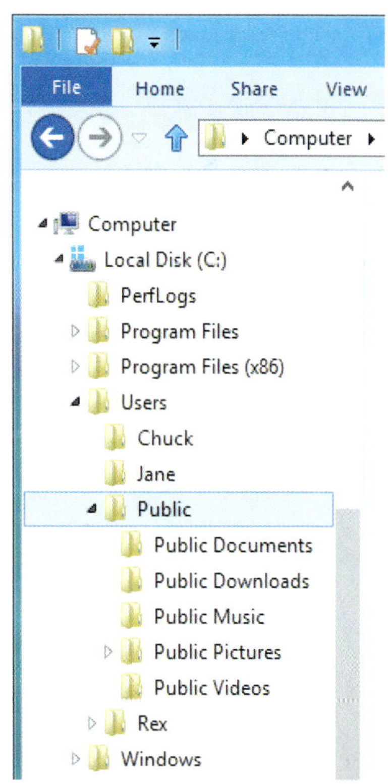

FIGURE 5-2 The Public folder on a Windows 8 computer.

WARNING!

If a network user is logged on to his own computer with an account with a matching username but different password, he will see a sign-in screen when he attempts to connect to your computer's Public folder. It's not a big problem as long as he can provide the correct password.

HomeGroups Versus Sharing the Public Folder

In HomeGroups, access is assigned per computer, not per user. When you share your Windows 8 Public folder, access is granted per user.

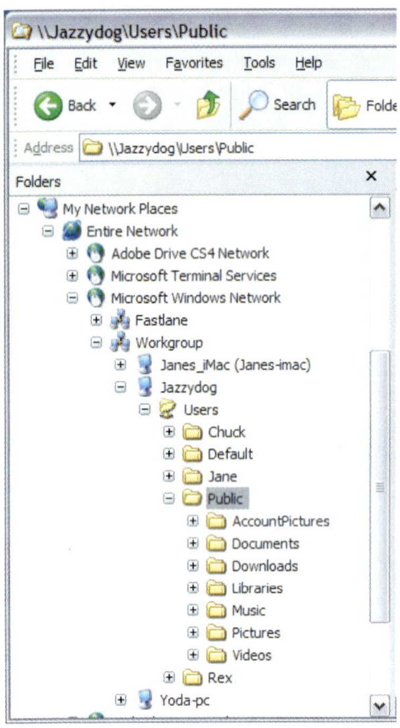

FIGURE 5-3 The view from a Windows XP computer.

The default Public subfolders have a special relationship with the default Libraries for each user. For instance, the Public Documents folder contains the files and folders all the users on this computer have placed in their Public Documents library folder. Recall what you learned about Libraries in Chapter 4. A library does not contain the folders that appear in the library, but rather has pointers to the locations for those folders. So, the My Documents folder in the Documents library points to the currently logged-on user's Documents folder, located in a folder with that user's name. Similarly, the Public Documents folder in the Documents library points to the Public Documents folder under the Public folder.

So, simply place or move files and folders into one of the public folders in your libraries, and people on the network who have local accounts on your computer can connect and access these files and folders, but they cannot access your other folders. Add the users to your local accounts by following the instructions for creating a user account in the Try This! in Chapter 4. If the username and password do not match the account with which a user logs on at her computer, Windows prompts her to supply a username and password to access the Public folder.

After you add a new user to your local accounts, that user can browse to your computer and see the Public folders, as shown in Figure 5-3, as long as the user is logged on to another Windows computer with a matching account. Users given this access to the Public folder can browse to the Public folder and have full control within that folder and its subfolders, meaning they can create files and folders and read, write, modify, and delete them.

LO 5.2 | Web Browsing in Windows 8

Many of us spend a good part of a typical day browsing the Internet for work or school research, or just for fun. We don't often think about the apps that let us do that. We will take time here to look at those apps—web browsers—in general, and then learn about **Internet Explorer 10 (IE 10)**, the web browser introduced with Windows 8 with two separate GUIs. We examine the features common to both IE 10 GUIs, including security features. Then we practice navigating the web with each GUI.

The Web Browser Back Story

Windows 8 comes with version 10 of **Internet Explorer (IE)**. IE is a **web browser**, software designed for navigating and viewing sites on the **World Wide Web**. A web browser is a client that accesses web services running on web servers on the Internet. These web services and related technologies create the graphical environment we know as the World Wide Web. The web is just one of many services that exist on the Internet, yet it is responsible for most of the huge growth in Internet use that began after the web's introduction in the early 1990s. Web technologies changed the look of Internet content from all text to rich and colorful graphics, and made it simple to navigate the Internet.

A web browser's ease of use hides the complexity of the Internet, as underlying protocols help to transfer the content of a web page to the user's computer. There the web browser translates the underlying plain-text markup language into a rich, colorful document that may contain links to other pages on other servers on the web. A **link** consists of words or an image that you can click on to open a new web page or to jump to a different section on the same page. When you use these links and menus within a website to move to other web pages and websites, you are doing **site navigation**, which saves you the trouble of directly entering an address for every page you jump to.

You can also go to sites more directly using an **address bar**, something that all web browsers have. What you enter into an address bar is a text version of a website's address, such as www.microsoft.com. This is a very simple address that includes a top-level domain (TLD) name ("com" in our example) and a second-level domain name (Microsoft in our example), which combine to form a domain name that Microsoft has leased from an Internet Domain Name registrar, an organization that manages the use of domain names. We won't go into all the details of domain names, but you have probably noticed other common top-level domain names, such as org, edu, gov, and biz. The period symbol separates the parts of the domain name, and people often talk about a TLD as "dot com," "dot org," and so on.

When you register a domain name, is it is associated with a numeric Internet address so that any traffic for that domain is sent to that address. It is up to an organization how it manages everything within its domain; it can even redirect traffic coming to its address. It can add names to the left of the domain name (such as the "www") that may point to a specific server or subdomain in its domain, and items to the right of the top-level domain name point to specific pages.

Finally, on the far left of an address in the address bar is the name of the protocol being used to transfer data from that website. Two protocols you should be aware of are **Hypertext Transfer Protocol (HTTP)** and **Hypertext Transfer Protocol over Secure Sockets Layer (HTTPS)**. HTTP is the core protocol used to transfer information over the World Wide Web. HTTP includes the commands web browsers used to request web pages from web servers. The second, HTTPS, is a secure version of HTTP that encrypts data before sending it. **Encryption** converts data into a code that requires a secret key or password before converting it back (a process called **decryption**) into a readable format. Why do you care?

HTTPS should be in use on any web page where you must enter your banking or payment information. Make sure it is. How will you know? Check out the **uniform resource locator (URL)** in the address bar. The URL is the complete text-based address to a website and web page, including the protocol. While you are browsing and adding items to your shopping cart on Amazon, the address bar will show the HTTP protocol, but when you click Proceed to Checkout, the protocol changes to HTTPS, and you might see an address such as this: https://www.amazon.com/gp/cart/view.html/ref=ox_sc_proceed. Knowing this bit of information, you can now look at a URL and pick out the protocol and the domain name.

Today, there are versions of web browsers for Mac OS X, Microsoft Windows, and Linux. Beyond the desktop, you'll find versions of these web browsers with scaled-down screens for smartphones and tablets. In short, just about any electronic device that can connect to the Internet and that has a display also uses some type of web browser.

In the past two decades, web content has become ever more complex, and the original markup language for web pages, **Hypertext Markup Language (HTML)**, did not keep up fast enough with the changes desired in web content. Today, web servers often include other types of program code to create active content. Browsers don't only interpret HTML code, but must be ready to interpret other types of code on web pages so that you can view animation and videos and interact with programs on the website. You are able to view and interact with such content on web servers thanks to small programs called **plug-ins** that you add to your web browser to bring the enhanced content to you. These plug-ins include Java, QuickTime, and Adobe Flash Player. One problem with how plug-ins traditionally work within browsers is that after a plug-in is activated to play web page content, it operates independently outside the control of the browser. This has made plug-ins a security hole, and the trend is to

There is more to protocols than meets the eye.
A **protocol** is a set of rules that software needs to comply with to perform a function. There are many different protocols that are used by software on the Internet.

A Plug-in by Any Other Name
Numerous terms describe program code that adds capabilities to a larger program. An incomplete list is plug-in, add-in, add-on, and extension. Sometimes we make a distinction between the types of code and categorize it under different terms.

change that model of plug-in independence. Today the latest version of HTML, HTML5, supports animation and interactive content, and many believe it is more secure to use HTML5 rather than plug-ins.

Internet Explorer 10

That background on web browsers brings us to Internet Explorer 10 and its features. The most obvious is that IE 10 is effectively two separate apps, each with a different user interface. The first is a full-screen Windows 8 version (Figure 5-4) that does not have an official name. For our purposes, we'll call it **Windows 8 IE 10**. Second is a windowed desktop version (Figure 5-5), which we'll call **Desktop IE 10**. We will examine the features common to both IE 10 GUIs, including security features. Then we will practice navigating the web with each GUI and look at how to configure security and privacy settings for both GUIs using the Internet Options Control Panel applet.

Microsoft designed IE 10 in both interfaces for the rich content of today's Internet written in HTML5, the latest version of HTML. Before releasing it, Microsoft announced that only Desktop IE 10 would support plug-ins, and

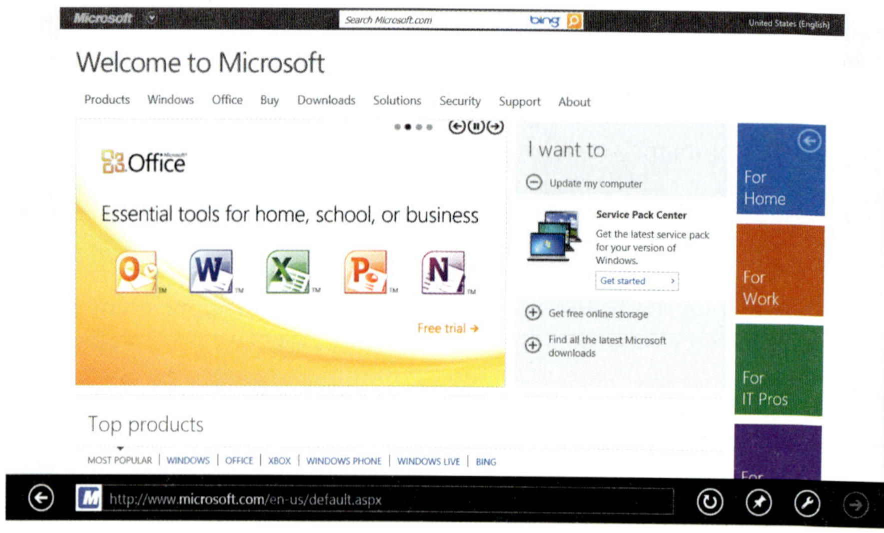

FIGURE 5-4 Windows 8 IE 10 is a full-screen app.

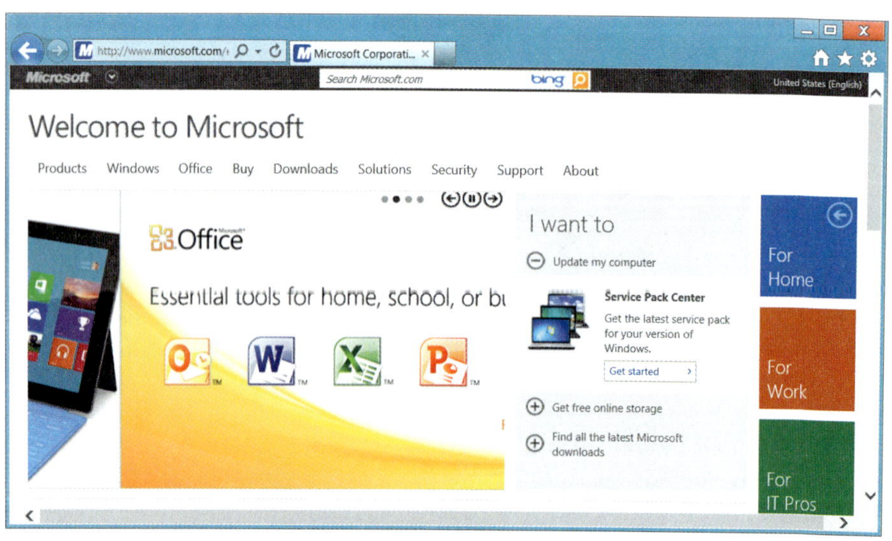

FIGURE 5-5 Desktop IE 10 is a windowed app that runs on the desktop.

Windows 8 IE 10 would support only HTML5 content. This led to a lot of negative feedback from many people who requested that Windows 8 IE 10 include support for the very popular Adobe Flash Player. Perhaps because of this feedback, Microsoft included Adobe Flash Player, not as a plug-in but integrated into IE 10. Microsoft and Adobe worked together to integrate it into IE 10 (both interfaces), just as Adobe and Google worked together to integrate Adobe Flash Player into Chrome (see sidebar to the right regarding Chrome). In each case, the integrated Adobe Flash Player also automatically receives security fixes and patches.

Another aspect of rich, complex, and active web content is that it requires fast Internet connections to download ever-increasing amounts of content, and it also requires more computing power than the simple text-and-picture content of the early days of the web. This is because it must interpret more program code from the web servers—especially for complex graphics. To help with this, Internet Explorer 10 takes advantage of hardware acceleration features in modern computers.

Launch Windows 8 IE 10 from its Start screen tile and launch Desktop IE 10 from its pinned icon on the desktop taskbar. They share some features and underpinnings, but each has its own unique features. You can configure the shared features through the legacy Internet Options Control Panel applet. We will explore Internet Options later in the chapter. With that background on browsers in general and Internet Explorer in particular, we will review the security features and then the two interfaces of Internet Explorer 10.

Other Web Browsers
Other web browsers are available for Windows—all free. The most popular competitors to IE are Mozilla Firefox and Google Chrome. In this section we explore both the Windows 8 IE 10 and Desktop IE 10.

Internet Explorer 10 Security Features

IE 10 includes the security features of the previous versions of IE, including SmartScreen, XSS filtering, InPrivate browsing, Tracking Protection, Pop-up Blocker, and Hang Detection and Recovery. It also includes a new feature, Enhanced Protected Mode. A brief description of these features follows.

SmartScreen SmartScreen prevents you from opening links, website content, and apps based on the reputation of the source. When applied to applications, this is called Application Reputation. As described in Chapter 4, you can change SmartScreen settings in the Action Center.

XSS Filtering Security holes in websites allow for a type of attack called **Cross-Site Scripting (XSS)** in which malicious code is placed on a legitimate website through a vulnerability in how the website handles incoming data. This typically occurs on a website that accepts user input, but does not check it for malware before allowing it to be output to other users of that website. Malware then installs on the receiving computer when the user inadvertently runs the contained script. **XSS Filtering** in Windows 8 checks all input to the browser from websites to ensure that it does not contain such scripts.

InPrivate Browsing InPrivate browsing is Microsoft's version of private browsing features commonly found in Internet browsers. Other browsers call it Private Browsing or Incognito Mode. During a normal browser session, the browser tracks information and saves it when you close the session (by closing the window or tab). This information includes browsing history, cookies, passwords, form data, addresses entered into the address bar, and temporary Internet files. An **InPrivate browsing** session works like a normal browsing session, except when you close the tab you were using for InPrivate browsing, it saves none of the gathered information, and so your browsing behavior cannot be tracked. Normally, websites can use this locally stored data for good or evil, as described in Chapter 4. At some sites, it is a convenience to you to allow this. For instance, have you ever visited a shopping site like Amazon, not logged in with an account, and selected items for your shopping cart? Then, without completing the transaction, you left the site. Did you notice that the next time you returned to that site from the same computer, things you looked at show up, and your shopping list is still there? If you considered that a convenience, you would not want to do InPrivate browsing at that site. But you may want it turned on for other sites or when using someone else's computer. That is when you select InPrivate browsing. When you start an InPrivate session, you are protected until you leave the tab page that was opened for InPrivate browsing.

Tracking Protection Many websites contain content provided by another website, a third-party website that may track your browsing across multiple sites. **Tracking Protection** blocks third-party sites from tracking you by blocking requests for your tracking data from a list of suspect sites.

Do Not Track The **Do Not Track (DNT)** feature, when enabled, sends a DNT signal to each visited website. It is up to the website to comply with the request.

Pop-up Blocker Configure IE 10's Pop-up Blocker on the Privacy page of Internet Options. You can then choose to allow or not allow sites to show pop-ups.

Hang Detection and Recovery Some graphical web page content can put a strain on your computer's graphics hardware, even causing it to suffer a severe error and hang, meaning that all processing by the video systems graphics processor stops. Windows 8 has a feature called **Hang Detection and Recovery** that detects when this occurs; it sends a signal to reset the graphics processor and restores the Windows environment and IE 10 tabs to their previous state.

Enhanced Protected Mode **Enhanced Protected Mode** isolates the content within each open IE 10 tab so that malicious code from a web page cannot access information in the other open tabs.

Navigating with Windows 8 IE 10

Windows 8 IE 10 is optimized for touch screens; when you're working on a touch screen this will probably be your preferred browser. It is certainly very usable without a touch screen, so you can become familiar with Windows 8 IE 10 on any computer running Windows 8. From the Start screen open Windows 8 IE 10 by clicking or tapping the Internet Explorer tile. It opens to your Home screen, and displays the **navigation bar** at the bottom of the screen, as shown back in Figure 5-4. This is a departure from other browsers, including the previous versions of IE and even from Desktop IE 10, all of which have a navigation bar at the top of the browser GUI. This can take some getting used to.

Exploring the Windows 8 IE 10 GUI Windows 8 IE 10 shares data with other Windows 8 apps through a mechanism called systemwide contracts. With Windows 8 IE 10 open, access the Charms bar and select the Share charm to see which apps have a sharing contract with IE. Windows 8 IE 10 will send the other app a link along with a preview image of the web page. Also, Windows 8 IE 10 accesses devices, such as printers, through the Devices charm. As with past versions of IE, updates are free and downloadable from Microsoft's website.

Notice that everything showing on the Windows 8 IE 10 screen has to do with the website, except the narrow navigation bar on the bottom, which displays when you first open a page, but disappears as soon as you click or tap on an empty area of the page. Unnecessary space is not taken up with a surrounding frame, menus, and buttons (visual objects that are part of an app dubbed "chrome" by Microsoft) so that every bit of your screen is used by the browser to display content. Figure 5-6 shows the Windows 8 IE 10 navigation bar as it appears when you first open a web page.

FIGURE 5-6 Windows 8 IE 10 navigation bar opens at the bottom when you open a new web page.

Let's take a closer look at the Windows 8 IE 10 navigation bar and its selection of controls (from left to right):

- Back button opens the previous page.
- Address bar contains the uniform resource locator (URL) of the current site, which is http://www.bing.com in our example. Manually type a URL in here, and as you type, the navigation bar expands and a results list displays above the address bar. If the correct address is in the results, click or tap it to move to that page.
- Refresh button sends a request to the current website for a refresh of the web page.
- Pin to Start creates a Start screen tile for the page. Like other Start screen tiles, these can display dynamic content, if supported by the linked web page.
- Page Tools opens a menu with three choices:
  - Get App for This Site will be an option when IE detects that to receive content from the site requires an as yet uninstalled app. Select this to have IE connect to a download site for the app.
  - Find on Page opens a Find bar where you can enter a string of characters to search for on the page.
  - View on the Desktop will open the current page in Desktop IE 10.

If you click or tap in the address bar, the Apps bar expands upward, covering over one-third of the bottom of the screen, as shown here. It now displays **navigation tiles**, graphical objects that contain links to sites that you have frequently accessed, as well as sites you have pinned to the Start screen. Click or tap a navigation tile to switch to that web page.

When using Windows 8 IE, if a website has content that requires a browser add-on, you will see a message similar to the one shown above the navigation bar pictured here. If you click or tap the blue Open button, the website opens in Desktop IE 10.

Within each website, use your mouse and keyboard as you have in the past, or use touch gestures to navigate the web. If you swipe left or right without touching the sides of the screen, you will switch between web pages. If you swipe up and down without touching the top or bottom of the screen, you will scroll through the current web page.

Access all the Windows 8 features with mouse, keyboard, or gestures. Open the Charms bar when you want to print, share content, or search. Step-by-Step 5.3 walks you through a tour of Windows 8 IE 10.

Step-by-Step 5.3

Browsing with Windows 8 IE 10

Practice using some of the features of Windows 8 IE 10 as you browse web pages.

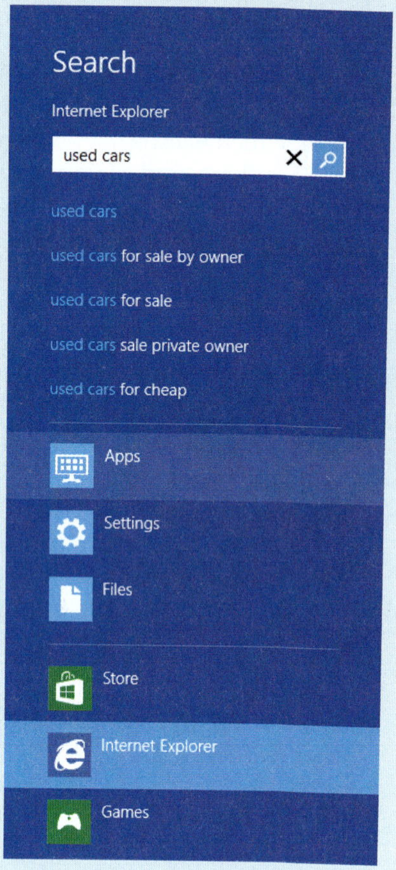

Step 1

From the Start page, click or tap the Internet Explorer tile to open Windows 8 IE 10. Open the Charms bar and click or tap the Search charm. Search focuses on the current Windows 8 app—Internet Explorer in this case—and it will use your default search engine. When you enter a search string, it will offer to complete the search string with topics it finds on the web. If you want to stay with the original search string, click or tap the magnifying glass icon (or press Enter on the keyboard) to complete the search. Or click or tap one of the suggested topics for a more targeted search.

Step 2

In our example, selecting "Used cars for sale by owner" brought up Microsoft's Bing search engine with search results. You can begin your search from your favorite search engine without using the Search charm. Most search engines list the paid advertisers first in the results list, and we normally recommend that you scroll down beyond the paid ads. However, the results for some topics, like "used cars," include many paid ads.

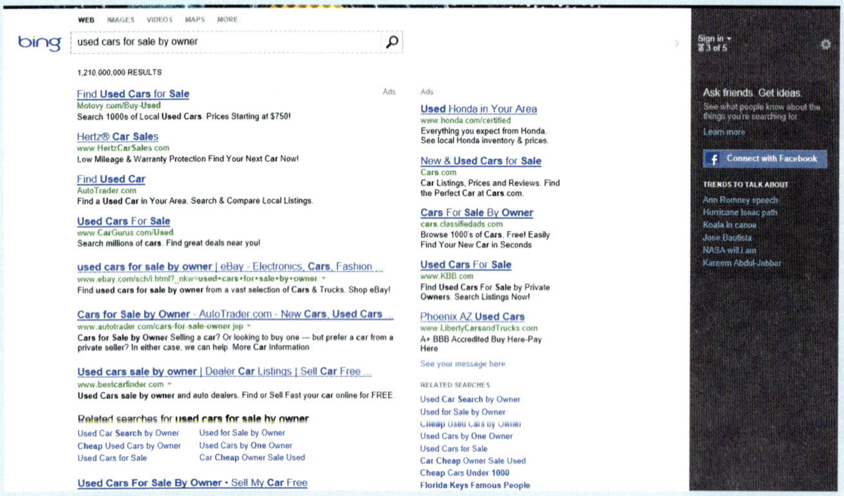

Step 3

Scroll through the results using gestures or mouse actions. Browse to at least two sites in the search results. Use the mouse or gesture on the left side of the screen to return to the results page to select additional sites.

Step 4

Right-click in a blank space or swipe a short distance from either the top or the bottom of the screen toward the center to bring up the navigation bar on the bottom and the **Tab Switcher** bar containing the open tabs on the top. The Tab Switcher displays tiles for the last 10 tabs you used.

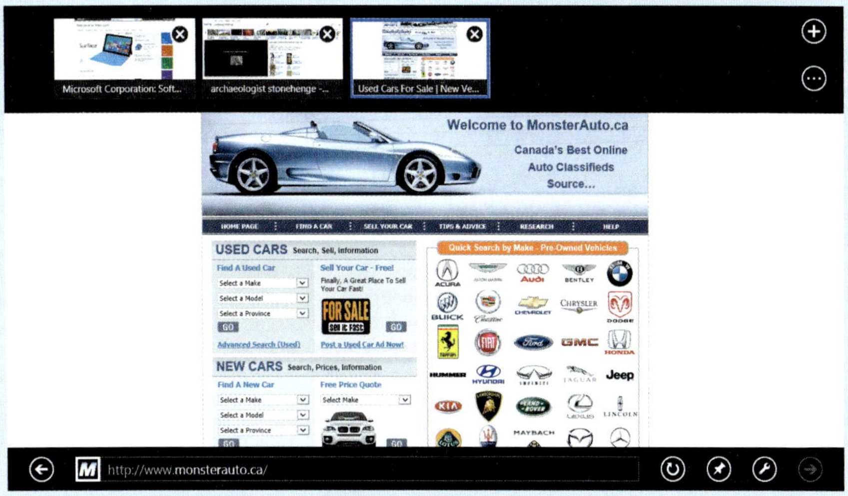

Step 5

In the Tabs bar, click or tap a tab to return to a web page. Then open the Tabs bar and navigation bar again and click or tap the New Tab button (the one with a plus sign) in the upper right of the Tab bar to create a new tab, or press Ctrl+T. The Tab bar closes and an extended navigation bar opens on the bottom, giving you three ways to open a new tab.

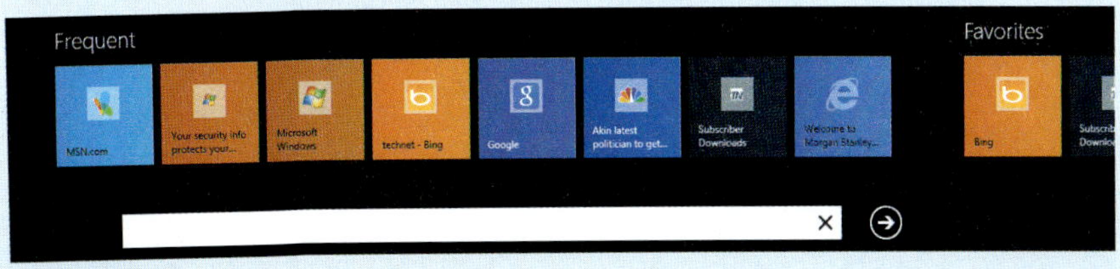

Step 6

Open a new tab now. You can open a new tab by selecting one of the frequently visited websites from the navigation tiles, or select a favorite site (if any are listed). Finally, you can enter a URL into the address bar by typing or, on a touch screen, tap inside the address bar and the pop-up keyboard will display, and you can enter the URL or a portion you remember.

Step 7

Find a web page with content you would like to print. Open the Charms bar and select the Devices charm. Then select the Microsoft XPS Document Writer.

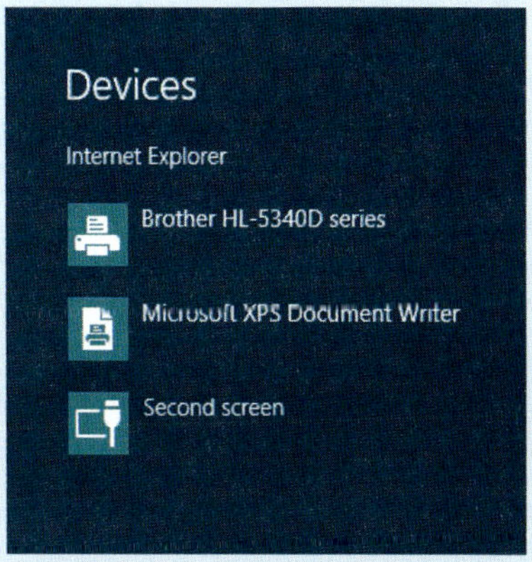

Step 8

When you select a printer, the bar expands from the right side of the screen, showing a preview of the document. On this page you can change orientation, and More Settings leads to other settings, including orientation (again) and paper size and quality. When you print to the Microsoft XPS Document Writer, it creates a file in your Documents folder with the name of the web page and an extension of "oxps."

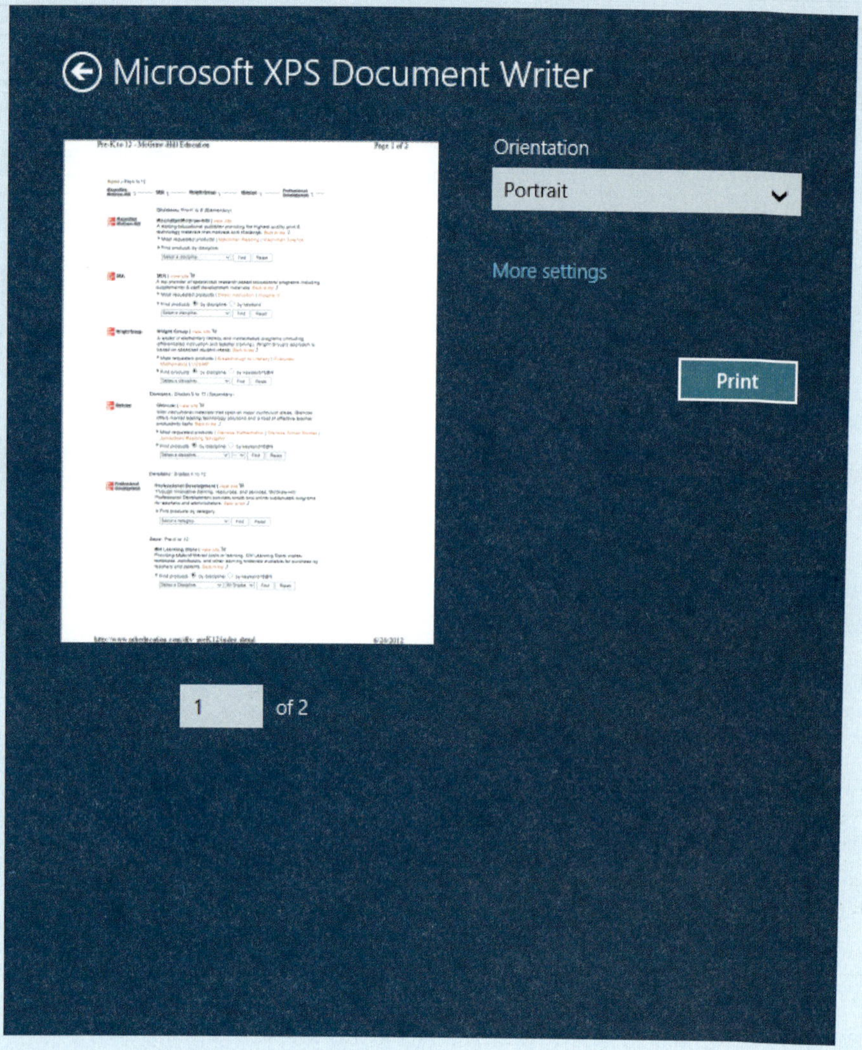

Step 9

Now open the Tab bar and navigation bar again. Close one or more tabs by clicking or tapping on the "x" button on the tab thumbnail. Return to the Start page by pressing the Windows key or swiping from the left bottom corner and selecting the Start screen thumbnail.

The Tab Switcher bar shown in Step 4 in Step-by-Step 5.3 also contains the Tab Tools button with three dots (...). Click or tap this button to open an InPrivate Browsing session in a new tab with the message shown here. Use the Windows 8 browsing tools to navigate to web pages. As long as you stay within the tab, your browsing will be private. If you switch to a tab from the Tab Switcher bar at the top of the screen and it is not using InPrivate browsing, you will be out of InPrivate browsing. If you are using InPrivate browsing and you navigate to another page using the navigation bar at the bottom (shown in the illustration on the next page)—even if you select one of the pinned or frequent tiles, you will remain in InPrivate browsing.

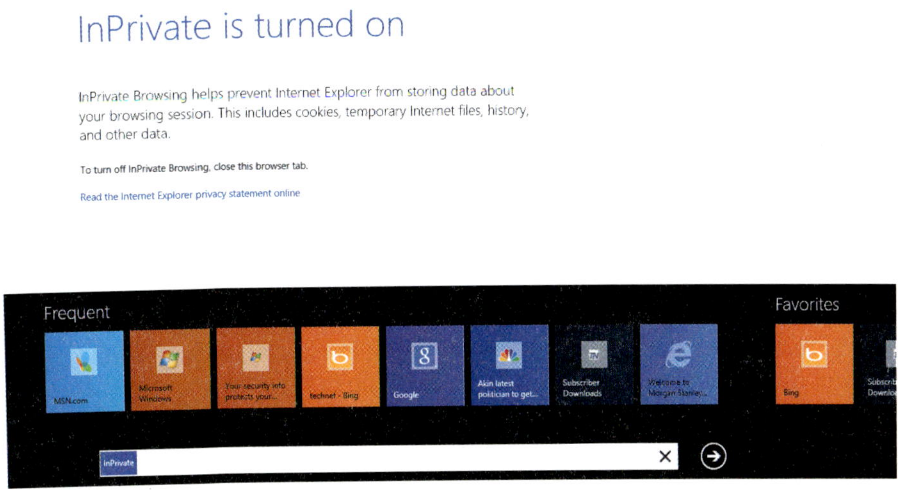

Configuring Windows 8 IE 10 Settings Windows 8 IE 10 and Desktop IE 10 share certain settings, and some settings are exclusive to Windows 8 IE 10. To access settings while in Windows 8 IE 10, open the Charms bar and select the Settings charm. This opens the Settings bar, (shown in Figure 5-7) focused on Internet Explorer. From here select Internet Options, which opens the Internet Explorer Settings bar, shown in Figure 5-8. It contains just a few of the many settings that affect IE 10. We will examine these now, and later in the chapter we will detail more settings available through the Internet Options Control Panel.

try this!

Try InPrivate Browsing in Windows 8 IE 10

Open an InPrivate Browsing tab and see if you can see a difference. Try This!

1. From the Start screen open Internet Explorer.
2. Right-click in a blank space or swipe a short distance from either the top or the bottom of the screen toward the center to open the Tab Switcher bar at the top of the screen.
3. Click or tap the Tab Tools button (with the three dots) and select New InPrivate Tab.
4. Try navigating by using the Tab Switcher bar. The experience should be very like normal browsing.
5. If you switch to a tab that is not an InPrivate tab, you will no longer be doing private browsing. Look for the InPrivate box to the left of the address bar to confirm that you are still protected by InPrivate browsing.

On the Internet Explorer Settings bar, select Internet Options to open the Internet Explorer Settings page, shown in Figure 5-8. This appears on the right of the screen; it is wider than the Settings bar, but not truly an entire page. It is confusing that the Internet Options choice on the Windows 8 Internet Explorer Settings bar is the same name as the traditional Control Panel applet, still a part of Windows 8, which we discuss later. For now, let's look at the settings available on this page:

Settings Bars Are Context-Sensitive
The Internet Explorer Settings bar, shown in Figure 5-8, appears only when you open the Settings charm with Windows 8 IE 10 open. Opening the Settings charm with Desktop IE 10 open will open the Desktop Settings bar.

- Delete Browsing History removes your browsing history, which contains information valuable to marketers and others who want to learn about you. This information also makes life a bit easier for you when you return to favorite sites. A system compromised by spyware or other malicious means could reveal this information to the wrong persons. Additionally, if you leave your computer unattended, but logged on with your account, anyone with access to your computer can look at your browsing history. Further, system administrators or others who have administrative access to your computer can do the same. Therefore, you will want to know how to delete browsing history in any web browser you use.
- Permissions allows or disallows a site to use your physical location, as determined by either Internet address or by data received from a built-in positioning device, such as found in phones and tablets today.

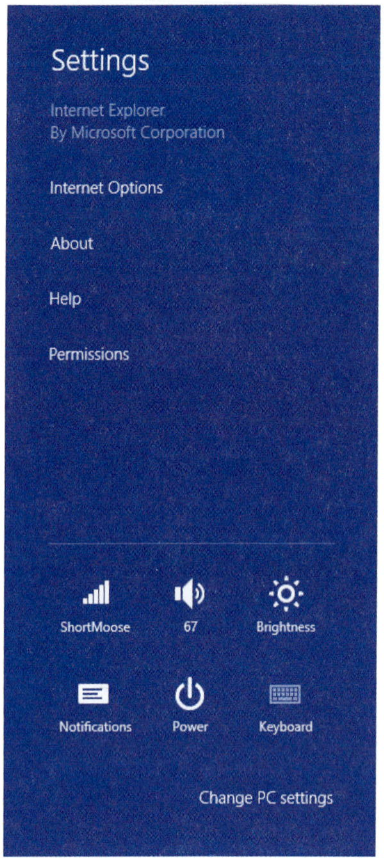

FIGURE 5-7 Windows 8 IE 10 Settings bar.

- Zoom allows you to specify the default web page size on your screen. You can dynamically change the current size while viewing a page.
- Turning on **Flip Ahead** lets you take advantage of a new feature in Internet Explorer 10 in Windows 8. When the browser detects that a web page is part of a multipage document, the user can use the swipe to the right or left gesture to page forward and backward within the document. With a mouse, move the pointer to the middle of the right edge and click the small arrow that appears. When Flip Ahead is off, these actions let you navigate among recent websites. Flip Ahead scrolls through a multipage document on one website.
- Encoding settings are at the bottom of the Internet Explorer Setting page, but are not visible in Figure 5-8. If encoding is set to automatic, it will automatically change the language settings for a web page so that you can view the page in the correct language. Move the selection slider to On or Off for automatic encoding. Another related setting is for a left-to-right versus right-to-left document.

We will look at a more comprehensive list of browser settings that affect both Windows 8 IE 10 and Desktop IE 10 after we tour Desktop IE 10.

Navigating with Desktop IE 10

Desktop IE 10, shown back in Figure 5-5, opens in a window and looks much like its predecessor, with toolbars, tabs, menus, and buttons. We will take a few minutes to explore the Desktop IE 10 GUI.

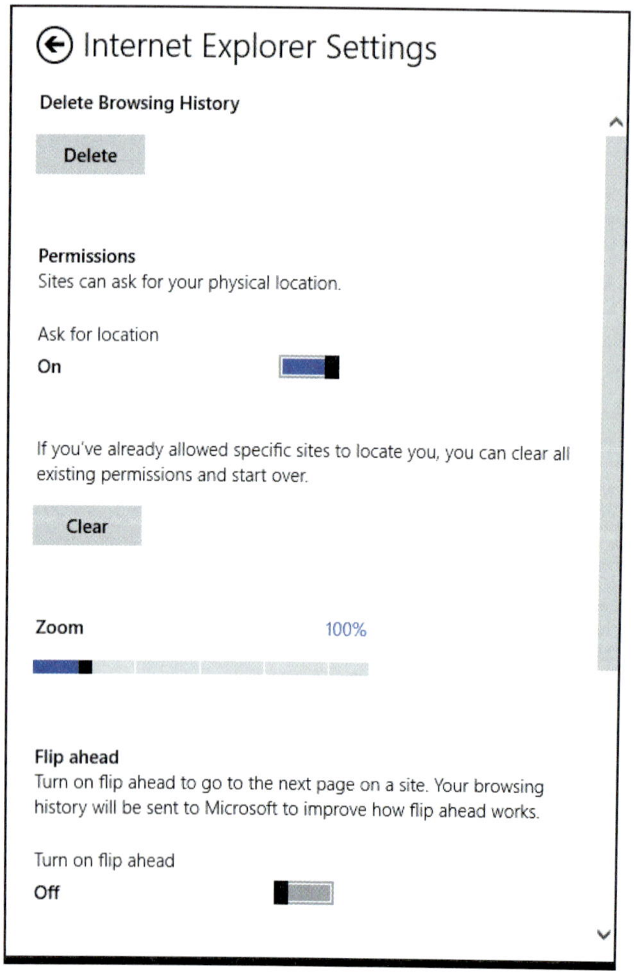

FIGURE 5-8 The Windows 8 Internet Explorer Settings page.

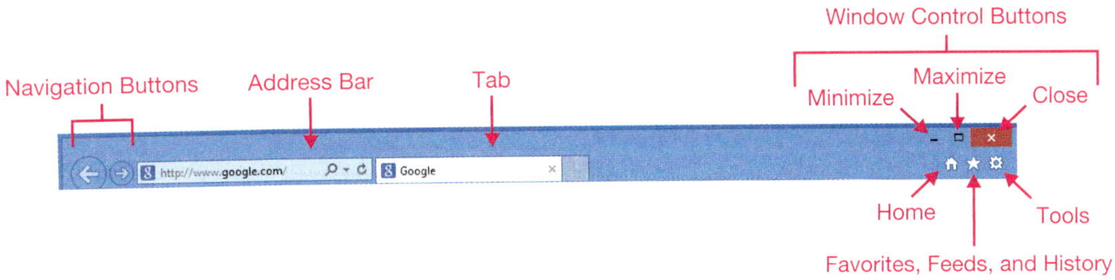

FIGURE 5-9 The Desktop IE button bar.

Exploring the Desktop IE 10 GUI The frame that makes up the Desktop IE 10 window can be as plain as in Figure 5-5, which shows the vertical (right side) and horizontal (bottom) scroll bars, which appear only when needed to view content beyond the window frame. It can also be a busy place, as we will see.

The bar along the top of the window was once the title bar, containing the name of the current web page and "Windows Internet Explorer," but version 9 introduced the clean "title-less" look that continues in Desktop IE 10. This bar contains the controls shown in Figure 5-9. They include (from left) the navigation buttons for previous and next web page, the address bar tab for a page containing an open web page (there can be multiple open tabs), window control buttons (Minimize, Maximize, and Close), the Home button, the star button (Favorites, Feeds, and History), and the Tools button. Considering that most, but not all of these controls are for navigation, this is Desktop IE 10's navigation bar.

The Home button (Alt+Home) returns focus of the current tab page to the Home page. Click or tap the yellow star-shaped button to open the menu shown in Figure 5-10.

When a website you want to return to is open in Desktop IE 10, click or tap the star-shaped button on the right of the bar (or press Alt+C) to open the **Favorites Center**, which includes tabs for Favorites, Feeds, and History.

If you would like to add the website to your Favorites list, click the Add to Favorites button in the Favorites Center. This will open the Add a Favorite dialog box, shown in Figure 5-11, where you can add the website directly into Favorites or create a folder within Favorites for saving several related links. The benefit of building a Favorites list is that you can click or tap the star and select the website, rather than browse to it.

Two other lists in the Favorites Center, Feeds and History, are similarly useful for keeping up with your favorite websites. History is, of course, the stored history of websites you have visited, but Feeds takes a little more explaining.

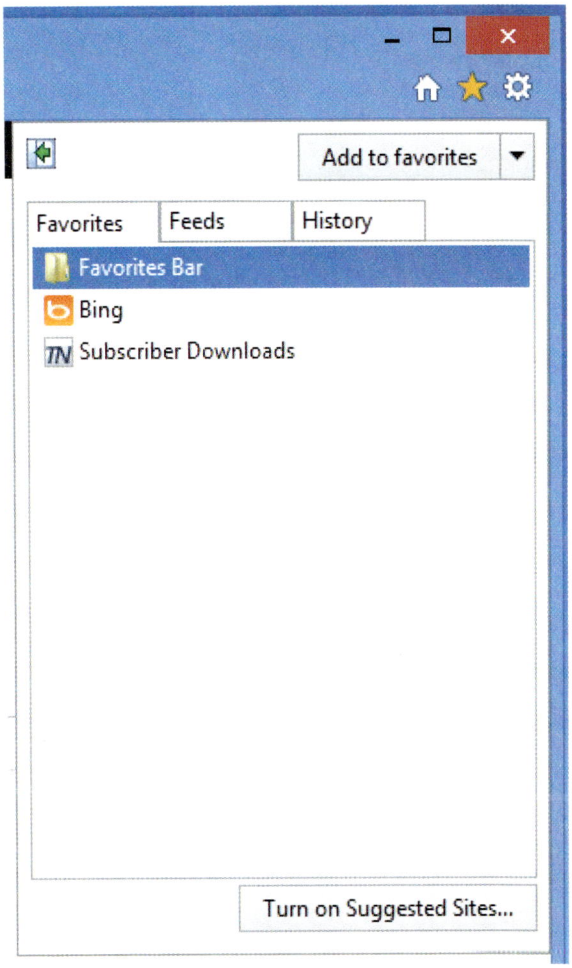

FIGURE 5-10 The Favorites list.

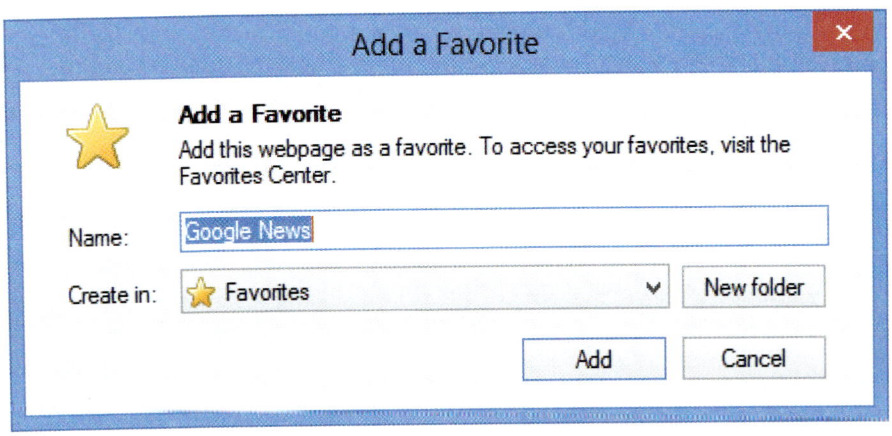

FIGURE 5-11 The Add a Favorite Dialog box.

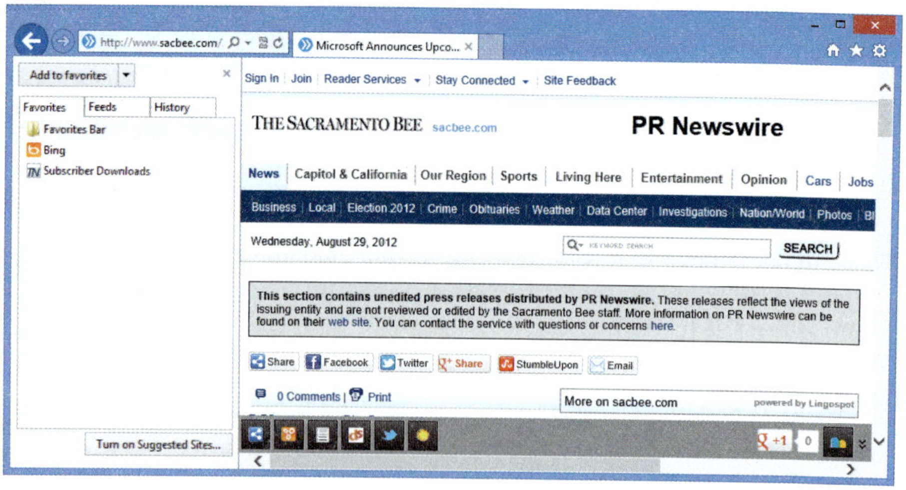

FIGURE 5-12 The Favorites, Feeds, and History lists in a pane on the left.

try this!

Add a Site to Favorites

It is easy to add a site to your Favorites list. Try This!

1. Click or tap the Internet Explorer icon on the task bar.
2. Browse web pages until you find one you would like to add to Favorites.
3. Click or tap the star-shaped button to open the Favorites Center, and then click or tap the Add To Favorites button to open the Add a Favorite dialog box.
4. In the dialog box, look at the name and change it if another name would be more helpful to you. Click or tap Add to add the website to the Favorites list.
5. Close out of IE and then open it again. Test your new favorite link by opening the Favorite Center and selecting the link you just added.

Feeds work through something called **RSS**, commonly thought to be an acronym for Really Simple Syndication or Rich Site Summary, but it is not necessarily an acronym. **Syndication**, in this case, means gathering content for publication to many destinations. This came about to solve a problem for people trying to stay up-to-date on specific topics. Many websites, such as news sites, update their content frequently—some even several times a day. You can go to the website frequently looking for changes, or subscribe to an email newsletter (not usually immediate enough), or you can take advantage of the RSS feature on these websites. Today's web browsers include a component called an RSS Reader, which displays the information from an RSS feed within the browser. When you turn on a feed for a certain topic on a website, you receive updates in real time. You can turn on an RSS feed at the website, by looking for the RSS symbol, shown at the top of this page in the left margin but it may be almost too small to recognize. Websites may show this symbol on a page or next to links to RSS feeds to which you can subscribe.

If you frequently rely on Favorites, Feeds, and/or History for navigation, click or tap the small green arrow in the upper left of the Favorites Center (see Figure 5-10) to open the Favorites pane on the left side of the window, as shown in Figure 5-12.

It's handy to use Favorites, and it may continue to be the place where you want to create a list of your favorite sites, because it can hold many more items than can Windows 8 Favorites. However, for those few most-frequently used web pages, use the Pinned Items list on the context menu for the Desktop IE 10 Taskbar button. Figure 5-13, shows two items pinned to the list. To pin a web page to the list, it must first appear in the Frequent list, which it will if it is frequently opened. After you locate the website in the list, right-click it to open its context menu, which includes choices to Open, Pin to This List, and Remove from This List. Select Pin to This List, and it will appear in the Pinned section of the menu.

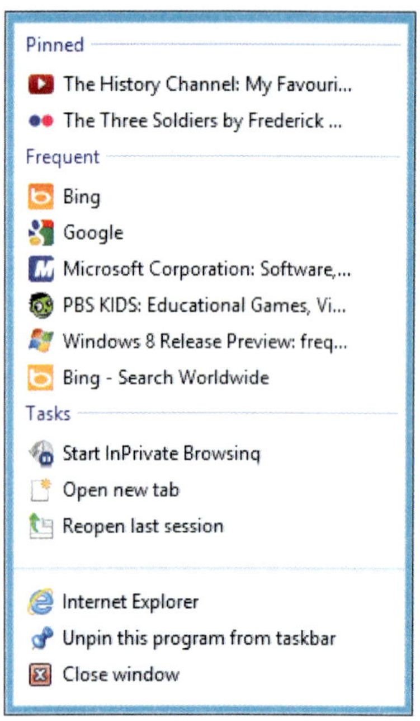

FIGURE 5-13 The context menu for the Desktop IE 10 Taskbar button.

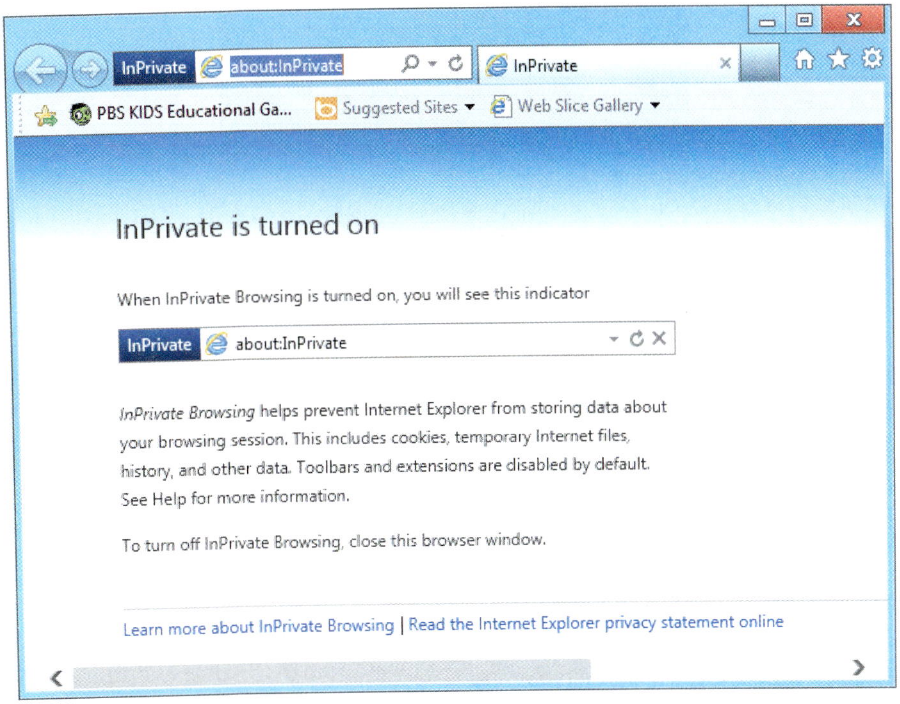

FIGURE 5-14 The InPrivate browsing page.

In Figure 5-13, notice the other choices on the context menu for the Desktop IE 10 Taskbar button. Even before you open IE, you can open this menu and select a web page from the Pinned or Frequent list. You can also start an InPrivate Browsing session, which opens the page shown in Figure 5-14. Additionally, you can open a new tab or reopen your last session from this menu.

When you are ready to print from Desktop IE 10, open the Tools menu (identified by the gear button on the Title bar) to access printers and other functions. Figure 5-15 shows the Tools menu with the Print submenu open.

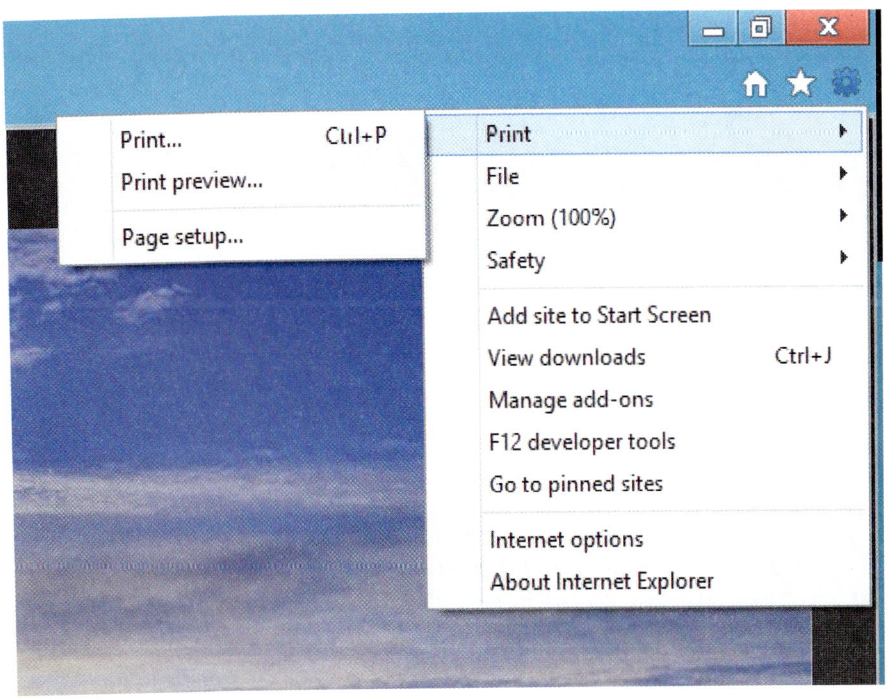

FIGURE 5-15 Desktop IE 10 prints via the Tools menu.

FIGURE 5-16 Start screen tiles: from left, a tile that will open a web page in Desktop IE 10, a tile that will open the same web page in Windows 8 IE 10, and the Windows 8 IE 10 Start tile.

try this!

Add a Site to the Start Screen

In Desktop IE 10, it is easy to add a tile for a website to the Start screen. Try This!

1. From the Desktop click or tap the Internet Explorer icon on the task bar.
2. Browse web pages until you find one you would like to add to the Start screen.
3. Click or tap the gear button on the Desktop IE 10 Navigation bar and select Add Site to Start Screen.
4. Close out of Desktop IE 10 and return to the Start screen.
5. Locate the new tile and tap or click to open the website in Desktop IE 10.

The option Add Site to Start Screen creates a Start Screen tile for the current website. When you select that tile from the Start screen, the website opens in Desktop IE 10. Figure 5-16 shows three tiles from the Start screen. They are (left-to-right) one for a web page pinned to Start through Desktop IE 10, one for the same web page pinned through Windows 8 IE 10, and a tile for Windows 8 IE 10. Practice creating Start Screen tiles for websites in the Try This!

LO 5.3 | Configuring Browser Security in Internet Options

So far you have seen where you can access a handful of settings while working in Windows 8 IE 10, and manage many settings in Desktop IE 10. You can go to another place for dozens of settings that affect both forms of the browser, called Internet Options, a Control Panel applet that opens on the desktop. The most important settings in Internet Options are security settings that you will find on the General, Security, Privacy, and Content tabs. We will explore the security settings on those tabs in this section.

Accessing Internet Options

Open Internet Options from the Tools menu in Desktop IE 10 or by opening Settings Search (Windows Key+W) and searching on Internet Options. Select Internet Options from the results and it will open on the desktop, as shown in Figure 5-17.

The General Tab

Internet Options is a multitab dialog box that looks much as it did in Windows 7, but there are some differences. First, they finally renamed it from Internet Properties to Internet Options—a logical and welcome change. We will focus on the Security and Privacy settings. Surprisingly, they are not all on the Security and Privacy tabs. The settings for Browsing History, which falls under both security and privacy, are on the General tab, as Figure 5-17 shows. Before you decide to have IE delete browsing history on exit, click the Delete button under Browsing History to open the

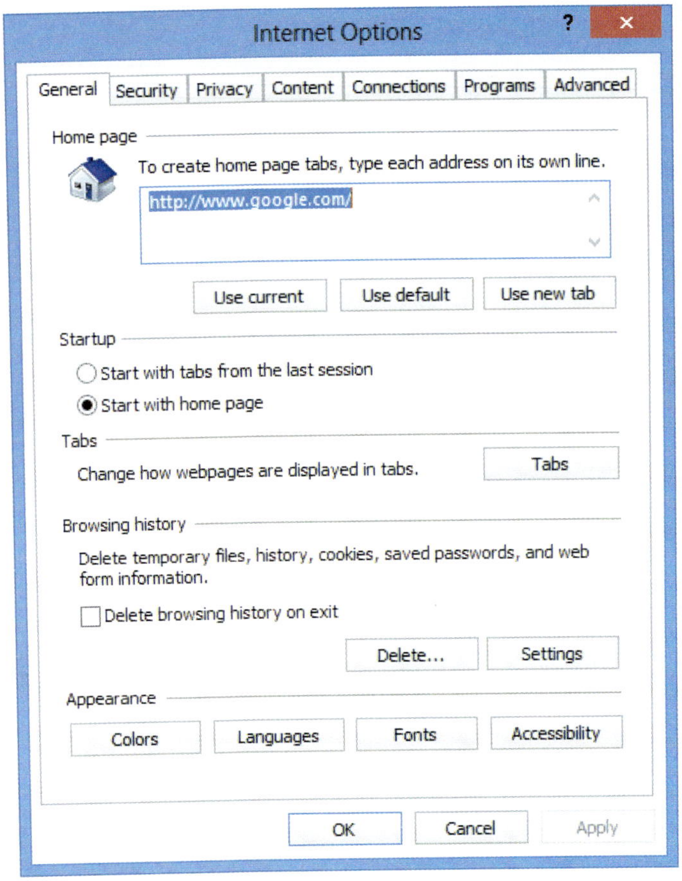

FIGURE 5-17 Internet Options General tab.

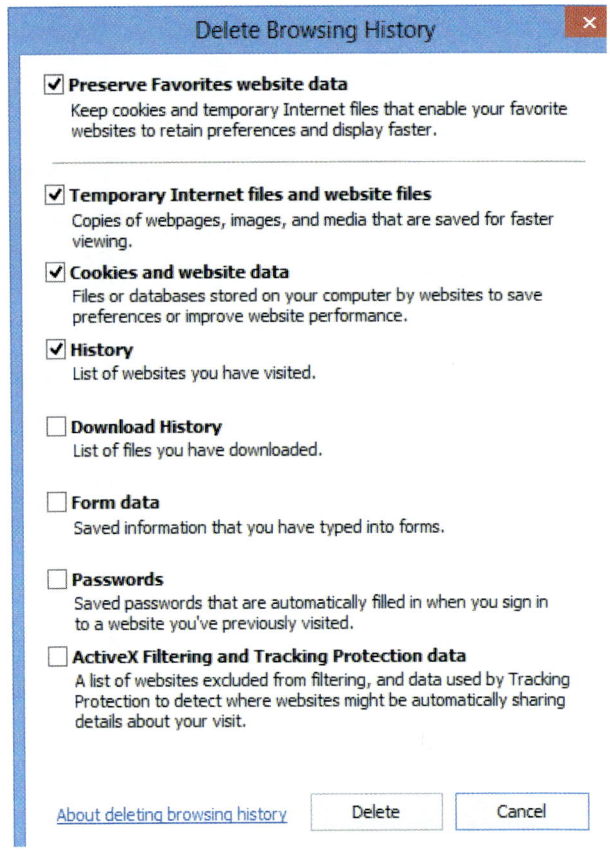

FIGURE 5-18 The Delete Browsing History box allows you to select many types of data for deletion.

dialog box in Figure 5-18. Here you will decide what type of data you want deleted. Notice that the data selected is most commonly used to track browsing habits, whereas the data not selected in Figure 5-18 is data most beneficial to you: download history, form data, passwords, and ActiveX Filtering and Tracking Protection data.

The Browsing History Settings button opens the Website Data Settings dialog box where you can control settings for website data. Normally, you should leave the defaults in place, because these settings do not directly affect security, but they determine how, where, and for how long these files are maintained.

The Security Tab

The Security tab (Figure 5-19) contains settings configured by zones. Many websites are notorious for attempting to install malware through your browser, so modern web browsers detect and block this type of behavior, and they can block sites known for attacking browsers. The Security page gives you options for how the browser handles known bad sites and when to warn you about suspicious behavior from a website. You can also provide domain names of trusted sites. IE has the notion of zones that it uses to assign security settings for selectively restricting activity from a website. A **zone** may be an area, such as the Internet or local intranet, or it may be a list of sites grouped together, as trusted sites or restricted sites.

FIGURE 5-19 Internet Options Security tab.

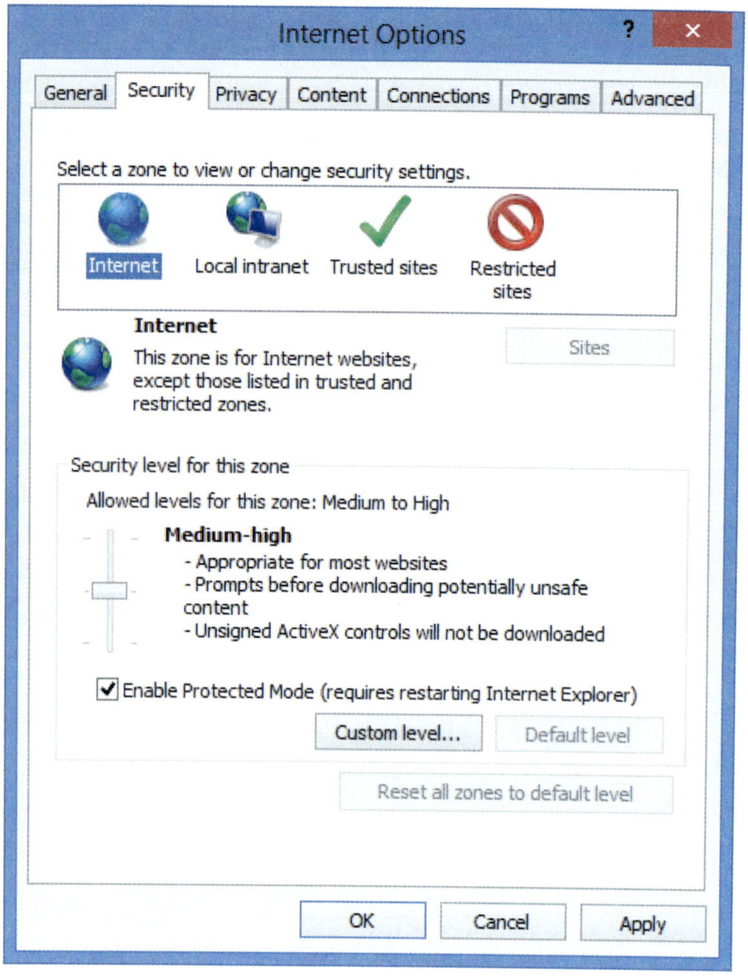

Protected mode is the feature that will alert you when a program is trying to run or install from the Internet. You can then choose to stop the program or, if you trust the source, let the program run.

try this!

View Custom Security Settings

Although we don't recommend that you get too ambitious about changing your Security settings beyond using the slider for Security level and ensuring that Protected Mode is turned on, it is wise to know where you can go to change settings for Protected Mode, should you need to. Try This!

1. Open Internet Options from the Tools menu in Desktop IE 10 or by opening Settings Search (Windows Key+W) and searching on Internet Options, and then selecting Internet Options.
2. Open the Security tab, and then click or tap the Custom Level button near the bottom of the dialog box.
3. In the Security Settings—Internet Zone dialog box, scroll through the long list of settings, noticing that by default some are enabled and some are disabled. Do not make any changes unless you are confident that you know the results. The default settings should be adequate.
4. If you make changes and want to remove them, click or tap the Cancel button. If you change your mind about settings after clicking OK, click or tap the Custom Settings button again, and click or tap the Reset button.
5. Use the OK or Cancel button to close out of the Security Settings—Internet Zone dialog box.

Figure 5-19 shows the Internet zone selected, and the settings below apply to it. These settings include the security level (modified by a vertical slider control) and the Enable Protected Mode settings. The Internet zone is set to the default of medium-high with Protected Mode enabled. There is more to Protected Mode than an on/off switch, and you can view the many settings applied in Protected Mode in the Try This!

On the Security tab, click or tap Local Intranet to see that the default security level for the local intranet is set to medium-low, because you normally trust computers on your local network. Select Trusted Sites anytime you want to add sites that you trust, and then configure the security level for the Trusted Sites. Do the same with Restricted Sites when you know of a particular site that you do not trust.

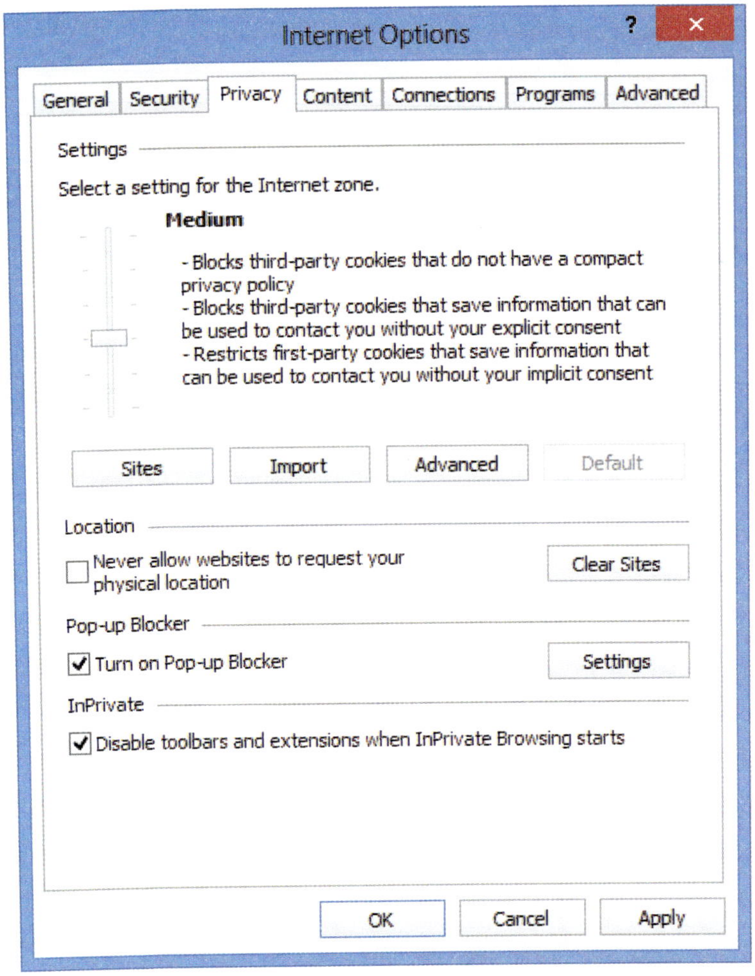

FIGURE 5-20 Internet Options Privacy tab.

The Privacy Tab

The Privacy tab, shown in Figure 5-20, has several important settings. The top Settings control blocking or allowing of third-party and first-party cookies in the Internet zone. This includes both a general setting, and the ability to set cookie handling by site. The example Privacy tab shown in Figure 5-20 shows the setting to keep websites from requesting your physical location turned off, but the Pop-up Blocker is turned on, and InPrivate browsing is set to disable toolbars and extensions. View and manage Pop-up Blocker settings in the Try This!

try this!

View and Manage Pop-up Blocker Settings

View and manage Pop-up Blocker settings on your computer. Try This!

1. Open Internet Options from the Tools menu in Desktop IE 10 or by opening Settings Search (Windows Key+W) and searching on Internet Options, and then selecting Internet Options.
2. Open the Privacy tab and then click or tap the Advanced button.
3. In the Pop-up Blocker Settings dialog box shown in Figure 5-21, notice that you can enter one or more sites and build a list of sites where IE 10 should allow pop-ups. Enter a website that you trust in the address bar and then click the Add button. Repeat this for any site where you want or need pop-ups to work.
4. At the bottom of the dialog box are settings for Notifications and blocking level. Notice that it will play a sound when a pop-up is blocked and that it will show a notification bar when that happens. Further, you can control the level of blocking. High will block all pop-ups, Medium will block most pop-ups, and Low will allow pop-ups from secure sites.

The Content Tab

The Internet Options Content tab shown in Figure 5-22 has four areas: Family Safety (formerly called Parental Controls), Certificates, AutoComplete, and Feeds and Web

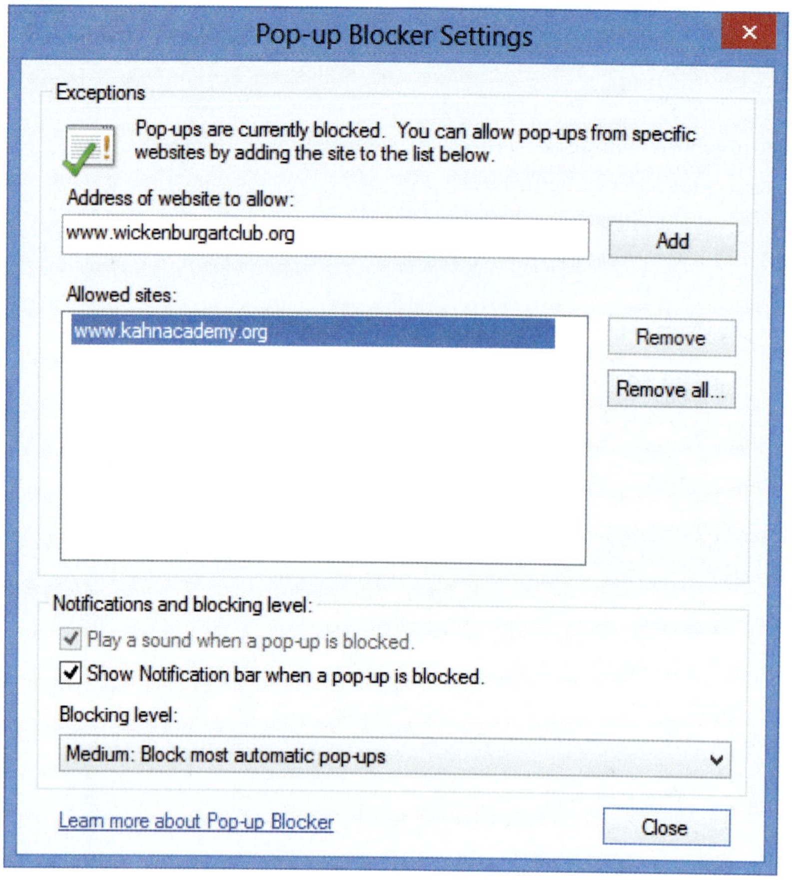

FIGURE 5-21 Pop-Up Blocker Settings.

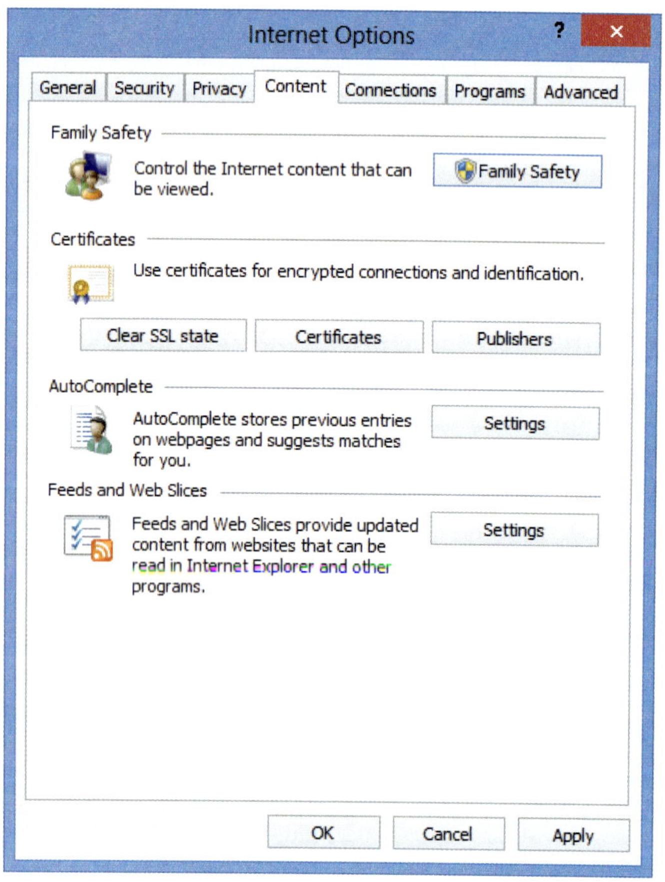

FIGURE 5-22 Internet Options Content tab.

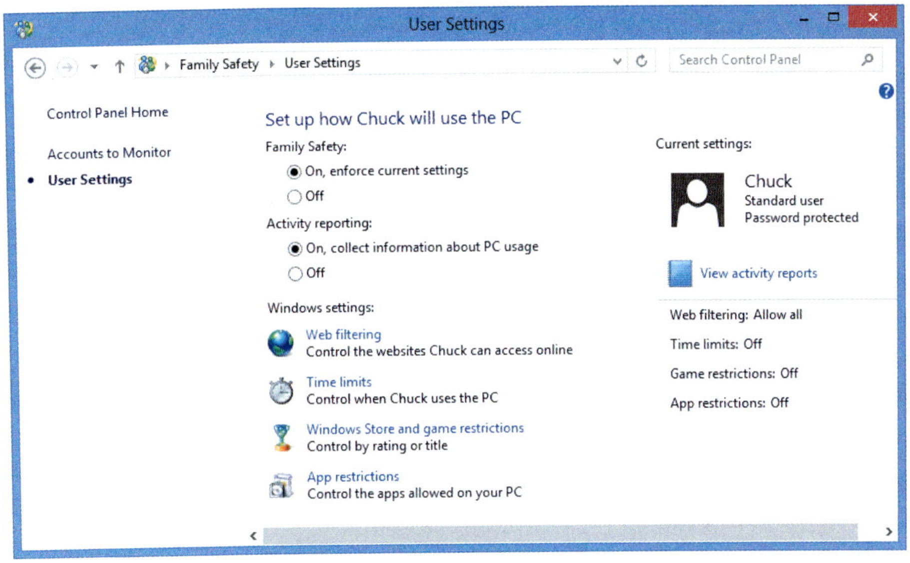

FIGURE 5-23 Configure restrictions and activity reporting on the User Settings page for a single user.

Slices. If you want to control the sites on individual visits, set time limits, and track the activities of a user, such as a minor child, click or tap Family Safety. This opens the Family Safety box with a list of users' accounts on the local computer. Click or tap the account you want to manage. This will open the User Settings box, shown in Figure 5-23, which shows Family Safety enabled. Here you can turn activity reporting on or off, configure web filtering to allow or block websites, set time limits on the person's usage, allow or block games and Windows Store apps, restrict usage to only certain apps, and view activity reports.

LO 5.4 | Using Email in Windows 8

The type of app that lets you manage your email is an **email client**, and Windows 8 comes with such an app, simply named Mail. In this section, learn how to create an account in Mail, add contacts in the People app, create email messages, add attachments to emails, and open an incoming email and attachment. You may have a different email app on your Windows 8 computer, but if it is a Windows 8 app, it will behave much like Mail, and interact with other Windows 8 apps in a similar fashion.

Like the Mail and People apps, the Calendar app works with all your accounts, tracking appointments it finds, such as those stored in any online social network accounts you add to the People app. You can also add appointments directly into Calendar.

Creating an Account in Windows 8 Mail

Before you can use an email client, you must have an **email account**, which is an account that represents you on a network and allows you to send, receive, and store email messages over the Internet or within an intranet. For instance, you may have an Internet mail account with Microsoft Hotmail or Google Gmail. Or you may have an account through your employer or school that is an Exchange account, which works within your employer's or school's intranet and, in most cases, is also available to use over the Internet. A newer service offered by Microsoft is Exchange Online, a part of the Microsoft Office 365 online services.

The People app manages all your accounts from different sources. By default, the Mail, People, and Calendar apps share data, including accounts, so you need to create an account only once to be able to use it in the other apps that share account data.

A contact is information for communicating with an individual person. Contacts may be stored and managed by a local app or may be stored and managed by an app on a server. If you have used an email client, like Microsoft Outlook, it allows you to access several types of email accounts. If you use it to access an Exchange email account, your contacts are saved both locally in Outlook and on the Exchange server in a location reserved for your data. A cloud-based email account, such as Google Gmail or Microsoft Hotmail, stores your messages as well as your contacts list. Many email clients will sync your contacts with these types of email accounts. The People app stores the information that other email clients store in a contacts folder, and it will synchronize your locally stored accounts with your cloud-based email accounts.

If you sign in to Windows 8 with a Microsoft account, you already have your first account in Mail, because the first time you sign in to Windows 8 with a Microsoft account Mail automatically adds that account. If you sign in to Windows 8 with a local user account, then the first time you open the Mail app, it will prompt you to create an account, which will be the first account in Mail. This account must be a Hotmail account. Step-by-Step 5.4 walks you through the steps for creating the second account. The scenario assumes that you have created a Hotmail account and have signed in to Windows 8 using that account. Now you want to add a second account. In our example, we will add a Google Gmail account.

Step-by-Step 5.4

Creating a New Account

This exercise will guide you through the steps for creating an account in Windows 8. This exercise works best on a Windows 8 computer on which you have signed in with a Microsoft account. You will need the address and password for another email account of one of the types supported by Windows 8 Mail (Hotmail, Gmail, or Exchange).

Step 1

From the Start screen open the Mail tile.

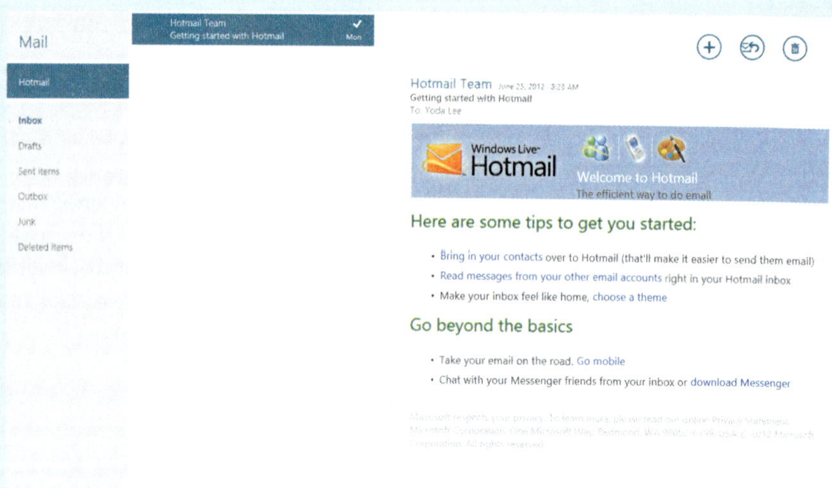

Step 2

On a keyboard, use the Windows key+I shortcut to open the Mail Settings bar. Using touch, open the Charms menu, and then select the Settings charm to open the Mail Settings bar. The settings bar will open on the right side of the screen.

Keyboard Shortcuts!
Windows key+I opens the Settings bar for the current app.

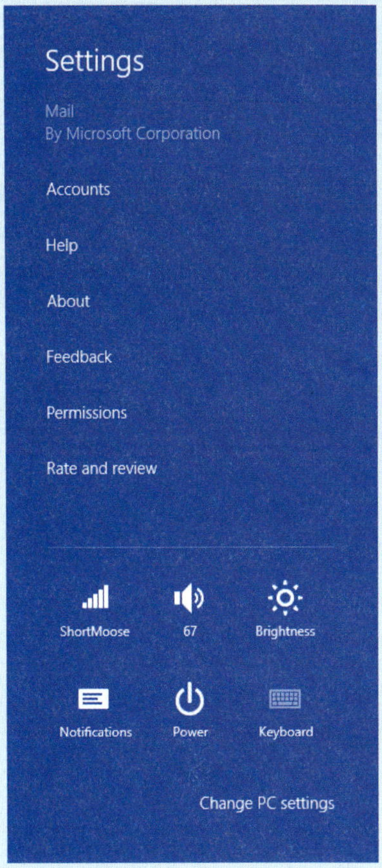

Step 3

In the Settings bar, click or tap Accounts to open the Accounts bar. In the Accounts bar, click or tap Add an Account.

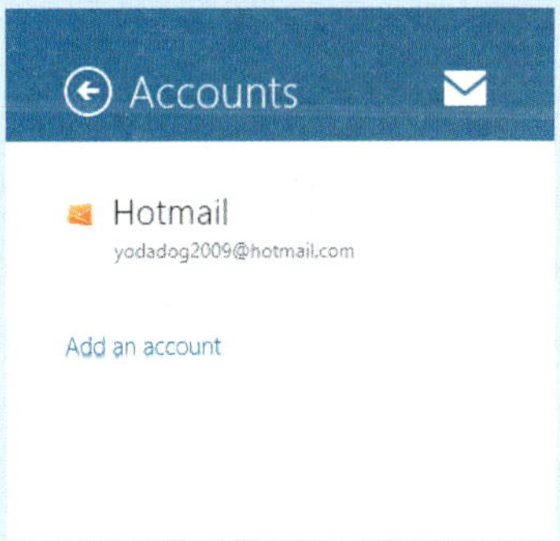

Step 4

Click or tap the account type from the list.

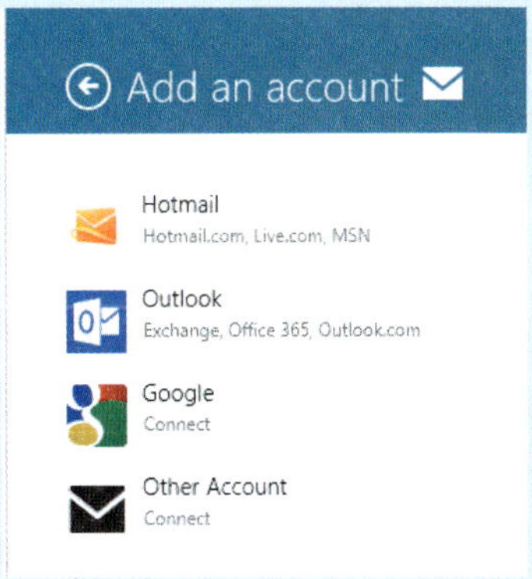

Step 5

Enter the email address and password for the account, and then click Connect.

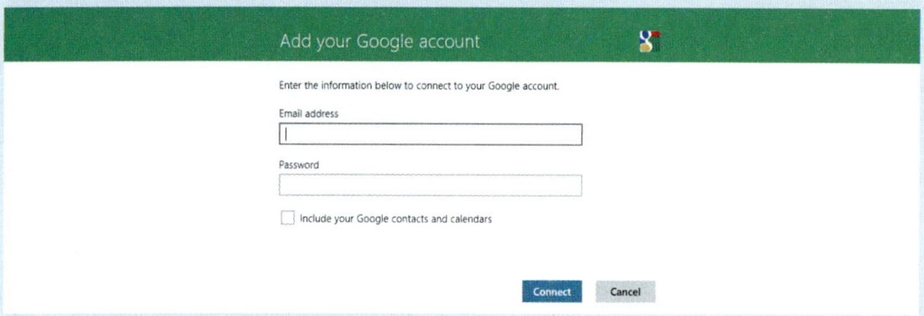

Step 6

Mail will connect to the mail service you selected, using the address and password you entered. If authentication is successful, the Mail page displays with the new account showing in the upper-left corner of the screen. In the example shown here, the Microsoft and Google accounts are installed, the Google account is selected, and therefore, the links below are for the Google account's folders. Any message you create while this account is selected will be sent using the Google account. Leave the Mail app open as you continue through this topic.

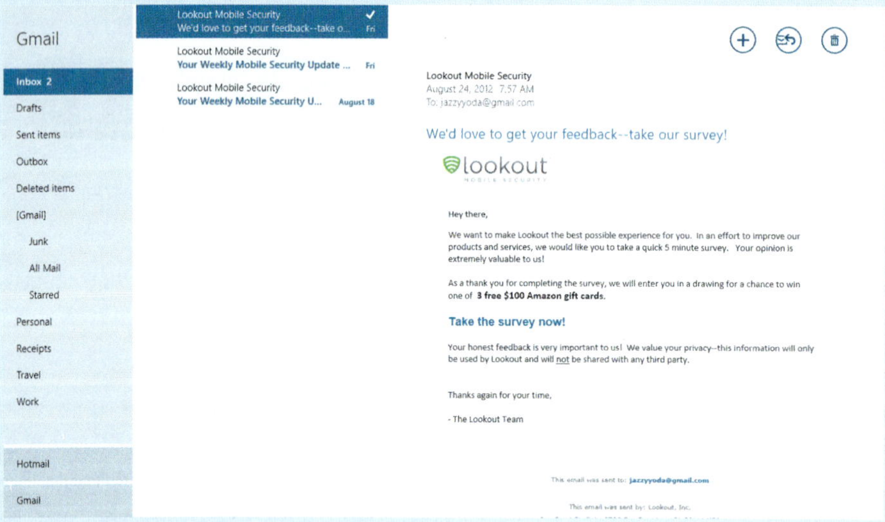

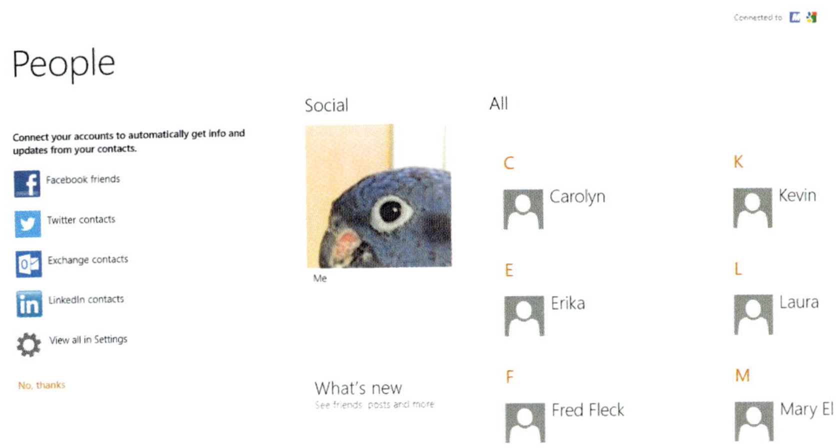

FIGURE 5-24 The People app contains contacts from all your accounts.

Adding Contacts to People

You won't find a contacts list in the Windows 8 Mail program. To add contacts, open the People app from the Start screen. The People app, shown in Figure 5-24, contains contacts from any account you have added to Mail, People, or Calendar. If you are using your Microsoft account or have already added other accounts, contacts contained in those accounts will appear in People. The icons in the top right of the People screen show that People is presently connected to a Microsoft Account and a Gmail account. The list on the left shows other account types you can add. You can add new accounts here or from the Settings bar for Mail, People, or Calendar. Therefore, click No Thanks at the bottom left to close the list so that you have more screen space for viewing your contacts. When you add contacts here, they will be added to your accounts.

While the Accounts list is open on the People screen, you can tap or click Add People to Your Contact List. If the Accounts list is not open in People, open the Apps bar, shown in Figure 5-25, and tap or click the New button (far right). This will open the New Contact form (Figure 5-26) where you can enter the information for a new contact. If you want to add more name information, such as middle name, nickname, title, or suffix, use the Name button to add boxes for this information into the form. Similarly, add boxes for other email types (Work, or other) with the Email button; add more phone numbers with the Phone button; add addresses with the Address button, and add other types of information with the Other Info button. When you are done, click or tap Save, and the new contact will be entered into the contact list. It will also update your associated online accounts. Practice adding contacts to People using the steps in the Try This!

try this!

Use People to Add Contacts to Accounts

It is easy to add contacts in the People App. Try This!

1. Open People from the Start menu.
2. Open the Apps bar and click or tap the New button.
3. In the New Contact form select the Account for this new contact.
4. Enter contact information into the labeled boxes.
5. When you have entered all contact information, click or tap Save, and the contact will appear in People.

FIGURE 5-25 The Apps bar for the People app.

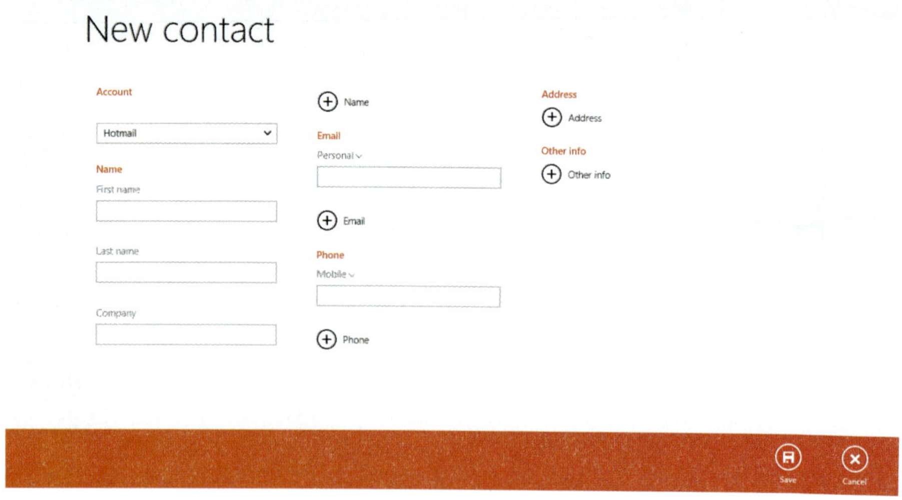

FIGURE 5–26 The New Contact page.

Creating and Sending Email

After you have created an email account, you can create and send messages. Step-by-Step 5.5 will walk you through the steps for creating an email in Mail and adding an attachment to it.

Step-by-Step 5.5

Creating and Sending an Email with an Attachment

Use Windows 8 Mail to create an email with an attachment.

Step 1

Open the Mail app, as you did in step 1 of Step-by-Step 5.4. In the Mail app, click or tap the plus button to open the form for creating a new email. Then open the Apps menu (right-click or swipe up from bottom).

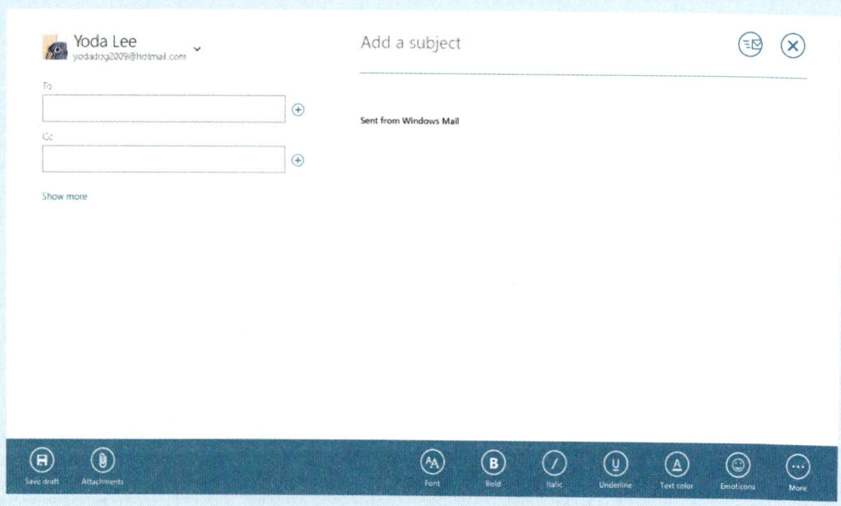

Step 2

We recommend that you add attachments and compose the message before adding an address in the To box in order to avoid accidently sending an incomplete message or one missing the attachment mentioned in the message. If you want to add an attachment, click or tap Attachments button on the left of the Apps bar. This will open a Files page where you can browse to the location of the attachment. As you find the files you want, click or tap each one; after selecting all files for a single message, then click or tap Attach.

Step 3

The attachments will appear as large thumbnails. Now click or tap Add a Subject and type the subject name (always a good idea). Then click or tap below the attachments and write your message. You can either keep or write over the line "Sent from Windows Mail."

Step 4

Open the Mail Apps bar again to use such features as paste, a variety of font choices and treatments, as well as a selection of emoticons for different occasions. We made the emoticons larger by selecting them and then using the Font button to make them a larger size. It works!

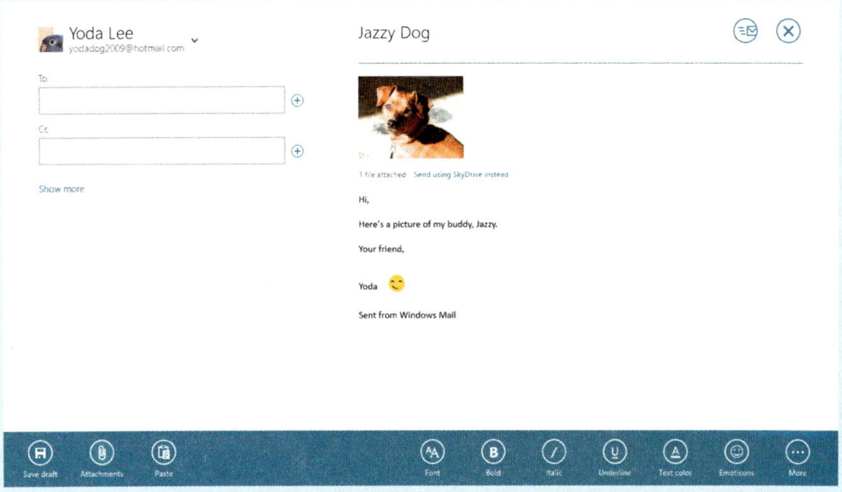

Step 5

Now you are ready to address your message. You can either type an address in the To box (upper left) or press the plus (+) button to the right of the To box to open the People app and select one or more addresses. Do the same to add addresses to the Cc box. If you want to send a blind carbon copy (BCC), hiding the addresses, select Show More to open the Bcc box, as well as the Priority box in which you can choose between Normal, High, and Low Priority. High Priority will be indicated on the recipient's end by a red symbol (usually an exclamation mark (!).

Step 6

When you are ready to send, click or tap the Send button in the upper right of the screen. The message will move to the Outbox until it completes the send; then it will appear in Sent Items.

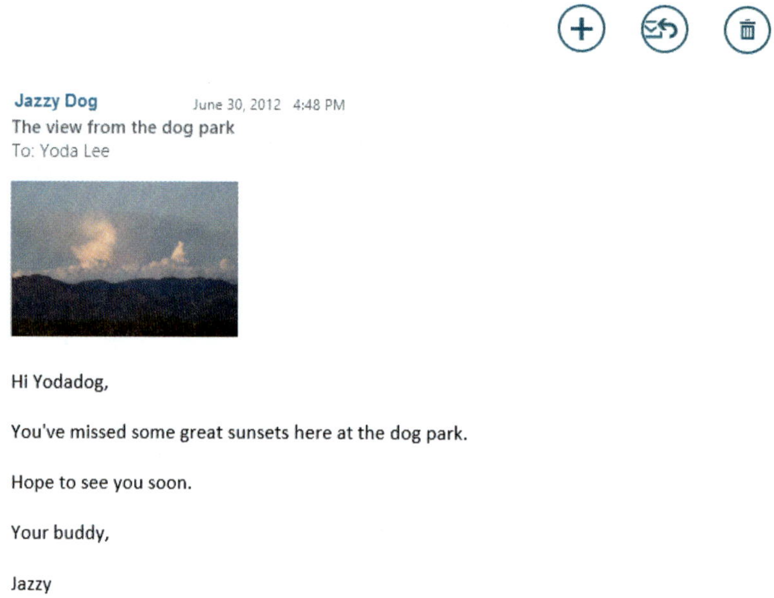

FIGURE 5-27 An open Mail message.

You can also receive and easily open email attachments in Windows 8 Mail. First, you will know that you have a new message if you look at the Mail tile in the Start screen. It displays the number of new messages. Open Mail, open the Inbox, and select a message. The contents will appear on the right of the screen. An attachment will show as a thumbnail of the contents. A document will look like a miniature version of the document, and a picture will display as shown in Figure 5-27. Double-click or double-tap the attachment thumbnail to open the file in the default program for that type of file on your computer. In our case, the Photos app is the default app for viewing a variety of graphic files, and the file opened full screen in Photos.

Chapter 5 REVIEW

Chapter Summary

After reading this chapter and completing the Step-by-Step tutorials and Try This! exercises, you should understand the following facts about using Windows 8 on a network:

Sharing Files and Printers in Windows 8

- Windows 8 allows you to share your local files and printers over a network and to connect to file and print shares on other computers.
- Windows 7 and Windows 8 computers can participate in a HomeGroup, an improved and easy way to share files and printers on small networks with a level of security that should be adequate for home use or in a small office environment.
- Local or network users with accounts in your local accounts database can access the Public folder on your computer, including all files and folders within it.

Web Browsing in Windows 8

- Windows 8 comes with Internet Explorer 10 (IE 10). IE 10 is a web browser, software designed for navigating and viewing sites on the World Wide Web.
- A link is an address or instructions that activate when you click certain words or screen objects on a website.

- Site navigation is the use of links and menus within a website to move to other web pages and websites.
- A web browser has an address bar where you can enter the text version of a website's address in the form of a uniform resource locator (URL).
- Common top-level domain names are com, org, edu, gov, and biz. A period separates a TLD from a second-level domain name, such as Microsoft.com.
- Hypertext Transfer Protocol (HTTP) is the core protocol used to transfer information over the World Wide Web. Hypertext Transfer Protocol over Secure Sockets Layer (HTTPS) is a secure version of HTTP that encrypts data before sending it.
- Hypertext Markup Language (HTML) is the original programming language for web pages.
- Plug-ins let you view and interact with web content that would not be otherwise available from your web browser.
- Windows 8 IE 10 is the full-screen Windows 8 version of IE 10. The IE Start Screen tile launches this app.
- Desktop IE 10 is the windowed version of IE 10. Launch it from its pinned icon on the desktop task bar.
- IE 10 includes many security features, such as SmartScreen, XXS Filtering, InPrivate Browsing, Tracking Protection, Do Not Track, Pop-up Blocker, Hang Detection and Recovery, and Enhanced Protected Mode.

Configuring Browser Security in Internet Options

- You can configure certain security and privacy settings from within Windows 8 IE 10 and Desktop IE 10, but the tool for configuring most security settings that affect both IE 10 GUIs is Internet Options.
- Security- and privacy-related settings are on four of the Internet Options tabs: General, Security, Privacy, and Content.
- Configure browser history settings on the General tab.
- The Security tab lets you configure the level of security based on zones, trusted sites, and restricted sites. This is also where you enable/disable and configure `Protect Mode`.
- The Privacy tab contains settings for cookies, Pop-up Blocker, and InPrivate Browsing.
- The Content tab contains Family Safety settings (formerly Parental Controls) and the Content Advisor.

Using Email in Windows 8

- Manage email in Windows 8 Mail. Manage contacts for email and other apps in Windows 8 People.
- Mail needs at least one email account, such as Microsoft Hotmail, Google Gmail, or an Exchange account. You may have multiple accounts.
- When you add an attachment to an outgoing message in the Mail app, it appears as a thumbnail at the top of the message.
- When you open an attachment you received in an email message, it opens full screen in the default Windows 8 app for that file type.

Key Terms List

address bar (145)
cloud computing (138)
Cross-Site Scripting (XSS) (147)
decryption (145)
Desktop IE 10 (146)
Do Not Track (DNT) (148)
email account (163)
email client (163)
encryption (145)
Enhanced Protected Mode (148)
Favorites Center (155)
Flip Ahead (154)
Hang Detection and Recovery (148)
HomeGroups (138)
Hypertext Markup Language (HTML) (145)
Hypertext Transfer Protocol (HTTP) (145)
Hypertext Transfer Protocol over Secure Sockets Layer (HTTPS) (145)
InPrivate Browsing (147)
Internet (138)
Internet Explorer (IE) (144)
Internet Explorer 10 (IE 10) (144)
intranet (138)
link (144)
navigation bar (148)
navigation tiles (149)
plug-ins (145)
protocol (145)
RSS (156)
share (138)
site navigation (144)
Syndication (156)
Tab Switcher (151)
Tracking Protection (148)
uniform resource locator (URL) (145)
web browser (144)
Windows 8 IE 10 (146)
World Wide Web (144)
XSS Filtering (147)
zone (159)

Key Terms Quiz

Use the Key Terms list to complete the sentences that follow. Not all terms will be used.

1. In a departure from other browsers, the Windows 8 IE 10 ____________ is at the bottom of the screen.
2. Using the ____________ feature, new in Windows 8 IE 10, the browser detects when a web page is part of a multipage document, allowing the user to page forward and backward through the document by swiping to the right or left.
3. ____________ converts data into a code that requires a secret key or password before converting it back.
4. A/an ____________ gives the complete address to the website and web page, including the protocol.
5. Java, QuickTime, and Adobe Flash Player are all examples of ____________.
6. ____________ are an easy way to share files and printers on small networks with a level of security that should be adequate for home use or in a small office environment.
7. When shopping on the web, the ____________ should be in use for the page in which you enter your payment information.
8. ____________ are folders and printers available to other users on a network.
9. In Windows 8 IE 10, swipe from top or bottom or right-click to open the ____________, an area at the top of the screen displaying tiles for the last 10 open tabs.
10. ____________ isolates the content within each open IE tab so that malicious code from a web page cannot access information in the other open tabs.

Multiple-Choice Quiz

1. To join a HomeGroup using Windows 7 or Windows 8, you merely enter this once, and then you can access HomeGroup resources without logging in again.
   a. username
   b. HomeGroup name
   c. PIN code
   d. HomeGroup password
   e. share name
2. What is the maximum number of HomeGroups a Windows 8 computer can join?
   a. 1
   b. 2
   c. 16
   d. 32
   c. 256
3. What acronym is used for the complete text-based address to a website?
   a. XSS
   b. DNT
   c. HTML
   d. HTTP
   e. URL
4. What Internet Security feature checks all input to the browser from websites to ensure that it does not contain malware in the form of scripts in incoming browser data?
   a. InPrivate Browsing
   b. XXS Filtering
   c. Pop-up Blocker
   d. Tracking Protection
   e. Enhanced Protected Mode
5. When needed or called up, the Windows 8 IE 10 navigation bar appears in this location on the screen.
   a. top
   b. bottom
   c. left
   d. right
   e. center
6. Right-click in a blank space in Windows 8 IE 10, or swipe from the top or bottom to open this bar at the top of the Windows 8 IE 10 screen.
   a. navigation tiles
   b. Tab Switcher
   c. Charms
   d. links
   e. ribbon

7. Use this Internet Explorer 10 security feature in either GUI when you do not want the browser to save information gathered during your browsing session.
   a. InPrivate Browsing
   b. XXS Filtering
   c. Pop-up Blocker
   d. Tracking Protection
   e. Enhanced Protected Mode
8. This desktop Control Panel applet is where you can make dozens of settings that affect both Windows 8 IE 10 and Desktop IE 10.
   a. Tab Switcher
   b. InPrivate Browsing
   c. All Apps
   d. Charms
   e. Internet Options
9. Before you can use an email client, you must have one of these.
   a. local user account
   b. email account
   c. Microsoft account
   d. Administrator account
   e. People
10. There is no contact list in Windows Mail, so where can you save contact information for use in Mail?
   a. Share charm
   b. Address bar
   c. Search charm
   d. People app
   e. Settings charm

Essay Quiz

1. Describe a difference between sharing data using HomeGroups and sharing data using the Public folder shared to local accounts.
2. Describe the difference between HTTP and HTTPS and explain when and where you should watch for HTTPS.
3. Explain the difference between mail accounts and contacts.

Lab Projects

LAB PROJECT 5.1

Practice copying files between HomeGroup computers.

For this Lab Project, you will need the following:

- A computer with Windows 8 connected to a network with other Windows 8 computers.
- A lab partner at one of the other computers.

1. Make sure that both Windows 8 computers are in the same HomeGroup. Because HomeGroups do not have names, the best way to do this is to confirm that both have the same password. To do that, open PC Settings and select HomeGroup. The password is near the bottom of the page. If they are not in the same HomeGroup, one should leave the HomeGroup, using the Leave button on the HomeGroup page, and then enter the password of the other computer's HomeGroup. Keep PC Settings open.
2. Make sure that both computers are sharing at least one public folder, even if you must enable sharing for the folder in the HomeGroup page.
3. On both computers, place a number of files in the shared folder. Then, each partner should open File Explorer and browse to the HomeGroup, locate the other computer and the shared folder, and copy the files from the other computer to their own. You can copy them to any folder you want on your local computer.

LAB PROJECT 5.2

Open Desktop IE 10 and browse to several news sites (or other sites that interest you) and scroll down, looking for an RSS feed symbol. In most cases, the RSS symbol will have a link to a list of feeds. Select one, open the Favorites Center (Star button), and click Subscribe to This Feed. When the Subscribe to This Feed dialog box opens, click Subscribe. Do this for several news feeds. Then go back from time to time and open the Favorites Center and select one of the listed news feeds. Notice that the current activity for the selected feed displays in the Desktop IE 10 window.

LAB PROJECT 5.3

Add an additional email account to your Windows 8 Mail app, and if you have contacts stored in that email account, verify that they are added to your contacts in the People app.

chapter 6

Music, Video, and Pictures in Windows 8

"Creativity is contagious, pass it on."

—Albert Einstein

The days of having to find storage space for your disc-based music, video, and photo collections are numbered, as more people collect music on their computers and personal players and as music, video, and photos are stored and shared in the cloud. An estimated 3.4 billion movies were streamed over the Internet in 2012 alone. In developing Windows 8, Microsoft made decisions reflecting the current trends that allow apps to share content from many locations and to play content on many devices.

In this chapter we first survey digital media basics and then look at several options for managing and playing media in Windows 8, beginning with an overview of Windows Media Center, a full-featured program. However, you don't have to buy an add-on like Windows Media Center for most of your need because programs bundled with Windows 8 provide most, if not all, of the tools you need for your media collections. We explore these apps, including the Windows Media Player desktop app and three individual Windows 8 apps for working with your media: the Music, Video, and Photos apps.

Learning Outcomes

In this chapter, you will learn how to:

- LO **6.1** Identify the media file types supported by Microsoft Windows.
- LO **6.2** Explain the features of Windows Media Center and how to add it to your Windows 8 computer.
- LO **6.3** Play and manage music in Windows 8.
- LO **6.4** View and manage videos and photos in Windows 8.

LO 6.1 | Digital Media Basics

Music, video, and graphic images/photos (in their digital forms, of course) are all **digital media** (most often simply called "media," which has several other definitions, such as storage media, transmission media, and broadcast media). **Multimedia** is a broader term usually used to describe a presentation that combines two or more forms of content, such as text, audio, photos, animation, and video. Multimedia also includes forms that allow interaction, as often used in online learning.

Digital Media Files

There are many standards for digital media files, and associated file name extensions for each type. Chances are you may never need to be concerned with what type of file you are using. You will generally become aware of a file type only when you attempt to play a file that is incompatible with your software. Tables 6-1, 6-2, and 6-3 list digital media file types supported by Microsoft, grouped by music, video, and graphic/photo. Some file types have more than one file name extension, depending on the version of the standard and features it supports.

When you take a photo with a digital camera, and if your camera saves the file in a TIFF or JPG format, it first processes that data from the image. Professional photographers often prefer to save their digital images in a format called **RAW**, which saves all the unprocessed data recorded by the camera for an image, allowing the photographer to then use specialized software, such as Adobe Photoshop, to process the image. If you save your digital photos from your camera in RAW format, you will not be able to view them in the software described in this chapter.

Why Buy Media Software?

Media software is included with Windows 8, so for most purposes you will not need to purchase media software. But something is missing that was previously included. Using the free **Windows Media Player (WMP)** in Windows 7, you could play music CDs and DVD movies, create slide shows of your digital photos, and stream all types of media to other devices on your network or from

TABLE 6-1 Music File Types Supported by Microsoft

Music File Type	File Name Extension
Audio CD format	.cda
Windows Media Audio (WMA)	.asx, .wm, .wma, .wmx
Waveform Audio (WAV)	.wav
MPEG 1 Audio Layer-3 (MP3)	.mp3, .m3u

TABLE 6-2 Video File Types Supported by Microsoft

Video File Type	File Name Extension
Windows Media Video (WMV)	.wmv
Windows Media	.wm, .asf
Windows Video	.avi
Microsoft Recorded TV Show	.dvr-ms
Movie	.mpeg, .mpg, .mpe, .m1v, .mp2, .mpv2

TABLE 6-3 Graphic/Photo File Types Supported by Microsoft

Photo File Type	File Name Extension
Joint Photographic Experts Group (JPG)	.jpg and .jpeg
Tagged Image File Format (TIFF)	.tif and .tiff
Graphics Interchange Format (GIF)	.gif
Bitmap (BMP)	.bmp
Windows Metafile (WMF)	.wmf
Portable Network Graphics (PNG)	.png

network locations to your computer. You could also organize and display your photos in Windows Media Player. This is still true today, with one exception: Windows Media Player in Windows 8 does not allow you to play DVD movies.

To play media of any type requires special software called a **codec**, which compresses or decompresses a digital media format for storing and playing the content. The program you use to play your digital media uses codecs, and many codecs exist for the variety of media formats. Although most of them are usable without any licensing fees, some, such as those required for viewing DVD movies, have licensing requirements. Microsoft was paying licensing fees for including the codecs in Windows 7 computers, while many users did not play DVD movies. This is due in part to the popularity of Internet sources for movies. Therefore, they removed just those codecs from WMP, which is a desktop app in Windows 8. The same is true of the built-in Windows 8 Video app. If you want to play DVD movies on your computer, you will need an additional program you can purchase and add to Windows 8. Therefore, you need to find a third-party source for the program, or purchase Windows Media Center from Microsoft.

LO 6.2 | Windows Media Center for Windows 8

In certain editions of Windows, such as Windows 7 Premium and Windows 7 Professional, Microsoft included **Windows Media Center (WMC)**. WMC is an app that manages and plays a variety of media on CDs and DVDs, and plays streaming content from the Internet and other sources, such as a TV tuner. It integrates with the **Xbox 360**, a specialized gaming and entertainment computer box, usually used with a **gaming controller** (an input device with joy sticks and buttons to control gaming actions). **Streaming** is the process of sending digital media data, such as a video or music, over a network and viewing it on the receiving computer or device before the entire content has finished transmitting.

Windows 7 with WMC runs on many home theater PCs (HTPCs). In addition to the previous features, WMC for Windows 8 includes the capability to play high-quality **Dolby Digital Plus**, the 8-channel standard in surround-sound digital audio that is included in the signals from many TV shows and used on Blu-ray and HD-DVD movies. However, WMC is not bundled with any edition of Windows 8. In this section, we describe how to add Windows Media Center to Windows 8 and we highlight some of the features.

Acquiring Windows Media Center for Windows 8

In addition to its ability to play movie DVDs, Windows Media Center is a more sophisticated home entertainment app than Windows Media Player. If you want WMC, you must purchase it as an add-on to Windows 8.

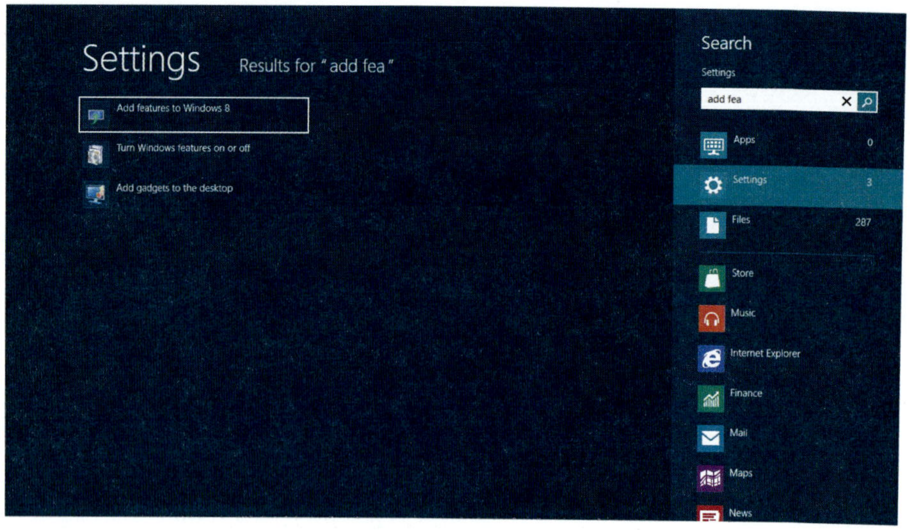

FIGURE 6-1 Begin typing "add features" in the Settings Search box on the right, and the list of results appears on the left.

try this!

Adding Windows Media Center to Windows 8

Use the Add Features applet in Windows 8 to add Windows Media Center. Try This!

1. From the Start screen, open the Charms bar and select Search, and then select Settings.
2. In the search box, begin typing *add features* until you see Add Features to Windows 8, as shown in the results list in Figure 6-1. Click or tap it to open it. If a User Account Control dialog box opens, click Yes or enter a password to continue.
3. Follow the instructions to provide a product key, or select the option to buy online when prompted.
4. Windows will install Windows Media Center and restart your computer.
5. When Windows restarts, look for the Windows Media Center tile on the Start screen, as shown here.

You can add WMC through the Add Features Control Panel applet available through Search Settings (see Figure 6-1). If you have the Windows 8 Pro edition you will add the Windows 8 Media Center Pack. If you have the Windows 8 edition you will need to add Windows 8 Pro Pack, which upgrades the OS to Windows 8 Pro and adds Media Center. In both cases, the result is Windows 8 Pro with Media Center. You can purchase a product key for WMC from Microsoft some time before downloading Windows Media Center, or you can purchase the product directly from Add Features. If you decide to add Windows Media Center to your Windows 8 computer, follow the instructions in the Try This!

After WMC is installed, click or tap the Windows Media Center Start screen tile to open it. The first time you run it, you will be greeted by the Welcome to Windows Media Center window. Press Continue, and it will guide you through your initial configuration. If you have a TV tuner in your computer, it will run the Live TV Setup to configure WMC to work with the tuner. When the configuration is complete, the Windows Media Center Start page will display.

As with much of Windows 8, there is more than meets the eye in Windows Media Center. If you hover your mouse over the titles (TV, Movies, and so forth) and move up without touching the upper edge of the window, an up arrow appears that lets you scroll through the media choices. For each media type there is a menu you can scroll through horizontally and click or tap to open. In the following sections, we will briefly review these choices, beginning with Tasks.

Windows Media Center Tasks

In addition to the various media menus in WMC, the one menu you should access as soon as you can from the Windows Media Center Start page is Tasks,

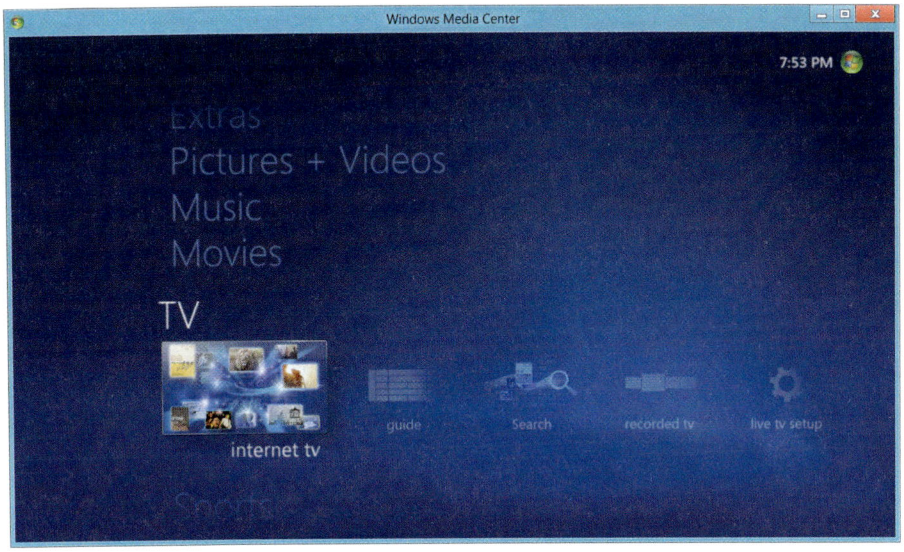

FIGURE 6-2 The Windows Media Center Start page focused on TV.

Internet TV, shown in Figure 6-2, was removed from Windows Media Center for Windows 8 at the time it was released in October 2012, but not available to us as we created these screenshots using WMC running on a preview version of Windows 8 before that date. Although Internet TV will no longer be in Windows Media Center, you can still download and watch Internet TV using Internet Explorer 10 or another Internet browser.

because Tasks gives you access to actions that affect changes to WMC across all features, and some affect Windows itself. To access Tasks, you need to scroll up or down through the list of media on the WMC Start page until you see Tasks, shown here.

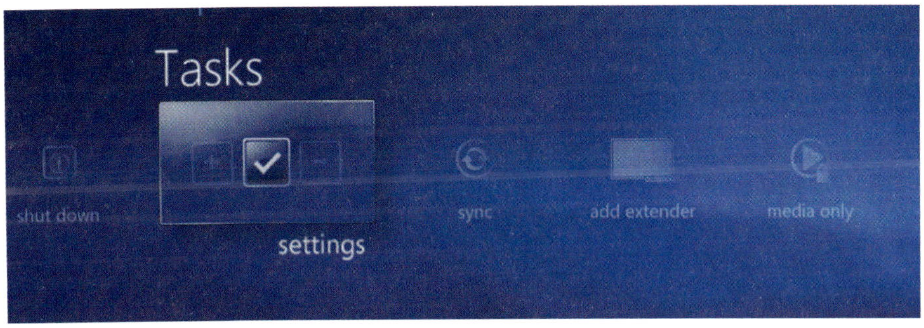

Shutdown

One option available in Tasks is Shutdown, which has a surprising number of options (shown here), including Close, which shuts down WMC, leaving Windows open; Log Off (the key button) signs off the currently logged in user and displays Lock Screen or Sign-in Screen. Shutdown (the center button) turns off the computer, Restart (the sunburst) closes all your programs and Windows and restarts Windows without a power down and power up cycle, and Sleep (the button on the far right) puts Windows in Sleep mode.

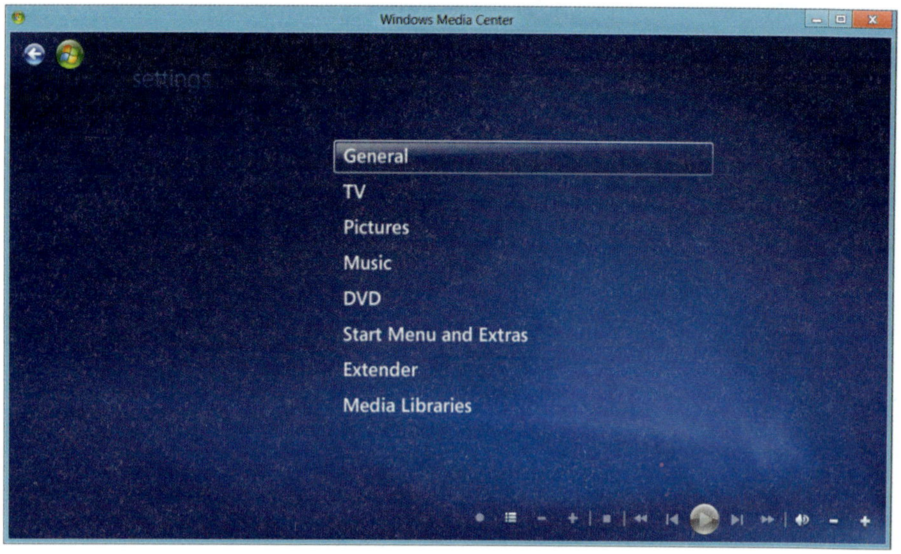

FIGURE 6-3 The Windows Media Center Settings menu.

Settings

As you work with WMC you will occasionally see messages to open Settings in Tasks. This is the go-to place for settings for each of the WMC components. Figure 6-3 shows the various categories of settings; you can also access settings within each media category by opening the context menu with a right-click.

General General Settings include the following:

- Startup and Windows Behavior
- Visual and Sound Effects
- Windows Media Center Setup
- Parental Controls
- Automatic Download Options
- Optimization
- About Windows Media Center
- Privacy

TV TV Settings include the following:

- Set Up TV Signal
- Configure Your TV or Monitor
- Language
- Audio
- Closed Captioning

Pictures Settings for Pictures include the following:

- Slide Shows
- Slide Show Screen Saver
- Favorite Pictures
- Ratings

Music Music Settings include the following:

- Favorite Music
- Ratings
- Visualizations
- Now Playing

DVD DVD Settings include the following:

- Language
- Audio
- Subtitle
- Remote Control Options

Start Menu and Extras Start Menu and Extras Settings include the following:

- Start Menu
- Extras Library Options
- Extras Library
- Clear List of Trusted Applications

Extender If you want to stream your media over a network to your TV, you need a **Windows Media Center Extender (WMX)**, which is either hardware or software. The software can be Windows Media Center running on another computer or device, whereas WMX hardware is a free-standing device connected to your network. Examples are set-top boxes available for purchase online and at consumer electronics stores, or the Xbox 360 game console.

Media Libraries You use the Media Libraries settings to set up your media libraries for the following type of content: Music, Pictures, Videos, Recorded TV, and Movies.

Sync

The Sync task lets you use Windows Media Center to Sync content to your portable devices. Connect a compatible device and select the Sync task.

Add Extender

The Add Extender button on the WMC Tasks page opens the Media Center Extender Setup, which will walk you through the steps to set up your Windows 8 computer to interact with a Media Center Extender, such as a compatible DVD player, TV, or Xbox 360, all of which must have Media Center Extender software built in.

Windows Media Center TV

The TV media menu has several choices, which we will look at next. The Internet TV option was removed in the version of Windows Media Center released with Windows 8, but not available to us when writing this chapter. We have removed all options that are obviously related to Internet TV, but this change may affect some of the screens shown in this section.

Search

From the WMC Start page, click or tap search to search for a movie or video title. You can choose search criteria, as shown along the left edge of the Search page in Figure 6-4. Clicking or tapping in the search box will open the onscreen keyboard.

Recorded TV

If you record TV shows using WMC, select Recorded TV, shown here, to open a list of shows.

Live TV Setup

If you add a TV tuner to your computer, open Live TV Setup, shown here, which will configure WMC to work with your TV tuner.

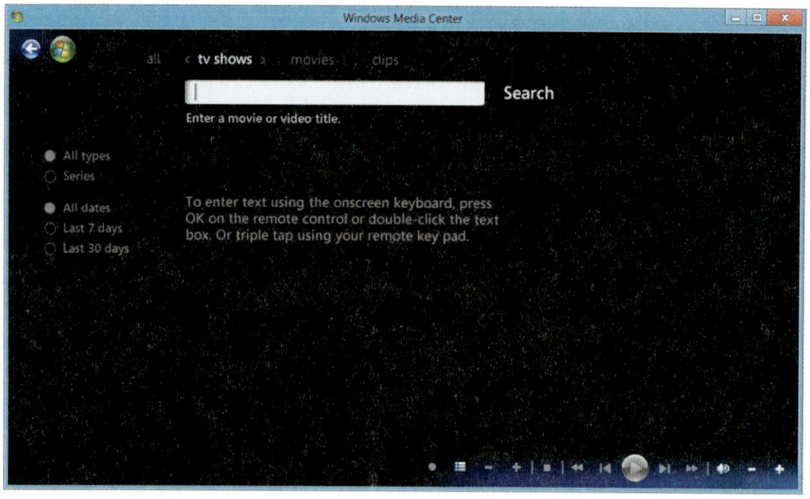

FIGURE 6-4 Search for a movie or video title.

Windows Media Center Movies

The Movies category, shown here, has several choices, including (at this time) Netflix, Movie Library, Search, and Play DVD. We look at these choices next.

Netflix

Netflix is a for-pay service. If you have a Netflix account, click or tap Netflix, log in, and select movies. If you do not have a Netflix account, you can use the Netflix choice to get a free one-month trial. To do that, you supply your e-mail address, a password you want to use with the Netflix service, and payment information (credit card or PayPal). Before the one-month trial period ends, you must decide whether to continue the service; unless you inform Netflix before the expiration of the free trial that you do not want to continue, they will charge your account with a monthly fee.

Windows Media Center is a windowed desktop app, but when you make it full screen, the window frame disappears!

Movie Library

Use the Movie Library option to select movies to play and to manage your Media Library for all types of media, including Music, Pictures, Videos, Recorded TV, and Movies.

Search

The Search option, shown here, opens a page similar to that shown above in Figure 6-4, except the title over the search box is "Movies" rather than "TV Shows." Enter a title to search your Media libraries.

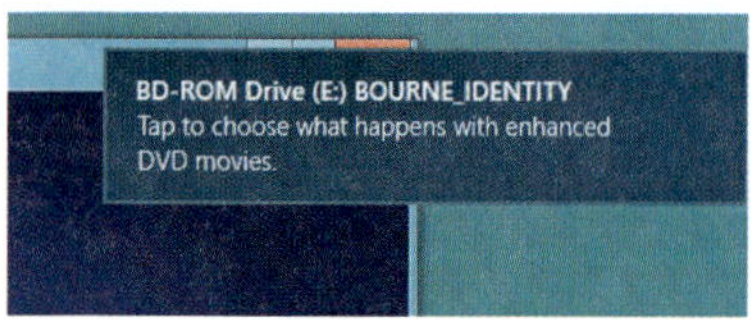

Play DVD

Play DVD will play your DVD or Blu-ray discs, supporting high-definition video and high-quality Dolby Digital Plus. When you first insert a DVD (or any type of storage), you will see a message similar to the one shown here.

Click or tap it and the message in Figure 6-5 displays. Almost anyone who has used Windows is familiar with this type of message. The choices will depend on the type of storage and the type of content. What should you do about this? The short answer is, if you are in a hurry and you simply want to watch the movie, select Play DVD Movie. However, if you would like to set defaults for AutoPlay, flip back to Chapter 3 and review the section titled "What to Do About AutoPlay." Figure 6-6 shows the AutoPlay Control Panel applet open to the settings for DVDs, Blu-ray discs, and CDs. You can set options so that certain actions take place for each type of storage and each type of media files contained on it.

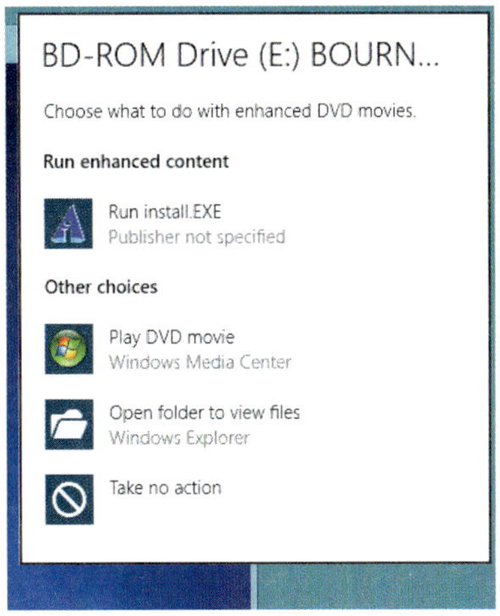

FIGURE 6-5 Select an available action (depending on the movie).

Windows Media Center Music

The Windows Media Center Music options, shown here, include Music Library, Play Favorites, Radio, and Search.

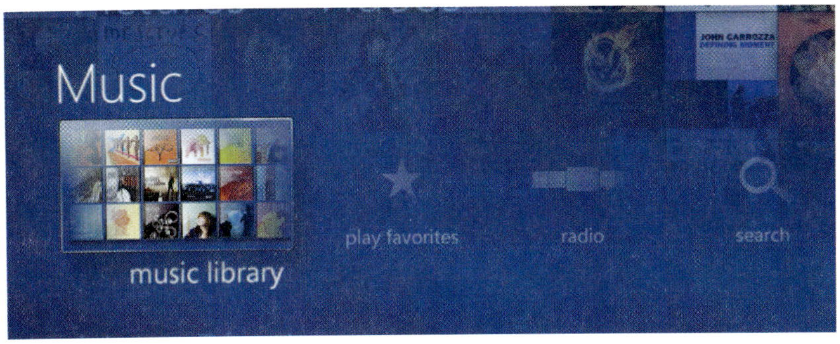

If the screen is locked on your Windows 8 computer or tablet while playing music in Windows Media Center, the music will continue to play and you can continue using the volume controls on your computer or tablet to adjust the volume without having to open the Lock screen and sign in. A small box displays on the Lock screen or Sign-In screen when you touch the volume control.

Music Library

Open the Music Library (Figure 6-7) to select songs to play and to manage your music collection. You can organize music by albums, artists, genres, songs, playlists, composers, years, and more. You can share your collection among your computers and other compatible devices.

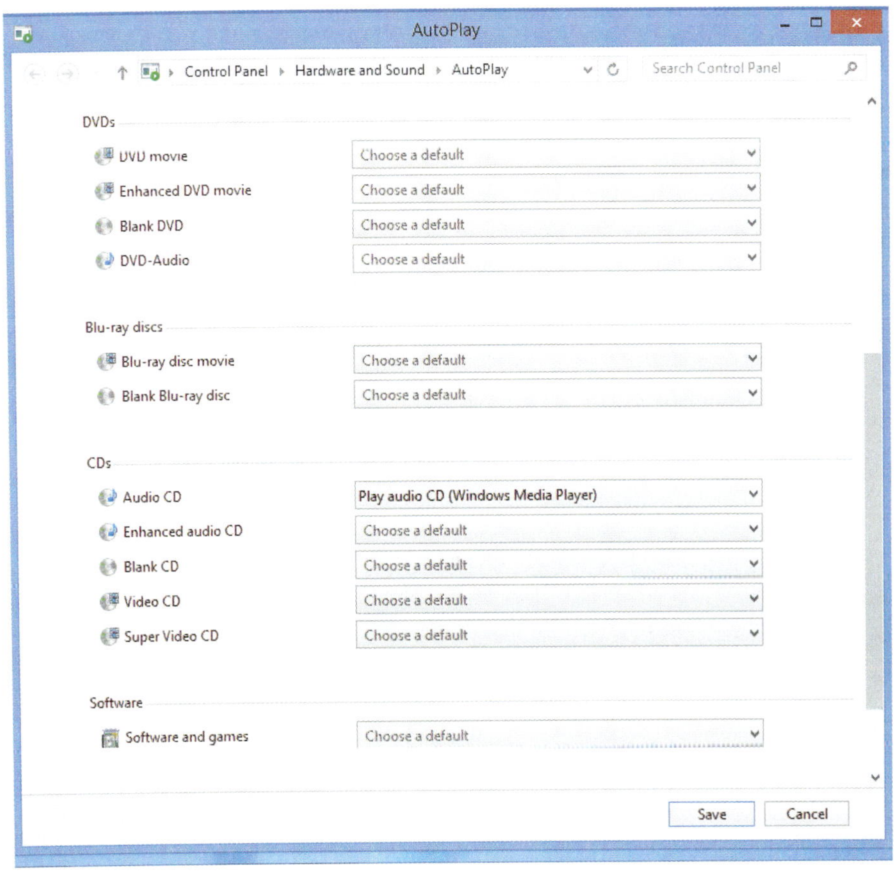

FIGURE 6-6 Select an action for each type of storage and each type of media file.

FIGURE 6-7 Windows Media Center Music Library.

Play Favorites

WMC Music Play Favorites (Figure 6-8) lets you select from a song list and set a playlist to shuffle or repeat. A **playlist** is a list of media files (music, video, or photos) you want to play or view together in one session. Two other options give you something interesting to watch while listening to your music: Visualize turns on computer-generated moving graphics, and Play Pictures plays a slide from your Pictures library, using many slide-show animation effects. The Buy Music option opens the Shop for Music page where you can browse for music from a variety of online stores. When you make a selection, a Choose Store box opens (if multiple stores offer that selection). Select the store, complete the transaction, and download the music into your Music Library.

> Right-clicking inside Windows Media Center will bring up a context menu of tasks.

Radio

The Music Radio option is available only if you have an installed radio tuner.

Search

The Music Search feature, shown in Figure 6-9, will search your music libraries.

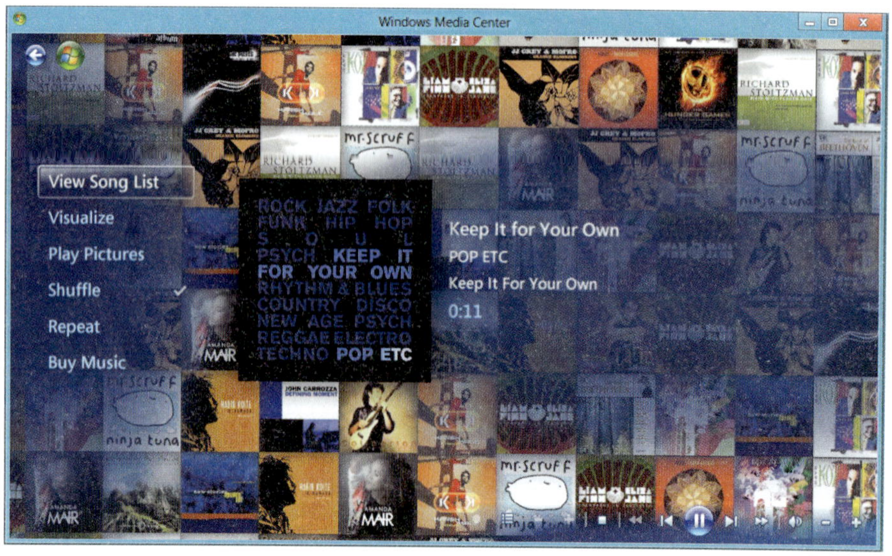

FIGURE 6-8 The Play Favorites page.

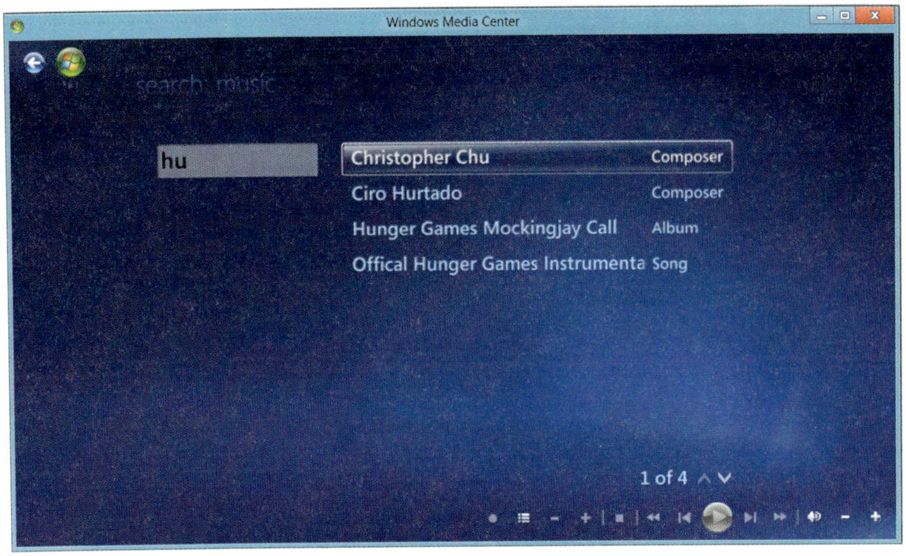

FIGURE 6-9 Search your Music Libraries.

Windows Media Center Pictures + Videos

WMC lets you manage and display your still photos and videos through Pictures + Videos options, shown here.

Picture Library

Use the WMC Pictures and Videos Picture Library to browse through your digital pictures and to create and play slide shows based on several criteria, including location (folders), tags, date taken, and ratings. You do need to add pictures before you can use some of the functions of the picture library.

Play Favorites

Open Play Favorites, and it will play a slide show of your favorite pictures. If you have not yet selected favorites, it will play recent slide shows. Right-click in Play Favorites (even with a slide show running), and the settings page for Favorite Pictures, shown in Figure 6-10, displays. You can add or remove pictures, add ratings, and browse your folders to find more pictures.

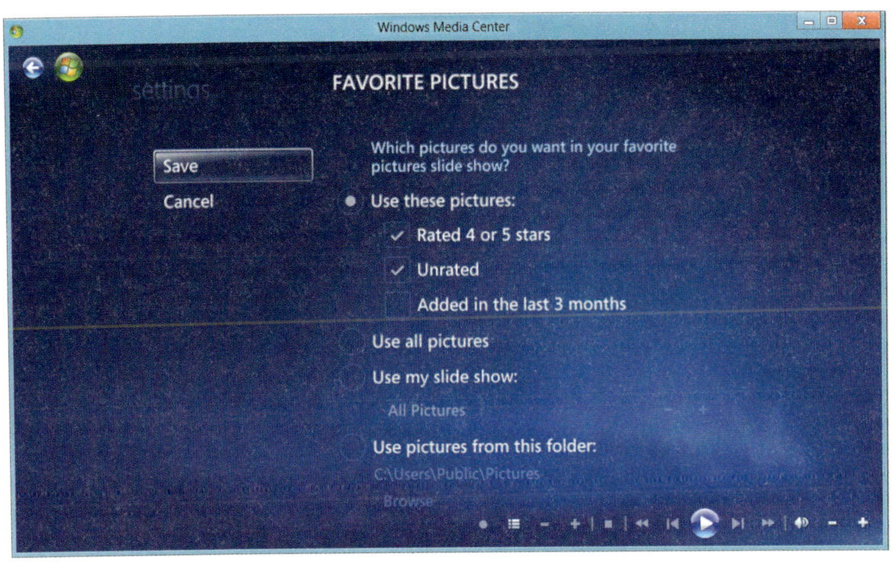

FIGURE 6-10 The Favorite Pictures settings page, where you can add or remove pictures, add ratings, and browse folders.

Video Library

When you open the Video Library, WMC will search for your videos. A pop-up box allows you to add videos.

Windows Media Center Sports

The WMC Sports menu, shown here, has three choices: Scores, Players, and Leagues. Open Scores, and it ties in with several services that provide up-to-date scores on major sporting events. Players opens a page where you can add players you want to track in both the real sports leagues and fantasy leagues. The Leagues menu choice opens a page where you can select a league, show current and future games, show scores, configure game alerts, and track fantasy players.

Windows Media Center Extras

Windows Center Extras are optional programs (often games) or Internet services by third parties (not Microsoft). The Windows Media Center Extras menu lets you manage how these extras are configured, add new extras, and add them to the WMC Start screen.

The Extras Library contains any extras you have configured. Because these are usually games or services that you pay for, the library will remain empty until you add extras to WMC. The Extras gallery contains links to a variety of games and services you can add to WMC as extras.

Windows Media Center and Xbox 360

Microsoft also includes Windows Media Center in the Xbox 360 game console, a powerful special-purpose computer (see Figure 6-11). The inclusion of Windows Media Center in the Xbox 360 means it is not just for playing games, but for all home entertainment, and it can therefore be a Windows Media Center Extender. If you have an Xbox 360 and Windows Media Center installed on your Windows 8 computer, WMC becomes an Xbox controller, allowing you to send your music, videos, and still photos through the console to your TV and other compatible media devices. Hence, the Xbox becomes the hub of your home entertainment system.

You can also download content using **Xbox LIVE**, a subscription service available as either a limited free service (**Xbox LIVE Free**) or as a for-pay service (**Xbox LIVE Gold**) that includes multiplayer games over the Internet. The Xbox 360 comes with lots of ports for multimedia output and networking (both Ethernet and Wi-Fi) as well as several USB ports and a game controller.

FIGURE 6–11 The Xbox 360 integrates with Windows 8.

Xbox SmartGlass and Xbox 360

Yet another media-playing option is **Xbox SmartGlass**, a free app that installs on a Windows 8 computing device and connects to your Xbox 360, which connects to your TV and other compatible devices via Wi-Fi or Ethernet. This requires that you log on to both your Windows 8 computer and the Xbox 360 console using the same Microsoft account. Then you can use your computer or tablet running Xbox SmartGlass as an interactive remote control to view movies, games, TV shows, and Internet content on your TV while viewing related content, such as maps or biographical information on characters in a movie, in Xbox SmartGlass on your computer or tablet.

In addition to running on Windows 8, Xbox SmartGlass comes in versions that run on two mobile operating systems: Google's Android and Apple's iOS.

LO 6.3 | Enjoying Music in Windows 8

You say you don't have an Xbox 360 console and do not plan to install Windows Media Center? That's okay. You can still use Windows 8 apps to play and manage your music, videos, and pictures on your computer. In this section we look at how to listen to your music, burn CDs, create playlists, and rip music from audio CDs to your computer. We will use two Windows 8 apps for working with music: Windows Media Player and Music.

Using Windows Media Player

As mentioned earlier in this chapter, Windows Media Player (WMP) is a Windows desktop app that you can use to play music CDs and stream all types of media to other devices on your network or from the Internet and other network locations to your computer. Use it to **rip** music from audio CDs, which means the music files are copied, and if necessary, converted to a different digital file format before being copied to a new storage location.

Using WMP you can select music files and then **burn** a CD, which means to copy music or other digital media to a CD in a media format that can be played on a CD player or computer. And, if you have a smartphone, tablet, or digital music player, you can synchronize your media files between your computer and that device, based on rules you define.

If the screen is locked on your Windows 8 computer or tablet while playing music in Windows Media Player, the music will continue to play, and you can use the volume controls on your computer or tablet to adjust the volume without having to open the Lock screen and sign in. A small box displays on the Lock screen or Sign-In screen when you touch the volume control.

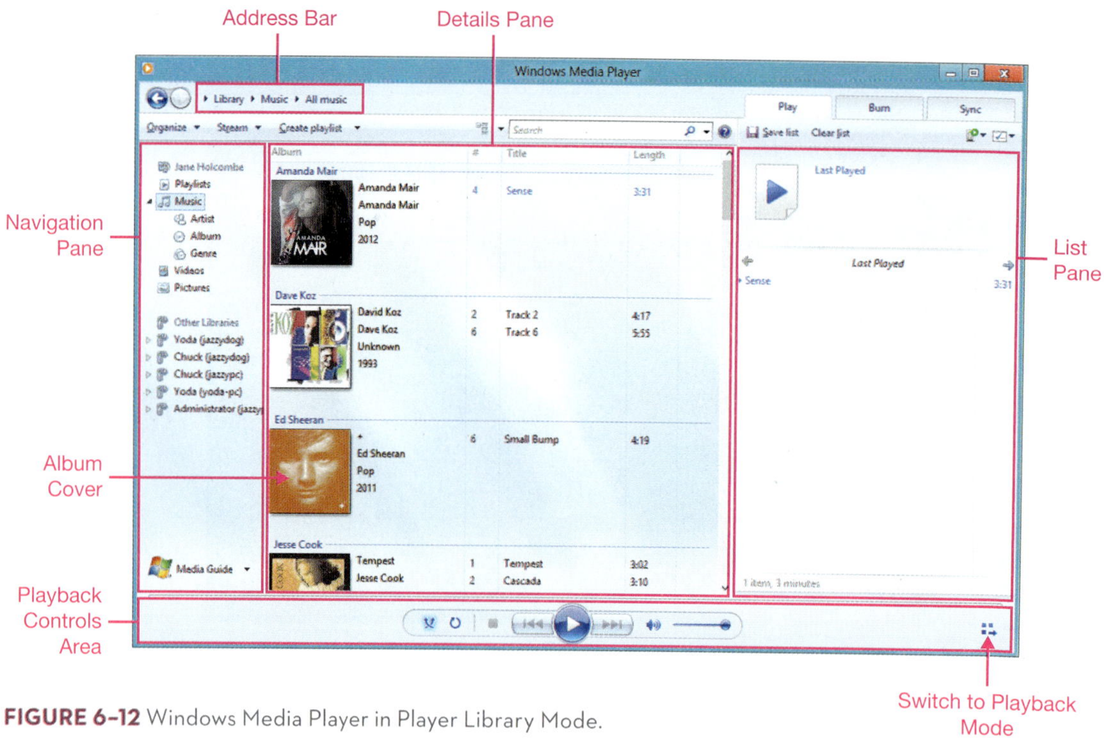

FIGURE 6-12 Windows Media Player in Player Library Mode.

WMP has two modes you can use while playing your music. The **Player Library Mode**, shown in Figure 6-12, gives you access to all the features for managing your media collections and selecting songs. From Library mode, click the Now Playing button on the bottom right to switch to **Now Playing Mode**, which closes the WMP desktop window and displays a tiny gadget-like window on the desktop that includes onscreen controls, as shown here.

Getting Started with Windows Media Player

Windows Media Player in Windows 8 is nearly identical to the version in Windows 7, so if you used that version, you will have no problem getting started. It is also pretty simple to use, in spite of having many features. Just remember that the new Windows Media Player cannot play DVD movies. Step-by-Step 6.1 walks you through starting and configuring Windows Media Player. Then you will add files to your Music Library, play a CD, and rip songs from a CD to your Music Library.

Step-by-Step 6.1

First Steps with Windows Media Player

Start Windows Media Player for the first time and add music files to your Music Library by copying them from other storage locations or by ripping them from a CD. You will need media files on some form of storage that you can access and/or a music CD to complete this exercise.

Step 1

Use the Search charm to search for media player in Apps, and click or tap Windows Media Player in the results list. The first time it opens, you will see the Welcome to Windows Media Player page. Select Custom Settings.

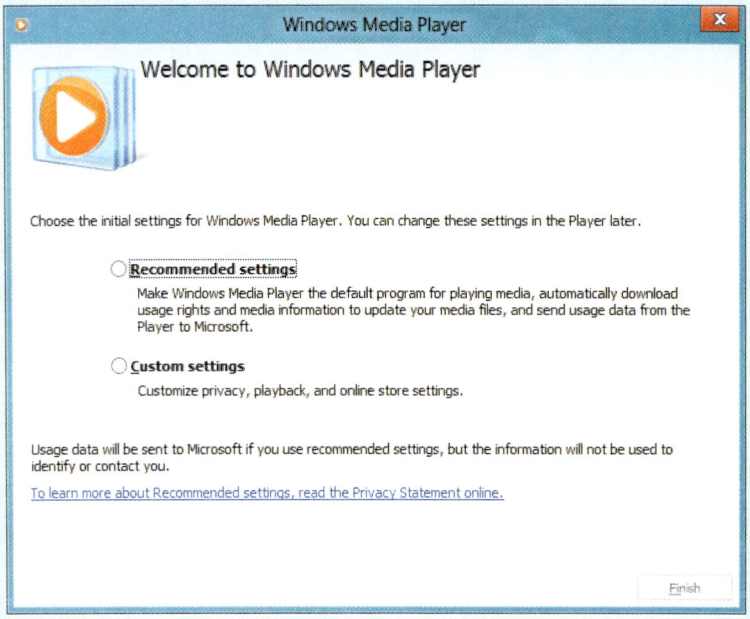

Step 2

In the Select Privacy Options page, we recommend that you select the options shown here.

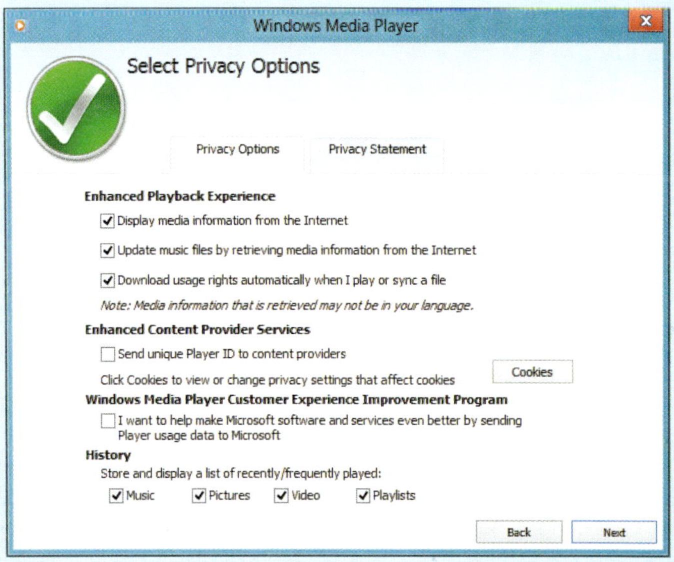

Step 3

In the Select the Default Music and Video Player page, select either Make Windows Media Player the Default Music and Video Player, which means that WMP will be used for all music and video file formats, or select the second option, which will require that you specify which media file types WMP will play.

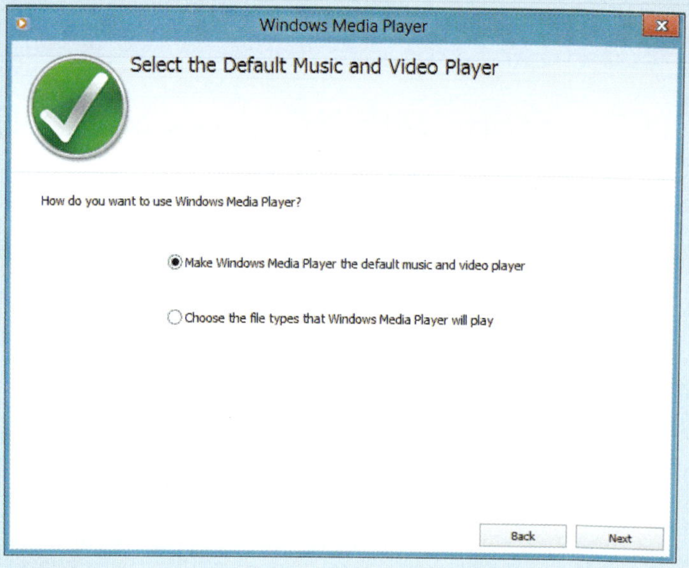

Step 4

In the Choose an Online Store page, select a store (only one is provided in our sample) or select the option to delay this choice until later in WMP.

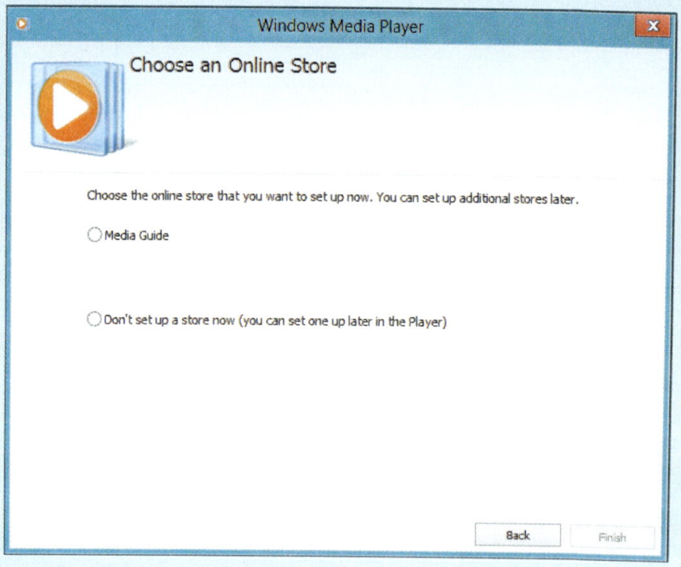

Step 5

Windows Media Player scans Music Library for media files. If your Music Library is empty, Windows Music Player will look like this. If you have media files in other locations, copy them into your Music Library. After files are copied into your Music Library, WMP will detect and display the music files, and you will see them listed in WMP, as shown earlier in Figure 6-12.

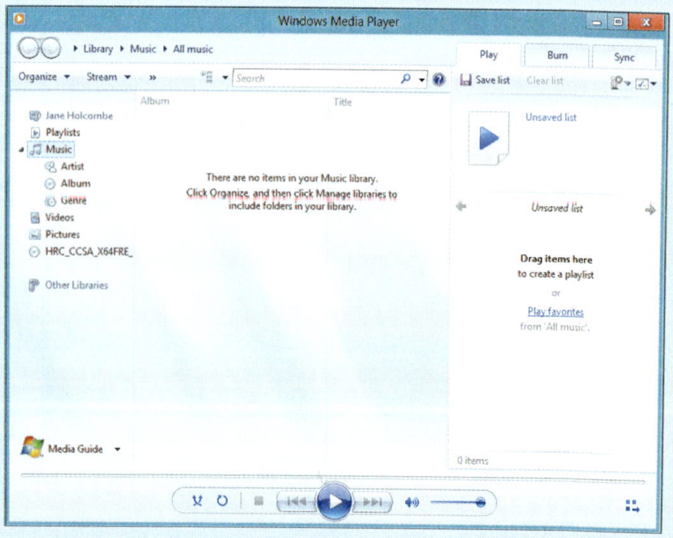

Step 6

You can also rip the music from an audio CD to the WMP library. With WMP open, insert a CD. It will start playing. Click the CD in the left pane of WMP and then click the Rip CD button in the button bar (it immediately changes to the red Stop Rip button). If the Rip CD button is not visible, click the chevrons (>>) in the middle of the button bar to access it. WMP will begin ripping the music as it plays, showing the progress in the Rip Status column, as shown here where ripping is almost complete. The last song shows a green progress bar as it completes.

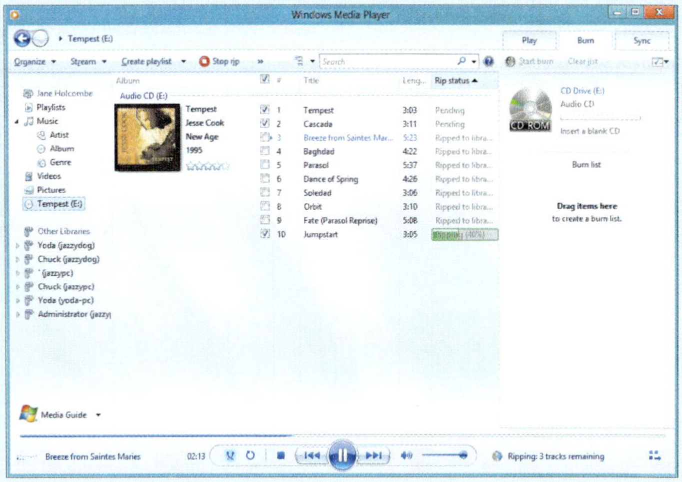

Creating Playlists and Burning CDs in Windows Media Player

To create a playlist in Windows Media Player, have the WMP window open in Player Library Mode. Then you can either use the Create Playlist menu shown here or open the Play tab in the List pane (Figure 6-13). Drag and drop individual songs or albums from the Details pane into the List pane, and enter a new name for the title of the playlist.

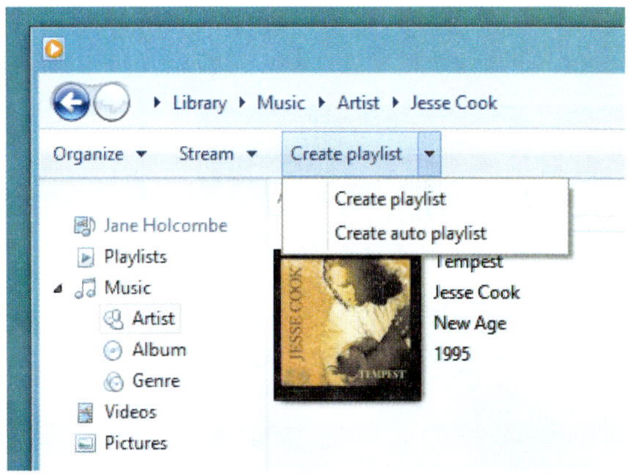

If you select Create Playlist from the menu, a new playlist folder will open under Playlists in the Navigation pane, as shown here, waiting for you to name the new playlist, which will replace the placeholder name of "Untitled playlist." From here you can drag and drop songs and albums from the Details pane onto the named playlist in the Navigation pane. You can create many playlists, and if you have a compatible digital music player you can open the Sync tab and synchronize all your media files, including playlists, with that device. Similarly, you can also open the Burn tab and select songs and playlists to drag and drop to the List pane to burn an audio CD.

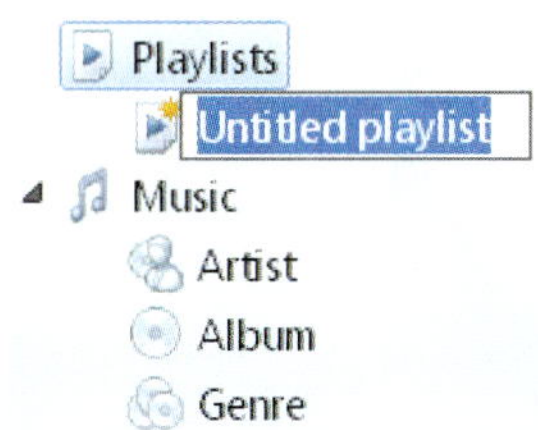

If you like the idea of a playlist that automatically adds media based on criteria you select and updates every time you start WMP, select Create Auto Playlist from the Create Playlist menu and the New Auto Playlist dialog box opens, as shown in Figure 6-14. Name the playlist and select your criteria. The Music in My Library options let you configure the following criteria:

- Album Artist
- Album Title
- Auto Rating
- Bit Rate
- Content Provider Genre
- Contributing Artist
- Date Added
- Date Encoded
- Date Last Played
- File Type

The And Also Include option lets you pick additional media type, such as music, pictures, TV shows, and video for your auto playlists. The last option lets you select restrictions, such as a limit on the number of items in a playlist, the total time duration, or the total size of a playlist.

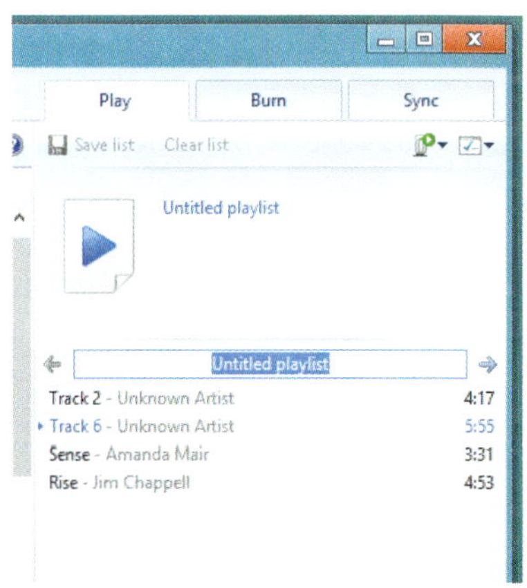

FIGURE 6-13 Open the Play tab in the List pane and drag songs and albums to create a new playlist.

Using the Music App

The Music app is a Windows 8 app that plays music on your computer or compatible connected devices. You can also play music through an Xbox 360 console. Using the Music app you can connect to the Music Store and buy

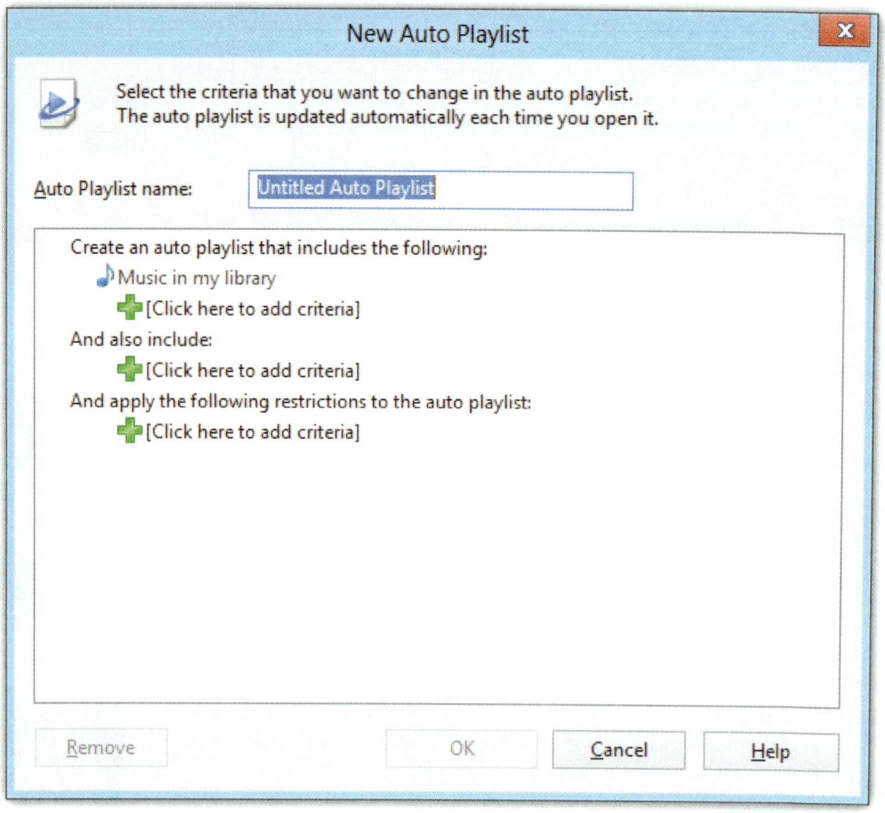

FIGURE 6-14 The New Auto Playlist dialog box.

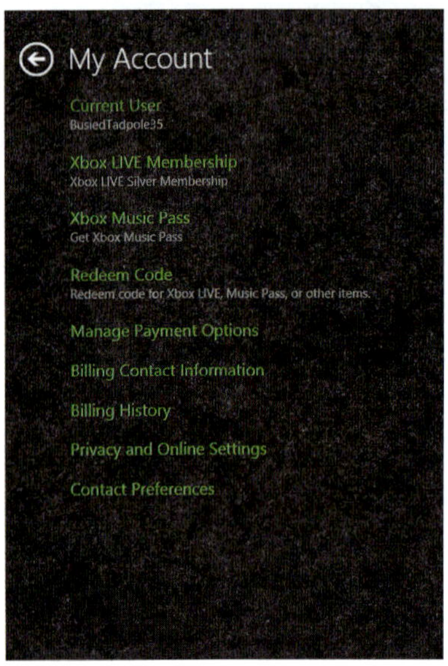

FIGURE 6-15 The My Account bar gives access to your account settings.

music. If you have Xbox 360 and an Xbox LIVE account, you can connect to the Xbox Music service and purchase music there. If you don't have an Xbox LIVE account, you can connect to the Music Store and search and preview music. You can also purchase an **Xbox Music Pass**, a subscription music service from Microsoft. The first time you connect to the Music Store through Music, you will be required to create an account. You manage your account settings from the My Account bar (Figure 6-15), accessed by opening the Music Settings charm and selecting Account.

Like Windows Media Player, the Music app will find music in your Music Library and display it on its home screen under the category My Music, as Figure 6-16 shows. Therefore, if you have music in other locations on your computer or network or on removable storage, transfer it to your Music Library using File Explorer on the desktop.

You can play your music by clicking or tapping a song's tile in the Music home screen or by browsing to your Music Library and selecting a song or album. Unless another app is your default app for music files (like Windows Music Player) the Music app will open and play the selection, as shown in Figure 6-17, where you see the normal controls for pausing, backing up, and advancing music. Click or tap the arrow in the small circle on the top left to return

try this!

Copy Music into the Music Library

Do you have a flash drive or other storage media containing music files? If so, copy files into your personal Music Library to play in Windows 8 Music. Try This!

1. Open File Explorer on the desktop.
2. Browse to the location containing your music files.
3. Select music files to copy.
4. Using the keyboard and mouse, right-click the selected files, select Copy, and then browse to the Libraries folder; right-click within the Music Library and select Paste.
5. Or, using a drag-and-drop operation with gesture or mouse, drag the selected files to the Music Library.

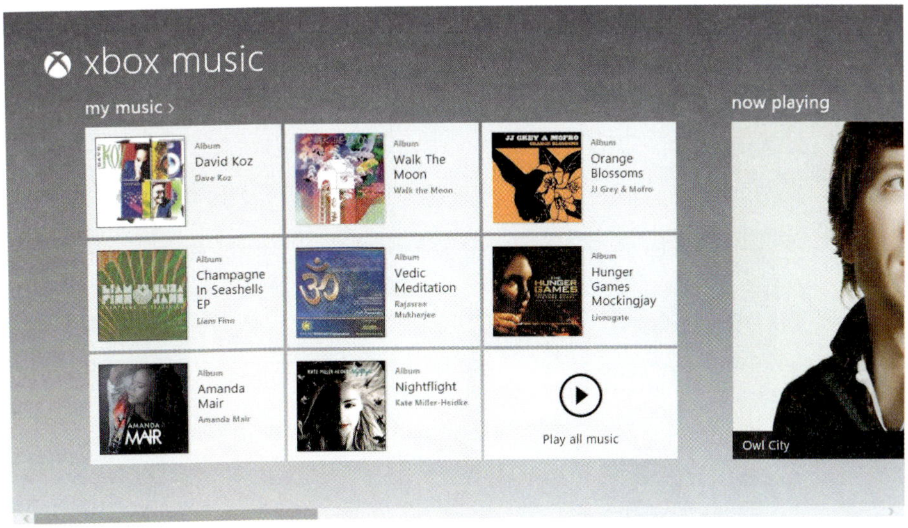

FIGURE 6-16 The My Music category contains tiles for music found in the Music libraries.

to the Music app's home screen while allowing the music selection to play. When you start music from within the Music app, the app bar displays, allowing you to add a song to a playlist, delete the song, shuffle the tracks, repeat a song, play the previous song, pause, or skip to the next song.

> The Music app will continue playing your music even when the screen locks on your Windows 8 computer or tablet. You can use all the music controls (not just volume) on your computer keyboard or tablet to adjust the volume and switch tracks without having to open the Lock screen and sign in. A small box displays on the Lock screen or Sign-In screen when you touch one of the controls.

Populate Your Local Music Library

As with Windows Media Player, Music will search your Music Library folders (My Music and Public Music). If you have digital music files in another location that you would like to add to your Music Library folders, do so with the help of the Try This!

Creating a Playlist

You can create your own playlists for playing in Music in Windows 8 from the Music Library in File Explorer. You can also add a song to the playlist while it's playing. Follow the instructions in Step-by-Step 6.2 to create a playlist.

FIGURE 6-17 The Music app playing a song.

Step-by-Step 6.2

Creating Playlists in Music

Create a new playlist.

Step 1

Open Music and select a song or album to play. Then open the App bar and tap Add to Playlist. The example shown already has one playlist named Rumba. You can add to an existing playlist or create a new one.

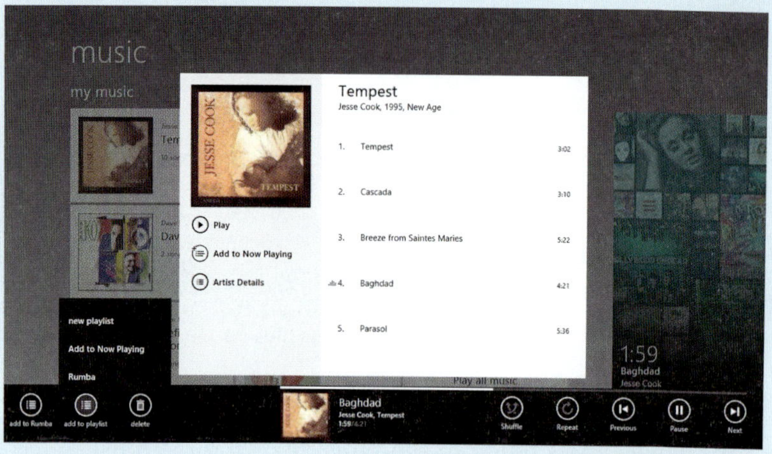

Step 2

If you select an existing playlist, the selection will be added to that playlist. If you select New Playlist, a box pops up and you enter the name of the new playlist and tap Save. This creates the playlist with your selection in it.

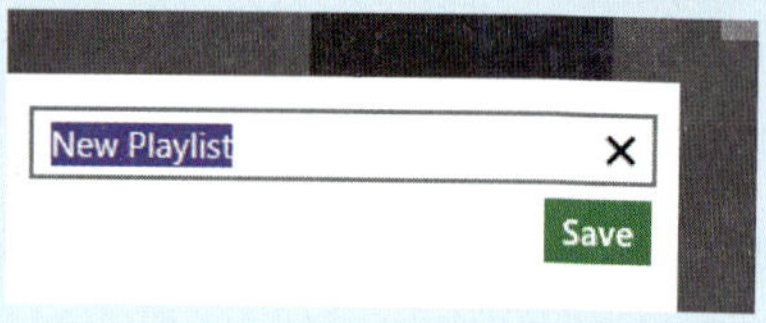

Step 3

The home screen of the Music app will contain a new playlist tile with the title you chose, and a tile will show multiple album covers. The two playlists in this example are Jazz and Jesse Cook.

Step 4

Now share a song or playlist. From the Music home screen, first select a song or album and then open the Share charm. The selection will be listed in the Share sidebar, and you can select how you would like to share from the choices listed below.

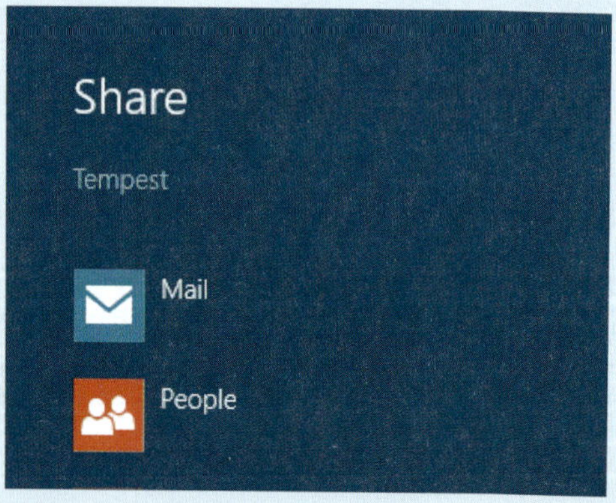

Step 5

From the Share bar, select Mail to send someone a link to the online source for the music. You can add a personal message before sending. Recipients can follow the link, and if they have an account, buy the song or album.

Step 6

If you add your social networking accounts to Windows 8 through the People app, you can share links to your favorite songs with your friends through Facebook, Twitter, or other services. Similarly, you can share information about a song through any installed Windows 8 app that shares with the Music app.

LO 6.4 | Viewing and Managing Videos and Photos in Windows 8

Although Windows Media Center and Windows Media Player allow you to work with a variety of digital media, three new Windows 8 apps are each limited to one type of media. You already learned about the Music app, created to work with your music collections, and in this section we will survey the other two apps. They are Video, for managing and running video media, and Photos, for your digital pictures.

The Video App

The Video app is a Windows 8 app that lets you play and perform simple management of your video content. Like the other media-related apps, it also can play content on your computer or compatible connected devices and through an Xbox 360 console. Through the Movies Store and Television Store links in the Video app, you can purchase movies and TV episodes using an Xbox LIVE subscription.

The Video app supports stereo 3D video and multiple audio tracks per video. As with the Music app, you can access media-related hardware controls on your computer keyboard or tablet when the screen is locked—a handy feature considering you are using your computer as a remote while sending content to other devices. After all, remotes don't go to sleep and quit working when you're watching TV!

Like the other Windows 8 media apps, Video searches your Videos Library and displays its results on its home screen under My Videos. Figure 6-18 shows the message that appears when Video does not find any content.

Recall the discussion of codecs earlier in this chapter. If you see a missing codec when you attempt to play any type of media, a little research will reveal that many websites offer free codecs, but you should be wary of downloading them unless you have a way of confirming that they are legitimate and that they are compatible with your software. The best rule is to use only codecs that the publisher of your media program approves.

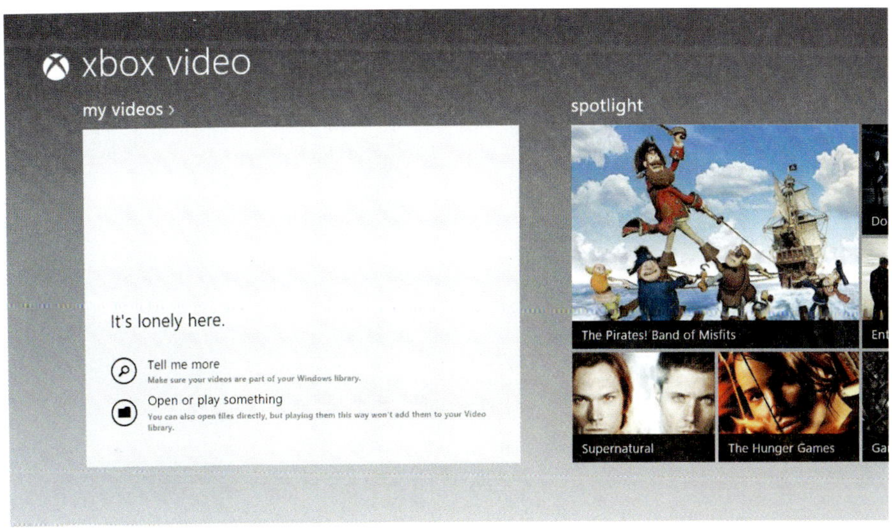

FIGURE 6-18 The Video home screen showing an empty video library.

FIGURE 6-19 Playing a video.

Click the link labeled Open Or Play Something and you can browse your local hard drive and network for a video. Then click the video and it will play on the device you specify. Figure 6-19 shows a home video running on the PC's computer screen. The controls for back, forward, and pause appear when you first start a video, but soon disappear. Bring them up again with a touch on a touchscreen, a mouse click, or a key press.

Use the back arrows to move back to the Video app home screen. Then scroll to the right to display the Movies Store. If you click the Movies Store link (at the top) you are taken to the Movies Store website and a screen of tiles displays, which is only the tip of the iceberg as far as the number of movies available through the Store. Scroll through the movies by category or open the Search charm and search on a key word for a movie, such as a title, name of an actor, the studio, and more. Figure 6-20 shows the Movies Store with the Search charm open. Notice the categories that Movies Store offers at this time (featured, new releases, top selling, genres, and studios).

Click a movie in the Movies Store and a box pops up, as shown in the illustration on page 197 with a brief description of the movie and a list of options for buying or renting it, movie details, playing the movie trailer, or playing the movie on Xbox. Selecting Play Trailer will run the movie preview in the left two-thirds of the screen while displaying an overview pane on the right with

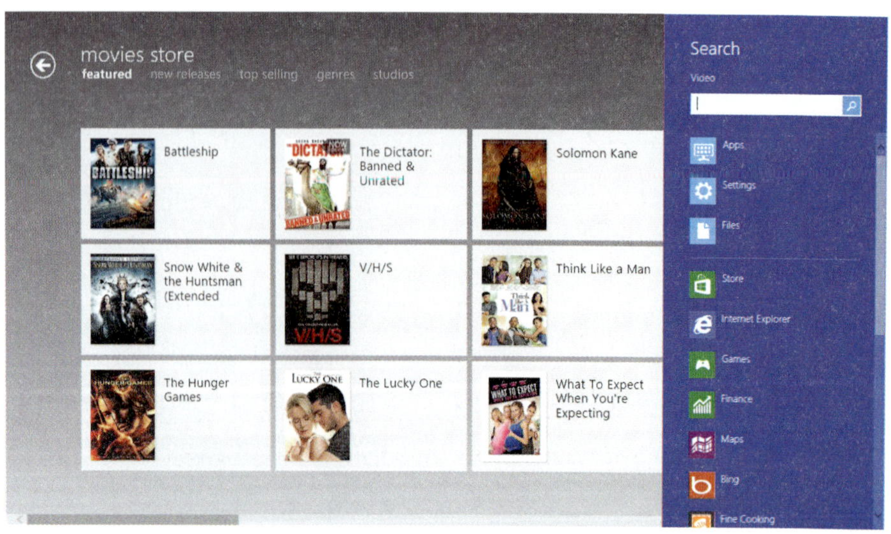

FIGURE 6-20 The Movies Store with the Search Charm open.

options for buying, renting, or playing in Xbox. Practice browsing and selecting movies by following the steps in the Try This!

Now let's explore the Television Store. If necessary, return to the Video home screen with one or more back swipe gestures or by moving your mouse and clicking the back-arrow button when it appears on the upper left. On the Video home screen, scroll the screen to the right until you see the Television Store, shown in Figure 6-21. As with the Movies Store, if you click the Television Store link (the title at the top) you are taken to the Television Store where tiles of some of the TV shows are shown (Figure 6-22) and, similar to the Movies Store, you can choose to browse TV shows by TV-centric categories, such as featured, last night's shows, free TV, top selling, genres, and networks. If you have an Xbox LIVE account, you can purchase episodes or series.

try this!

Browse the Movies Store

Use the Video app to browse the Movies Store and view trailers.

1. Locate the Video tile on the Start screen and open the app.
2. In the Video home screen, scroll to the right to the Movies Store.
3. Tap or click the Movies Store title/link near the top of the screen.
4. Browse through the selections, using search if you have a certain movie in mind.
5. When you locate a movie of interest, tap or click its tile.
6. In the resulting box, select Play Trailer to see the promotional trailer for the movie.
7. When finished, swipe or use your mouse to return to the Video home screen.

The Photos App

Although we know people with huge digital music libraries, we believe a far greater number have unmanageable collections of digital photos scattered on computers and devices all over their homes and offices. We do, and we have tried other methods for organizing this mess, but we may have found our solution in Windows 8, SkyDrive, and the Photos app. This Windows 8 app gives you access to all your digital

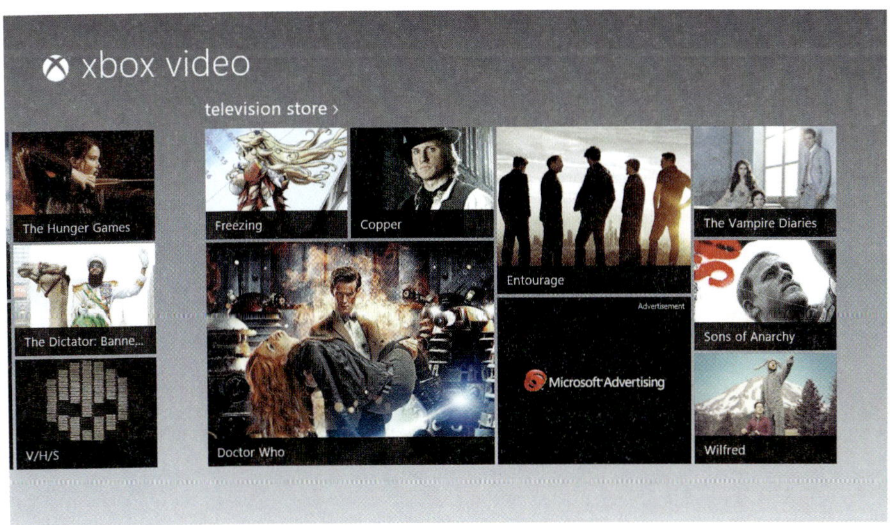

FIGURE 6-21 The Television Store on the Video app home screen.

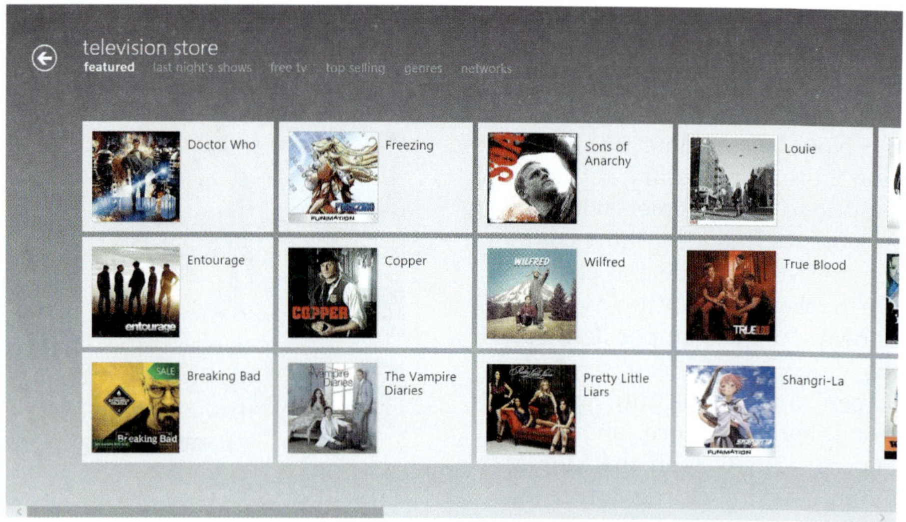

FIGURE 6-22 The tiles from the Television Store website.

photos almost anywhere. Locations include any local media, Facebook, Flickr, shared libraries in a HomeGroup, and SkyDrive.

Accessing All Your Photos

Install the SkyDrive app on Windows computers. It installs as a desktop app on the older Windows (Windows Vista and Windows 7) and as a Windows 8 app on Windows 8. Then, let the SkyDrive app automatically back up your photos, music, and videos (and other data files) from those computers to your SkyDrive in the cloud. Then the files are available to you from any Internet-connected Windows computer SkyDrive, as well as from your Windows 8 computers using its new apps. Figure 6-23 shows the Photos home screen with tiles to the local Pictures Library, SkyDrive, and libraries on a PC in the same HomeGroup. The other tiles are for Facebook and Flickr. If you have those accounts, add them to your Windows 8 People apps and use the Photos app to share photos with your friends on Facebook or Flickr.

Click one of the tiles on the Photos home screen to open a collection and view multiple photos onscreen. Pinch to zoom out for thumbnail view, and back in to enlarge. To zoom out with a mouse, hover it on the bottom right of the screen until minus (–) and plus (+) signs display. Click the minus to zoom out and click the plus to zoom back in.

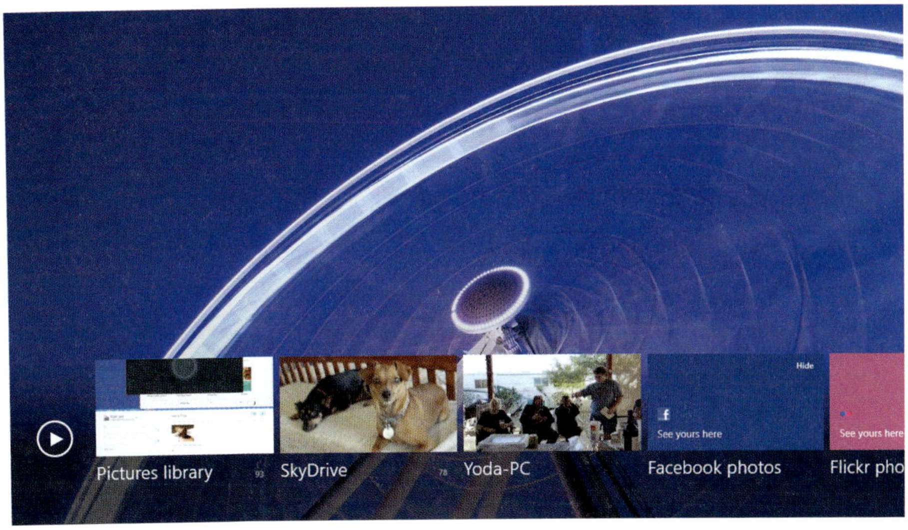

FIGURE 6-23 The Photos app home screen shows all the locations for photos.

Importing Pictures from a Camera

You don't need to install software that came with your camera in order to download your photos. You can import photos directly from your camera into your Pictures Library using Photos, and you can create new folders in the Pictures Library for your photos. The Photos app sees each folder as an album. Step-by-Step 6.3 walks you through this process.

Step-by-Step 6.3

Using the Photos App to Import from a Digital Camera

If you have a camera with photos that you would like to download, you can download those photos to your Windows 8 computer.

Step 1

At the Photos home screen or in an album, open the App bar.

Step 2

With the App bar open in Photos, connect your camera's USB cable to your computer and turn on the camera. If you have not yet set AutoPlay options, a box labeled Removable Disk will open in the upper right of the screen, requesting that you choose what to do with memory cards. If you select Import Photos and Videos, it will proceed with the import. If you select Take no action, you will need to click the Import button on the far right of the App bar in Photos. You will then be asked to choose a device, click or tap the device and click the Import button again.

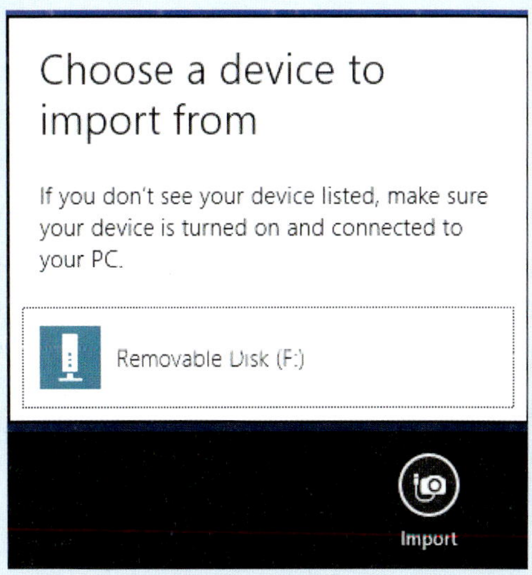

Step 3

In the next screen you select (right-click or tap) the files you want to import and name the folder for importing. The default name is the date the pictures were taken, but you can enter a new folder or an existing folder name. The Photos app will create the new folder in the default folder of the Pictures library. When you have chosen the files, click the Import button.

Step 4

A progress bar displays while the files are being imported. If you need to stop the import, click the Stop button. When the import is complete, the progress bar will be colored its entire length, and a message will show the number of files copied. The Stop button will become an Open Album button.

Step 5

Click the Open Album button. Your album will display and you can scroll through the photos or open the App bar.

FIGURE 6-24 The Photos home screen after adding our own background photo.

Using Your Photos for the Windows Lock Screen, Photos Start Screen Tile, or Photos Home Screen

To use one of your photos for the Lock screen, the Photos Start screen tile, or the Photos home screen background, select the file from one of your albums and open the Apps bar. Then tap or click the Set As button at the bottom left of the Apps bar; in the pop-up menu (shown here), select Lock Screen, App Tile, or App Background. Figure 6-24 shows the Photos home screen after we added our own background photo. We also removed the links to Facebook and Flickr by opening the Settings bar, selecting Options and removing the checks by the two social networking sites.

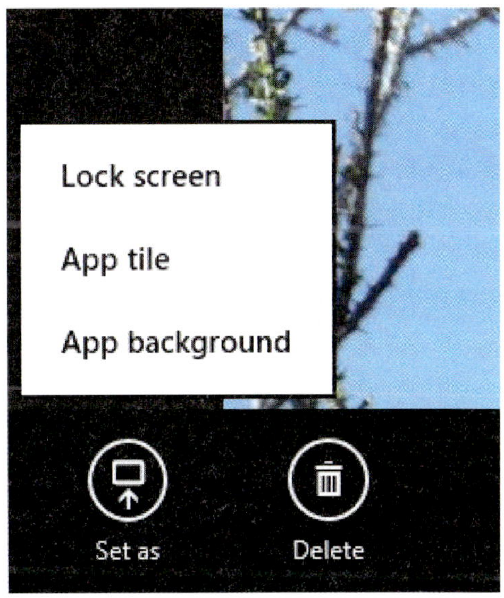

More App Bar Features

You can use a button (not shown here) on the far right of the App bar to add the selected photo to a slide show.

Sharing and Devices The Photos app can share with other apps. For instance, use the Share charm to e-mail photos as attachments or as SkyDrive links. Use the Devices charm to display photos on any compatible device (referred to as a Windows certified Play To device) that is either directly connected or available over a network, such as your TV.

Chapter 6 REVIEW

Chapter Summary

After reading this chapter and completing the Step-by-Step tutorials and Try This! exercises, you should understand the following facts about working with music, video, and pictures in Windows 8:

Digital Media Basics

- Music, video, and photos in their digital forms are digital media.
- Multimedia is a broader term usually used to describe a presentation that combines multiple forms of content, such as text, audio, photos, animation, and video.
- There are many digital media file types that can be divided into the following categories: music, video, and graphic/photo. Microsoft Windows supports several file formats in each of these categories.
- A codec is software used to compress and decompress a digital media format for storing and playing the content.

Windows Media Center for Windows 8

- WMC manages and plays a variety of media on CDs and DVDs; plays streaming content from the Internet and other sources, such as a TV tuner; and integrates with the Xbox 360. WMC for Windows 8 also supports Dolby Digital Plus 8-channel surround sound audio.
- Windows Media Player is a free Windows app that, in its Windows 8 version, will not play DVD movies.
- Windows Media Center (WMC) is an add-on for Windows 8 that is more capable than Windows Media Player because it includes the codec to play DVD movies. To install WMC, you first purchase a product key from Microsoft and then download and install WMC through the Windows 8 Add Features Control Panel applet.
- If the screen is locked on your Windows 8 computer or tablet while playing music in Windows Media Center, the music will continue to play, and you can use the volume controls on your computer or tablet to adjust the volume without having to open the Lock screen and sign in.
- You can add third-party Windows Media Center Extras, which are usually games or services that you pay for.
- Windows Media Center is integrated into the Xbox 360 console, and Windows 8 with Windows Media Center installed can control the Xbox 360 console, sending content through it to play on your compatible devices.
- Xbox SmartGlass is a free app that installs on a Windows 8 computing device and connects to your Xbox 360.

Enjoying Music in Windows 8

- Use the free Windows Media Player to play all types of media files except for DVD movies.
- Manage your media files, ripping music from CDs, burning music to CDs, and creating playlists.
- Windows Media Player in Player Library Mode is a desktop window in which you can do all types of tasks to manage and play media files.
- Switch Windows Media Player in Now Playing Mode to reduce the window to the size of a gadget on the desktop, but still have controls visible.
- If the screen is locked on your Windows 8 computer or tablet while playing music in Windows Media Player, the music will continue to play and you can continue use the volume controls on your computer or tablet to adjust the volume without having to open the Lock screen and sign in.

Viewing and Managing Videos and Photos in Windows 8

- The Video app is a Windows 8 app that lets you play content on the local computer or on connected devices.
- The Video app supports stereo 3D video and multiple audio tracks per video.
- You can access media-related hardware controls on your computer keyboard or tablet when the screen is locked so that you can continue to remotely control playing of videos on other devices.
- Use the Video app to search the online Movies Store and Television Store to buy and download movies and TV episodes for viewing on your computer or TV.

Key Terms List

burn (187)
codec (177)
digital media (176)
Dolby Digital Plus (177)
gaming controller (177)
multimedia (176)
Now Playing Mode (188)
Player Library Mode (188)
playlist (184)
RAW (176)
rip (187)
streaming (177)
Windows Media Center (WMC) (177)
Windows Media Center Extender (WMX) (181)
Windows Media Player (WMP) (176)
Xbox 360 (177)
Xbox LIVE (186)
Xbox LIVE Free (186)
Xbox LIVE Gold (186)
Xbox Music Pass (192)
Xbox SmartGlass (187)

Key Terms Quiz

Use the Key Terms List to complete the sentences that follow. Not all terms will be used.

1. When you ______________ a CD you are copying music files to it in a format that can be played on a CD player or computer.
2. A group of media files selected to play together is a ______________.
3. When you ______________ music you are copying the music files from audio disc and, if necessary, converting them to a different digital file format.
4. When you send digital media data, such as video, over a network and it can be viewed on a receiving computer before the entire content is finished transmitting, the action is called ______________.
5. When you play music in Windows Media Player and switch to ______________ the Windows Media Player window shrinks to the size of a gadget.
6. Purchase a license for ______________, an add-on to Windows 8, if you want to use a Microsoft product for managing and playing all your digital media, including DVD movies.
7. The ______________ of Windows Media Player opens in a desktop window and gives you access to the libraries for managing all your media content, burning CDs, and ripping music.
8. Digital music, video, and photos are all forms of ______________.
9. ______________ is a standard for high-quality 8-channel digital audio surround sound.
10. A/an ______________ is software that compresses or decompresses a digital media format for storing and playing the content.

Multiple-Choice Quiz

1. This list of media files (music, video, or photos) will play together when you select it.
   a. rip
   b. burn
   c. playlist
   d. extender
   e. Xbox Music Pass
2. What type of software component is missing if you cannot play a movie DVD?
   a. extender
   b. digital media
   c. streaming
   d. codec
   e. extra
3. You can add a third-party game or Internet service to Windows Media Center as a Windows Media Center ______________.
   a. WMA
   b. codec
   c. extender
   d. extra
   e. playlist
4. What free software turns a Windows 8 computer or tablet into an interactive remote control, working through an Xbox console to control compatible devices, such as TVs?
   a. Windows Media Center Extender (WMX)
   b. digital media
   c. streaming
   d. codec
   e. Xbox SmartGlass
5. Which built-in Windows 8 app can you use to purchase movies and TV episodes online?
   a. Photos
   b. Movies
   c. Video
   d. Dolby Digital Plus
   e. Xbox LIVE

6. Which of the following is a digital music file format?
   a. WMP
   b. WMC
   c. WMA
   d. WMX
   e. WMV
7. Which of the following is a digital photo file format that cannot be viewed in the Microsoft software included in this chapter?
   a. JPG
   b. RAW
   c. TIFF
   d. PNG
   e. WMF
8. Which of the following is a digital video file format?
   a. WMP
   b. WMC
   c. WMA
   d. WMX
   e. WMV
9. Which of the following file name extensions indicates that the file is a recorded TV show?
   a. .cda
   b. .wmf
   c. .mp3
   d. .dvr-ms
   e. .tiff
10. To copy photos from your digital camera using the Photos app home screen, connect the camera to your Windows 8 computer and click this button on the Apps bar.
    a. Copy
    b. Import
    c. Move
    d. Transfer
    e. Sync

Essay Quiz

1. Describe the basic function of the Xbox 360 console and briefly detail what the Windows Media Center software built in to the Xbox 368 console adds to the console. Then explain the benefit of adding the Xbox SmartGlass software to a Windows 8 computer with a network connection to an Xbox 360.
2. Describe the differences between ripping, burning, and streaming.
3. Describe the SkyDrive app and explain how it would help you in managing your media collections.

Lab Projects

LAB PROJECT 6.1

You would like to play DVD movies on your Windows 8 computer, and you would like to find an alternative to Microsoft's Windows Media Center. Research the options—both free and for purchase. Find three, and write a short description of each of them, describing features and explaining which one you would choose and why.

LAB PROJECT 6.2

Build a fantasy playlist. Using Windows Media Player or the Music app, browse through the Music Store or use the Search charm. Select songs of interest and use the Preview button to listen to samples of each song. Then decide which songs would make a playlist you would enjoy. Write about your playlist. Do the songs in your playlist have something in common? Write a list that includes at least six songs you would put together in a playlist.

LAB PROJECT 6.3

Almost everybody has digital photos somewhere. Locate some of your favorite digital photos—whether on a smartphone, a digital camera, or stored somewhere on a computer. Copy them into your Pictures Library and create a slide show using an app available on your Windows 8 computer. If you have a choice between more than one app that can create slide shows, explore the slide show features in each. Does one have more features than another? Can you add music to your slide show with an app that is on your computer? Write up your results describing the differences between the apps you tried, and then show the slide show to your classmates.

Appendix A

Mouse and Keyboard Actions and Shortcuts

Mouse Action or Mouse+Key Combination	Result
Hover	The object the mouse pointer hovers over will display a tooltip, infotip, or similar information, if enabled for the object.
Single left-click	Selects or activates an object, depending on the current context and location of the pointer. For instance, if the pointer is in a document, this action sets the insertion point.
Single right-click	Selects the object and displays its context menu.
Double left-click	Selects or activates the object, performing the default command. If the pointer is in a document, this action selects the word at the insertion point, and a third click selects the sentence or paragraph (depending on the application and the version of the application). The third click for selecting an entire paragraph disappeared from Microsoft Word several versions ago.
Ctrl+Press middle scroll wheel	Semantic zoom (in and out).
Shift key+single left-click	For selectable objects, this action contiguously extends the selection.
Drag and drop	After pointing the pointer at a graphic object, hold the primary pointing device button down while moving the pointing device to visually drag the object. At the destination, release the mouse button to drop the object.
Keyboard Shortcut	**Action**
Ctrl+A	Select all.
Ctrl++	Semantic zoom in.
Ctrl+–	Semantic zoom out.
Ctrl+F1	Expand or minimize the ribbon in File Explorer or an app.
Ctrl+Shift+Esc	Opens Task Manager.
F1	Opens context-sensitive Help within a File Explorer app or on the desktop; the app Help opens. It does not work in Metro apps or the Start screen.
Windows key+F1	Opens Windows Help and Support (a File Explorer app) from anywhere in Windows 8.
Windows key alone	Return to Start screen or return to last app from Start screen.
Windows key+PrntScn	Captures the screen and saves it in the Pictures folder.
Windows key (hold)+Tab key (repeat)	Cycles through open apps.
Windows key+.	Snaps current app to the right.
Windows key+shift+.	Snaps current app to the left.
Windows key+Shift+left arrow key	Moves desktop window to left monitor.

(Continued)

Keyboard Shortcut	Action
Windows key+Shift+right arrow key	Moves desktop window to right monitor.
Windows key+Shift+right arrow key	Moves desktop window to right monitor.
Windows key++	Opens Magnifier to magnify all or part of the screen.
Windows key+Esc	Closes Magnifier.
Windows key+– (hyphen)	Restores screen.
Windows key+, (comma)	Peek at the desktop.
Windows key+. (period)	Snaps open app to right; repeat to move snapped app to left, repeat again to toggle app to full screen.
Windows key+; (semicolon)	Reveal desktop.
Windows key+Home	Minimize nonactive desktop windows.
Windows key+Enter	Turns on Narrator.
Windows key+Alt+Esc	Turn off Narrator.
Windows key+Spacebar	Switch input language and keyboard layout.
Windows key+Tab	Cycles through Metro app history.
Windows key+left arrow key	Snaps desktop window to left.
Windows key+right arrow key	Snaps desktop window to right.
Windows key+up arrow key	Maximizes desktop window.
Windows key+down arrow key	Restores/minimizes desktop window.
Windows key+PgUp key	Moves Start screen to left monitor.
Windows key+PgDn key	Moves Start screen to right monitor.
Windows key+1–9	Opens desktop app at the given position on the task bar.
Windows key+C	Opens Charms bar.
Windows key+D	Opens the desktop.
Windows key+E	Opens a File Explorer window on the desktop.
Windows key+F	Opens Search focused on files.
Windows key+G	Cycles through File Explorer desktop gadgets (if they exist)
Windows key+H	Opens the Share bar allowing Metro apps to share data (if they support this feature).
Windows key+I	Opens Settings bar.
Windows key+K	Displays connected devices in the Devices bar.
Windows key+L	Locks the PC displaying either the Lock screen (if enabled) or the Sign-In screen.
Windows key+M	Minimizes all File Explorer windows.
Windows key+O	Toggles the device orientation of mobile devices on and off.

Keyboard Shortcut	Action
Windows key+P	Projection/second monitor options.
Windows key+Q	Opens the Apps Search bar.
Windows key+R	Opens the Run box.
Windows key+T	Cycles through open desktop apps.
Windows key+U	Opens Ease of Access Center.
Windows key+W	Opens Settings Search.
Windows key+X	Opens Start context menu.
Windows key+Z	When in Start screen or a Metro app, opens Apps bar on bottom of screen.

Appendix B

Installing Windows 8

Windows 8 Hardware Requirements

The minimum requirements to install Windows 8 are just that, minimum requirements, especially in regard to memory and disk space. You should have more memory and MUCH more disk space on a computer on which you plan to install applications and save data.

- 1 GHz or faster processor
- 1 GB RAM (32-bit) or 2 GB RAM (64-bit)
- 16 GB available hard disk space (32-bit) or 20 GB (64-bit)
- DirectX 9 graphics device with WDDM 1.0 or higher driver
- 1024 × 768 minimum screen resolution (1366 × 768 resolution required for the Snap feature)

To use the touch features, you need a multitouch-capable laptop, tablet, or display. Windows 8 supports up to five simultaneous touch points, and if your hardware doesn't support that, you could have problems with the onscreen keyboard and certain controls. Microsoft upgraded the Microsoft Touch Mouse to work better with the multitouch capabilities of Windows 8.

An Internet connection is required to synchronize settings and files from one W8 PC to another.

Installing Windows 8

At this time Windows 8 is only available in two forms: preinstalled on new computers and tablets or as an upgrade available from the online Microsoft Store or from other retail locations.

To install Windows 8 on an existing computer that meets the above minimum requirements, purchase it as a download from the Microsoft Store or at retail. If downloading, allow about 20 minutes for the complete installation, and follow the instructions from Microsoft to install it, either as an in-place upgrade to your existing installation that will transfer all your settings and keep your data files intact, or as a clean installation. An in-place upgrade will get you back to work faster, but you may want to do a clean installation in order to leave behind problems with the old version of Windows.

You can also install Windows 8 as a dual-boot installation and continue to choose the version of Windows you want each time you restart your computer.

Here are general instructions for downloading and installing Windows 8.

1. From your Windows computer, connect to the Microsoft Store or another source, purchase Windows 8, and initiate the download and installation. Write down or print out the product key, because you will need it to activate Windows 8 during the installation process.
2. The Windows 8 Upgrade Assistant will automatically run compatibility tests on all your installed and powered-on hardware.
3. The Upgrade Assistant may prompt you to choose between a 32-bit installation and a 64-bit installation. Unless you are installing Windows 8 on a very old computer, you should select 64-bit.

4. After the Upgrade Assistant completes its tests, it will display a compatibility report. Review the report and take any necessary actions, such as acquiring new drivers for some of your hardware. Continue when you are ready.
5. Next, the Windows 8 installer and appropriate Windows 8 files and drivers will download.
6. Follow the instructions on the following pages. Select your language, enter the product key, and agree to the license terms.
7. Choose between an Upgrade or Custom installation.
   a. An Upgrade is an in-place upgrade that will install over the top of your old installation, keeping files, settings, and applications.
8. Consider the Custom installation if you are an advanced Windows user and need advanced features. A Custom installation gives you many options, including deleting, creating, and formatting drive partitions. You can even shrink the existing partition, if room permits. A separate partition is ideal if you want to install Windows 8 and keep your old version of Windows intact for a dual-boot configuration. The most important rule to know to do this is that you should install the newest OS last.

   The Windows installer runs and restarts several times, displaying a progress screen with check marks appearing by each installation task as it completes them.
9. At the end of the Windows installer's tasks, Windows restarts, the Personalize screen displays, and you can choose the colors for the Start screen and name your PC. From this point on, follow the instructions in the section in Chapter 1 titled "Start Fresh in Windows 8."

Photo Credits

Chapter 1

page 1: © Purestock/Alamy
page 3: © Ryan McVay

Chapter 2

page 25: © PR Newswire

Chapter 3

page 57: © Stockbyte/Getty Images

Chapter 4

page 97: © Jonathan Kitchen/Getty Images
page 98: © Image Source/Getty Images
page 101: © John Lund/Blend Images LLC
page 104: © Images.com/Corbis

Chapter 5

page 137: Dieter Spannknebel/Photodisc/Getty Images

Chapter 6

page 175: © Doug Ross
page 187: © PR Newswire

Index

D

P

Q

R

S

X

Z